John McNeill

Sermons

Volume 1

John McNeill

Sermons
Volume 1

ISBN/EAN: 9783337285487

Printed in Europe, USA, Canada, Australia, Japan

Cover: Foto ©Lupo / pixelio.de

More available books at **www.hansebooks.com**

SERMONS

BY THE

REV. JOHN McNEILL

INTRODUCTION
BY
REV. A. T. PIERSON, D.D.

VOLUME I

FLEMING H. REVELL COMPANY
NEW YORK   CHICAGO   TORONTO
Publishers of Evangelical Literature

Entered according to Act of Congress, in the year 1890, by
FLEMING H. REVELL,
In the Office of the Librarian of Congress, at Washington, D. C.

CONTENTS.

No.		Page
	American Introduction—Rev. A. T. Pierson, D.D.	
1.	Mary and Martha; or, Stable and Unstable Equilibrium	1
2.	The Conversation of Lydia	17
3.	A Short Walk over "Redemption Ground"	33
4.	Shammah and Benaiah	49
5.	The True Physician	65
6.	Found Out	81
7.	The Burning Bush	97
8.	Working out Salvation	113
9.	How God's Election Works	129
10.	"How Well Horatius Kept the Bridge in the Brave Days of Old"	145
11.	The Queen of the South *versus* The Men of this Generation	161
12.	Remarks Preliminary to an Ordination of Elders and Deacons	178
13.	Jacob's Crisis	193
14.	Fear Not	209
15.	The Three Crosses	225
16.	The Lord Our Shepherd	241
17.	The Worth and Worthlessness of Music	257
18.	Concerning Audiences, Preachers, Sermons, and Conversions	273
19.	"Sans Eyes, Sans Taste, Sans Everything"—But God and Hope	289
20.	Bread to the Full	305
21.	The Transfiguration	321
22.	Naaman, the Syrian	337
23.	The Farmer who Fed His Soul with Corn	353
24.	The Imperial Standard for Measuring Recruits	369
25.	Awake! Arise!	385
26.	The Salvation of Zacchaeus	401

INTRODUCTION TO THE AMERICAN EDITION.

Some men, like their master, cannot be hid. John McNeill is one of them: he needs no introduction. On both sides of the sea, he has won the ears of men, as any man will win them who thinks and speaks in dead earnest.

There is a grand difference between having to say something and having something to say. He has shown that he has much that is worth saying and therefore worth hearing. Those who read these sermons will not need to be told that the man who follows Dr. Dikes at Regent Square is a full, fresh, thoughtful, helpful preacher. But those who have heard him will know that the printed page can neither catch nor convey the charm of the action and attitude; the flashes of the eye, the tones of the voice, the magnetic sympathy, that make up the living speaker. As was said of Bishop Andrews and the seraphic Rutherford, "they might steal his *sermons*, but they could not steal his *preaching*." John McNeill must be heard to be appreciated.

Pulpit oratory is a divine art: it has three essentials; simplicity, sincerity, spirituality. In these sermons there is a marked simplicity, alike of thought and language. We found on one page, of nearly four hundred words, that over four-fifths of them were monosyllables, and three-fourths of them were of Saxon origin. As for clearness of thought, the "London Fog" does not seem to hang about Regent Square Pulpit. Mr.

McNeill's sincerity is transparent: he is a genuine man who speaks from the heart, and so to the hearts of others. As to spirituality, few preachers have a truer insight into divine truth, or a more effective way of putting it before the people.

John McNeill uses "great plainness of speech." Like John Knox, he seems to say, "I am in that place where I am demanded of my conscience to speak the truth and therefore the truth I speak—impugn it who list." But it is "speaking the truth in love," for a generous, sympathetic heart beats back of that utterance.

This preacher is a man of the people. Like the horse that will not go in blinders, he cannot endure the trimmings and trappings of ecclesiastical ceremony. Even a Geneva gown is irksome to him, and he casts it off as he gets into the sermon. When we watch the growing tendency to ritualism, we remember that "when the crozier became golden the bishops became wooden;" and that nothing is more lifeless than a mechanical religion. It is well to have men in these days whose whole life is a protest against forms and a plea for reality; who would not give up their hold upon the hearts of the lowest and poorest for a "garter" or "mitre," a palace or a throne. John McNeill is a true man, and nothing that is human is alien to him. May he long be spared to tell the "Old Story!"

ARTHUR T. PIERSON.

2320 SPRUCE STREET,
    PHILADELPHIA, PA.

Regent Square Pulpit.

MARY AND MARTHA; OR, STABLE AND UNSTABLE EQUILIBRIUM.

A Sermon

Delivered on Sunday Evening, Nov. 10, 1889, by the

REV. JOHN McNEILL.

"Now it came to pass, as they went, that he entered into a certain village: and a certain woman named Martha received Him into her house," &c.—Luke x. 38.

I should like at the outset to say that it is my desire in dealing with this simple village idyll to get as far away as possible from the unhappy discussion that has been started here to this effect: Was Martha really unconverted? Does the Lord mean to say at the end of the narrative, or does He mean to suggest, that only one of these sisters had really found the one thing needful, while the other had not? I think the better way will be for us to take the story as it comes, and try to gather what we can from the actors in it.

The Lord, we are told elsewhere, loved Martha and Mary, and the story as it has been given to us was intended to teach us mainly the diversities and varieties of character that may exist, and that do exist, within the household of Faith

No. 1.

amongst those who do really know, and love, and desire to serve the Lord Jesus. In the spiritual world, as in the natural, there is great variety in the midst of unity, but in this variety we are to ascertain what is to be commended and what is to be severely pruned and pinched off.

Mark how simply the story is told. "Jesus entered into a certain village," &c. If we would honestly follow the lead of the story, we would not get into those weary, vexing discussions, but would get the real gist of the question into our very hearts, so as to tell upon our lives. "Jesus went into a certain village." The story is told, first of all, because Jesus became incarnate, and actually stood here incarnate God. If He had not been the incarnate Son of God, this Jesus wandering about the roadsides of this weary world, then this story never would have been told. But seeing He is still with us, there ought to spring up in our hearts this earnest hungering: Oh, that He might come into my house, and make Himself as much at home under my roof as He was under the roof of that old home in Bethany long, long ago! That will come about if we are careful to notice how Martha acted. For this heavenly and homely narrative can as little be told without Martha as without her Master. The Lord came to her door. True. But she let Him in. "Behold I stand at the door and knock. If any man hear My voice and open the door, I will come into him, and will sup with him and he with Me."

"Jesus entered," &c. Ah, my friends, that is still true, and needs but very little explanation! The narrative is quite simple, and its spiritual meaning should not present difficulties to any of us, because there is Jesus, the incarnate Son of God, living our life here amongst us. He comes along the roadside, and here and there He enters; doors are opened to Him, homes are placed at His disposal, and not only homes, but also hearts. The expression, you will notice, is "Martha *received* Him into her house." The The word in the Greek, used to describe "received," has a much deeper significance than simply to offer a mere polite invitation to come in and rest Himself a little. She received Him into her house. Now the Lord is the same Lord still, and if He is not manifesting Himself to us, then we must know the reason why. It is because He has never been heartily invited. You cannot put off the Lord Jesus, any more than you can put off me, with a mere formal, a mere polite invitation. He must have earnestness, just as you and I must have it. You could stand up here and tell this people, whose houses you have never been in, and that it is not because you have never been invited, it is simply because of the coldness of the invitation, and you have not the slightest intention of going even when you are again asked. When the next politely worded note comes in requesting the favour of your company to dinner, the invitation will go into the waste-paper basket quicker than all the rest. You are not impressed by these invitations. Now in the case before us, Martha, in receiving Him into her house, gave Him a heartiness of welcome that pleased our Saviour, a heartiness that made them the recipients of those great and wonderful blessings which afterwards came out of Christ's visit to this home of Martha. And if you want Christ, (I am preaching a family sermon, which applies to lodgers as well), if you want Christ into your family (and even the best of landladies need Him), then receive Him as Martha did, with open arms and open hearts.

You remember that story of how one evening, when walking with His disciples, in coming to a certain place He made as if He would go farther. He had no intention of going farther. From all eternity He meant to enter there. And yet Scripture says, "He made as if He would go farther." Christ is just like ourselves—He likes to be pressed, and to be made welcome. Like one of your own friends, perhaps, whom you know to be of a shy and retiring disposition; one who does not like to force himself upon anybody. And when you ask some one who knows him, "Did you ask him to come?" he, perhaps, tells you "Yes"; and you say, "But did you press him?" "No." "Will you just press him the next time? Be hearty, and he is sure to come." That is just the same as Jesus of Nazareth. He still goes about the roadsides of this world, and oftentimes He makes as though He would go farther. Let us receive Him at such a time, and show Him that in deed and in truth we really want Him. Now, friends, none of the old treatment, none of the treatment we sometimes give to our Master. I have been treated anything but heartily sometimes amongst my own friends, and have, when passing their door, been asked to "Come in; it's just about supper-time. Will ye no come in? But perhaps you had better push on, it's getting late." Let us stop this "Come-in-but-push-on" invitation.

Lord, come in; we virtually say, I believe that *now* is the accepted time, and *now* is the day of salvation, but *again* would suit me as well. Ask Him in heartily, and He is in before you know it. There is nothing in all your house that He covets. He does not want to stretch His feet under your mahogany. There is nothing in all your house that is a treat to Him. There is just one thing that He wants, and that is you.

Long ago His enemies called Him a gluttonous man and a wine-bibber, meaning that He was a man that loved a good dinner. It was an infamous lie. The dish on the table, the dish at the dinner that Christ wants is you; not anything on the table, but the host himself, who has invited Him in.

So Martha received Him into her house. Let us consider more closely this wonderful thing, for thereby hangs a tale. When we are put under the fierce glare of that electric light of Heaven, no masks, no guises, nor disguises can prevent our very selves from coming out into the light of Christ's presence, which is the touchstone and the "test" of character, both at home and abroad everywhere. She had a sister called Mary, who also sat at His feet and heard His words. I like to have the names mentioned here as elsewhere in Scripture. It is beautiful to think that in God's Book our names are written; not in this, that, or the other book, but in God's own Book. There they all are: the husband and the wife, and the widow it maybe, and our Johnnies and Jennies, Marys and Bessies, and Katies and Tommies. Their names are all there—He knows them every one; they are all His family. There never was one so human and so Divine as the God who has revealed Himself to us in His dear Son. "Mary sat at Jesus' feet and heard His words." Perhaps the house may have belonged to Martha.

There was a man in Glasgow, a genius of a preacher, and because he was that, and said things out of the usual track, some people called him daft Wully Anderson. He made a remark once that amounted to genius: "I always think of this home in Bethany after a Scotch fashion. I think that Martha was a widow with property, and after her husband's death her sister Mary came to live with her, and brought with her their brother Lazarus, who was what the Scotch call 'silly' (that is weak physically), and in time he dwindled and died." Let this way of putting it help to bring home to us the real state of things, so that you can almost picture the scene in your own imagination. It is not at all an unlikely idea, and we can further imagine Mary taking a somewhat inferior or secondary position in the house. And so it came about that as Martha bustled about, Mary took up a position near the Master, went out of the kitchen in fact, and sat at Jesus' feet as He discoursed, and heard His word. "But Martha was cumbered about much serving, and came to Jesus and said, Dost thou not care that she help me?"

Here is where the great contrast and diversity of character is revealed. Martha busy and bustling, Mary sitting at the feet of Jesus, then the little outburst of temper, then the appeal to the Lord, then the Lord's final verdict upon this whole business. Now I do not want to say much against Martha. In some respects she was a very good creature—

may her number be increased! I do believe that if you could get a Martha and a Mary combined, you would get a perfect wife, or mother, or sister; but as we cannot get both, let us have each at her best. Martha, despite her faults, was a most excellent character. She was observant, and she could mark Christ's weariness—for the Son of God could get leg-weary on His journey, even like ourselves, and He needed kindness and attention at these times as we need them—and Martha went on the right track; she did the right thing and at the right moment.

Speaking of myself as God's servant, I have found after doing Christ's work in a certain neighbourhood, I won't say which neighbourhood—I don't want to make anybody's face red—I missed Sister Martha. In order to do Martha's work, you have to leave the drawing-room or the sitting-room and go away into the kitchen, and be perhaps covered with flour up to the elbows; still, I must say you never look better than when doing even such domestic work as that. Don't be ashamed of the kitchen. Let me say a word to those who are superfine ladies: don't be so ignorant of the duties of the kitchen, as some of you unhappily are. Your education is not finished unless you have gone through the training of a cookery school, and can work like Martha. Bless God for the Marthas, and I say again, may their number increase! Probably, some of you here thought I was going to run down Martha. You are enlightened by this time—I have done nothing of the sort. I wish Christianity would teach some people to boil a potato readily, and to cook a bit of food. Still, poor Martha made a mistake. She was cumbered about much serving, and she came to Him to say, "Dost thou not care that my sister has left me to serve alone? bid her therefore that she help me." She made the mistake that we are all apt to make. She was a handy and a clever woman, and she believed herself, or thought herself, to be the *type and model*—and that is a peculiar mistake to which every one is liable.

One Martha in the house is a great blessing; but when there are two or three of them hurrying and scurrying about the house, it is too much for one man. They never rest, they won't sit down and speak to a body. It is no doubt done from a very good motive, but all this fussiness only upsets and irritates. Martha, dear, betimes rest; take a leaf out of Mary's book; try to understand that when Christ comes this flurry and this tendency to fly in the face of other people is sin, not service. That was where Martha went wrong, when she burst so suddenly upon Christ. Having been busy bustling and fussing in the kitchen with no one to help her, her temper had been touched, and she broke in upon Christ, and, without giving herself time to think, she gave utterance to this wild speech, "Lord, dost thou not care?" &c. Ah, yes! there are many of us who like Martha would always like to be in the right, and would always like the Lord to stand by and hear Him say, "Mary, take to your feet and go into the kitchen."

If we could only get the Lord to endorse our own certificate about our own mighty service, how glad we would be. No, the Lord will dare to tell a Martha that she is wrong. What a poor speech she made. Just think for a moment who that Man was, Jesus the Incarnate Son of God. The same words as used by Martha were on another occasion used by His disciples in tones almost blasphemous. And such words sometimes are not very far from our hearts if not from our tongues.

"Master, carest Thou not that we perish, whilst Thou art lying sleeping there?" What awful thing is this which has come upon us? Let us set a watch upon the door of our lips, that we sin not with our tongues.

Brother, sister—for in this business there is neither male nor female—a great deal of your fussing, which is not working, has it not this complexion in it: a great deal of grumbling not at each other, but Him—"Dost *Thou* not care?" Martha was cumbered about much serving. The word "deacon" has the same meaning in the Greek. Might I be allowed to constitute the Deacon's Court, and to say to some of them—Is there not just a little of this fussiness in our Deacons' Courts, is there not just a little of this fussiness in all of our Church service? What an ado we make. I was preaching to a magnificent audience in another part of London one day, and I noticed how fussily the deacons were going to work, so much so that they nearly spoiled everything. They were bringing in piles of chairs, though the people were quite content to be as they were, but Martha must be flouncing here and there! Serve if you like, by all means; do all that is in your heart; *but let other people alone.* Don't think that there is no other way of showing kindness to Jesus but your way. I need this truth taught me; we all need it. The Lord thanks no man for turning His service from being a pleasure into a burden. "My burden" (and it is true in every sense) "My burden is light."

"They also serve," says John Milton, "who only stand and wait;" and they may keep up a waiting, restful attitude who yet are full of activity. In the spiritual, as in the natural world, there is what is called stable and unstable equilibrium. Let Mary represent the one, and Martha (after her adjustment) the other.

> "Oh, Perfect Pattern from above,
> So succour us, that ne'er
> Prayer keep us back from works of love,
> Nor works of love from prayer."

Yes, our Lord Himself is the Perfect Pattern. In Him we see "perfect peace subsisting at the heart of endless agitation."

What more shall I say about Mary? Mary is difficult to understand, and Mary is difficult to preach about, because she is so deep, because her spirituality is so simple and so profound! When Christ entered the house, Mary put aside her work. Her heart at once enters into a peace and a rest that the world cannot give and the world cannot take away. Mary represents the profound, adoring, contemplative side of the Christian character.

But may there not be spoiled Marys as well as "riled" Marthas among us? There are those who are too quiet; there are those amongst us who do too little; there are those who are not too spiritual, but are always running to meetings when it would perhaps be more proper for them to stay at home and wash the dishes. You understand? I am glad you do. I shall hope to see a great improvement in domestic economy after this sermon. The Lord save us from the woman, the Lord save us from the man, who talks as if household duties and secular things were becoming to them unholy because they are getting so profoundly spiritual! Out upon such spirituality! I am not speaking to Mary; I am speaking to you. There are many of us who are finding excuses for laziness. It is much nicer and easier to come to meetings and sing, "All hail the power of Jesu's name," &c., than it is to set to work like Sister Martha. It is not so nice to go home and roll up your sleeves and set to work. Who knows but that some of you here might have been better employed than in coming to this place of worship! You might have been keeping the bairns of some poor woman who never more will be able to come to the church unless some one takes the bairns off her hands for the time being.

Now what did Jesus say in reply to Martha's speech? "And Jesus answered and said to her, Martha, thou art careful and troubled about many things; but one thing is needful: and Mary has chosen that good part, which shall not be taken from her." What really is the meaning of Christ's words? Some would say this, that Christ meant to say, "Martha, you are troubled about many dishes; you are doing too much. You don't understand Me. I don't need many dishes and the great work you are making about Me. I don't want you to put yourself about. I don't thank you for offering me such great service." In the East it is quite common to make a meal off one dish, and perhaps that is what Christ wished Martha to understand. "One dish is enough for Me." Well, that is, perhaps, too literal an interpretation. But, my brother, my sister, you never met anybody so easily pleased as the Son of God—never, if you only take Him the right way.

Some of us are bursting ourselves trying to do great things for Him, and we are utterly out of our reckoning. There is a sense in which He is hard to please, but on this side of the question the giving of a simple thing, even a cup of cold water in His name, pleases Him. You remember the time when a poor widow woman passed Him one day as she went into the Temple, and she dropped into the treasury two mites, and the Lord's face lit up with a great light as He seemed to say, "I am best served by simplicity and heartiness such as this." Let us get rid of our foolish ideas; let us not be like the man in the parable who came to his master on his return, giving him back the pound rolled in a napkin, with the words, "I knew that thou wast a hard man, ill to serve, reaping where thou hast not sown," &c. I knew there was no pleasing of thee, so I never tried it. "Lo! there thou hast that is thine."

There is nobody so easily served as Jesus. You will find this in your family circle. Anybody who loves you is pleased, easily pleased. Your master, your mother, your wife, your sister, your friend, your minister, your Saviour, if they love you they are easily pleased. Now Jesus loved Martha and her sister; let us get the benefit of that idea in our Church service, and cease striving after great things. Do simple things, and do them from the heart.

But I think Christ's language has a wider application. I think He lifted His eyes far beyond Bethany, and beyond His own day and generation His eye swept down through the Church, and He looked grand and noble and solemn almost to severity, with the warning tone in His voice to keep us all right here, as if He would say, " Martha, Martha, take care ! You may make a god of your service in the midst of all your dish-making. In the midst of your preparing for Me you may lose sight of Me." The Christian system is a splendidly simple system. It focusses all its faith and all its creed and all its conduct upon one, and only one thing, blessed be God, and that one thing you may miss. " Mary hath chosen that good part that shall not be taken from her." Before I let this family go, let me be what is called evangelistic. Before I let you go, let me preach Christ to you. One thing is needful. In the midst of this dinging out of life to keep it in, to study what we shall eat and drink and wherewithal we shall be clothed, there come straight from the Eternal Glory the ringing words to lift us up from the turmoil and bustle of the world : One thing needful — one that is really needful. What a helpful thought !

How it gladdens our souls. How it girds up the loins of our minds! How it delivers us from the distracting power of the thousand voices that rush upon us and say, " Here, here, here is the thing you need !" " Nay, nay, nay," says another. " In this direction is what you require."

"No, no," says another; "it **is** here you will find satisfaction."

But Christ says they are all liars; they are all cheats; they are all deceivers. One thing is needful, and I have got it, and I only. Yea, I am the one necessity for the soul of man.

It was the salvation of a very busy man in a country village. He gave a good deal to the church, and he was very useful in many ways, and his minister had watched him for some time and decided to test him. And one day he chanced to meet this man, and spoke to him. This man spoke about the great things he was doing in the church, and how well the church was getting on, &c. The minister looked at him and said, "One thing is needful, John; and I am afraid you have not got it," and he passed on. That night John came to the minister's door, not sad and anxious, but in a state of assurance and gladness. He almost wrung the minister's hand as he said, "Minister, I thank you for your word at the roadside. It was the very thing I needed. I didn't know the one thing. Now I believe I have got it," and he dropped down into his native Scotch, and said, "Aye, sir, it is hard to put us richt. Speak to them a' like yon, sir; say 'yon' to them a'."

There are some here who are fond of praising their church; even of praising their minister; even of bringing people to hear their minister. I will dare your wrath. I will look into your eyes and say that before God I stand in doubt of you. One thing is needful, and I fear you are as yet without it. Your heart is not yet resting in and on and with the Son of God. I am clear of your blood after to-night, for I have told you how you may have this thing. There is time even here; and when you seek it, ask for it in simple, fervent prayer.

Even in the whirl of London's traffic some hearts are glad, for they continually behold the face of God and hear His Word.

> "There are in this loud, stunning tide
>   Of human care and crime,
> With whom the melodies abide
>   Of the everlasting chime;
> Who carry music in their heart,
> Thro' dusky lane and wrangling mart,
> Plying their daily task with busier feet,
> Because their secret souls some holy strain repeat."

Regent Square Pulpit.

THE CONVERSION OF LYDIA.

A Sermon

DELIVERED ON SUNDAY MORNING, NOV. 17, 1889, BY THE

REV. JOHN McNEILL.

"And from thence to Philippi, which is the chief city of that part of Macedonia, and a colony: and we were in that city abiding certain days. And on the Sabbath we went out of the city by a river side, where prayer was wont to be made; and we sat down, and spake unto the women which resorted thither. And a certain woman named Lydia, a seller of purple, of the city of Thyatira, which worshipped God, heard us: whose heart the Lord opened, that she attended unto the things which were spoken of Paul. And when she was baptized, and her household, she besought us, saying, If ye have judged me to be faithful to the Lord, come into my house, and abide there. And she constrained us."—ACTS xvi. 12-15.

I MUST cast myself upon your indulgence to-day. Let me say at once that this is not the subject from which I meant to preach. I had prepared myself, because this is College Day, on a subject which brought in some special and particular reference to professors and students. I have no heart now to make the remarks.* My subject is taken from me; and so I ask that you and I alike may to-day feel that the Lord Himself gives us the message. He has taken you and me into His own hands, and I trust that out of this, which certainly puts me very greatly about and which reduces me to the very uttermost, He may bring glory

---

* The preacher had only learned half an hour before of the death of Professor Elmslie.

No. 2.

to Himself. That, at any rate, is what one might reasonably expect—that when a man feels himself utterly confused, and utterly at an end of what little power he may think he has, then is the time when God may be glorified. May it be so. We are going forward to our communion service this evening, and I should like to take up this subject because we have here the elements of the Gospel, and if the Lord applies it to our hearts it will be the best of all preparations for sitting down at His table.

"On the Sabbath day," says the narrative, "we went out of the city by a river side, where prayer was wont to be made; and we sat down, and spake unto the women which resorted thither. And a certain woman named Lydia, a seller of purple, of the city of Thyatira, which worshipped God, heard us: whose heart the Lord opened that she attended unto the things which were spoken of Paul." This narrative brings out one side of the work of grace very plainly. Other narratives bring out other sides; but this narrative seems to be put here to emphasize that the human heart naturally, the human heart even at its best, the human heart even when it is, so to speak, religious, and, in a sense, possessed of the fear of God as the one Lord and Creator, the Ruler and Disposer of all things, is still shut against the indwelling of that same Lord, as He has revealed Himself for purposes of grace and salvation in Christ Jesus.

Before we come to that point let us see, however, how the narrative itself leads us up to it. This is a critical time, I had almost said, in your history and in mine. When we open the Bible at this chapter we open it with peculiar interest, for here the Lord of grace and of salvation is on His way to us. The Lord is bending His steps westward, and, so to speak, committing Himself to cause the channel of His grace, which ultimately is to bless all the earth, to be cut through Europe first instead of through Asia. It is a critical moment. Just suppose that Paul and Silas had been ordered the other way instead of this way. Then very likely, if everything else had happened as it has happened, these lands of ours would have been the India and the Asia and the Africa that now are; and away in those lands the Gospel would have been abundant, and ministers would be doing their best to get their people to contribute to foreign missions, to evangelize the barbarians of Europe and all over this way. It is a critical place. We ought never to open this page without having that in our minds. God is committing Himself to come this way. Behind that shut heart of Lydia lies Europe, with these islands of the sea. It is a thrilling narrative. How silently it begins. How quietly the story is told; so quietly that unless you read and think and examine the history and drift of things, you do not see the great departure that God is taking. Slowly God does His work; but let us always be interested in it, for whatsoever He does is from eternity and has consequences to eternity.

Leaving that high aspect of the question and coming to the human side, as the narrative is told here, see what has to be taken in. They had been staying in Philippi for certain days, as you might be sojourning in London, and on the Sabbath day they went outside the gate to the river side, where they supposed there was a place of prayer. So then, humanly speaking, the Gospel came to Lydia, and the Gospel came to us, because Paul was a man of fixed principles and fixed habits. Paul was not a man who was a devout worshipper when he was in Jerusalem, but who when he was in Philippi spent his time on Sundays as the Philippians did. Not he. I am not straining: I am not exaggerating. We are warranted to look minutely into every point in this wonderful narrative, remembering its place in the Divine purpose for a great mass of mankind; and looking at it in that way, we are warranted in condescending with some force and insistence upon this—that had Paul been as loose and uncertain in his observance of the Sabbath day as some people whom we know, this story would not have been written under his name. It is very hard to do what Paul did. It is not a little thing. It requires purpose and determination. He had to gird up the loins of his mind, if on the Sabbath day he would turn his back upon Philippi and upon all its wonders. Unlike us, Paul, true to his training and true to his habits, this old-fashioned, narrow-minded, prejudiced, bigoted Jew turned his back upon Philippi, and went outside to where he expected that, following their usual custom, his countrymen and countrywomen would be gathered together for their peculiar religious rites and ceremonies. Do I speak to strangers who are among us to-day? My friend, let this lesson be for you. Forget not your God to-day. Forget not the ways of worship in which you were brought up in some place else when you are sojourning here in London to-day. Remember that God is with you to-day. Remember that God is watching you to-day. Remember that for this Sabbath you shall be responsible. To-day you are not in your accustomed place. You are not in your accustomed church. You are not to-day in your usual Sabbath-school work, or in your usual Christian work of whatever kind; but God has not given you the holiday to spend as you please because of that. Remember that perhaps you were brought here to-day to open some door which, but for your arrival, would have remained shut. Look up to God to-day, and ask Him this day as earnestly, yea, perhaps more earnestly than ever before, to use you for His glory in this strange city, and amidst the strange surroundings in which you feel yourself at this very hour.

"Lord," says the Psalmist, "I have loved the habitation of Thy house, and the place where Thine honour dwelleth." Can we say the same? Is the love of worship, the love of the old familiar round of worship, so strong in us that when the worshipping day comes round our heart almost by itself wakens up with strong desire to engage in the dear and familiar round? Sometimes we have to speak severely, lest the routine of worship may become the end in itself. Sometimes we have to speak severely against an observance of the Sabbath day which is an observance only in form and in dull, monotonous routine.

But here we are at the other side of it. Never delude yourself into believing that I—to speak for myself—am saying a single word against the Sabbath day: the need for the Sabbath day, and the need, if you will, for steady plodding attendance on the ordinances of grace as these are conducted on Sabbath particularly and peculiarly. Out of Paul's steady-going habits there came this wonderful story of grace and salvation.

What a wonderful scene is presented to us! "Outside of the city," the city away back there, with its sin, and its bustle, and its sprightliness, and its gaiety, and its multitude. They turn their backs on the city, and go out here to this quiet place by the river side. What a picture after all of all congregations! Where are we to-day? "Along the river of time we glide" all the other days of the week, floating down to the vast sea of eternity. Some who were with us last Sabbath, it may be have gone into the great sea. But on the Sabbath day we reach a little quiet creek, and God's own hand thrusts our boat in here; and while the river goes speeding away on to the sea, we disembark for a little. This is a resting day. We get out of the swim and the stream and the current. We disembark, and quietly, for a little time, while our boat rocks idly in this little bay, we rest ourselves. We land, and we sit down, and lo! God's servant providentially comes among us, and he lifts up his voice, and he speaks of things that belong to eternity and to the kingdom of Jesus Christ; and we open our hearts, or rather our hearts are opened for us, so that we attend to the things that are said to us, and receive inestimable blessings thereby. May that scene be repeated while we sit here, and as this service goes on this forenoon. May it have a thousand thousand illustrations all over the land on this blessed Sabbath day.

What a boon comes to the world when the Sabbath day comes! What a blessing came to Philippi that Sabbath day, although the great city back there knew nothing of the Lord Jesus Christ, or only knew Him to scoff at Him. What a blessing was on the road to that city; and it came, humanly speaking, by means of a well-kept Sabbath day.

> "A Sabbath well-spent brings a week of content,
> And health for the toils of the morrow;
> But a Sabbath profaned, whatever be gained,
> Is a certain forerunner of sorrow."

"A certain woman named Lydia, a seller of purple, of the city of Thyatira, who worshipped God, heard us: whose heart the Lord opened, that she attended unto the things which were spoken of Paul." What a quiet congregation! I do not suppose they were even roofed in. There was the river gurgling past in front, and this little company of women—no men mentioned. Can you imagine a more unattractive programme? Remember that the Lord is on His way to Europe, and see in what an anti-climax and unheroic way He begins. A vision appeared to Paul—a man of Macedonia cried, "Come over and help us." Paul takes that as the Lord's guiding, and he goes over. He crossed over from Asia into Europe, and lo! as Dr. Andrew Bonar used to say, the man turns out to be a woman. Here is "the man of Macedonia." You can imagine Paul going about the city and wondering and saying. "I wonder where the man is? Where is the man whom I saw in the vision?" And on the Sabbath day he goes outside of the city, and the Lord brings him to the person whom he is seeking. But, I say, how unlike the way in which we would act. I do not wish to be hard on anybody except myself, but I am compelled to say how unlike the Lord's "Forward" Movements are to some of which we hear. And this was a Forward Movement on a magnificent scale; and yet how quietly it was done. No big bills—and I believe in bills; I believe in "sandwich" men. Here was no beating of the drum. Maybe the Lord would like us to take a leaf out of His book, and whether we do things in a quiet way, or whether we do things in some more overt and public way to be very intense, to make sure that we are aiming at individuals and not at a blurred and confused mass, for that will come to nothing. God says in the very forefront of His purpose here, that if Europe ever is to be saved, it is to be saved man by man, woman by woman, family by family. That is God's programme. That is how He has been coming along ever since. He begins at one woman, one household—and so it spreads. How quiet. No men there. People, perhaps, taking a stroll by the river side would cast a strange, wondering eye upon that little group, little knowing what was there. Paul was there, Lydia was there, God the Father was there, God the Son was there, God the Holy Ghost was there, the Word of God was there. "Who hath despised the day of small things." No wise man; but fools do it continually—and that is a folly that you and I are apt to be guilty of. It is a folly that we London ministers and Christian workers are apt to be guilty of. We come to some meeting, and God knows that our hearts were set upon the meeting, and we meant to do good; and when we "turn up" there are only a few women, and the very look on our face says, "Only a few women! The meeting is a failure. None of the men of the district! This is not the class of people we wanted to get at," and so on. When will we learn to get rid of these phrases that have so much unbelief in them? One might have said, "Oh! Paul, Paul, Paul, you are off the track. Man, you have lost yourself! You are out of it now altogether. You are swinging about aimlessly." Paul did not think so, but he sat down and spoke unto the women who resorted thither. I am not saying a word against big crowds. I like to preach to a big crowd. If you do not fill this church for me every time I come to preach I will let you hear about it on the deafest side of your head! Let me say that it is very difficult, as I have often told you, to convert sinners. It needs Almighty power. But it is utterly impossible to convert empty benches, and I never want to see dead wood. The Lord save me from preaching in a wood yard. No, I say nothing against multitudes. Often a bad use is made of Christ speaking to the woman at the well. How often that incident is quoted against those unfortunate beings (I disclaim being among the number) called "popular preachers." "Oh, the popular preachers," it is said, "have an unholy lust for crowds; they forget that Christ spoke to the woman at the well." Did He? Yes, He did; but He so spoke to the woman at the well that she went and raised the town about Him. The next day came the whole city nearly to hear Him. I say nothing against preaching the Word to multitudes; but what we have to learn this morning, whether we be dealing with the multitude or with a small number, is that the Lord saves individually. All that He seems to claim is this: "Let Me get in anywhere, and I will be glad. That is a beginning. Let Me get into the heart of one woman, and there will be a church in Philippi coming out of that"—as there was. What a blessing now to learn the lesson! Sabbath-school teacher, Christian worker, Bible-class teacher, preacher, aim at the individuals. "God has much people in this city," but this is how He gets at the multitude — through means of quickened individuals; and if your company this afternoon should be small because the weather is foggy, or because it is wet, do not let the light die out of your face, and do not let despondency and fog creep into your heart, and do not let God see that your heart is saying, "What a small meeting! only a few women and children." God bless the women who give us meetings! for sometimes if it it were not for Lydia we should have no meeting at all. Do you understand that, you men, greyheaded men as well as young men? Where would some of God's poor preachers be if it were not for women? It is not that you are engaged. It is simply that you will not come. You consider it beneath you to come. It is not that you stay at home in the evening. You do not. You go out in the evening, but you do not come this way. Suffer that word just as sharply and as heartily as I am saying it, for you need it. I want to pierce through all disguises and to blow away all misconceptions. We ought not to be left many times as we are. Still, accepting the situation as it is, if there are only a few women, let us, like Paul, say to ourselves, "This is God's opportunity, and this is my work."

Notice the condition of the heart of this worshipper. She was a devout woman according to her light; not a Christian as yet, in our sense of the term, but a devout woman, one who worshipped God. She had come into contact with Jews, and the Jews had taught her the one God who made heaven and earth and the seas, and all that are in them. She knew after some dim and distant fashion the God of Israel. She was not an idolater. She had turned away from paganism in which very likely she was born, she had turned away from all its vanity, and she had turned away from all its abominations. She was one who worshipped God. I am speaking to some Lydias here. It is not enough to be devout. It is not enough to be religious after the ordinary fashion. It is not enough to believe in one God. It is not enough because of your belief in God to depart from open and flagrant iniquity. It is not enough to be diligent in your calling, as no doubt Lydia was, and to owe no man anything, and to pay twenty shillings in the pound, and to attend to the affairs of your own household, and to be decent and upright and regular, while others are indecent and bad and altogether depraved. That is not enough. Even Lydia with all these things in her favour needs to have her shut heart opened. Now, in God's name, before I let you go to the communion table to-night, my brother, my sister, has that mighty change, do you think, passed upon you? Has your shut heart been opened to let the Lord in? Why, you are still only a decent Jew; a worshipper of the one God who made heaven and earth, the main element in your worship being a kind of fear of Him, that He does live and He is not to be too flagrantly sinned against. I am afraid that is all that is in the thoughts of many people. They are not converted; they are not Christians in sincerity and in truth. The Lord is still outside their hearts. Whatever they do religiously is only what Lydia did before Paul came, bringing the revelation of God in Christ with him.

But still we have to notice that she was there, and she was using the light which she had; and by using the light which she had she came to more. "Whose heart," says the narrative, "the Lord opened, that she attended to the things which were spoken of Paul." Notice, then, how here in this narrative the preacher is suppressed, and notice how the sermon is suppressed, and notice how the hearer is lifted up into prominence. This is a grand subject for a preacher. This subject takes your eye off me, and turns your eye upon yourself, my hearer. The next story of conversion, or the next again—the story of the Philippian jailor—elevates into prominence the preacher of the Gospel. In that story you have the sum and substance of the Gospel eternally: "Believe on the Lord Jesus Christ, and thou shalt be saved." That is our message; but in this story see how Paul is set aside, and the sermon is set aside, and the hearer is lifted up and analyzed once for all: "Whose heart the Lord opened, that she attended unto the things which were spoken of Paul." Notice, then, that attention, humanly speaking, is the avenue by which the Lord Jesus Christ, with all blessings of His Gospel for time and for eternity, comes into the human soul. Attention. It is a small thing, but I am afraid a rare thing. Why are there so few conversions in Regent Square? There may be two answers to that question. It may be because you do not get much to attend to. That may be. I am willing to bear my share. It may be because you have not Paul preaching, and because you have not the Gospel that Paul preached. If that be so, may God shut my mouth and take me hence, and send a man in my place who will give you Paul's Gospel to attend to. But the other side may also be true, that even supposing that you had that great Apostle, and even supposing that you had him preaching the Gospel as he knew it, and as he felt it, and as he preached it, with fervour and vigour, with all the resources of a great big mind and heart, and a burning desire for the salvation of souls, still conversions in Regent's Square might be very scanty indeed if the audience did not attend to the things which were spoken by the preacher. And it is not so easy as we are apt to imagine. It needs the power of the Holy Spirit to enable Paul to preach, and it needs the same power to enable the hearer to hear. Just look for a moment at the thousand and one things that make attention difficult. Remember the awful issues that hang upon simple absorbing attention to God's message, and then the whole aspect of sermon-hearing is changed. The preacher stands up, and he begins to preach. The person sitting next you may want to get the Gospel. He may not have had the Gospel. He may never really have attended to the Gospel, and he is just beginning to attend to the Gospel with personal, breathless, thrilling interest for the first time as a message which has some personal reference to himself, when the devil starts a tickling in your throat as you are sitting next him. You begin to bark and cough, and the attention is broken, and the enemy wins. He could not attend, and he went away without having heard, and without being saved. I want to put it as broadly and bluntly and plainly as that, for that is the truth. That is only one thing. There are many other 'things. The more we try to attend, the more we shall be made to find that it is not easy. The more we shall be made to find that every time we gather into the church to hear God's Word, it becomes a kind of theatre on which contending forces display themselves, trying to carry off the soul of the worshipper. While I am speaking, how many things help to distract attention. Although your face is to me, where is your mind just now? Thinking of the state of things at home? Thinking of something that was in your business yesterday? Thinking of something that is to be in your business to-morrow? Thinking, thinking, thinking. Even while it is "eyes front," and there seems to be "attention," you are thinking of everything rather than the Lord Jesus Christ, who speaks to you wherever the Gospel in simplicity is being proclaimed. Ah, how many of us are like the wayside hearers! Who are the wayside hearers? Those who hear the Word, but do not attend. "Hail makes as much impression on a slated roof as the preaching of the Gospel makes upon your mind," for you do not bring your mind with you to the church. You bring your Sunday looks and your Sunday books. But your immortal soul? God knows what you do with that. You do not give it to me. You would have been converted like Lydia—you might have been converted like Lydia long, long ago, if ever once you had listened with attention and intention for five minutes to the poorest preacher who ever stood here. It was not want of the Gospel. I will say that for myself, and certainly I can say it for the grand men who went before me. It was not want of the Gospel. You are unconverted, not because of a poor preacher here, but because of a mighty poor listener down there. "Whose heart the Lord opened that she attended." Send your soul up to your ear. At that gateway listen and watch for Almighty God as He passes by. That is what we have got our ears for. That is what we have got our eyes for. That is why we are here, *compos mentis*. That is why we are here with a sound mind in a sound body, that God may have us in the best condition for getting simply but entirely into our being. "Hear," says the prophet, "and your soul shall live."

Then see how this simple narrative brings out the mystery of conversion. The plainness of it: "She attended unto the words which were spoken by Paul." The mystery of it: Her heart was opened by the Lord. Do not ask me to explain that. I cannot explain it. I can only point you to the fact, but what a blessed fact it is. For this comes to me and says to me as it says to you, and as it says to all of us,

"Oh, human soul, hast thou ever really attended to the word of the truth of the Gospel? Dost thou think that thou dost know Him who is its message, even the Lord Jesus Christ? Do you know Him? And if you can honestly say that you think you do, "Then," says the narrative, "Blessed art thou Simon Barjona, for flesh and blood never revealed that unto thee." It was not the preacher, although he had the eloquent tongue of men and of angels. It was not a wonderful sermon, though it may have been preached by Spurgeon or Moody. It was not the earnest, eloquent, pointed sermon that revealed Christ Jesus to thee. His own hand unlocked thy shut heart. It was Himself who stepped in through the open door and took possession. This work God will not give to another. This first, last, essential work of opening the shut heart and opening the blind eye, and unstopping the deaf ear, and quickening the dead soul, is God's glorious prerogative. He, and He alone, opens the shut heart of even worshipping men.

I say that that is a comfort. I am glad of that. I am glad of that little bit of spiritual analysis—spiritual psychology. If my heart has been opened, it was divinely done. I have been the subject of a mysterious but Divine operation. Never again can I be what I once was. My heart has been opened. Would, God, it might be done to-day! Oh, what a strange thing is the heart of man! Not long ago, in sport, a man handed me a purse with money in it, and I felt it and I heard it jingle. He said, "Open it"; and in spite of my doing my utmost, I could not. I turned it over and over, end for end; tugged it now this way, tugged it now that way; pressed what seemed to be one spring, pressed what seemed to be another; but it was too cunningly and too curiously contrived. It absolutely baffled me. Such is the heart of man. It is worth the opening. The Son of God would like to get into it. Lift up your heart, man, woman, where you sit. Lift up your heart in your hand to God and say, "Open this mystery; for, O God, it is true what the preacher is saying. My heart is shut against Thee — shut hard and close and fast, double bolted, double locked, double barred. Oh, take me in hand Thyself, for this McNeill, of Regent Square, will never get the Gospel into my heart. I am too cunning for him. I am too subtle for him. I am too deep and tortuous and twisted for him. I am too intellectual for him. He might save some sinner in the slums; but, O God, I am going down to hell—to the hell of the critics who attend only to " pick holes and tear to pieces." If there is a hotter hell than another, you are on the road to it, my friend! May God save you from it. Hand up that round, black, cold, shut heart of yours which I have gone all round in my stupid, blundering way. I have tried it here and I have tried it there; and I have pushed here, and I have touched the other place—reason, will, conscience, affection, love, fear, hate. God knows that I have touched all the springs about you which I know, and I have failed. Hand it up to God. Do it yourself. Do not be put off any longer. Hand up your heart to God, and say, "O God, do for me what Thou didst for Lydia. Open my heart." If I may use the figure, God will hold your heart down in front of you in His hands, just before He opens it, and He will say to you, " I will open it; but would you care to see in? Would you like to see what is in it?" Out of the heart proceed evil thoughts, murders, adulteries, thefts, fornications, blasphemies. These are the things that are in it. Do you want to see them ?—that is another reason why it is hard to attend to the Gospel. If the heart were empty—but it is not, it is packed full. Oh, that God might open our hearts to-day, as He opened Lydia's, and that He would let us see them, for I rather fear that our first thought when our hearts are opened will be, "He will never come in!" Ah! but He will. He will. I think I see the Lord Jesus Christ doing what I did out in the country one day some time ago. I came to a little cottage away out in a lonely moor, and I went round, but the shutters were up against the windows, and I went round to the door, but the door was fastened. However, it did open; and you know the uncertain, cautious way in which you push open the door of an empty house and peer into the darkness. But I went in. So the Lord Jesus Christ to-day is coming to your heart, and He knows all the springs and locks in it, and He is opening it, and He is looking in. God help us! What a place! It is hanging with cobwebs; shivering draughts flying through it; unclean things wriggling and squirming about the floor; everything dark and desolate and dirty, for it has been God-forsaken ever since you were born. Oh, human soul! it is not a small text; it is a great text. The Lord opened the heart of Lydia, and, decent woman outwardly and all as she was, that is what He saw inside. That is but a faint description of what He saw, and yet He opened it, and yet He came in. So it is with Him to-day.

May He use His great power; may He come in all the more that this sermon was not to have been your sermon to-day; all the more that it is coming upon you and upon myself with pretty much of a surprise. May He come in— that blessed Lord who opens the heart, that Lord at whose girdle hang the keys of all hearts here. May He pass through these pews. Listen! listen to the jingling of the keys at His girdle as He is looking for the one key that will open your heart; and look up, and help Him, and say to Him, "Lord Jesus Christ, put in the key and open my heart, and take possession of me."

"And when she was baptized, and her household, she besought us, saying, If ye have judged me to be faithful to the Lord, come to my house, and abide there. And she constrained us." First the heart, and then the home. She kept them; she lodged them; she fed them; she bore all charges for them at the very beginning. We need this very day to have all this revived in our hearts. We need to get back to our first faith and back to our first love. Listen. We are wanting between this and the end of the year over a thousand pounds, and Lydia can do it, but only

Lydia. If the Lord gets into your heart to-day the money will come tumbling out to-morrow. You have been keeping it by far too long. Remember Lydia at once became a contributor to the Sustenation Fund! She took in Paul, and took in his companion, and in a true sense she sustained them for days. That is just a type and picture of what we all should do, and what we all should be: first of all our hearts opened by the Lord Himself, then our house opened, our children given over to Him, our business given over, and all that we are and have devoted to His service. Oh, to be minister to a congregation of Lydias who open their hearts to the Lord, and open their houses to the Lord, and lay their whole substance at His disposal for the carrying on of His cause at home and abroad.

May the Gospel—the old Gospel—spread among us here and everywhere in the old way. May we get the women truly converted to Christ; for when we get them, we get the children and the servants and the money; and as for the men—well, they aren't so all-important as we have been making them out to be, and so *place aux dames!* May the Lord surprise us with His salvation, through this "surprise" sermon.

Regent Square Pulpit.

A SHORT WALK OVER "REDEMPTION GROUND."

A Sermon

Delivered on Sunday Morning, Nov. 24, 1889, by the

REV. JOHN McNEILL.

Text: Exodus xiv.

We cannot, of course, go into all the minute detail given here; the chapter is thirty-one verses long. But you will notice that our translators have put paragraph marks through this chapter, as they have done all through Scripture; and although sometimes these are not very well planted, in this chapter, at any rate, they really mark paragraphs, and are real and helpful divisions, and we might get most profitably through the whole of this narrative by simply taking a striking word or expression out of each paragraph.

The first paragraph contains the first four verses, and the striking expression there is, if you will allow me to come at once to this subject, "And Pharaoh will say of the children of Israel, They are entangled in the land, the wilderness hath shut them in." Of course this was written for our instruction, upon whom the ends of the ages are resting. These people were redeemed from the bitter bondage of Egypt. We are redeemed from a still more bitter bondage and severe task-master. As with them, so with us: with a high hand and an outstretched arm the Lord has broken our bonds, and is leading and guiding us to a place of which

No. 3.

He has spoken to us in the Word of the promise of His Gospel. He is bringing us to a goodly land and a large. He is bringing us, though it be through fire and water, to a wealthy place; and all this history of Israel, from their redemption from Egypt to their possession of the promised land, is but a picture of our progress from justification to final sanctification and eternal glory. Now here, where in this chapter the curtain rises upon Israel's national history, and where the spiritual curtain rises upon our spiritual history, the analogical teaching is very strong.

And I want you to centre your attention on that expression, "They were entangled in the land." Just precisely as it was with them as living, breathing men and women, and as a nation with such and such a history in the past, and with such and such a prospect in the future, and the present immediate surroundings; so it is with us. A great deal of our distress, a great deal of our present panic and uneasiness, and misery and gloom, comes from the voice that whispers in our ears, "To leave Egypt was a mistake." True, you were not exactly well off there; still, what better have you made of yourself by the change? You have escaped one kind of trouble only to land yourself in another. You have avoided Scylla and fallen upon Charybdis. True, you are delivered from the lash of the task-master; you are not so sunburnt and baked, body and soul, as you used to be; but what more have you made of it? "You are entangled in the land." You are all in a muddle and mess; you don't know where you are, a kind of neither lost nor won state, neither redeemed nor altogether let alone. Now, in our hearts, this morning, many of us are very much like this. We are entangled in the land; the wilderness hath shut us in.

When I was trudging through the mud of London to Regent Square, and thinking of my subject, I thought the very grim, wretched London brick walls said it to me, and the miserable atmosphere repeated to me, "You redeemed? You a believer bound for glory? You a pilgrim going home? No; you are entangled in the land; hemmed in, shut in." At one time you may have had some idea of guidance and direction, but it is over already. Before the blessedness almost began it has vanished. Like many of us, yea, like all of us, when we consult with flesh and blood, and take counsel of our fears, we all give up hope and sink into despondency, and say, "I shall never see the goodly land. This Gospel, when it came to me, spoke in my ear great words; but it has broken its promises. The word that was spoken to my ear has been broken to my hope. The Gospel said 'Redemption,' the Gospel said 'Salvation,' the Gospel said 'Freedom,' the Gospel said 'Victory.' Where am I now? Am I redeemed? am I free? am I victorious? am I saved? I am simply entangled in the land."

The next paragraph shows us the very opposite state of feeling, the very opposite state of mind on the part of Israel's enemies. The Israelites seemed to be without compass, without guide, without direction, without strength. Their enemies were full of purpose, full of energy, full of guidance, knowing precisely what they would be at, and that was to recover Israel. Look at the paragraph. We need all to get both sides of this great question of salvation fully efore our minds.

"And the heart of Pharaoh and of his servants was turned against the people, and they said, Why have we done this, that we have let Israel go from serving us? And he made ready his chariot, and took his people with him; and he took six hundred chosen chariots, and all the chariots of Egypt, and captains over every one of them. And the Lord hardened the heart of Pharaoh, King of Egypt, and he pursued after the children of Israel: for the children of Israel went out with an high hand. But the Egyptians pursued after them, all the horses and chariots of Pharaoh, and his horsemen, and his army, and overtook them encamping by the sea, beside Pi-hahiroth, before Baalzephon."

Israel is presented to us in the opening paragraph like a little purposeless company of sheep or lambs, and their enemies are presented to us in this second paragraph as strong in purpose, with the chariots and the horsemen, and with might and majesty and power. And, my brother and sister, does it not often seem to us, although we try to cheer up our flickering courage by calling ourselves the redeemed of the Lord, and by looking back and saying, "I was redeemed; I am redeemed"—does it not often seem to us as if while we are feeble and soulless and purposeless, *the enemy is for ever strong and firm and solid and forcible?* Does it not seem as if all our troubles come like horses and chariots, as if they had all manner of strength, and all manner of attendants at hand, and the vigour of an army; and we all the opposite? Our enemies come with a "rush," and we never seem to get ourselves drawn up into line of battle. God help us! Before we can struggle to our feet, and set the battle in array, we seem to be overborne. If we could only get pulled together and have breathing time! Instead of that we are harried and worried, and never seem to get girt, and rallied and able to make a fight of it, but are for ever scattered and dispersed. Look at the assembling of the hosts, and tremble for Israel! See them coming—

> "The trumpets sound, the banners fly,
> The glittering spears are rankèd ready,
> The shouts of war are heard afar,
> The battle closes thick and bloody."

All that might and majesty seems on the side of the enemy, and all this weakness and wretchedness on our side. Plan and purpose there: *Pharaoh made ready his chariot;* panic and sheepishness here. It is so for a time.

The paragraph between verses 10 and 12 still further deepens it: "And when Pharaoh drew nigh, the children of Israel lifted up their eyes, and, behold, the Egyptians marched after them; and they were sore afraid; and the children of Israel cried out unto the Lord. And they said unto Moses, Because there were no graves in Egypt, hast thou taken us away to die in the wilderness? wherefore hast thou dealt thus with us, to carry us forth out of Egypt? Is not this the word that we did tell thee in Egypt, saying, Let us alone, that we may serve the

Egyptians? For it had been better for us to serve the Egyptians than that we should die in the wilderness."

I wonder if people are as inconsistent still? I wonder if Christians, for example, are as hypocritical still as on this occasion? "They cried to the Lord." I do not suppose they cried all this blasphemy to the Lord. Oh, no; they would cry to the Lord religiously and piously. They would cry to Him, " God save us!" *and turn round on Moses and tell him what they actually thought.* So people stand in congregations, and sing to the Lord great psalms and hymns, and then turn round and worry the minister. I do not say that is the case here; but there is such a thing going on. Let us be consistent. If we are in trouble, let us go to the Lord, all of us. It is a common trouble, a common distress. What a senseless speech the children of Israel made to Moses—"Is not this the word that we did tell thee in Egypt? Let us alone, that we may serve the Egyptians!" So they did, I believe. The Lord redeemed some of the most useless rubbish that ever took human shape when He redeemed these down-trodden Israelites. Just the poorest rubbish that ever was called man. I sometimes dare put it that the Lord never met with such useless, cantankerous people as these Israelites until he met with you and me. We are just the same. How shall we get over this paragraph? For when I read this bristling narrative of Israel's history in which so often you have the faithfulness of God set over against the unfaithfulness, even the blasphemy, of His people, the marvel always is to me that Israel's history, as a redeemed people, still runs on.

The marvel is that the history does not stop at the 12th verse of the 14th chapter of Exodus, that God does not just leave these poor people and pitch them back to Pharaoh again, saying, "I made a mistake; take them and keep them" Do not you sometimes wonder about yourself, my brother, that God puts up with you? First of all, you were not willingly redeemed. It is sadly and simply true that if God had not come to us, and kindly coerced us, we had been in Pharaoh's hands yet. We did not walk out with trumpets and banners as men who were glad the standard had been raised and the hour of redemption had come. No; we went laggardly and reluctantly; for, although there was a sense in which we were in bondage and always bound with chains, there were fat stews and dishes to be had—cucumbers and leeks and garlic—and how we revelled in these! There were theatres and balls and dances, and bad books, and books not so bad, and things that gratified and glutted the sensual and the carnal and the selfish and the self-willed within us. There were always plenty of these in Egypt; and since we left it all, we are bound to testify that many a time we have acted as though God's religion, God's faith and fear, have been barren where Egypt was gren, and lean where Egypt was fat, and gloomy where Egypt was bright and dazzling.

I say the wonder is that Israel's history still runs on, that it does not come to a stop, and that God does not fling them over and go away to some other savage tribe and take them in hand, and commit to them His purpose for all mankind, *for they could not have done worse.* And yet, full of pity, He forgave their sins. As David said long afterwards, when he was thinking about it, and making much more of his thoughts than I, and turning them into holy psalms full of beauty: " He forgave their sins and did not slay them, but ofttimes turned away His anger. For He remembered that they were but fading flesh and wind that passes away and returns no more. In His love and in His pity He redeemed them, and put up with them all the days of old." Oh, my friend, that is your salvation yet, and mine. God stands amongst us to-day, and sorry specimens we are! He sees what we are, and what does He say? What He says is this, if we may with reverence say so, " Well, let Me not be disappointed; after all, what can I expect from these poor creatures?" As a man said to myself who had sorely vexed me—I had laid hold of him in

Egypt's bondage, a sore, wretched, sorry creature, a drunkard and a wifebeater, and a terror to his children, and he had listened to the Gospel, and I had believed he had been redeemed by its power, that the Lord had brought him out; but then he had terrible slips and lapses, and wore through my patience, which is a very uncertain quantity. And I remember I spoke to him one day rather bitterly, and the poor fellow looked in my face, and said, "What can you expect from public-house sweepings?" Well, that is true. What can you expect from public-house sweepings? "O God, have pity on us! What canst Thou expect from such dregs and moral rubbish as we were when Thou didst come to us, broken down and demoralised everywhere?" Oh, man, you may stand up and talk great things about the dignity of human nature. I have never seen it in here—the Bible. Even when redeemed by grace there is nothing to be proud of, not only because it is "all of grace," but because, for a time, grace makes human nature look worse than ever. The light that God kindles only shows how dark the place was.

Gather round that paragraph lying between the 10th and 12th verses, and see your own photograph, and there in the background the great overshadowing, pitying face of God, as He listens to us in all our petulance and miserable unbelief, and says to us, "But I won't let you go back." "Yes, I know that although you took the Sacrament last Sunday evening, there were times last week when you would often have gone back, times when the world seemed to be everything and to contain everything that could satisfy the desires of the soul; but I did not let you go, and won't.' "Sinner," He says, "Look and live! When I took you in hand this was My covenant—that, first of all, I would come and awaken you, then make you willing, then keep you, and never leave you and never forsake you until all My purposes of grace and mercy should be fully accomplished." That is our salvation, that God has taken us in hand—and, wonder of wonders, I do not expect eternity will explain *why God began.* Why He ever began with this wreck called McNeill, to make a saint of him, is what eternity will not disclose! I have put in my own name to encourage you to put in yours: it is as dishonoured as mine in this connection! Nothing, nothing in us; everything to be put in us, and put in again and again, or not a soul of us but will be back to Egypt!

Let me recite in this connection the terms of the Covenant: "I will make an Everlasting Covenant with them, that I will not turn away from them, to do them good; and I will put My fear in their hearts that they shall not depart from Me."

The man that tampers with "Covenant Theology" is a fool: he is sawing off the branch he is sitting on!

The 13th and 14th verses constitute the shortest paragraph, but the strongest. This is the keystone of the chapter, and it needs a keystone, and gets it. "And Moses said unto the people, Fear ye not, stand still, and see the salvation of the Lord, which He will show to you to-day: for the Egyptians whom ye have seen to-day, ye shall see them again no more for ever. The Lord shall fight for you, and ye shall hold your peace." Now in the fulness of time the Lord takes His place upon the field of this narrative: "The Lord shall fight for you, and ye shall hold your peace." How sadly Israel forgot the Lord! How sadly we also forget Him! We can hear every whisper of the wind, and occupy ourselves with everything that is against us seemingly, never appearing to understand that all this is part of the Divine plan and purpose, not for our destruction, but salvation, and the final overthrow of all the power of the enemy. For you remember in the opening of the chapter it was God who said, "Speak to the children of Israel, that they go along this road;" and in the 13th chapter we find, "God led them not through the way of the land of the Philistines, although that was near; for God said, Lest peradventure the people repent when they see war, and they return to Egypt." That ingrate thing has always to be reckoned with ("that they return to Egypt"). "But God led the people about through the way of the wilderness." So the sum and substance is that the trappers are trapped. Pharaoh has not got Israel in a corner. Israel was not entangled in the land. That was Pharaoh's thought about them, and their own thought about themselves; but when God rose, when we see His programme, it was all of His ordering and doing, that, once for all, He Himself might rise upon the view as God Almighty, Invincible, Unconquerable, who had all things in His hands and in His power. The trappers trapped, the biters bitten, the pursuers pursued, the insulters mocked and laughed at. So was it at a much later day, when that young manservant of Elisha stepped out one morning and beheld the town of Dothan, in which he and his master had taken refuge, surrounded by the chariots and horsemen of the enemy. Elisha was calm and cool; but the young man, the servant, was like the Israelites here, sorely shaken and distressed: and deliverance came then as here, by such a paragraph as this, that occupies the 13th and 14th verses. Elisha, you remember, prayed, and said, "Lord open the young man's eyes." And the Lord opened his eyes, and he saw the situation, that behind the beleaguring forces, the mountains were filled with the chariots and horsemen of Jehovah. Again the trappers were entrapped. Again the enemy was taken in flank and rear, and contemptuously driven out. It is so with us. The Lord is fighting for us. The Lord has the battle in His own hands. He fights, and we hold our peace, and if we open our lips it should be only to say, not "woe," "woe," "woe," in this wretched unbelief, but "Bless the Lord, O my soul, bless the Lord, and forget not all His benefits, who forgiveth all thine iniquities and healeth all thy diseases, and redeemeth thy life from destruction."

The next paragraph shows no falling off in thrilling interest. You notice the opening part: "And the Lord said unto Moses, Wherefore criest thou unto Me? speak unto the children of Israel, that they go forward," and so on. "Wherefore criest thou unto Me?" What does that mean? It is very, very singular to see God at this place muzzling the mouth of prayer, putting the closure upon Moses. What does it mean? Well, I just take this big meaning out of it. I can hardly preach it, for a big sob is in my throat the more I look at it. Here is God so wrought upon by the distress of His people, that when Moses comes pulling at His skirts, as well as all the children of Israel, He so wants to deliver them that He sets back Moses: "Unhand Me, children of Mine. Stand back from Me; you are only hampering Me. I want to break out on Pharaoh. You do not need to ask Me to do this. I have heard your pleadings, and have seen your helplessness under the insulting pride of Pharaoh. Unhand Me, and let Me get one stroke at your enemy and mine." That element is in God yet. Hear it, brother, sister, sorely badgered by the world, the flesh, and the devil, and oftentimes tempted to speak unadvisedly with your lips and think foolishly in your heart, and say, "My God has forgotten me, and the blackest day that ever come to me was the day when I professed the faith and fear of Jesus Christ. It has brought me nothing but trouble and distress and ever-threatening disaster." *It has not.* The very pity of your case is rousing God, if I may so say it, to do His best for you. God loves you. He stands among us as a great Father, as a great, strong, loving father would stand in the midst of his children. There he is, and some enemy is attacking his home and his loved ones. Here is his wife clinging to him, here are the bairns crying and clinging about him, and there is the enemy in front, and if that father is to do his best he has to get disentangled. If he is to strike out, and strike out in all his loving, manly strength, he has to be a little firm with them, and grip them and set them back, and say to them, "Hold your peace." I like to see a strong man in a righteous rage. You have heard of one of our literary characters who loved a good hater. That is why I am getting to love God more than I used to do. God has perfect love and perfect hate. I like to see God rising in His wrath. So did David. It was the inspiration of some of the grandest Psalms we have—Psalms that put our sugary hymns out of sight. " For the oppression of the poor, for the sighing of the needy, now will I arise, saith the Lord." You can feel it. Human and far back as we are, we can feel it; and then, remember, that this Divine indignation has not a taint of sin in it. It is a splendid sight, the God of Israel rising to meet blow with blow, to take up the challenge that has been so insultingly thrown down. "The Lord is a Man of War."

In the paragraph from the 19th to the 22nd verse we see God's plan, " And the angel of God, which went before the camp of Israel, removed," &c. If you go back to the 10th verse you read, " And when Pharaoh drew nigh the children of Israel were sore afraid; " and in the 20th verse we find that " the one came not near the other all the night." That paragraph is a paragraph of restraint. God could simply have come in a moment and annihilated these Egyptians. He did not do that then, that was not His way at that time nor since. The marvellous thing is the time God takes. The marvel is that God takes the trouble to restrain, when He could finish His work of judgment and mercy in a moment. He first restrains them, and makes the wheels of their chariots to drive heavily, and then He utterly overwhelms them. There we have the whole conflict of the Church of God vividly represented. Why is Israel not utterly swallowed up? The answer is that the Lord restrains in a marvellous way the wrath of the enemy: " the one came not near the other all the night." It is night with us, in a sense, until the eternal morning breaks; but even in all the darkness and vicissitudes and uncertainty let us lay to heart for encouragement, if we are really Israel, if our heart is really throbbing with faith and hope in the Lord Jesus Christ:—"Although the enemy may be near me, although I may feel his breath upon my cheek, there is an invisible but impenetrable wall between me and my spiritual adversary." And what is true of the individual is true of the whole Church: "the one came not near the other all the night." It must amaze the devil, as I remarked in connection with the 23rd Psalm one previous Sunday morning, that he has not gotten us. That after all, and when everything seems to be in his favour, and we seem to be selling ourselves to him, there is an invisible but impenetrable wall erected between us; and, to God's glory be it told, he has not gotten us yet. No, nor ever will. "The one came not near the other all the night," and their defence was a pillar of fire; and still "the angel of the Lord encompasseth all those about that do Him fear, and them delivereth."

How blessed were we if only we had more confidence in the Lord our God, in our Jehovah—Jesus. How blessed, how sure, how safe. The saints in heaven are happier, but not more secure than the saints upon earth: "the one came not near the other all the night." You cannot kill the Christian if you try, nor hurt a hair of his head. You may catch him and imprison him, you may behead him, but you have done him no harm, nor once come near him—not once.

> " Surely when floods of waters great
> Do swell up to the brim,
> *They shall not overwhelm his soul,*
> Nor once come near to him."

Oh, what an encouragement it should be to some souls here this morning! I wish I knew the history of some of you; it would do us all good. If any one here is pursued by old sins, which are seeking to drag you back and pull you down, although you are so weak and defenceless, yet you are preserved. There is a wall round about you. You cannot be got at.

"And the Egyptians pursued and went in after them to the midst of the sea, even all Pharaoh's horses, his chariots, and his horsemen. And it came to pass that in the morning watch the Lord looked unto the host of the Egyptians through the pillar of fire and of the cloud, and troubled the host of the Egyptians. And took off their chariot wheels, that they drave them heavily; so that the Egyptians said, Let us flee from the face of Israel; for the Lord fighteth for them against the Egyptians." Oh, man and woman, hard beset, fix your eyes on that sight, and see how God fights. Try to get it into your imagination, and never lose sight of it—that great wrathful face of Almighty God looking through the pillar of fire upon the Egyptians; and the very look of His eye picked out the linch-pin from the chariot wheels. The look of God's face is annihilation, and the look of His face on the other side is heaven for ever. By the look of His face He shook the Egyptians till the stoutest heart began to tremble with nameless terror. What is this? This is God, the God of Israel. Your poor atheists and superfine unbelievers scorn Him, but the day is coming when they too, and the stoutest heart, shall cry, "God, God, God is against me, and I am but a breath before Him!" I am no more against God than the mists which strive (and fail) to battle down the rising sun. The sun looks at them, and laughs at them, and at meridian day the clouds of the night are utterly annihilated. That day is coming for the Church. It has very much to bear just now. But her travails and pains and pangs shall come to an end in due course. We are afflicted, and we mourn and weep now, but says our heavenly Leader, "Be comforted, for your mourning shall be turned into mirth. And the mirth of every enemy of God and God's people shall be turned into endless mourning." The end of that mirth is heaviness.

The power of Pharaoh is great to-day. The power of all the things leagued against God's Church is great to-day. Look at the power of unbelief as represented in literature. Look at the clever, the devilish clever pens leagued against God upon the philosophic and scientific side; the impure literature that is leagued against God's cause. Look at the drink traffic, that damned power of Pharaoh that is leagued against God's people. Look at everything, and all the power of the enemy, and yet, while you look, never doubt that all this power is tottering to its fall. God's eyes are upon it, and it is not. That is the strength of the Church. The Lord is with us. Yonder He is. Lift up your eyes; behold Him, as represented in the New Testament, the Lord Jesus Christ sitting down upon His throne, from henceforth expecting—take it literally—from henceforth looking out until His enemies be made His footstool. All is right with the Church, therefore, for the Lord is on His throne, and the power of the enemy is steadily being disintegrated.

And in the last paragraph we have the final victory. That which became the salvation of Israel became the destruction of their enemies. "The sea returned to its strength when the morning appeared." The very powers of nature seem to be set forth here as in sympathy with the God who gave them their place. The sea, as if it was instinct with life and meaning, as if the sea knew what it was doing, the sea rose upon them, and again and again, while an Egyptian head appeared, the sea in its strength swept over it. "There remained not so much as one of them."

And the waters were a wall unto the Israelites on the right hand and on the left. Before you go, take that picture with you. What a wall! A paradoxical story all through. The visible and the strong and the palpable and the material met and checked and held back by the immaterial and almost invisible—a cloud and a pillar of fire opposed to horsemen and chariots of iron. Yes, and successfully opposed; and here again seems to be a paradox: "And the waters were a wall." You could drive your fist through it up to the elbow. No; you could not; not through that kind of wall. What is weaker than water? A very proverb. But the wall was firm, solid, terrible—nothing could shake it until God removed it. What these waters were to Israel, that faith is to every spiritual Israelite. Faith seems to be as feeble as a wall of waters: faith is as strong as a wall of iron. As long as we are in simple and real fellowship with the God of salvation, we are so surrounded that the devil cannot get at us to vex or slay us. And that same thing which was Israel's salvation became the distress of their enemies. "By faith the Israelites passed through the Red Sea, which the Egyptians assaying to do were drowned."

I have kept you too long; just one word more in closing, and it is a word of warning.

I do not think that this narrative ends so brightly as one would like for Israel. We are told that Israel saw the dead upon the shore, and they believed and feared the Lord, and His servant Moses. That is the faith that will not last. Soon shall we have them in the "wilderness of Sin" again. Faith that springs up because I see my dead lying there—that is an uncertain faith; and very soon afterwards you will find Israel at the old trick of grumbling again. They were walking by sight when they thought they were walking by faith. Israel saw the dead, then believed the Lord and feared Him. But by-and-bye, in the wilderness, the vision of the dead will grow dim, and their eyes will see things temporal that will discourage their faith, and it will melt away. It should be the other way about: Israel, from the first, should have *believed to see* the enemy dead upon the shore.

That faith will hold, and that is the only faith that will hold. Thomas made the same mistake, and said, "Unless I see the print of the nails," and so on, "I will not believe." And Christ said, "Thomas, because thou hast seen Me, thou hast believed; blessed are they, Thomas—blessed are they that have not seen, and yet have believed." Thomas, that is the cheapest kind of faith and the poorest kind of faith that believes because it sees. The right kind of faith is that which believes to see. "I had fainted," said the Psalmist, "unless I had believed to see the goodness of the Lord in the land of the living." I end, then, where all God's lessons should have their end. Fear not, only believe; and although we do not see all things by the eye, still, by faith, we see the Lord upon His throne, and in that there is the sign and the sure promise that we also shall overcome, and sit down beside Him there.

May God bless this exposition to us. Amen.

Regent Square Pulpit.

SHAMMAH AND BENAIAH.

A Sermon

Delivered on Sabbath Morning, Dec. 1, 1889, in

REGENT SQUARE CHURCH,

and on Monday Evening at

THE "THIEVES' SUPPER," ST. GILES,

by the

REV. JOHN McNEILL.

---

2 Samuel xxiii. 8.—"These be the names of the mighty men whom David had," &c.

11 and 12.—"And after him was Shammah the son of Agee the Hararite. And the Philistines were gathered together into a troop, where was a plot of ground full of lentils; and the people fled from the Philistines. But he stood in the midst of the plot, and defended it, and slew the Philistines: and the Lord wrought a great victory."

20.—"And Benaiah the son of Jehoiada, the son of a valiant man of Kabzeel, who had done mighty deeds, he slew the two sons of Ariel of Moab: he went down also and slew a lion in the midst of a pit in time of snow."

22.—"These things did Benaiah the son of Jehoiada, and had a name among the three mighty men."

I wish you for a little while to look at the deed of this man Shammah, who stood in the midst of the plot of lentils and defended it, and slew the Philistines, and Benaiah who slew a lion in a pit on a snowy day.

These, of course, are instances of individual valour. These men are called mighty men—" the mighty men whom

No. 4.

David had;" and in each case is given a sample of their mighty deeds—something to suggest that they were worthy of the names they carried, worthy of the great hero with whom they had been in association, even the mighty David himself, and worthy of the renown which was attached to their names for many a day afterwards in the land of Israel.

Very likely when the writer of the Epistle to the Hebrews breaks off from his detailed narrative and says, "The time would fail me to tell of them all," these are some of those whom he had in his mind. We will take a little time where he had none, and look for a moment at the brief narratives of these mighty men. How did Shammah's deed come about? The Philistines were gathered together into a troop where there was a piece of ground full of lentils, "and the people fled from the Philistines. But he stood in the midst of the ground and defended it, and slew the Philistines: and the Lord wrought a great victory."

The one idea that leaps up from this narrative is that which you often find through Scripture, that in the day of defeat and disaster all God wants is one whole-hearted man. If the Lord can only get a beginning made, if He can, amidst all the disgraceful stampede and rout, get but *one man* to stop running, one to stop flying, one soul to cease from unbelief and panic and fear, and begin to trust in Him, there and then the tide of battle shall be turned. You see how this glory came to Shammah the son of Agee the Hararite. Some men are born great, it has been said; some achieve greatness; and others have greatness thrust upon them. Our hero of this morning, while he certainly achieved greatness, yet, in another view, had greatness thrust upon him. I mean that the occasion, the opportunity, seems to have come suddenly and unexpectedly and to have been used by Shammah in the same way. It was not sought, but sprang upon him by surprise. I have no doubt he was well through with the conflict before he came to himself, and understood what a wonderful thing the Lord had done by his hand. And that same element might give heroism to your spiritual life and to mine to-day. For as these were mighty men under David, who won their honours and proved their right to the title, so we are under the heavenly David, the Lord Jesus Christ. Now, granted that many things connected with Christ and His cause, in ourselves and in the world round about, are very dark and disastrous-looking; out of that darkness and disaster is continually coming the very opportunity that the Lord wants to recover the defeat, if only we would play the man, as did these true men of Israel long ago.

Israel under the power of the Philistines! That happens often—Israel disorganized and scattered, and the Philistines, for the time being, strong and triumphant. Israel was here dispirited, weak, helpless, and Philistia strong, victorious, insulting. One day a little group of the Israelites are going out in a feeble way to reap a wretched little patch of lentils, the seed of which they had sown in the spring; but lo! as they step out to reap it, down come the marauding, plundering, ravaging Philistines, and the people flee before them. It was expected. The Philistines did not suppose they would have to fight, and their expectations were answered: the people flee. That had been the state of things for a good while. Philistia has simply a walk-over; Israel was so "all-gone" they did not think of rallying for the conflict. On come the Philistines, and off go the Israelites shamefully before them—all but one man; that one man Shammah the son of Agee the Hararite, who in that dark and shameful day pulled himself together, and with a great cry in his heart to God, and a big sob, half rage and half sorrow, for himself and countrymen, instead of flying, stood in the midst of that plot of lentils and defended it, and slew the Philistines, and the Lord wrought a great victory.

Shammah did, that is to say, the unexpected. Fleeing had been the order of the day for Israel, and pursuing had been the order of the day for Philistia. A very pretty game, truly! We shout, and you run. We appear, and you disappear. You sow in the spring—it was very kind of you, Israelites—and we step in in the autumn and take the harvest. It is a wonderfully nicely arranged system for Philistia, whatever it may be for Israel. And, just so; don't we seem to make nothing of our Christianity (meaning by that, *Christ*), as against the powers of Philistia?

Look at them in London to-day. What are we doing? Where are we gaining? Speaking broadly, it is invisible. Where are we defeated? Everywhere. The world laughing at us, scandal upon scandal, tale upon tale, wreck upon wreck, ruin upon ruin. Drink, lust, uncleanness, commercial dishonour, everything that belongs to the Devil, strong and vigorous, successful and sweeping; and everything that belongs to Jesus Christ, like those dispirited Israelites, weak and scattering as a flock of sheep. It is bad enough. But just as then, so I believe still, if here and there some man would only understand that in all this there is a trumpet being blown for rallying, times for the individual and for the community might be mightily changed. There is Shammah, and what seems to be sweeping through the breast of—I was going to say the poor man, the noble man

—was this: "This is too bad! I am sick and tired of this. Are we for ever to sow in the spring, and are these Philistines to reap our crop in the autumn? Are we for ever to be at their mercy? Are we for ever to be trodden under foot and scattered like sheep? Death is preferable to this running and running and running; and in God's great name I stand to-day—Death or Victory!

If some of us would do that, we would be big Christians (I speak in no carnal, boasting sense) before night; we would be what we have not been for a long while, we would be triumphant, we would be successful. Just where you have always yielded, my hardly beset brother or sister, try how it will work to stand to-day. Resist this onset that always before has made a clean sweep of you, and what will happen? It will be what always happens: "Resist the devil, and he will flee from you"—he is a bigger coward than you are. "Whom resist steadfast in the faith." Brave old Shammah, tired of running, a sense of blame and shame for himself and countrymen so working in him, that at last he stands firm, and God stands in him and for him and by him; and between them twain, if I may say so, they wrought a great victory.

Then, it was a big fight for very little. "He defended a plot of lentils." One could easily have criticized him and said, "Ah, this is zeal without knowledge"—I am afraid he was not a Presbyterian, he was so reckless—"this man is making a great fight at the wrong time and at the wrong place. Now, if he had gathered together a little committee of souls like-minded with himself, and if they had laid their heads together—ah, that's the plan!—if they had laid their heads together, then what a lot of wood there would have been in one place! If they had taken counsel together, and struck on some plan, and adjourned—until next century!" No, he did not use the committee system; he just made himself a committee of one, with power to add Jehovah to his number, and made himself very active to the extent of such power and opportunity. Shammah, *plus* the Lord, means, Tremble, Gates of Hell!

Not much to fight for, a plot of lentils! But, coarse horse-food after all, as I believe it was, it was Israel's lentils, and Philistia had no right to them. It was God's, and not theirs; and little as it seemed to be to make a fight for, Shammah stepped into the middle of the plot, like one who would say, "It is mine, it is my countrymen's, it is my God's, and ye shall not have it if one man can prevent it."

I wish some one here, young or old man, would, like Shammah, *stand in the middle of the wreck that is left*, and have one fight for it. Although what is left may have no more proportion to what used to be or what might have been than a patch of lentils has to a broad-acred farm, yet in God's name stand in the middle of the wreck, and see what will happen. That is all God asks: Stand, stand in the midst, and then see! If the Church of Christ would only get possessed of Shammah's spirit, and in all the howling wreck that is at home and abroad, if she would stand and fight, there would be such a central victory as would tell to the furthermost circumference.

"Oh, the drink," we say, "it is there, and it will always be there! This social impurity, this army of fallen women, it has always been, and it will always have to be! Oh, this commercial rottenness; it belongs to a system of things on this planet — it has always been, and will always be!" That is what we ought not to say. That is what Shammah might have said: "Oh, those Philistines have come up! Well, sometimes we have our turn, and sometimes they have theirs. It is their turn just now, and there is no use trying to change it. They are too strong, and we too weak." He dismissed all these carnal calculations, and no doubt, with a cry in his heart to the God of Israel, he laid hold of whatever was near him, and laid about *him* lustily.

I think I see him. He is a sight for sore eyes, a sight for dispirited Christians, a sight for all poor backsliders who have come in here this morning mere wrecks. The Lord has sent a message to you by my stammering lips to-day. You are defeated, overcome, overborne. Old sins, like Philistines, have come back on you; redeemed though you call yourself —and I believe you are—old sins have come back for the last month or year and more, and they have been driving you before them pitiably, somewhat contemptuously—secret sins, or open sins, or both combined. You have lost heart, the roaring flood in its strength has swept you away, and you came in here this morning the weakest thing that ever was called man—especially the weakest thing that ever dared to call itself Christian man, believing man, redeemed man. Now, what are you to do? In God's name let us all try it, let us all do what Shammah did—stand in the middle of what is left. Do not propose some great plan that you are going to carry out by-and-bye, some big plan of campaign; but just to-day as we are, where we are, let us put our foot down and say in God's name, looking at all the wreck and the strength of evil that is gathered round about us, "*We will do or die.* This wretched kind of life is not worth living, and I am going to make a bold stroke—Death or Victory."

"Who would be free
Himself must strike the blow;"

but if we are striking out, the very power of the arm of the Lord is transfused into our poor arm of flesh. Let me be still more urgent and particular here. Let me speak to some old, but backslidden, believer — fifty, sixty, or seventy years of age; you have made nothing of your Christian profession; you are a wreck, and you know it; your day is nearly done, and you know it; there is a black account for you in the reckoning day, and you dread it. What shall you do? My brother, late in the day as it is, and although night is coming near, although you are not now the man you used to be, and a hundred voices in your ear say to you, "It is too late to retrieve the past," those hundred voices are a hundred lies and liars. It is *not* too late: stand in the middle of the wreck left, in God's great name. If I were you, I would make a fight yet; stand, although the few years left to you are like this patch of lentils, and do not seem to be worth fighting for. Stand, stand! you might die more than conqueror yet. Over you, there may yet be heard in Heaven the shout of victory: *Stand!* And what I say to you, I say to every *young* fellow. There may be here some mere youth of twenty-five years, or less, and though actually not twenty-five, *you are a wreck*. You have been to the house of shame and sin, though you still come to the house of God. Alas! alas! I cannot tell what I am getting to know about the fearful compromises with sin that some young men are making here in London. You are a wreck, secretly, or openly, or both, and to you also the voices come that whisper, "Give it up, yield to Philistia altogether, quit this sickening hypocrisy." Let those voices also be liars. Wrecked and all as you are, with drink, with lust, with gambling, with lying, with untrustworthiness down in the office; wrecked and all as you are now, my brother, to-day, *to-day*, put down your foot. *Have out* the battle with him who besets you through these sins of yours: fight, for the Lord is with you, and He will turn the battle to the gate.

Shammah stood in the midst of it—I think I see the rage of battle in his face—and though it was not worth two half-crowns of any man's money, he defended it, and slew the Philistines, and *God came down from heaven* to win a patch of lentils! For the Lord loves victory, and the Lord hates defeat, and the only thing He wants is to get at His adversary through some faithful, upright, believing soul.

And those flying Israelites, at last their breath became short and they had to stand. They were tired of running, and stood and looked back. I think I hear them saying, "Great God of Israel, Shammah is fighting!" They heard the shouts and saw him dashing here and there, and the sight rallied them. I have no doubt a blush of shame swept across their faces, and quicker than I am taking time to tell it, they went back to the place where victory had already begun, and where the shadow of death had been already turned into the morning. Ah! if only one Christian would get a little bit of victory, it would help us all: if only one denomination would get to be successful, it would rally us all. How greatly we are needing to see some well-done deed, just to encourage us all, and to cause the shameful stampede and the sickening sense of being dispirited to come to an end. My brother, might you not try it to-day? There is a district round about you filled with the power of Philistia: the world, the drink, I don't know what, all raging and ranging and ravaging in every direction. I wish you would land down on it somewhere with a shout, and in God's name display your banner. The whole tide of war might be changed in that district. *If just one soul* would go down into some one cottage meeting in some slum or mews-lane, without any committee, without any blowing of trumpets, without any pre-arrangements, go and stand in the middle of the wreck somewhere, and in God's great name take the sword of the Spirit and begin, begin! We might hear wondrous things. Perhaps this way of working that we carry on inside the Church here will never tell on that field of wreck and defeat round about us. Try you the other way. Take a walk through the district, feel the blush of shame on your cheek that such things should be in a great city, with churches everywhere, and the Gospel so much preached; so much *form* of Christianity and so little *power* of it. Feel it, and especially if you are a young brother and the blood is hot, give Christ your hot and fiery youth.

See the Sabbath day, the holy, beautiful Sabbath of the Lord, how it is utterly wrecked in London by the power of Philistia! Oh, that we might get the same victory for the Sabbath that Shammah got for his countrymen on the occasion of which we have read! Oh, that each one of us might be a Shammah to redeem the Sabbath day! Stand in the middle of the wreck that is left, and the Lord will stand for you and His holy command and his holy and beneficent purposes through the command; and God alone knows how the tide of war as regards Sabbath desecration may be rolled back.

I wish some Shammah would stand up *in your dear old*

Church of England just now in the midst of the little that is left that is worthy of the name of Protestantism within her bounds. May God send Shammahs to all the Churches, men who are tired of fleeing and are sick at heart of the misery about them, and must do something. The enemy has come in like a flood. Oh, Spirit of the Lord, lift up a standard against him!

Now, let us go away and try to be like him. At home—how is it with you at home? Your home is a wreck from a religious point of view: no family prayer, no worship, no sign of being a covenant Israelite as regards your wife, your children, and your household: Philistia has invaded your home. Go back to-day, man; quit your sneaking and shuffling; go back to-day to stand in the middle of the wreck left at home, to build up a family altar, to call your servants and your children round about you, and to assume the position for God and His truth that you ought to have at home. If that were multiplied in ten thousand instances London's religious problem would be altered before night.

Oh, the little taste of victory, how it would change all our notions and all our outlook! May God give it to us to-day! Go down to your Sabbath-school class this afternoon, or your Bible-class, my brother, with the shout of Shammah, saying to yourself, "Go to, this defeat and making no headway, and being for ever tied in and tripped up by Philistia," this is not to be—Arise, and God will arise in you like a mighty man, and God will refresh you as a giant is refreshed through wine, and the power of God will be displayed even yet in connection with your work.

We rejoice to find that God is using our inartistic, inelegant, structureless sermons to His glory. A man wrote to me the other day, saying, "We are in the midst of a most successful work, and, under God, it was you who did it." He heard me talking like this, not in this church, but elsewhere, and he was just going to give up the work he was doing in a London slum. Instead of that, he went back with Shammah, shouting; and to his own great surprise, as he said in his letter, God came down and gave him blessing beyond his utmost expectation.

Now, I have scarcely any time left for the case of Benaiah, "who went down also and slew a lion in the midst of the pit in the time of snow." That is a man worth looking at! I thought as I came here somebody would be saying, "What are you going to make of that man?" That is what my wife said this morning when I told her of the subject. Well, he was a brave man. Why? He was in a sense unlike Shammah. To Shammah the Philistines suddenly came; they swept down on him; he stood firm— and it was death or victory. He had to slash and cut and hew in the best way he could. But this is a different kind of thing. It is a snowy day, think of it. A snowy day; a cold day! It is not like a day in spring; not like your spring morning that makes you heroic, when the sky is bright, and the birds are whistling, and your own blood is tingling in your veins, and you feel as if you are the strongest man on earth; you want to go and advertise challenges to anybody your height and weight, to come into grips with you. It was not that kind of morning—but a wet-blanket kind of morning, with nothing to stir the blood, nothing to cheer the poor fellow. "A cold, dull, miserable day," the neighbours come in and tell you, and while they are speaking through the thick, heavy air, there comes the muttering of the lion fallen into the pit. Very likely because the snow concealed the entrance, the brute as he ranged about tumbled in; and the very roaring makes the whole neighbourhood feel thankful that they have houses to go to and stay in.

It is difficult to be brave on a day like that,

> '' When Dick the ploughman blows his nail,
> And milk comes frozen home in pail.''

But that was the day when Benaiah, the son of Jehoiada, the son of a valiant man of Kabzeel, who had done many mighty acts, went and did another.

On a snowy day, when all others were in, sitting over the fire, burning their knees, he arose, went to the door and listened. Ah! while other men's faces grow long with fear, his brightens. "I have been wanting to kill that lion for the last six months, and never could get the chance. Thank God, this day has come, and that we know where he is." Look at him trudging through the snow! Think how there was nothing to help him, nobody to cheer or encourage him; and as he goes through the air so thick and so hurtling with the flakes of snow, you feel here is courage not less than that of Shammah. And he went on and on and on; and nearer and nearer came to the pit with the lion in it. He comes to the edge of it and looks down, and sees the ranger and ravager and destroyer, the terror of the countryside for many a day; and with a prayer to the God of Israel, he leaps down beside the lion, knowing that out of that pit only one will come up alive. It was a big deed by a big man. God never puts a nobody into His Word. This man was worthy of his name— a mighty man. He leapt down;—there is a roar and a spring; then a mortal groan. The lion is down; Benaiah has put his foot on his neck; "he went down and slew the lion in a pit on a snowy day."

Did it ever occur to you that that man was wonderfully like another Benaiah? Did you ever think he was wonderfully like the Lord Jesus Christ, who, on one of the dullest and darkest days that ever the world saw, went down into the pit, and encountered, face to face, the devourer and the destroyer of men. And He had nobody to encourage and nobody to cheer. All His disciples forsook Him and fled; and single, unaided, and alone, He went down into the pit, and slew the lion, the dragon, the devourer. He fought and He won.

> " Up from the *pit* He arose
> With a mighty triumph o'er His foes,
> He arose a Victor from the dark domain,
> And He lives for ever with His saints to reign.
>   Hallelujah, Christ arose ! "

Did it ever occur to you that that man down there in the pit, in that deadly conflict, is a type and figure, in his action, of what every believing soul has to go through?

My dear brother, my sister, there is a lion-like strength of evil in every one of us, and we are not saved till our foot is upon its neck, and its power is broken. With some, the lion is out, ranging and roaring, as that lion might be supposed to have been before this snowy day when he fell into the pit. That is to say, the power of sin is apparent: they are notorious drunkards, they are notorious sinners in some form or another. But with others, the lion is in a pit, and—God help such foolish people!—they think they are all right when they have driven sin in out of sight. If only they can keep sin from breaking out openly in their faces, in their speech, in their conduct—the poor dupes think that all is well.

No, my brother, the big work is to be done yet. Go down into the pit; go down into the deeps of your own fallen nature, the depths of Satan in you; go down there quick, in the strength of Benaiah, and win that fight, or you are not saved yet. None of us, old or young, ignorant or learned, has a right to feel safe until he has done Benaiah's deed, and gone down into the depths of sin that are in himself with the lamp of God and the sword of God, and stabbed to the heart the life of sin that is in the very deep places of his soul.

That is to be done; and that is why some of us are so far back, because it is not done yet. That lion is not slain; that battle is not fought between me and my own sin down in the pit. Go down to him to-day. Where you sit, go down; listen to the growlings of the brute in you. Listen! Feel, almost, the lashings of his tail. Go down and fight, and in God's name win down there. "He slew the lion in a pit on a snowy day."

Shammah's "Waterloo" came to him, Benaiah had to make his. Don't wait for that wonderful day that is to be, so you fondly think, when you will find your opportunity, and rise to the occasion, and come out bright and bold for God. Nay, but on this dull, unheroic, December day, unseen, untrumpeted by man, find and fight and win your soul's Waterloo.

The last thing I want you to notice is the little point of extra light that comes from the name. What does Benaiah mean? Benaiah means, literally, the man whom God built. There is something in a name, after all! The man whom God built from the protoplasm upward and onward, the God-built, God-strengthened, God-nerved, God-sustained man. May God grant that all of us shall have that pedigree! May God grant that out from this church to-day a multitude may go of whom this is the generation: "Born not of blood, nor of the will of the flesh, nor of man, but born of God." Born again! Spiritual men, whose foundations God hath laid in Christ Jesus; and out of whom God is making strong, stalwart, heroic, spiritual men, because He has built them and founded them on the Eternal Rock of His own dear Son.

Have we that strength, my brother, my sister? Men whom God hath built! Otherwise, no wonder we are weaklings, and no wonder we are continually overcome in the day of battle and the shock of conflict.

May the Lord Himself appear to us to-day in all His saving strength, and turn, for all of us, defeat into victory and the shadow of death into the morning! All appearances to the contrary notwithstanding, the Lord is with us. There is no cause for fleeing, and the very dark condition of things will only give us opportunity to glorify God, and to do something—to do *something* that shall find for us an honourable mention in the great day. Cease to be dispirited; cease to talk despondingly; let us lift our hearts into the light of the face of our great Captain and King. "Cry out and shout, thou inhabitant of Zion, for great is the Holy One of Israel in the midst of thee."

It is a day of splendid opportunity for the individual. The battle is the common soldier's battle, and the Great Captain's eye is searching the field that He may show Himself strong in the behalf of every one who is making a stand against sin.

HENDERSON & SPALDING, Printers, 1, 3 and 5, Marylebone Lane, London, W.

Regent Square Pulpit.

THE TRUE PHYSICIAN.

A Sermon

Delivered on Sunday Morning, Dec. 8, 1889, in

REGENT SQUARE CHURCH,

BY THE

REV. JOHN McNEILL.

Mark v. 22-23.—"And there cometh one of the rulers of the synagogue, Jairus by name; and seeing Him, he falleth at His feet, and beseecheth Him much, saying, My little daughter is at the point of death: I pray Thee, that Thou come and lay Thy hands on her, that she may be made whole, and live."

35-36.—"While He yet spake, they come from the ruler of the synagogue's house, saying, Thy daughter is dead: why troublest thou the Master any further? But Jesus, not heeding the word spoken, saith unto the ruler of the synagogue, Fear not, only believe."

How the sovereignty of grace, to use a good old phrase, comes out in this chapter, as in all the narrative of God's dealings with the children of men ever since that record began! We have the Lord, in His grace and mercy, landing upon human wretchedness, which has its fount and spring in human sin; landing upon it as He pleases, where He pleases, and when He pleases: gracious truly; yet sovereign in the exercise and manifestation of His grace. In this same chapter we see His grace and mercy lighting down upon a madman, curing that sorely vexed lunatic. Then we see His grace and mercy lighting down upon just the other extreme —a very, very wise man, as wise as any of ourselves, a ruler of the synagogue, Jairus by name; a naturally calm and self-possessed religious man. And also we see His grace lighting down upon that poor, unknown, nameless creature in the midst of the crowd, who stretched her hand forward to touch the hem of His garment, thinking within herself, "If I may touch but His clothes, I shall be made whole."

> "Sovereign grace o'er sin abounding,
> Ransomed souls, its praises swell,
> 'Tis a deep that knows no sounding,
> Who its depth or lengths can tell?
> On its glories
> Let my soul for ever dwell."

May this Jesus in His sovereign grace visit us to-day, and exercise His saving power when and where and on whomsoever it may please Him! Only let us do our part; even as this poor man who cried, and the Lord helped him and saved him out of all his distresses.

Looking at the narrative which occupies us to-day, how true it is that "a little child shall lead them." The story opens darkly for Jairus, as he thinks of his child; but we who stand at this late date, and quietly and calmly look back on what has so long been finished, can easily see how that remark is illustrated. That little girl was being used through her sickness and sore calamity, in the purpose of God, to bring to Christ a man, a household, who without this powerful, providential leading very likely would not have come. Remember, this man by his ecclesiastical position, by birth, blood, and upbringing, naturally belongs to Christ's murderers: to the class who put Christ to death, who inflamed the multitude against Him, who seduced the people from their Messiah when He came and when they would have received Him gladly. The rulers of the people, the elders of the synagogue, the chief men in Israel after watching Him for a little, took sides against Him, and, naturally, "like priest like people," the mass of the people took the side of their religious leaders, and cried, "Away with Him: crucify Him!"

But we are dealing, remember, with sovereign grace; and the Lord and Saviour Jesus Christ will claim for Himself out of such an unlikely quarter some trophy, some specimen of His love and His gracious power. From between the devil's fingers, so to speak, He will pick this man and this household and set them on high, safe from all danger arising from natural tendency and environment. And it was the death of the little girl that did it. I cannot think of this Jairus— neither can you, when you remember all that belonged to his position, and all that was just beginning to "hatch" against Christ in connection with the rulers of the people,—you cannot think of his coming to Christ and worshipping Him, and becoming one of His disciples, unless he had been driven to it by the lash and thrash of the heavy whip of this affliction. It was the trouble of his little daughter that drove him to Christ Jesus. I rejoice to think it is true to-day, and that it has been true of many of ourselves; and if nothing less than that will do, may it be done again. If nothing less than the taking away of your pet lamb will draw your heart to the Good Shepherd, then may it be taken. My poor, proud, self-contained brother, if nothing less than this will bend your knees in true prayer, and bring from your heart the bubbling cry, "Lord, help me!" then may this come. It seems to be hard, harsh, heartless; but it is uttered not only by a man who loves you, but by the Lord behind the man, who through my lips is expressing His deep heart's desire that your formality may be broken up, and that it may be said of you in heaven, "Behold, he prayeth!"

I fear there are not a few rulers of the people in all our Churches to-day, who, if ever they are to be really brought to a real Christ, will need this same strong and seemingly harsh treatment. How many of our elders, how many of our deacons are, like Jairus, this ruler of the people, this elder in the synagogue. If—*if* they are to be born again into a true, throbbing, palpitating faith in the dear Son of God Himself; if they are to be delivered from synagogue trammels, and from the down-dragging power of the mere form and routine of the worship of God in connection with which they have an honoured and honourable place—it is, perhaps, only to be done by the sharp spur of some keen, lacerating affliction. It is hard to bring Jairus to Christ's feet; but Christ can do it. It is hard to bring some people, who are compelled to take an official position in connection with religion and the worship of God in the land—it is hard to get some of these to be brought in reality into personal relation with the personal Saviour.

But the Lord can do it, and in His marvellous and ever-to-be-adored, though often inscrutable, wisdom, He brings Jairus, one of the rulers of the synagogue, to fall down at His feet. Praise the Lord for sharp strokes, my brothers, if they bring us to ourselves!

And here let me interject a prayer for all Church officials. Lord save the beadle, save the precentor, convert those excellent men, the deacons; and let our ruling elders know Thee in their own hearts! Yea, Lord, save the minister, save the bishop: and bring priest and Pope, by some means, to know their own sore and their own grief!

I do not know anybody in the congregation who needs this more than the man who is speaking; I do not know any persons in London to-day, religious professors, who need this more than the men who occupy pulpits. For it may be that we ourselves are like Jairus, so concerned with the form, the order, and the routine of worship; so concerned with you, that—God help us!—unless some sharp stroke of distress comes upon ourselves, we might go sleeping along, getting more and more of the form of religion and less and less of the power of it. And unless the Lord checks and corrects us, by teaching us our own need, and by some home-coming visitation, swift and personal, making us to feel that *we* have a soul to save, and that *we* have a little family circle at home as well as the Church and congregational circle to pray for, and who need to become the subjects of Christ's saving grace, we may miss Him altogether.

And then when Jairus did pray, how well he prayed! When he is brought into living and naked contact with the reality of religion, whether it be in Old Testament synagogue or Presbyterian kirk, that is *Christ*—how real he becomes! " My little daughter lieth at the point of death, I pray Thee come and lay Thy hands on her that she may be healed, and she shall live." I do not believe he could have said that in the temple. If you had put him there or into the synagogue and removed the incarnate Christ from him, and said, " Now, my friend, your little daughter is very ill, pray for her," we know how he would have begun. He would have begun away back I don't know how far; he would have entered into all manner of things, very much as we do ourselves; he would have quoted a very great number of texts of Scripture—and I suppose they would have been all well quoted—and at last he would have mentioned that he had a little girl at home who was very ill! How this sharp stroke delivered him from a great many things; how well he prayed, to be an office-bearer, if you will allow the expression; how urgently, swiftly, how much to the point! He sees it all in his mind while he is speaking; he has a picture before him of Christ going with him, and of the way in which He will heal her. "He will lay His hands on her, she will be healed, and live."

O God, that we might learn from him! I made a remark just now that caused a smile; I did mean it to cause more than that—I speak to myself and you, and I do not want to ruffle any souls, yet what am I to do? I have got to stand here and plead and beseech you that this matter of prayer might become more urgent and real. Fathers, mothers, Sabbath-school teachers—you, woman, who wrote to me after last Sabbath, saying, your patch of lentils was a flock of young people, and that you had a hard battle with the Philistines—is this how you prayed for them? Is this how we pray? Is this how we realize the case? Do we realize what death means, whether temporal or spiritual, as Jairus realized what temporal death meant in all its desolating power to his own heart and life? and do we come into the Master's presence with these prayers, these broken, pleading supplications, as Jairus did? I think you know that well-worn story, yet it is worth telling again, for it is true: it is of a countrywoman of ours who had a little child at the point of death, and she and her husband, and I think he was an office bearer in the Church, went to the throne of Heavenly Grace to intercede. But John prayed in the temple style of prayer, in the synagogue style, in the prayer-meeting style. He began away far back, and recited to God the doctrines of grace—and they are very true; then he took in "Thine ancient people Israel," and the good woman could stand it no longer. She took the office of intercessor out of her husband's hands, and she plucked him by the elbow and said, "Oh, John, ye're sair drawn oot aboot thae Jews, but oor bairn's deein'." It was a needed rebuke, and I hope it did John good, and that it will do us all good.

It requires a great deal of courage for me to say what I am going to say next—*courage*, not impudence; we can be impudent without grace, but it needs much holy boldness for me to say this next thing. We have a little time on the Wednesday when we meet with Christ to supplicate, to plead, to beseech with Him greatly for blessings. I wonder if Christ has heard the great beseeching which is recorded here? I wonder when we shall have in our little gatherings for prayer more condensedness, more piercing and penetrating cries, and then sit down to let the next burdened believer get his or her turn? This prayer was short; it was weighty; it came from the heart, and went to the heart. What of ours?

After Jairus' prayer, there follows the story of the woman with the issue of blood. We won't dwell on that just now

—I think we have taken it up before; but sometimes I have thought that if Jairus had stayed at home, and sent his wife, this woman would have been cured second instead of first. Urgent as he was, she would have done it still better; woman like she would have fairly carried the Lord with her through the crowd, and the woman with the issue of blood would not have been neglected—oh no, no! she would only have been second instead of first. May all of us, especially fathers and mothers, take away this lesson, at any rate— Oh for urgency at the throne of grace!

The narrative resumes, so far as Jairus and his little daughter are concerned, at the 35th verse.

"While He yet spake," that is while He lifted up His voice in benediction on the poor woman, "there came from the ruler of the synagogue's house certain which said, Thy daughter is dead: why trouble thou the Master any further? And as soon as Jesus heard the word that was spoken, He said to the ruler of the synagogue, Be not afraid, only believe."

When I bend over this narrative at this turn in it, I seem to hear Christ saying, "It is expedient for *you* that I should go away." We oftentimes speak as though it were a great drawback to us that we did not live in the times when Christ was here in the flesh. That is not a wise saying. We are vastly better off than if we had lived then, for various reasons, and for this among the rest: there is now no danger of any hitch of this kind, no seeming breakdown like this. If the Lord were to stay among us always in the body, then He would always need to be subject to bodily conditions, and to ordinary conditions of space and time; one would need to go in his turn, and another to stay back, with all the misery that comes through hope deferred. But we are not under this law, with its long delays; we are under grace, with its immediateness and swiftness, and do not need to trouble ourselves as did poor Jairus. Glad as he was to see that woman go and get her blessing, yet, as he witnessed that wonderful incident by the roadside, his heart would be just going like an engine;

"Oh, but my girl! Lord," he would be saying to himself, "be quick; Lord, push through, let us get on. This is very grand for the woman, and very kind of you, but it is interruption—my daughter, my little daughter!—when will *my* turn come?" We are saved from that. I do not need to stand beating my breast because Christ is at *your* door, and because my turn will not be for half an hour or a full hour yet.

No, blessed be His Name, it was expedient for us that He should go away. Now all of us can grip His skirts at once, and get the help we need immediately. I am glad He is not here in the flesh. We have Christ, in the fulness of His power, risen to God's right hand; and apprehended by the right hand of faith by any soul that lives throughout the whole breathing, sin-sick world. I want the living Son of God, and He is here by His invisible spiritual presence,—with us always and everywhere to the ends of the earth.

Somebody came and said, "Thy daughter is dead: why trouble the Master any further?" Oh yes, that voice is still in the world. A great part of the business of us poor preachers is to contradict that voice, and we are not getting on very well; a great part of our work is to stand before those who are believers, and are wanting to believe better, but are being sadly inclined by the actual fact and condition of things to give in to that voice which says, "It is too late for you. Thy daughter is dead." As a preacher of the Gospel, let me stand here, let us all stand in London to-day, and contradict that. That was a poor messenger; a poor speech that he made! We see to-day how far wrong he was. Let it help the application of the point that I am trying to make. Do not take counsel of sad surroundings that vex you. It is *not* too late. Thy daughter is *not* dead. And instead of ceasing to pray and to be earnest, be more urgent and more earnest than ever. Do not let death win with the Lord of life near by! Do not let death win without another try, without another cry, without another struggle. It is not true. Gather over that verse and underline it; unless your Bible is too sacred to be pencil-marked, somehow or other emphasize it, especially those who have dead children in the awful sense of the word *dead*. You who wrote to me with the tear-blot on the page—I know what blotted it—it was not something in your ink, it was the great splash of a tear. My dear brother, my sister, your father, your mother, your daughter, your son is not dead. It is a lie as deep as hell. Don't believe it. I don't care what the appearances of things may be, don't give in, don't give up; hear Christ, as he said swiftly—as soon as Jesus heard that word He said—" Be not afraid, *only believe.*" *That* is the cure. *That* is the balm for this family heart-ache, is it not? What a great word! May its music ring in all our desponding hearts to-day! Preachers, parents, Sabbath-school teachers, those who have charge of the dear lads up in the gallery, don't give in to those words: " It is too late: death hath seized them, and is bearing them down to the pit." Nay, nay. As soon as Jesus heard the word that was spoken, He said to the ruler of the synagogue, " Be not afraid, only believe." " Weep not," He said to one on another occasion, " only believe."

Read the 38th and the following verses. How this story repeats itself to-day! Verily, this is the word of God that liveth and bideth for ever. I think I see the blessed Master coming. I think I see Jairus trying to dry his eyes, and not succeeding very well, trying to comfort his heart, trying to hold himself as between Christ and the messenger who said, "Thy daughter is dead: don't bother." Oh, how cursedly cool some people can be when it is not their daughter! Jairus holds himself between hope and fear, but I imagine his heart goes suddenly down, for appearances are that the messenger spoke truly, and that

Christ had misunderstood or had miscalculated the urgency of the case. He finds those that weep, those that bewail greatly; the hired mourners, and those who were not hired, making a great ado.

Somehow or other, the world does not like to be interrupted at a funeral. The world gets a kind of pleasure in connection with this funeral business, and does not want to stop. We have not given it up yet—no, we have not; we try to hold this Gospel, and with it this old-world, humbugging paganism. You have had the two at most of the funerals that ever I have been at. We endeavour still to combine the two. I think it is rare to find a Christianly-conducted funeral. Not often is a funeral service conducted at Church or grave, I had almost said, as Christ would have it. Not that the tear is inadmissible; He wept Himself; we are often too dry, often too cold. But we might dispense with much of the ordinary mummery and flummery that gathers around a funeral. How I rejoice to read that word of Christ, "He put them all out." While His heart was filled with pity for the poor father and mother, at the same moment the same heart could be filled with holy scorn for this post-mortem profanity: and "He put them all out." Let our funerals then, in ordinary circumstances, be marked by quietness and Christian simplicity. Dismiss everything that is incongruous with the so'emn, hopeful, awful scene. Especially do I wish that professing Christians at such a time would banish intoxicating liquors. Put them all out! To many of us the text "what concord hath Christ with Belial" comes into mind where Bacchus is associated with Burial. God grant that the same Spirit, the Spirit of Jesus Christ, might come still, and sweep out from our chambers of death and from our houses of sorrow all those things that offend the Master, that offend against the very spirit and power and hope of Christianity.

The very sight at some of our funerals makes one ask, "Do we believe in Christ yet? Have we got rid yet of the stupid, bewildered notions of our heathen ancestors when death comes?"

He said to them, "Why make this ado and weep? the damsel is not dead, but sleepeth. And they laughed Him to scorn." Shall we stand and bear that laugh to-day? Let us think of it. Bring forward your dead, my friend. Let us remove, let us dare to remove this controversy not only from the chamber where death is newly begun, not only from the interrupted funeral procession, as in the case of the widow of Nain, but let us carry it down to the graveyard itself where the dead had been lying for days unmistakably dead and buried. Let us shift the problem down there, and even there dare to say, with Christ, "Not dead, but only sleeping." The moment you say it, even although you say it in Christ's name, and although you say it in the 19th century after He is gone to the glory, the laugh and scorn rise in our ears. Our men of science, our materialistic philosophers, our would-be wise people of to-day gather around us, and as we say, "Not dead, only sleeping," they say, "Ha, ha, ha!" They laugh us and our Master to scorn; they say, "this is the sheer infatuation of your religion." "Man," they say, "Preacher, take that in your hand, is not that death? Doctor, come here and certify that this is a corpse." And we dare the doctor and say, "*No*, not dead, but only *sleeping*." We stand with Christ, "*not dead*, only sleeping." As His own grave is empty, so shall all graves one day be. We do not say that all shall have the Blessed Awakening, but certainly all shall awake. It is grand, it is awful, it is terrible.

See here also the blessed place and function of the servant of the Lord Jesus Christ when the doctors have finished with the case. You understand? When the doctor has written his certificate and goes out, there is no more need of him—only to settle the bill. Now, have you not often felt, minister, servant of Christ, in going to the house of pain and disease, as though the doctor had the better of you? As long as there is life *he* seems to be the man. We are often made to feel this. The doctor only is allowed in. I have only newly wiped my feet on the mat when the nurse slips down and says, "She cannot be disturbed." Exactly! I am a disturber; the doctor, a friend, a power—everything. This poor man with his prayers and the reading of the Scriptures—*exit* preacher, enter doctor! Oh, you smile, but you do it: I would excite your patient, I would kill her; *he* is the cure-all, the doctor! Ah, it is a shame, a burning shame, but it is deep in the heart of some. If your child, if anybody belonging to you, is dangerously ill, keep out the spiritual man—he will excite, he will hasten the death; send for the doctor, with his pill-box and drugs—he is the man. Now, I would advise you to send for both of us. I won't scorn the doctor till he gets out of his place, then I am ready for him. He is the second, *not the first;* and when he has done his best and has failed, and when death reigns, then the preacher gets his chance. In came Christ when the doctor had done, when there was nothing to do but to bury and have the ordinary kind of funeral; and Christ said, "It is My turn now." Oh preacher, oh elder, oh man, who go down to the families of the people, bearing this Gospel in your hands, do not be ashamed of your position! Take a look at the face of Christ, and go to the house of mourning; go to the house of death, and stand and read the Bible, stand and lift up the heart to the Lord and pray: you are the very men needed, your words are the words needed, and your cure is the perfect cure for bleeding hearts in the chamber of death and bereavement. "Comfort one another with these words."

I like this story, because of that; it encourages me where I have often felt, and have often been *made* to feel, I was a nobody because I had not a prescription.

We forgive Tennyson for any encouragement he has given to the *dishonest* doubter, because of the splendid way in which he has pilloried the mere dissecting doctor.

You will remember how he holds him up once for all, "The man," as he describes him—

> "Fresh from the surgery schools of France, and of other lands,
> Harsh, red-hair, big voice, big chest, big merciless hands:
> Wonderful cures he had done ; oh yes ; but 'twas said too of him
> He was happier using the knife, than in trying to save the limb."

Then our poet goes on to tell what this kind of medicine-man said to the nurse at the bedside of a lad who had been fatally crushed in a mill—

> "And he said to me roughly, 'The lad will need little more of your care.'
> 'All the more need,' I told him, 'to seek the Lord Jesus in prayer.
> They are all His children here, and I pray for them all as my own.'
> But he answered me, 'Aye, good woman, can prayer set a broken bone?'
> Then he muttered half to himself ; but I know that I heard him say,
> 'All very well, but the good Lord Jesus has had His day.'"

Just so; they laughed Him to scorn. But the nurse takes her stand with Christ, and says—

> "'Had? Has it come?' It has only dawned. It will come by-and-bye;
> Oh how could I serve in the wards, if the hope of the world were a lie?'"

They laughed Him to scorn. They do it yet: God forgive them! Oh, that we might rise in the strength of this old narrative, and say, "Miserable comforters are ye all." Send for the minister. Send for the missionary. Send for the *spiritual* man. And there is no doctor here who is on the right side who can possibly feel offended. I do not mean you, my brother. God bless you, are you not all ministering spirits sent forth to be ministers to those who shall be heirs of salvation? And, like your coadjutors the angels, you do your work in many cases as gratuitously as they. The Lord will reward you: "Inasmuch as ye did it unto one of the least of His brethren, ye did it unto Him." Still my point holds good. That laugh, that taunt has not died away yet. That controversy—which side do we take in it?—still exists, still rages round about the dead. And still let me ask you, On which side do you stand—dead or sleeping, which? For your own soul's sake, I press the question, and for the sake of your dead—Dead or sleeping, which?

They laughed Him to scorn; and a great many to-day of our superfine unbelievers who would sneer at these very people, yet show themselves to belong to them in spirit, for they laugh at the hope of immortality and resurrection life through faith in Jesus Christ.

"And He entered in where the damsel was lying, took her by the hand, and said unto her, Talitha cumi; which is, being interpreted, Damsel, I say unto thee, Arise. And straightway the damsel arose and walked; for she was of the age of twelve years. And they were astonished with a great astonishment." How did He do it? What I am struck with is the mingling of infinite power with infinite tenderness and ease; the calm, quiet, and confident way in which Christ suited Himself to the whole situation. With the firm grip of His almightiness, He swept out these scorners. "He that sitteth in the heavens shall laugh, the Lord shall have them in derision." He will have it out with the sneerers; don't lose sight of that. Then calmly, as though He put on another face, He unbent His brows, the look of indignation passed from His face, and He just looked the very Man needed for a time and place like that—the very God-Man. He looked so hopeful and tender that the father and mother, Peter, James, and John felt their hearts beating within them. He walked to the bed, took the damsel by the hand, that cold clay which when any doctor had felt he would have said "dead." Christ took her by the hand and raised her, somewhat after the fashion of your own mother when she used to say to you, "Sleeping, my little lass? It is time you were up! Maid, arise!" "And she that was dead sat up, and they were filled with a great astonishment." Those who were there never forgot the word that was used. I am glad they did not, for there are some folk who would forget the very words that raised the dead. They would remember any trifle, and forget "Talitha cumi." That is a word never to be forgotten. As one of our able modern expositors has said, "If it were not that the question of the miraculous is involved, the dullest critic in Europe would admit that this story was a simple, natural relation of fact from beginning to end."

Now a word for our own dead before I let you go; physically dead. "Fear not, *only believe*." There is no cure but that; none is needed but that. "Comfort one another with these words." But as I indicated before, there is another meaning to the word *death*. This miracle becomes a spiritual parable and sermon. My father, mother, dear friend, it may be true of you, your daughter is dead in an awful and spiritual sense. What does this miracle teach? It teaches us to believe in Christ, to trust in Him—only believe in Him, only come to Him and ask Him, tell Him all about it, show Him your living sorrow and your dead sorrow, and believe! Only believe, and remember the mighty power that this Saviour hath! Think of that woman when her daughter was restored, and say to yourself, "That joy shall yet be mine," here or hereafter.

And I close by saying, all appearances to the contrary notwithstanding, "Oh fathers, oh mothers, oh Sunday-school teachers, oh you who are working among the young, you who are mourning because your sons and daughters are showing no signs of life, but of death and deepening corruption; they are not dead; it cannot be: do not believe it; do not give in. Call in Christ and pray, and pray, and pray to Him." Let us say of the worst—

> "She is not dead; it cannot be,
> That one who glowed with love to Thee,
> Can all that's past renounce, forget.
> Oh, speak, and she will hear Thee yet.

> "She is not dead; Thy voice Divine
> Can still revive, and seal her Thine;
> And 'neath Thy wing she yet may dwell
> More meek, more safe, than e'er she fell."

Lord, speak! Thy servant can do nothing; Thou hast the power. Lord, speak! and let Thy word go crashing through the blocked-up ear, the blocked-up door of death, and waken up life in the silent chamber. Lord, speak! Say, "Lazarus, come forth!" say, "Young man, arise!" say gently, according to the conditions of the case, "Talitha cumi. Maid, dear maid, arise." Amen and amen.

Regent Square Pulpit.

FOUND OUT.

A Sermon

DELIVERED IN REGENT SQUARE CHURCH,

BY THE

REV. JOHN McNEILL.

Text: JOSHUA vii.

THIS is a judgment story. I wish to use it as an illustration of the processes by which sometimes, even in this world, and certainly in that Great Day, God shall gather out of His kingdom, as Christ said, all things that offend, all things which to His own eye, secretly, were all along the explanation and the reason of the Church's slow progress, her dismal failure, when she seemed just about to wave the palm of victory. As here, so there. "From this one, learn all."

But first of all, let us firmly believe that the day of judgment is coming. God hath appointed a day, not simply, as on this occasion, for finding out Achan and for taking away from His people that stumbling-stone over which they tripped and fell, but a day in which He shall take the whole world before him, and finally, once for all, thoroughly winnow and purge His floor, and gather the wheat into the garner, and burn the chaff with unquenchable fire. Of that day let no soul of us be in ignorance or dubiety. It is spoken of all through Scripture. Everywhere the Bible lifts up the solemn index-finger and singles out "*that day.*" Enoch, the seventh from Adam, spoke of that day· "Behold, the Lord cometh with ten thousands of His saints," to do a work, not of mercy, but of judgment, "to execute judgment upon all, and to convince all of their ungodly deeds which they have ungodly committed." Solomon, at the close of that wonderful book of his, with its strange, thorough-going, almost despairing philosophy, brightens up at the close—thus showing that he had the thread in his hand all the time, and says, "Fear God, and keep His commandments, for this is the whole duty of man; for God shall bring everything into judgment with every secret work that men have done, whether it be good or whether it be evil." And, again, saith the Apostle, "He hath appointed a day in the which He will judge the world in righteousness by that Man whom he hath ordained, whereof He hath given assurance unto all men, in that He hath raised Him from the dead." And last of all, when we come to the Book of Revelation, we have a vision of the judgment-seat, the great white throne, and Him that sits upon it, with the dead, small and great, standing before God. You have no vivid instance like this, because it is not needed. All through, from here and onward, the Bible has been solemnly saying that the judgment without mercy is coming; and, instead of bringing forward at the close any more instances, it solemnly and finally says, "There shall in nowise enter anything that defileth, neither whatsoever worketh abomination, nor loveth or maketh a lie."

To come to the historical narrative, how vividly it illustrates that Scriptural saying, that "one sinner destroys much good." One day in this place, not long ago, we dealt with the former chapter, and how bright and glorious and gladsome that was. All God's people brought together into line, more than into line, into a unity and compactness and solidarity of thought and feeling and purpose by the work of God's Spirit. And just because they were so solid and compact there was a splendid momentum in their movement. Nothing could stand before them. Jericho's walls fell, and Jericho's inhabitants lay at their mercy. And now, in the turning of a leaf, what a change! Israel smitten before her enemies just when she was thinking she was so strong that, as we have read, all her strength was not needed for taking this Ai. It was a mere *et cetera*. The great work had already been done, and this was a mere trivial detail, and a mere handful of the host would succeed. But suddenly, to their own great surprise and Joshua's utter amazement, Israel is smitten before her enemies. Joshua lies flat upon his face, and cries out to God in an honest, earnest agony of soul, "O God, what am I to say? O God, what art Thou to say?" Very honest; very earnest. None but a whole-hearted, devoted, consecrated man like Joshua could have been in such a state of panic, or could have spoken words so wildly earnest. God said, "Wherefore liest thou upon thy face? Up, sanctify the people. Bring them before Me to-morrow. Israel hath sinned." And, as the whole story shows, one sinner destroyed all their solidarity.

One sinner destroyed all united effort. As I see in the chapter before how beautiful, how swift, how strong Israel was, because in all their hearts there was a single undivided faith and fear of the Lord God Almighty; and as I see in this chapter how they have broken all to pieces, I stand in awe, I bring myself out of the time of Joshua into the Church in Regent Square, and I ask myself, "Am I the cause?" Why are our works of faith and labours of love so seemingly abortive. Why is our work, our size in one direction, so large, so imposing, but behind it all such discomfiture, such confusion, such defeat? Why? Let every soul of us examine himself, is the solemn word that comes from this awful story of judgment without mercy. Is Regent Square not the power for God in this district that she ought to be—the power for truth and righteousness, the power for grace and salvation, the power to overcome sin and the devil, and lift up Christ in this end of London— because I am in the pulpit—because you are an elder— because you, sir, are a deacon—because you stand in the Sabbath school or somewhere in the ranks of the communion roll? There is a sweep in this sword that takes in all.

Who is to blame? What is wrong? I might easily apply it to the whole church, but I want to keep nearer. Let every church do it. We will do it in here for ourselves. Who is to blame? One man spoiled the unity, spoiled the success. It is put in plain English: for the sin of one man the anger of the Lord was kindled against Israel, and they all suffered. For that unity, that solidarity, is a reality far more than we think. God counts a great deal upon it. If one member suffer, the whole body suffers. If there is health, there is general health. If there is sickness, we are all enfeebled and hurt by that sickness. It is somewhat like what takes place in connection with our electric telegraph system. Messages and communications are flying to and fro, say, between the different parts of an army in a foreign country engaged in a foreign campaign, one being in complete accord and close communication with the other, when suddenly there is a breakdown. Suddenly the generals in each host cease to be able to communicate with each other. United movement is impossible; united counsel is impossible. Why? Because, at some one place the enemy, by means of a spy, has tapped the wire; and all this communication of theirs is being turned not for them, but against them. At some place the wire is tapped and the communication is taken off and is used by the enemy. So with Israel. At one point the tide of the Spirit's power that was circulating through them all was deflected. By one unfaithful man the whole tide of God's energy was shed helplessly down to the earth. Now, in God's name, let the question go round, for it is time it went round. Israel is in a shameful state before the enemy. Who is to blame? Let each man examine not his neighbour, but himself—himself, each soul, every one of us.

God rose for judgment. This is God's method to bring home to us our own responsibility, our own guilt—to give us also space and place, room and time, for repentance. "Let a man examine himself," is a favourite text in connection with the Lord's Table, but it is a text for all our Christian connection, and all our Christian relationship, and it is often misapplied. To far too great an extent, in the country from which I come, the idea is, "Let a man examine himself, and so let him stay away from the Lord's Table. Let him back out of fellowship. Let him keep back." That is not the Scripture. Let a man examine himself, and so let him stand in; so let him eat, not abstain from eating. Examination is made to be a merciful work, to discover ourselves to ourselves, to save God from going through these fierce processes of His fiery indignation, to lead to honest confession, to putting away of sin, and to restoration to our place in God's sacramental host. As God worked then so He is working still. So shall He work on that great day of judgment. God took the process in hand. "Though hand join in hand, the wicked shall not be unpunished." It seems to be a sore problem; it seems to be an utterly unsoluble problem; but this story shows us that it lies as plain before God as that book-leaf lies before you and me. There is no problem in the sad condition of God's Church as she is in the world just now. There is really no problem from God's point of view. All things are naked and open, lying plain before the eyes of Him with whom we have to do. Still, it is worth while for us to see what the problem is.

The problem on that day was this. There was one man who had broken the chain. A leakage was taking place at one point, at one particular man, an ordinary man, a man who but for his sin would never have been heard of in the world. Oh, see how staring, glaring, conspicuous a man becomes by sin; not by cleverness, not by intellectuality, not by wealth, not by culture, not by rank, not by wearing clothes, and taking positions, but by this dirty thing—sin. Sin makes a man conspicuous who otherwise, as I have said, would not have been heard of—an ordinary man in the ranks of men. There is that missing link; there is that break; there is that leakage; there is that sinner. The problem is, *how to find him out*—how to have the damage repaired, how to have that man detected, and either put right or put out. And the problem is intensified thus. The man knows what he has done, and the man will not tell. Do you not feel that you are sitting for his portrait, my friend? He knows who he is; he knows what he has done; he sees the judgment processes creeping closer, closer, closer to him; and there he stands braving it out to the last, and then he blurts out his confession, when it is too late. We have the same thing still. I take up this subject because I find this in my heart and in your heart. This accursed thing is in us, namely, that our heart shall depart from the living God; our heart shall forget its purpose; our heart shall turn aside to sin, and outwardly we shall brazen it out with our very Leader and defy Him, and deny so far as we are concerned, that we are responsible—that the blame lies at our door.

It has fearful force, this, for any congregation that I know of. Instead of meeting in conferences over "the lapsed masses," and this and that and the other thing, let us meet over the story of Achan, and let every man's own face grow white with fear. Let the question go round, "Lord, is it I? Master, is it I?" The best men and women in this church to-day are the men and women who already are feeling that in this mirror of God's Word their own face is beginning somewhat to shine out.

There was no confession. The Lord was not helped in the least. He had to take judgment in hand. Joshua was nonplussed; and if God Himself had not come, Israel's history as a successful people would have come to a close at this very point. We talk in our homely proverb of the difficulty, the impossibility, of finding a needle in a haystack. That familiar phrase receives a moral illustration here. What God has to do is to find out the one sinner among these assembled thousands, *when he is keeping as dark as the grave.* Again, I say, do you not feel it? Alas, alas! there are men and women in this church to-day, and their whole attitude towards God and heaven up to this hour has been a brazen-faced defiance. You virtually say, " What is all this noise and rumpus about sin? It is only a name in a preacher's mouth—a word. It has no reality.

It is at most and best an exaggeration." There might have been men in Israel who would have said that this was an exaggeration. In the end of the day nobody said that. All Israel stoned that man with stones. All Israel became executors of God's vengeance on the offender.

"Joshua rose up early in the morning, and brought Israel by their tribes; and the tribe of Judah was taken." What a process! How vividly it is presented in Scripture before our mind's eye. See that host. Remember the charge that hangs over them, "There is an accursed thing in the midst of thee, O Israel, neither will I be with thee any more till that thing be taken away." And there are the gathered hosts drawn up in their regular companies. What relief to the eleven tribes as the twelfth is taken! In those eleven tribes, all those honest souls knew that they had not taken the forbidden spoil. Yet when God comes to judgment, whose heart does not tremble? "God help me, it may be that I may have done the accursed thing, for the very stars are not clean in His sight, and in spite of itself this treacherous heart may have turned aside." "What a sigh of relief as eleven of the tribes breathe freely." What a concentration of their eyes upon the twelfth, the tribe of Judah.

How vividly, how unerringly, God makes His mark. The tribe of Judah, the family of Zerah; and the family comes man by man, *and Achan is taken*. Be sure *your* sin will find *you* out. This story is not so merciless as I have said already that it was. There is mercy even in this judgment. How? Well, in this way. God could have come and simply taken that unclean thing, Achan. He could have taken him "neck and crop" without all this process. God could have gone straight to him, and put His hand upon his shoulder, and hurled him out into the outer darkness at once. Why take all this time—tribe by tribe, family by family, man by man? Surely, my friends, that was mercy. That was in Achan's interest. He gave the poor, infatuated fool time, space, place, room to repent; and as he saw Nemesis evidently on his track he had time to cast himself down before Joshua, and to exclaim, "Stop! I confess! I am the man." Had he done so, this story, I am convinced, would have been one of the brightest stories of mercy in God's Book, instead of one of its darkest, almost without a ray of light. For thus saith the Lord in His Holy Book, " He that covereth his sin shall not prosper, but whoso confesseth and forsaketh shall find mercy." May the Achan, may the Judas in us clutch at these terms!

When will you and I learn the infatuation of sin? There are men and women in this church to-day just like Achan. Why does not God break out upon you? Why does He not somewhat vividly and visibly lift you almost from where you sit, and send you spinning into hell? It is not because He cannot do it. It is not because He is not here. It is not because you are not a troubler of Israel. It is simply because the forbearance of God is meant to lead you to repentance. Judgment is His strange work; and He delighteth in mercy. Oh, in a day, in an hour, God could come to us, God could come to all England, and to all this world, and bring in at once eternal heaven and eternal hell; and if He does not, He holds off simply and purely in our interests. The Lord is full of pity and of tender mercy, and He desires not the death of Achan, but would rather that Achan would turn, for turning means living; turning means confession, forgiveness, salvation. Let me ask the poor drunkard, the poor covetous man, the poor lad or older person sitting here, all leprous with secret uncleanness, why are you permitted to live? Why are you permitted to be the hypocrite on some communion roll that you are? Simply because God's patience is not yet exhausted; *but it has an end.* Let us be wise in time; and may the goodness of God send some of us home to-day—ay, do not wait until you go home, for it is a perilous world for an Achan to live in—where you sit, within these hallowed walls, hand up the sin out of your heart. As the stolen stuff was dug up out of Achan's tent, so allow me to dig up your heart for you. Disgorge; confess; forsake thy damning guilt and sin!

Achan was taken. That same God is the God of the New Testament church. I do not know, my friend, how it may be with you; but this is the kind of preaching I was brought up under, and I have seen no reason to turn from it—a God of inflexible righteousness and holiness, who will not allow sin to go unpunished. Now do not stand up blatantly and ask whether I have ever heard of the Cross and the New Testament. *I have been to the Cross.* This story is intensified by the Cross. At the Cross we behold at once the goodness and the severity of God. At the Cross we learn the exceeding sinfulness of sin, the dazzling, blinding holiness of God, as well as the mercy that is intershot through all. That God is our God. That God is near to you and me. His breath is every day upon our cheek. How fares it with your heart, my friend, as God comes in and makes His goings seen and known in His sanctuary to-day? Judgment begins at the house of God. How is it with us? Are some of us here confessing, doing what Achan did not do? Or are some of us sitting in grim, desperate, fatuous silence, daring God to do His worst, for we shall never yield—we shall never confess?

"And Achan, the son of Zabdi, was taken. And Joshua said unto Achan, My son, give, I pray thee, glory to the Lord God of Israel, and make confession unto Him; and tell me now what thou hast done; hide it not from me. And Achan answered Joshua, and said, Indeed I have sinned against the Lord God of Israel, and thus and thus have I done: when I saw among the spoils a goodly Babylonish garment and 200 shekels of silver, and a wedge of gold of fifty shekels weight, then I coveted them and took them; and behold they are hid in the earth in the midst of my tent, and the silver under it. And Joshua said, Why hast thou troubled us? The Lord shall trouble thee this day. And all Israel stoned him with stones, and burned them with fire." Again let me remind you, that all this trouble was not for nothing. Now, there was a moment when, very likely, wise, sagacious people might have said, "What is all this for? What is all this about?" There was another moment when the man stood forth in all his ghastly, hideous sinfulness; and I tell you, men and women, and I try to tell my own heart, this sin is, in God's sight, an awful reality. Sin is no metaphysical abstraction. It is not a mere arrangement of the letters of the alphabet. It is not a mere thing of theology or of philosophy. It is a deep, dark, abominable thing found in the hearts of men and of angels; and if God spared not the angels that sinned, how shall he spare us? No, it was no exaggeration. It was no "trouble for nothing." It was no mere cry. God was justified. There was a stone in the machine, and God found out the stone and took it away; and then the wheels ceased to grate and jar and move heavily. There is a stone in the machine yet, in the moral machinery of God's Church and of God's world. I may be that stone, and I may be concealing what I am—concealing it behind the profession of the ministry, concealing it behind preaching to you on this very subject. You may be concealing it behind the office of the elder. You may be concealing it behind a great anxiety to keep the table of the Lord and the communion roll pure—desperately concerned about those who are coming in, that they shall be pure, and that they shall be right; and I say that this is needful, and it is a good sign and a good thing that the Church should conserve and be anxious about her purity before God and man; and yet it may be part of the dress that we put on, to look as Achan looked. For while the judgment processes were going on, Achan, very likely, held up his head and looked round. "It is not I, at any rate;" and the nearer it came the more brazen he looked; "It is not I." So our very scrupulosity and care in connection with God's house and Book and Day *may* belong to the Pharisee within us, the Achan, the hypocrite. God Almighty alone could have detected this man, and God Almighty Himself had to take the judgment work in hand. He was justified in what He did, justified in all His processes, justified in the judgment. So God is justified in the Cross of Calvary, and justified in that great day which is coming, when sin shall be visited by judgment without mercy.

How mean—not to give it a greater name—how mean was the sin of Achan. What a sin this was in a soldier, when he ought to have been filled with enthusiam, with patriotism, with love to God, with great desires for his tribe and people. He saw a goodly Babylonish garment, and the shekels of silver, and a covetous gleam shot through his eyes, and all the soldier in him withered up, and he became a sneaking thief. What a contemptible figure—an Israelitish soldier a thief! I tell you, friends, sin, departure from God, never looks well in this book. Is it not exemplified in ourselves? We belong, or we profess to belong, to the Lord Jesus Christ. We profess to have the highest and holiest name named upon us. We say that it is our greatest pride, our glory, our one and only boast that we are His, and that we are travelling on to heaven, and we say that the one object that unifies all our life purposes and plans is this—to be His, and to see Him at the end; and last week, how did we do? In the midst of all our big preaching and praying and praising—in the midst of our high lofty profession, behind the counter we lied: at the counter we stole, one side or the other. Out there, young fellow, you saw the flutter of a skirt, and your heart went after lust and uncleanness. You fell from heaven to hell in a moment. Men and brethren, turn your face Godward, and then down upon your knees in confession, quick! Quick! ask God if there is blood to wash you, for you need it! ask Him. The narrowest lust that ever entered the heart of man is the lust for gold. Covetousness is idolatry. Which of us has not been guilty of that same gleam of the eye, that same baleful light, that shone in Achan's face, and led him to deeds of shame and an awful doom?

It is a heavy subject, my brethren, but I did not write the Bible. It is there, and I must deal with God's Word as it is, and with your life and mine as God's Word shows them to us. I close the Bible. That is all. There stands Achan. He made confession, soon enough to glorify God, but too late to avert God's temporal judgment. So I fear in the Great Day there will be many belated confessions. Then wailings, then gnashing of teeth—but *too late!* Oh, my brother, my sister, that day which you are daring, that day which you are defying, is the Day of Judgment. Why will you call it and look upon it as though it were a day somehow of mercy? *It is the Day of Judgment.* *This* is the day in which there is a chance, and in which there is room to turn and get mercy. "Now is the day of salvation."

I leave Achan where the Bible leaves him. All Israel stoned him with stones, and burned him with fire, and raised a great heap over him. That is the end, and I shut the Book. I preach to-day a doleful word. I preach to-day—hear it—a Christless sermon. Does not the very house get darker at the awful sound. A Christless sermon! you say, "What preacher? Don't shut the Book. Don't send us away like that." Ah, I know what you expect—that after all this dolefulness and all this gloom and doom, I am utterly to turn it upside down by bringing in the Cross, and mercy and peace. I do no such thing. I must stick to my text; mercy refused; mercy despised; the time and place for it rejected and neglected; then doom at last. I am speaking to Achan here, and I want to let you know that you will get all you are working for. The day comes when the sweet gales of mercy no longer shall blow—when you will hear no more about cleansing blood—when there will be nothing but "a fearful looking for of judgment and of fiery indignation that shall devour the adversaries"—when your sin shall be proved on you, and in you, and to you, and before an assembled world, with no chance for ever of getting its curse and its power lifted away. It is coming. God will here lead us now to confession, or there to too late confession and doom beyond remedy. You remember how vividly our poet describes the clinging curse of sin. One had committed murder, and he went away with the murdered corpse and laid in the woods, and covered it with leaves: and he went back again, and the wind had blown away the leaves—there was his sin before him. Then, you remember he took it to the river and he flung it in; and again it came back, and

> "I saw the dead in the river's bed,
> For the faithless stream was dry.
> Then down I cast me on my face,
> And first began to cry.
> For I knew my secret then was one
> That earth refused to keep,
> On land or sea, though it should be
> Ten thousand fathoms deep."

God will drag out thy lusts and spread them like dung upon thy face, for thou hast dared Him to do it, and He shall! Judgment without mercy. Achan was burnt and all that he had. Too late! Too late! A Christless sermon! An awful word to say: is it not? It is an awful word to utter in the ears of poor, lustful, covetous men and women in pulpit and in pew. It is an awful word to utter in the few brief hours between us and the morrow—the morrow when God shall come to make inquiry. So I take back that word. I repent. Will you hear it yet again, Achan?—there is mercy with God, not that He may be presumed upon, but there is mercy with God that He may be feared, and there is plenteous redemption that He may be sought unto. I draw back that ominous sound lest it may ring in your ears as you go home, and be the death-knell of all hope, like the tolling of the execution bell—"A Christless sermon!" But oh, remember, remember that the sands are rapidly running through, and it may be that this is the last opportunity for some hypocrite, some Achan, some backslider, some man or woman with a name to live while the heart goes to the world, and to all its worldliness and godlessness — the last opportunity. Oh, now, now I spoil the harmony, the continuity of my text. I trample upon its thoroughgoing exegesis, and I bring in the Cross, and Him who hangs upon it, and lift Him up before you. Sinner, backslider, thou whose heart has gone aside from the living God, the Lord Jesus Christ, the great Sin-Bearer, stands again among us, and He says to us, " I, even I, am He that blotteth out thy transgressions, and will not remember thy sins. Return, oh return unto Me."

May the Lord plead His own cause, and may the hearts of not a few be opening, and may the hidden silver, and the hidden gold, the hidden lusts, the hidden vanities, the mockery, the hypocrisy, the malice, the guile, the hate, the envy, may they be dug out and poured out before the Lord. Then shall the valley of Achor be a " door of hope"; and " our strength be as the strength of ten because our heart is pure."

Regent Square Pulpit.

THE BURNING BUSH.

A Sermon

DELIVERED ON SUNDAY MORNING, DEC. 22, 1889,

BY THE

REV. JOHN McNEILL.

"Now Moses kept the flock of Jethro his father-in-law, the priest of Midian: and he led the flock to the backside of the desert, and came to the mountain of God, even to Horeb. And the angel of the Lord appeared unto him in a flame of fire out of the midst of a bush: and he looked, and, behold, the bush burned with fire, and the bush was not consumed. And Moses said, I will now turn aside, and see this great sight, why the bush is not burnt. And when the Lord saw that he turned aside to see, God called unto him out of the midst of the bush, and said, Moses, Moses. And he said, Here am I. And He said, Draw not nigh hither: put off thy shoes from off thy feet, for the place whereon thou standest is holy ground."—EXODUS iii. 1-5.

How naturally, and yet how supernaturally, the God of Abraham, and of Isaac, and of Jacob revealed Himself to His servant Moses, for Moses' own sake, and for the sake of his oppressed countrymen. Moses one day—shall I say one afternoon?—was keeping his sheep, attending them just as he had been doing for long years—just as we, during the past week, have been attending to our secular and worldly affairs, with all their natural tendency to

No. 7.

engross us and to swallow us up. Moses was not engaged in any unworthy work, or any career of sin. He was tending the flock of his father-in-law, and he led the flock to the backside of the desert, and came to the mountain of God. Here, perhaps, he had been often before, but as he led the flock along that familiar track, suddenly there came to him, in the calm and quiet of that lonely place, this wonderful sight, this wonderful revelation of the Lord, which became a point of departure in Moses' own heart and history, and in the history of the people of God. So, I say, that which makes life worth living is this—we will come to the point at once—the great glory of our life is that God comes into it and reveals His presence; that God opens our eyes to see that there is more in the world than simply our daily calling, our flock of sheep, and our temporal interests; that life is more than a day's work, no matter how diligently and conscientiously performed, and a night's sleep. God, the personal God, is here to greet our own eyes with the kindling glory of the manifestation of His own presence. He will change our life, its whole current, its whole outcome. Let us open our eyes, and see that this Sabbath day and every Sabbath day—but the past Sabbaths are gone, and coming ones are not here—but let us see that *this* Sabbath day, which *has come*, may be to us a time when, like Moses, we are round at the back of the desert. We have come to the mount of God, we have come to this calm and quiet, this solemn and holy place. Oh, may God lift Himself up, and reveal Himself to us!

And I would like at the outset to waken up an expectation in those who are rather apt to think that the day is gone by for them either to expect or to receive such visions and revelations of the Lord. My friends, Moses was an old man when this took place. Therefore let not those growing old, either in years or in cares, give in or sink down. Many a long day and year Moses had trudged about this very region, when suddenly *one* year, *one* day, *one* hour, *one* particular moment, he lifted up his eyes, and, as we all know now, Lo! *there was God*. And out of that occurrence came new life and new days for Moses, and for a great mass of people in connection with him. Now, my friends, business men, business women, middle-aged folk, elderly folk, you have often been to Church, and have gone a long way through life, and you are beginning to say. " Well, I must have missed it! Life is not turning out to me what I expected when young. I must have gone past the place. The show is all gone; I have seen and been through it all, and I begin to get, if not exactly sordid and sodden, at any rate down to the level of the world, and of the world's work and swing and routine." Ah, my friends, say not so! Especially say not so, those among us who have never yet seen the sight of sights—God revealing Himself as a personal God, as a personal Saviour, to our own heart and understanding. For there may be such here. There may be people in Regent Square Church this morning who have been here for forty years, and yet it is possible that I am interpreting your own thoughts when I repeat what I said a moment ago, "I have missed it!" "Yes," you say, "that is just it. I begin to fear that I have missed it—the glory, *the glory!* There is no glory in my life," you say, " in me, in my church-going. There is diligence and faithfulness and steady plodding, as in all other departments of my work on week days; but, preacher, the glory, *that* is where I challenge you. Man, there is no glory in my life, there is no glory in my soul, there is no heavenly wonder in my heart or on my face." I thought that; and that is why I said it so plainly, and perhaps I am speaking to myself while pointedly talking to you.

Now, let us turn to this subject, for I see no reason why the glory may not come to-day. I see no reason why the vision may not come to-day to some; and be vividly renewed to others, to whom former revelations have been fading into the light of common day. Let us begin where Moses began. "And the angel of the Lord appeared unto him in a flame of fire out of the midst of a bush: and he looked, and, behold, the bush burned with fire, and the bush was not consumed. And Moses said, I will now turn aside, and see this great sight, why the bush is not burnt." Well, it seems to me that the way by which, ordinarily, we travel straight into the secret place of the tabernacles of the Most High is a very ordinary way, at the beginning. "I will now turn aside and see," said Moses. The knowledge of God as my own God, and the God of my fathers before me, the Saviour and Redeemer of His people; God the invisible, the eternal, the uncreated God, the personal Friend, speaking with His voice to my own heart, so that I hear, and I understand; I believe, and I yield myself to all His will—it begins often at this simple, lowly point. In the midst of all the *ordinary* humdrum and routine of life I see something. There is a glimmer, a something *extra*ordinary somewhere, sometime, and *I open my eyes*. I was often there before, and saw *nothing*; but now there is a gleam, a light, an Epiphany. My very soul is engaged, led on, and on, and on, until the end of it is God as man speaking to me, lifting up my life by the grappling-hooks of His own purposes, and using and glorifying it and me for ever and ever.

I want to show, for example, that you might have had a man, another shepherd, and that man might have been going on for seventy or eighty years of age like Moses, and he never would have seen this revelation. He would have got so down to the level of a shepherd's life and a shepherd's experience that when he saw the bush burning he would have got some natural explanation for it, and passed on. It would have come too late in the day for him to say, "That is worth looking at. It is a *little* extra, there is a *scad* there (to use a word we have across the Tweed), an extra blush on that bush; but it cannot be a fire, it is only an extra glow of the sunlight on the furze. I do not think I ever saw it just so before, though." Meantime the sheep give a bleat, and he turns his face away, and on he goes—a mere shepherd, like that waggoner of whom we have heard;

"A primrose by the river's brim,
A yellow primrose was to him,
And it was nothing more."

Oh, friends, it is hard to waken up some of us! We are so unlike Moses. Moses, old as he was, and though he had been keeping sheep in that part of the country for years, did not look up and say, "No; it cannot be a burning bush. Dear me! I have tramped along this part for years, and know every bush and everything in the landscape, right on to the horizon. I know everything on the plain, and everything in the glens, and everything on the very mountain-tops, and it cannot be a bush burning. It is just some kind of trick or touch of the sunlight upon that bush there, and I am going on." No; old as he was, he was as curious as a bairn. He had still the faculty to open his eyes and see wonderful sights, and clap his hands, and wonder what they were. May God take away the oldness of some of us, and give us the freshness of youth! It will be the beginning of salvation.

Open your eyes! The world is not done, and you are not done. Your days are only in the beginning, and if you only get your eyes open to see what is here, they will never close again. When once God shows Himself to us in Christ, we, at last, have our eyes open. Are you beginning to understand this? Then keep them open, for they shall see greater things than these. There shall be an expansion of this revelation for ever. I wish I could waken up myself, and get out of my trammels and ruts, and then my preaching to-day would be what it had always need to be, the old thing would become a new thing, a superadded something, and that something *God, God Himself.* That something, *the flame in addition to the bush* I have seen all my days, ever since I saw anything. The flame, the glory, the God revealed! That is what I want to see as a preacher, and you want to see as hearers. The flame, the glory, the personal God, the elevation, the uplifting, the heaven—*there!* Not millions of miles away, but heaven—*there*, and *there*, and *round about me.*

> "Earth's crammed with Heaven,
> And every common bush afire with God;
> But only he who sees takes off his shoes—
> The rest sit round it, and pick blackberries."

Curiosity! a human thing;—and God pulled Moses by that little thread—curiosity. And this great chain cable came after it—faith, clear, strong faith in a personal God, speaking to him, and giving him a personal message and mission. "And Moses said, I will now turn aside, and see this great sight, why the bush is not burnt." Now, turn aside; get off the track, oh man; step out of your way; turn aside. Go, go, go along this new course; it is not far to go. Do not sit still and let things go past. It is a wonderful world; it is a wonderful church; all life is just bursting with wonder, if you will only turn aside. "Oh come, oh come, all ye faithful," people all this Christmas week will be singing, and I trust it will be more than singing, "Let us go even now to Bethlehem, and see—and *see*—this great thing that is come to pass;—this *new* form of the burning bush, God in Christ revealing Himself in all that tender manifestation to open eyes and expectant hearts. What a world it is!

what a Church it is! What a day it is, if you could see the glory in the midst of the material and common and familiar. A burning bush! Once we get our eyes open, as Moses did, it is easy to see that the burning bush is everywhere. That is to say, you have the bush—the common, the natural, the ordinary—with this blaze, this extra thing, this wreathing, wrapping flag of flame coming out of it. The common, the physical, the natural, being made the pedestal, so to speak, the pedestal or platform on which the uncommon and the supernatural reveals and displays itself. That is everything. From this point of view, the whole world of nature is a burning bush. But not everybody sees the burning. Everybody sees the bush. It is only Moses that becomes aware of the "glory on the grass"; "the silence that is in the starry sky"; "the sleep that is among the lonely hills."

The world is more than mud or atoms brought together fortuitously, or in any other way. The world is a burning bush. It is so far earth—solid, material. I can handle it, and become a man of science, and say, "What is in it?" And, God help me, I can become so much a mere scientist as only to see the bush and leaves and berries, and the shape of the leaves and the shape of the stem, and tell you how it grew, and then say, "There is no flame." Just so; there is a way of looking at that bush, man—a way of looking at the bush that *puts out its light, or your light,* which is the same thing. There could have been a kind of man come tramping along here with the sheep, and with one single look he would have quenched that flame; and the same damnable thing may be in you and me. We may look at nature, and look at our own bodies, and look at Christ in the Bible; and look at the Bible itself, with such a blank look and stare of unbelief that God withdraws Himself, and never comes back. Never! There is a way of looking, a trick in the eye, that is an abomination to God, and He simply withdraws. And we may become great scientists and great scholars (and God forbid I should say a word against science—I never did—or against scholarship) and yet become as blind as bats, or 'howkin' moles, as we say in Scotland—scraping and scraping the earth, and getting darker and dirtier the farther we go.

The nineteenth century is full of moles, calling themselves men of science, and a bonnie wee moudiewart (molehill) of a world they have made it. They have been here, and there, and everywhere, and they have explored everything, and tell us there is no God, no Spirit. "If there is," they say, "we do not know." Very well, we never expected you would. Go and sit down. If any man had dared to go to Moses in after years and had said, "Yon was not a burning bush," I think Moses' keen temper would have come back, and he would have said, "You lie! It was; I have no doubt about it." "Well, but," says the man, "I saw the bush, yet I did not see any flame." "Well, that does not matter," replies Moses, "*I did.*"

> "Like a man in wrath, the heart
> Stands up and answers,
> *I have felt.*"

Now, in these days, let us take care. We have a great deal of this. There is a way of looking at this bush which will put out its light, or yours. There is a spirit to which God will never show Himself, in nature, in science, or in the Bible. He will quietly withdraw, and hide Himself, and leave us the letter, and withhold from us the spirit, the glory, the knowledge of Himself. Everything is a burning bush. Nature is such a burning bush. Nature is full of the supernatural, everywhere ready to burst forth, but you must not push forward, but stand back if you wish to see it. The more we push in irreverently, the more it flies from us. Our own bodies—a burning bush! Have you ever thought of that? Here is the physical, the material, the natural, but in it and on it the immaterial, the spiritual, in a true sense, the metaphysical. Streaming out of it, and above it, and beyond it, is that which lifts itself up from the mass of blood and brain and bone, and says, "I, I am." The burning bush: the natural and the supernatural; and the one the basis and the platform simply of the other, the two of them so linked together that you cannot separate them. I cannot find out where they leave each other; it is too inexplicable to be known. So with the world; so with this little world—man. Then, again, here is a burning bush for you—the Bible. So much of it natural: the boards, and that means the binder; the print, and that means the printer; the thoughts, and that means the thinker—like any other book.

Like any other book, but, God be praised, more than any

other book. For the glory, the voice, the "Thus saith the Lord," comes out from this, that comes from no other book. Well says our hymn,

> "A glory gilds the sacred page,
> Majestic as the sun."

Such a burning bush is the Church of Christ, and I speak not now of her survival of fiery trials. Now, a congregation, a Church, either in the large sense or the sectional sense of the word, is just like any other corporation or society. It has its laws and purposes, and there is so much in it of man's planning and guiding and ordering. Yet a Church is not a mere guild like any other; a corporation of people like any other gathering. No, no, no! It is like them as that bush is like any other bush; but, man, there is a glory in it, there is a wonder in it! The Lord is in this place. "In all places—*all places*—where I record My name, there will *I* come, and *I* bless them."

"Oh, thou that dwellest in Thy Church, shine forth." For some of us it is becoming only a bush, an institution like any other. We are in it, we have offices in it, and are greatly concerned about its work, its extension and development, and that it should realize a beneficent function among the institutions of the earth. But, O Christ, show us Thyself. Oh, shine forth this day, blessed Lord, in Regent Square, and let us see the glory, above and in and through the preaching, and the Psalm singing, and the sermon hearing, and the dispensation of the Sacrament. Lord, let us not lose Thee. Shine out, O Christ, on Thy Church, and in Thy Church; and what Thou doest here, do everywhere.

Oh, angel of the Covenant; Oh, Thou who dost dwell in the bush, let Thy Church so appear to the wondering eyes of men that they shall say, " Who is this that looketh forth as the morning? fair as the moon, clear as the sun, and terrible as an army with banners!"

And I see coming to us *Christ Himself as a burning bush*. There He lies, a baby, like your own, my good woman; but, unlike your own, there is a glory, there is a flame. Wherever you come across Him, as babe, or as boy, or as man, or as crucified, there is the flame, there is the extra superadded something, and that something is the eternal and uncreated Godhead. Worship Him, wherever you meet Him, from Bethlehem right on to the cross, on to the glory. Worship Him—God in human flesh. Turn aside and see *this* great sight: why human nature can exhibit this mystery—why the bush is not burnt.

But further, all this came to Moses, humanly speaking, this wonderful revelation, *because of reverence*. When the Lord saw that Moses turned aside to see, He called to Him, and said, "Put off thy shoes." Now there is a spirit abroad to-day, in the world and in the Church, that goes clean contrary to all this. When God saw that He had got Moses to act, when He had caught his eye, and when Moses was going to see the bush, then in Moses' interest, and in His own, He flung upon him this saving mantle of a reverent and devout spirit. "Moses," He said, "Draw not nigh hither." Moses, come near enough to see; Moses, come near enough to hear; Moses, come near enough to fall down and give an intelligent reverence and an intelligent worship, *then no nearer*. Nearer than that you cannot come and live; nearer you cannot come to any good purpose.

Now the spirit that is abroad to-day would say, "Moses, that is a very remarkable sight you are looking at, and in a spirit of bold yet reverent inquiry, go forward and subject this phenomenon to frank and fearless criticism. We are told to-day that the Church is greatly indebted to men of this spirit—men who have gone up to the burning bush and fingered the thing, and told us about it.

Now I am not indebted—I speak for myself—I am not in any part indebted, either as regards methods or results, to the Strausses, and Baurs, and Rénans, and Darwins, and Huxleys—I am indebted to no man who does not bring me nearer God. I am the very opposite. If the spirit of Moses did not dictate his method, the " Glory of God " will not come out in his results. Any man who makes the glory to be dim, how shall I be indebted to *him?* And they *do make the glory dim;* the glory on the grass, as well as the glory on the page, and the glory of the Person. They make it dim. When Moses might have come in the spirit, if it can be got up, of bold and free and candid—to use these cant words of to-day — candid criticism, God said, " Moses, keep back." As I put it before, " Come near enough to see and hear and give an intelligent worship, and then if you are not to turn your blessing into the blighting of the lightning, do not come nearer!"

Our modern critics go, and you know what happens. I

cannot quote poor Darwin's own words, but nothing can be sadder than his own words as to what happened to him because he went too near without the reverent spirit. He virtually tells us that his scientific studies put his eyes out. That is the sum and substance of it. He came too near the bush without the reverent spirit, and his light went out. His mind, he says, became a mere machine for grinding out general laws from masses of ascertained facts. God pity all such as have come too near the flame! That is what you get for coming too near. Let us take care. We are only human at the best, and even the man with the microscope is only human, and should not be worshipped nearly as much as he is. The tone of to-day is, because a man has a microscope and has found out some extra things with it, worship him, all ye gods!

"Draw not nigh hither: put off thy shoes from off thy feet, for the place whereon thou standest is holy ground." He was *near enough*. I can quite well understand that very likely no man more than Moses would feel, "Oh, I would like to see this great sight, and get to the bottom of it." But he could not, and we should not. God has set bounds to the inquiries of the human spirit, not cramping bounds, but wise and safe ones. "I want to know all about this. There is purpose in that burning bush, and I should like to have it explained." And God says, "Take care; be reverent. Go so far, and go no farther, for you cannot go beyond a certain length and prosper."

So with many other difficulties. How am I at once

body and spirit? But I am warned by this, that many men who have gone into that question in order to find out about it have put out their eyes. They come back from the examination of the human frame, from wonder upon wonder, they come back and say, "We have found no spirit, no breath of God; all that has no warrant from our researches." Out you go with your researches! And they go to this Bible and say, "It is a very wonderful Book, and we have examined it in the spirit of frank, candid, and fearless inquiry. We have not scoffed at the Book, nor scorned it; we have examined it in the spirit of frank and fearless inquiry, and we find the glory is gone." It is just so.

There is only one method—the reverent; and one result—and that is to know God better and bow down flatter before Him.

You cannot take away the hyphen that holds the "*burning*" and the "*bush*" together. When even Moses would have gone forward *to see why*, he was kept back, and his thoughts turned in more profitable directions. So you are forbidden to go nearer; you are near enough to see and to know and to bow down and to give an intelligent, whole-hearted adoration and worship of obedience. And any spirit that enters into you and me, and makes me go beyond the point where Moses had to pull up, is a dangerous spirit, alike in method and result. May God breathe upon all of us the spirit that He gave to Moses! "Draw not nigh: put off thy shoes from off thy feet, for the place whereon thou standest is holy ground." And so, keeping my true distance, curbing and checking my mere natural curiosity (that will disguise itself with marvellous names), standing back where God would have me, I see better, I hear better; coming out of the Church, and out of nature, out of man's body, fearfully and wonderfully formed, out of the Bible, and out from the God-Man, that One Voice that assures *me* of the "Good-will" of Him that dwelt in the bush! *That is what I want to know.* May God bless us all. Amen.

Regent Square Pulpit.

WORKING OUT SALVATION.

A Sermon

Delivered in Regent Square Church,

BY THE

REV. JOHN McNEILL.

"Work out your own salvation with fear and trembling. For it is God that worketh in you, both to will and to do of His good pleasure."—Phil. ii. 12.

You notice the setting of this familiar text. Paul had been preaching in Philippi; the Lord had blessed his word; sinners had been converted; a Church had been called together. Paul is writing to his converts, as he always did, and you find that all through this Epistle there breathes a great affection for them, which he is sure is reciprocated in their breasts. He had fallen very warmly in love with these people, and they had with him; both for the Gospel's sake and for his own.

But Paul's is not a fond and foolish love, that will simply over-indulge itself in warm, gushing, affectionate expressions. His is a love which carries wisdom along with it, in all its warmth and impetuosity; it is always taking counsel with wisdom, so as to be wise as well as warm. And it is here I think that the wise warmth, the sober-tempered affection of this spiritual father for his spiritual children, comes out. "Wherefore," he says, "my beloved, as ye have always obeyed, not as in my presence only, but now much more in my absence, work out your own salvation with fear and trembling." It is as if the great Apostle had heard that although these Philippians were getting on very well; still there was a danger coming to them through their affection for him, who, under God, had brought the Gospel to them; and gently, yet firmly, he disengages and disentangles himself from them, and them from him. He seems to overhear what they are saying, "Ah, well, we certainly had great times when Paul was with us; but we are suffering now that he is no longer with us; if we had only Paul back again, and could keep Paul among us, and have Paul always with us, then we would be about perfect; our heaven below would be about as full as any one can expect on this side of the abundant entrance into the actual heavenly state." And Paul here says to them, "Now, Philippians, let us be fond, but don't let us be foolish. After all," he says, "I have nothing to do with you, and you have nothing to do with me; do not defeat all my fond expectations, and all my labours among you and concerning you; but as you obeyed in my presence, now in my absence, instead of sighing and feeling yourselves at a disadvantage, be all that you were when I was with you, only more abundantly. Much more in my absence prove to yourselves, prove to all who care to look at you, that you do not depend on me, that you do not hang upon man or angel; but that you hang on God, who brought the Gospel to you, although He brought it on my lips. It was He who brought it, and He has not gone; He worketh in you both to will and to do of His good pleasure. Oh, ye Philippians," he says, "you are at no loss, you are at no disadvantage; true *I* am not with you, though I fain would be; but *God* is with you, and He is now working in you."

I sometimes think that this verse receives its fullest emphasis by taking it from Paul's mouth and putting it into Christ's. We hear it as coming not from Paul the servant, but from Christ the great Master within the veil as He looks down on us. Oh, how it fits us! We are so apt to say —if He were here, then how our sanctification and our Christian work would get on. Sabbath-school teachers are saying this morning and thinking, "Ah, if Christ were our

Superintendent at Aldenham Street; if only Christ stepped in to superintend at Regent Square, or Compton Place, our hearts would be on fire, our teaching would be better done. If Christ only gave me my commission to climb that stair, and to read to that old bed-ridden woman, how it would be done!" *If* He were here with us! And Christ says to us, to *us* His Philippians here in London, speaking down from the eternal glory, "Wherefore, My beloved, as ye have always obeyed not as in My presence only, but now much more in My absence, work out your own salvation with fear and trembling, for I am working in you both to will and to do of My good pleasure." Are we not sometimes liable to the same snare as that which was going to entangle these Philippians in their onward path? Sometimes our eyes see the teacher too much, and cannot get past the teacher. Now, teachers come and go, but the great Teacher abides; and so for ever may our eyes be open to Him, and our ears receive this message as from His own lips—"Not as in My presence only; do not ask Me back; do not show to the world that you are weak and languishing because your Leader is not actually at your head, but prove to the world that faith finds its freest scope and its loftiest exercise *because it is faith.*" Christians, we *are* walking not by sight, but by a spiritual vision of Him who has gone before us, and is drawing us surely and certainly into His own presence. "Not as in My presence only, but now much more in My absence, let there be intensity, let there be individualism; let every man feel that this is his own affair; and while you receive all ministries and all gifts of that kind helpfully and thankfully, rise superior to them all; reach out and forth to Me Myself, your Saviour, your Sanctifier, your All in all."

Work out your own salvation—*your own* salvation. I sometimes like to dwell on this in what I venture to call the original English—for we need original English as well as original Greek—in the simple actual English that is here. Suppose we just take it as it stands. I know it is scarcely the idiomatic Greek, but we will take it in this idiomatic

English sense. And this all the more because, as Alford virtually says, our translation seems to countenance the very dangerous idea that salvation, after all, is not of faith and grace, but of merit and reward. Let us take this expression, "Your own salvation," in the light of Scripture teaching elsewhere, so that our somewhat unfortunate English may not mislead us. "*Your own salvation;*" what does that mean? That is a rare word in the Bible; the Bible is not fond of calling anything our own. It rather comes to us in all our pride of possession, strips us bare and says to us, "You have nothing that is your own; your friends, your health, your strength, are not your own. There is nothing your own but sin; that is yours in actual possession, and in all the entail of guilt and misery here and hereafter that belong to such an inheritance. Ye shall be filled with your own ways, ye shall eat of the fruit of your own doings." Alas, sin is the only thing that is mine! *My* sin, *my* guilt, *my* misery, *my* curse, *my* condemnation. "My sin is ever before me," said a man when he began to realize that that was his only actual absolute possession—sin, and the clinging curse through sin; "my sin is my own, it is ever before me, I can no more get rid of it than I can of my shadow." Now that is the Bible, and yet the same Bible makes out salvation to be our own.

Dwell on that a little—how does that come about? For until we get that fastened in our hearts, I do not think we shall feel able to obey the Apostolic injunction, "Work out your own salvation." I must realize that I have in my heart the salvation I am to work out. Let me enhance this thought in your mind, the thought that salvation is made over to us as our own, in a Book which from beginning to end strips us of all real ownership. "This is mine," says a man here, or a man not here, "this is my pile, I scraped it together; I rose early, I sat up late," and as he says it he jerks his money-bags or turns over his bank-book to the balance. "Mine arm," he declares, "and the greatness of mine industry have gotten me this wealth, to have and to hold and enjoy. It is not yours--hands off, or I will send for the police—let this alone, this is mine, *mine*, MINE, MINE!" And as we have seen in Glasgow some years ago, in the case of the City of Glasgow Bank, the bank breaks and he is a beggar—*he is a beggar!* This that he was calling his, even while he clutched it, it left him; for riches take unto themselves wings, and prove to us that that possessive word was foolish; it is disproved by bitter fact. If your wealth was really yours, why did you let it go? It is gone, simply because wealth is not ours in any absolute sense of possession. "My property," says a man. "See that? See that fine row of buildings? that is mine. These title-deeds mine, securely mine," and the next morning he is poking among the black ashes with his stick; *his property* has gone up in a chariot of fire, and come down in a shower of soot! Oh, how sarcastically the chapter of accidents disputes with us this expression: "My own." How did that happen if it was really yours? "My own"—let us push it on, and forward—"my, *my*, MY friend," says a man; "there he is, and a friend is a great blessing. My friend in a special and peculiar sense; mine, always there, always handy," and alas, alas! the chapter of facts disputes that use of this possessive adjective pronoun:

> "Friend after friend departs—
> Who hath not lost a friend?
> There is no union here of hearts
> That finds not here an end.
> Were this frail world our final rest,
> Living or dying, none were blest."

Ah! a friend is a great gift, and when you find him bind him to your heart with hooks of steel. But you cannot, there is a Power without us that gives no account of matters to us, that snaps the hook of steel; and in a time of need, when we turn, our friend is gone; he is not here, even though we called him "Mine."

"My child," says a mother, "my own, my firstborn, the latest thing in babies, did you ever see his like? My own," and she draws him to her bosom. I can imagine some mother saying, "Now, preacher, you can surely allow the expression here—*My own* baby;" No, I dare not; I must be true to God's Word, and true to the facts of life. There is a Power that dares to come in between the babe and the bosom; and that is close work, is it not? And that fair flower withers, and is buried out of sight. Our children do not belong to us in any absolute sense of possession. If they did, they would never die. Why did death come? Why did you bury your child out of sight? No; everything of that kind contradicts this—"My own." It will not do! It is stripping us naked and bare. We have nothing that we can call our own; or if it is our own, why do these things happen that make us hearten-broken? "My wife," says a man." "Mine. I won her, and I'll wear her. I'd crowns resign to call her mine!"—and next week he walks a broken-hearted man behind her coffin. "My health and strength," says a man—and this is my last use of this ringing of the changes on the expression, "Mine—my own." "Health is a great help and a great wealth. After all, I can do without money, I can do without friends; only secure to me health and strength, soundness of body, and soundness of brain." *Mens sana in corpore sano*—a sound mind in a sound body;—what more do we need? Just about all: sound in mind and limb. Yet what beggars we are! What bankrupts we are! What feeble folk we are, that dwell in houses of clay, and have our foundations in the dust! What vain, conceited creatures we are, flaunting before Heaven as though we, as though "poor worm, Jacob," had anything of his own except the worm and the slime! No. Let me give you a severe illustration. There is a widow woman in London; she wakes up one morning, and although her husband is gone, that has not ruined her, or the children. No; for she had just one thing left, and that was enough—health and strength; and if you only secure to her health and strength as her own, she will get through. And yet so beggared are we, we cannot even claim that, and say, "My own." She rises in the morning, there is a busy day's work before her, there are those hungry mouths to feed; and she girds herself for the work, and goes at it with her great, warm, motherly heart and motherly strength, feeling that that will carry her through; but before noon she lies down, dead beat—and it is washing-day, with all that that means. God help us, nothing that we can call our own, so that when the pinch comes we have nothing—nothing, absolutely *nothing!*

And then I come to this word, or idea rather, " My *own salvation;*" and I have to rub my eyes to see. Show me that place again. Where is it? Ah! there it is, "Your own salvation." Is not the Bible contradicting itself? Oh, maybe it is, but I will let it contradict away at this rate of it. Here is this, that makes the beggar a millionaire, given to me on the stamp and seal and authority of the Word of Him that cannot lie—" Your own salvation." That thing, if I may so say, for which you had neither right nor claim nor title, handed over to you, and as it is handed over, this word along with it—" Now that is yours." " The gift of God is eternal life, through Jesus Christ our Lord;" " The wages of sin is death, but the gift of God is eternal life;" " He that believeth *hath* "—open your arms, man!—" everlasting life." There, he has it; it is his. It was Thine; it is mine because it was Thine and Thou didst give it me.

Now, thou black, grim, doubting devil that dost for ever whisper thy words in my ear, I will fight thee here. " My own salvation"—mine because it is a gift. Do you understand that yet, my hearer? Salvation is yours. This expression is on the line of the whole analogy of the faith, and gives salvation, pardon now, peace now, purity begun and growing now, and the eternal glory for ever. Salvation from beginning to end is made over to thee in a gift, not by working, not by meriting, not by striving, but by coming as a poor beggar, having nothing but sin, and getting that entail broken and taken away, and instead of it given eternal life. Salvation is ours because it is a gift, and from One who will never withdraw it. " The gifts and calling of God are without repentance." He will never change His mind, never go back and say, " You have proved so unworthy, hand me back My gift." So, then, let me be very evangelistic; let me say, my church-going friend, if you have not got salvation as a gift from a hand with the hole of a nail in it, you are not saved yet, and it is time you knew it. There is no other way. Free gift! You hold out the beggar's hand and you get the King's bounty—eternal life, the gift of God. Have you got it? The Christ of God—have you got *Him*? Answer: Yea, mine own God is He.

Now let us get on to the command, "*Work out* your own salvation with fear and trembling." That is what I wanted to get at. You have to be active. God's sovereignty and power evoke human responsibility and activity. You have it, therefore work it out. To use a common illustration: there is a load of bricks here, a load of timber and some slates. That is not a house. No; but there is the making of one, and you can make the house out of it. Now the Lord lays all down at our door; He puts it into our hearts; He comes with the plan and the specification and the material, and says, "Now work them out." Rise to the work; you have got to build a temple for your God, and a house for yourself in which to live and dwell for ever; you have to build a spiritual house; you have got to raise in your character and life a spiritual fabric, a copy of the Lord Jesus Christ—work out this business. The Greek has at its root the idea of " energy." Oh! what a pulsing word—*energize* your own salvation. Now there are just a number of people needing the word "energize." The doctrines are lying on your souls like great unwrought lumps of dough that you have not worked out—I speak to house-wives—and no man can feed on dough; it will kill him! Many of you are dyspeptics, feeding on Gospel doctrine that you have not kneaded and fired—and I don't know what—but you understand what I mean! "Work out your own salvation." Get up now, put your feet below you, fling off your coat, turn up your sleeves, and go at this business like the work of a lifetime, and never stop it, this work of saving yourself, if I may be as contradictory as the Bible is. What a work needs to be done! When the Lord comes to me in all the light of His saving grace, He shows me what to do. He brings all with Him that is needed; but I am not to be lazy; I am not to lie back and do nothing. There is a kind of teaching of the "higher life" abroad, and I do not say a word against higher life if it means being holier and working out your own salvation more diligently. But there is a kind of teaching abroad that is too passive. Its favourite illustration of the fact that you are in Christ, and Christ is in you, is the sponge. The sponge is in the sea, and the sea is in the sponge, and there you are! There you may be, but I prefer to come here. "Work out your own salvation with fear and trembling." *Work*, because as the text shall afterwards show, you are not working in your own strength; behind all your energies there is this eternal mainspring that enables you to work easily, swiftly, without friction, and without failure—" God worketh in you to will and to do of His good pleasure."

Now you know what to do. You have a bad temper— work out your salvation. You are getting to be a fair pest in the house because of this temper. You are not to go and cuddle up this temper and say, "I am a child of God, though I have a little infirmity." Be saved from your infirmity, oh sweet child of God! "I do believe," says another, "I am in a state of grace, but I have a weakness for a dram." Save yourself from that weakness, or, as Christmas is coming, you may be as drunk as any pagan! Another says, " I do believe that I am saved, but I am inconsistent." Well, save yourself from this inconsistency—work out your own salvation. What would you think of the man who went about with his hands in his pockets whistling and joking, because he had a load of bricks and stones and timber lying all around there; and wanting shelter on a wintry day, he creeps under the bricks and says, " This is my house: here will I dwell." Are not some of us doing so? Why, if you could see your spiritual house as the Lord sees it, you would get in an awful fright I grant the house has a foundation; if you are in Christ, you are on the foundation, and, maybe, there is a wee bit of the first course of masonry beginning to rise, and a sort of indication of where the windows are coming, and where the doors are to be, and there is just a faint look as if there was a plan; but ye have stopped, and though it is without a roof, and without walls, ye are living as if the work were done. Oh man, work out your own salvation!

Now, blessed be God, His great gift will work out. There is a grand "furthiness"—if you don't know that word, so much the worse for you—in the grace which comes from Jesus Christ, which will expand and extend and yield as long as you make demands upon it. There are many gifts we get that have none of this furthiness in them. You have them in your house. The first day that gift came to you—some ornament, it is on the mantelpiece—when it came first *it told on you*, it told of your friend's kindness, and for a little time there was much in it. But as time went on it did not expand, its gold became dim, and there came some day, some dull, dark day, that you were doleful and needed help, and you stood and looked at that gift, and it utterly failed to do you good. It came to an end. And all earthly gifts, at the best, come to an end. But this will work out and expand every day you live, and the more you draw upon it the fuller it becomes. "Work out your own salvation." Oh, what a gift Christ is!

Up to-day, and at it. So, we built the wall, says Nehemiah; with the sword in the one hand and the trowel in the other, now working, now fighting, but never idle. "Perfect holiness, without which no man shall see the Lord;" "Looking diligently lest any man fail of the grace of God;" "giving all diligence," says Peter; "add to your faith virtue, and to virtue knowledge, and to knowledge temperance, and to temperance patience, and to patience godliness, and to godliness brotherly kindness, and to brotherly kindness love itself." That is the work to do. First the foundation, and then all these rising tiers of solid, graceful masonry. "Work out you own salvation."

The next question is, How? Here is the *modus operandi*—

"with fear and trembling." Do not make the mistake that many are apt to make, who think this a queer text, partly because it calls them to work, and partly because it says "with fear and trembling." They have made it a kind of gloomy ogre, and do not like to come near it. It is like this dull, foggy time of the year, when we would rather go to bed like the bears, and sleep through it, to wake again in the spring. "With fear and trembling"—what does it mean? It does not mean that we are to go through life with our knees for ever smiting each other because "in such an hour as we think not" we will drop into the pit again. Many take that meaning out of it, and that paralyzes work. It does not mean a fear that brings you into bondage, which brings the frost and chill on your soul, that disjoins you from the Almighty resources of the Father's love and the Saviour's grace and the Spirit's sanctifying power; but the fear rather which makes you work sustainedly, eagerly, strenuously, unfailingly. It is a Bible expression, and it is only the Bible which can expound it; it occurs in no other literature under Heaven, except as a quotation from this old Book. "Serve the Lord with fear, and rejoice with trembling," says the Scripture; "Happy (not *miserable*) is the man that feareth alway;" "The fear of the Lord is the begining of wisdom;" and so on. Take a Bible Concordance and look down all the passages in which "fear and trembling" is mentioned, and you will have an exposition of Paul's words better than any I can give.

It is like this: salvation is full; salvation is free; it is a gift, and it is a gift from God without repentance. He will never change His mind. "That is just where it will spoil itself, preacher, don't you see?" says somebody. "Men will take this salvation that is in Christ with eternal glory! and then they will go away and live as they like. What have you to say to this?" Well, ever since the beginning, the advocates of my Gospel have just had to say to that, "*It is not the fact.*" It is those who take this salvation as the free gift of God who show the greatest hatred of sin, and greatest perseverance in striving against it. We might misuse it so, it is a wonder of grace that we do not, but we do not, and if any man here says, "I will take this eternal salvation, and will go away and wallow in sin,"—you "evil beast," you will never get the chance, never! No soul thinks thus who has ever been made the recipient of Divine Grace, none. We may slip, we may go back; but we will be ashamed of it, suffer for it, repent of it, and return.

"Work out your own salvation with fear and trembling." The cup of salvation is so full, it is so brimming, it is so sweet, that it would be "too sweet to be wholesome;" it *would* go to the head and make us reel and stagger, and become unwatchful and hilarious, and defeat its own purpose. But, wherever Christ gives the cup of salvation, He puts in an infusion of these tonic bitters, "fear and trembling," so that Grace may not cloy and clog. These are the bitter herbs with which we eat our Passover. The more freely you take of Christ, the more careful you become in life and conduct; the more you look diligently, the more you walk circumspectly, looking where to put your foot next, for it is a dirty world, and the most careful may go over into the mud. "Walk circumspectly, redeeming the time, because the days are evil."

It is like the ballast to the ship. You have seen those yachts of ours, designed by Watson, and built by Fyfe— things of beauty, and almost instinct with life. There it is; the sea is sparkling in the sun; there is a splendid, crisp breeze blowing. Watch that squall of wind as it strikes the yacht with its great mass and breadth of canvas that would do for the mainsail of a man-of-war. See what happens! You would expect the very breadth of the sheet is going to spoil all. That squall will strike the sail and the vessel will careen and go to the bottom. Not at all: that squall strikes her, and most gracefully she yields to it and heels over on to her very beam end; but look at the cut-water. See how she is tearing through! For deep down there is the keel, and a great weight upon it; in these modern days tons of lead are run along the keel; or, as in

America, there is a great centre-board sent away down into the water which gives tremendous leverage; and no matter how the yacht heels over, it holds her steady and prevents disaster. So with religion: spread your sails to the gales of Gospel grace; take Christ in all the fulness of the Father's gift as He is, and the Gospel doctrines will not sink you; you will not grow giddy and light-headed, but this fear and trembling will give you rest, weight, grip, ballast, solidity, and you will urge your course forward across these seas of time and sin with splendid speed.

It is just like what you have when a man has been saved who was drowning, and all his kicking and struggling were only hastening it. And when this kicking and struggling were over, some one has reached from above and drawn him out, and there he stands on the solid land, saved. Ah! but it was a narrow shave. Rejoicing, but it is not a hilarious rejoicing, is it? He is not cracking his thumbs and jigging, but he is rejoicing "with trembling." He is altogether saved, and he was so nearly altogether lost. Saved, blessed be God, saved!—cannot some man shout Hallelujah?—saved, but no thanks to us! He sent from above and drew us and landed us on the rock. We are saved, therefore we rejoice "with fear and trembling," and after we have shaken the water off us, we go steadily, calmly, circumspectly, never forgetting that if it had not been for Grace we must have perished.

"With fear and trembling." Take another illustration— I have used it before. An eminent French surgeon used to say to his students when they were engaged in difficult and delicate operations, in which coolness and firmness were needed, "Gentlemen, don't be in a hurry, for there's no time to lose." Time to make that incision once and well in the vital place, not time to dash at it with over-confidence. Before you have recovered yourself a precious life will have been spilled.

So, my believing brother and sister—I do not care what your years may be—it is a word for all of us this morning. Caution, diligence, a girding-up of the loins. a wider opening of the eyes. "Work out your own salvation with fear and trembling"—no swagger, no bounce, no bravado, no cocksureness, yet every confidence that He who hath begun this good work will carry it on to the perfect day. All confidence in Thee, my God, and none in myself; that is the way in which I do the best work towards God, or my brother man. Oh for sobriety to-day! How may converts begin and go on, and then—then comes a collapse. There are some here: you were converted, and with what splendid speed you began the Christian course—you did run well. What did hinder you? Ah! it is not the distance, but the pace that tells. You started off at too big a pace to keep it up; or, rather, you got away from your base of supplies, and you soon came to an end of yourself. It is just a few years since you began so well; and where are you to-day? You may be a Christian—you may be; but as regards activity, no one would know it. Your name is not found on the rolls of any Sabbath-school Superintendents in Christendom: not one. You never come with tracts now; you never lift up a word of testimony for Christ now, and this is what spoiled you. Too confident, you began in the Spirit, and you went on in the flesh, and that which is born of the flesh is flesh, while that which is born of the Spirit is Spirit, and alone will endure and grow to all eternity. Come back, then, you who are nerveless and strengthless; you who are lying down in the middle of the course long before you have reached the end, come back to lowliness, to watchfulness, to self-distrust—"work out your own salvation with fear and trembling." Only one life, no second chance for evermore; and into this one life, into this one day we are to crowd, to pack the utmost of holy living in every direction that we possibly can, "with fear and trembling."

I have left myself no time to deal with the 13th verse. "For it is God that worketh in you;" but I just wish to recite it before I let you go. You work out, as one has said; for God works in. There is the mainspring, there is the unfailing Source, of all the believer's energy for sanctification, and for personal effort in the Church of Christ to promote His cause. It is God who worketh in us both to will and to do of His good pleasure. Then let me say at once, we can be holy, we *shall* be holy, for it is *God* who worketh in us. I will not stay even for a moment to discuss the question of sinless perfection. *That* is not your danger. Poor drunkard, thou canst give up drink; lustful man, thou canst be clean; for it is God, it is *God* that worketh in you. Do not be a football of the world, of the flesh, and the devil, for it is God that worketh in you. What tremendous emphasis we should bring to bear on that text. After all this calling on you to energy and to activity, I know that perhaps I depress you, for you said to yourself, "Ah! it is true, it is all true; but what can I do?" Now we come back to the Power: "It is God;" and what can He not do if you will only let Him? God is the Source See how He puts it. It is God that worketh in you. How? Listen: "both to will and to do." The first thing is to get the will right, and then the deed, don't you see, will follow. Is it not your complaint and mine, that the will is wrong, the will is twisted, the will has been led captive by the devil? There are times when we can all enter into poor Augustine's complaint, "Lord, I began to love Thee too late: the devil was too long in me, the will got too much twisted, for although my heart goes after Thee, my *will* —that is the mainspring, that is the rudder that turns the boat ofttimes as I do not want it to go." God has gone down and down and down, deeper than the devil; God has bottomed thy will, and got down to the very spring of being; down at the spring and fount of thought and wish and imagination and effort, there is God. God is in thee to will and to do. Therefore again I say, we can be holy, we shall be holy, we must be holy, for it is God that worketh in us. We will not go back like a dog to his vomit, like the sow that was washed to her wallowing in the mire. Never!

In the day when God converted us—and with this I close —whether we knew it or not, in the day when God changed us, whether it was done calmly or with a great volcanic outburst and eruption, He did a greater work than ever we have given Him credit for. It was not a mere surface-touching of you, when God came to you and quickened you : God came in, *in*, IN to you. Wherever sin was, there He is.

There is an engine, a railway-engine—one of the finest sights on God's earth, and I can never understand John Ruskin finding fault with engines and trains, whether in town or country; they beautify and set off any scenery, do they not? Well, there is an engine—that splendid creation of the engineering faculty of the 19th century ! But did you ever see an engine which was allowed to drive itself ? There is a splendid horse, but did you ever see a blood horse that was allowed to drive itself? Your engine needs a driver, and your horse needs a rider; and your converted man has a God in him, managing him in every direction. There is the engineer; he steps on the foot-plate : with one hand he holds the reversing-rod, that sends the engine backwards or forwards; with the other hand, he holds the throttle-valve, the opening of which lets the steam into the cylinders. So with God: He holds the will and the doing. Thou art managed, splendidly managed. God will drive thee. God will see to thy supplies, and will keep up the Divine pressure. Thou shalt be filled unto all the fulness of God. Oh men and women. do we believe in the magnificent resources for holiness of heart and life, and the resources of power that are ours, since it is God who worketh in us ? And do not ask metaphysical questions as to how God can work on my will, and yet leave me free. The fact of the matter is I feel I am free, and yet I believe that my will lies in God's hand, and He gives it its permanent set and bias towards holiness and goodness for ever and ever. "In this," says Dr. Candlish, " the will of man finds its highest exercise, its fullest freedom, when it becomes the engine for working out the will of God." " And this is the will of God, even your sanctification." May God bless His Word ! Amen.

Regent Square Pulpit.

HOW GOD'S ELECTION WORKS.

A Sermon

Delivered in Exeter Hall,
On Sunday Evening, Jan. 5th, 1890.

BY THE
REV. JOHN McNEILL.

Text.—1 Sam. xvi. 6-13.

Our subject is the choosing of a king from among the sons of Jesse the Bethlehemite. The royal seat, just like my chair, was vacant, or was soon going to be. The Lord had rejected Saul from being king over Israel, and He sent His servant Samuel to choose Him a king to fill the vacancy out of the family named. This narrative shows how the choosing was done. In the same way, I like to think that I am here to-night, and great things—although it does not look like it—are in my gift. I magnify my office, I have a situation to offer. There is no doubt about the offer or about the gift; the only doubt lies with yourself, as of old the difficulty lay among the sons of Jesse. For what is the office of the preacher, but always to be on the errand on which Samuel went to that glen in Bethlehem of Judæa?

No. 9.

We are ambassadors for Christ; we are here to offer to men a crown, a Kingdom that never fades away. We offer you this, that you shall be believers in God's dear Son, which means co-workers with Him down here, and co-heirs with Him in the eternal splendour of the great hereafter. That is the Gospel as I understand it. A mighty programme, is it not? and a programme the reality of which it is absolutely impossible to exaggerate—impossible. I am not drawing the long bow; I am not exaggerating nor straining things when I say that, from the temporal and human side, what Samuel brought to David that afternoon was a small and temporary thing compared with that which the preacher brings to every young fellow, who has eyes to see and ears to hear of the great largess that is brought to him in the Gospel offer.

Let us bring the whole scene before us. I think I see Samuel going to the house of Jesse, and he tells his errand. He called the sons of Jesse before him; in they came, and then wonderful things happened, rather upsetting individual calculations. And all through the story gets increasingly thrilling with intense dramatic interest, right on to the very end; and let me say that that same thrill, that same throb, that same interest, that same sensation should be wherever the Gospel is preached—the same kind of breathlessness. If you could see a gathering like this with angels' eyes, you would have the same breathlessness to see how near the kingdom comes to one man—and, God help him! he goes past it, while it lights on another sitting beside him—one young fellow here to-night saved, as the eternal day shall show, saved with an everlasting salvation; redeemed, crowned, sealed, baptized into Christ; all done by the Word of God and the Spirit of God, and his consenting faith, on the spot; and the young fellow sitting next him as blind as a bat to it all.

Ah, wake up and listen! "The King has come in the cadger's gate," if you understand that phrase; the King has come very near to people who could have had no expectation that He would come so near, when the preacher stands before an audience in London or anywhere else.

In came the sons of Jesse, and first Eliab. He was the biggest, the "brawest," as they would say over the Tweed; a big, broad, buirdly chiel was Eliab, and he came in all his inches, feeling "the situation is for me. I have only to show myself, and whatever Samuel has to give, I will get it." In he came; and Samuel came near to be misled, I believe; for even prophets, if left to their own spirit, will go wrong like other men. Samuel was going to yield to the dictates of his own spirit. You see the need of inspiration, don't you?—a real inspiration, a miraculous interposition and assistance of the human mind by the Divine mind. He was about to yield to his own inspiration and to the look of things, when he was pulled by the sleeve, and the Lord said to him, "Samuel, look not upon his height, look not upon his countenance, seeing I have refused him." Samuel, the Lord sees not as man sees; man can only see face deep and skin deep and looks deep, but the Lord looks in upon the heart. Exit Eliab—the Lord hath not chosen him. I think I hear Samuel say to himself, "Ah yes, what a foolish old greybeard I had nearly made of myself. Is not this precisely the mistake that the whole nation made, when they chose Saul who has turned out so badly." What was the outstanding thing? It was his dimensions; a great, big, strapping fellow, seven by four, is Eliab. Now, this is very taking, very fetching, especially when a king is wanted, and in those old days a king did not spend all his time sleeping on a big chair you call a throne, with all manner of flunkeys around him telling him what a great man he was, and hoping he would live for ever, and so on. No, a king had to justify his selection. He had to go out at the head of the army; he had to fight, to show some extra fighting power. It was very natural, was it not, that Samuel should choose Eliab? And when the Lord whispered to him, or made him conscious in some way or other of His mind and His deeper insight, "I have refused him," I rather think that Eliab went out in a frightful rage. How his eye would flash and his cheek burn, as with bowed head, he who came in so full had to go out so empty!

Why did not Eliab get Samuel's gift? "Ah!" says the Spirit of God, virtually, "just because he was *too big*, too big for the place, too large; he made too big a show in the flesh, and too little a show in the spirit. And a number of us are kept from Christ, and kept out of the kingdom, for the very same season up to this good hour. My brother, yes; and my sister—for in this matter of pride there is no distinction—if ever you come into the kingdom you must bow yourself a little. You pull yourself up too much, and strut about with too great a display. Let me, as your friend, tell you that neither God nor man will ever make much use of you at this rate. The days are coming—bless God, the days are come!—when with all the badness of our times there is a kind of rough, ready, genuine sincerity about us, and I think it is going to deepen, so that no man will be selected for high place who has simply show and appearance and name. It was not a walking policeman for a pantomime who was wanted, it was a king; and Eliab would not have done for a policeman even. If you are going to be proud and lifted up, man, you will do for the devil, and will come to the devil's reward at the end. But the Son of God will do without you.

If there is anything, my brother, that God sets Himself against, it is this. Listen, I am not exaggerating, "A high look is an abomination unto God;" and that is what makes me tremble for some people when I am preaching the Gospel. Unless my judgment utterly fails me, you have not a gracious look, my poor lad; it does not seem as if the humbling and subsequently elevating grace of God had ever scratched the surface of your pride. There is a veneering over you, and would to God, as your friend, I could strip that paint off! That is why I say the straight thing. There is to be "A Straight Talk," as I read in the notices, next Sabbath afternoon; I will give it you before that time; the straight talk is on, and I hope you are listening, for nothing else will do in these days but very straight talking indeed. I sometimes wonder, as a natural man, that the people come back to me at Regent Square. But they do. It is a wonderful thing that straight talking, in God's name, does not empty churches; no, blessed be God! it fills them. People come back to be battered and pounded where you struck them last week; to get it all over again; for I do believe that where we are honest with the sure truth of God, though men may feel badly, and even say hard things against the preacher, in the secret soul there is a bell ringing responsive to the truth. I know it is rasping, it is irritating to be made to feel "I could pitch my book at that Scotchman's head, although he is, I believe, telling the truth. Fire away, my friend! only let me be faithful.

Eliab lost the throne, not because election is favouritism and selection of a capricious and arbitrary kind, but in mercy to himself, and the kingdom, and cause of God, Eliab was sent out; he would not do.

Now, will you remember that the Lord Jesus Christ, for whom I plead to-night, looks upon the heart, and a high look and a lofty look are an abomination unto Him. He will go past us, notwithstanding all our physical inches, and all our intellectual endowment, and He will take somebody out of the gutter, lift up that soul, and show that He is beholden absolutely for nothing to pride of mental or bodily girth. He is beholden to Himself, and to Himself alone. Be humble, my brother, be lowly and resist pride. "He giveth grace unto the lowly." If you won't take it from the Bible, turn up your Shakespeare and his splendid list of king-becoming graces; and as you read them, you will very likely come to the conclusion that Eliab was very poor in their direction.

But before Samuel got to David he had more to do with other sons of Jesse. In came Abinadab, the second; and he said, "Neither hath the Lord chosen thee." Then came Shammah—he passed by and out. And seven sons of Jesse, in they came, and out they went—*exeunt omnes*. Now, why did these seven lose it? Look at that procession— shall I call it the "rogues' march"—and I ask, what was wrong in them? Well, I think this is it: Eliab lost it because he was too big, too much concerned with himself, too proud; he would not do. And I rather think these other sons lost it because they were away at the other extreme; while Eliab was too big, they were "ower sma'"—too small, too little. Do not go about flaunting about like a peacock, drawing all eyes to yourself and your strutting. But, on the other hand, and as much on the other hand—would God I could be as "straight!"—do not be a nobody. Do not be a round O, a mere decimal; and do not be thus, because life has in it one splendid, golden, glorious opportunity that should compel every man to be bright and eager, and on the outlook for it, as it comes within his reach.

But these seven sons of Jesse—oh, well, I suppose they were just like a great many of ourselves. They were not proud like Eliab, not ambitious with an unholy, blown-up ambition; we can think of them as being too far the other way. When they heard that Samuel had come to choose a king from among their father's sons, Eliab went and "sorted" himself, and came in to look his best. These others came in to grumble that they were taken from the plough tail, and they would say to the servant who came to call them in, "We don't want to be kings; we have no ambition for this vacant situation; it will introduce us, supposing it is real and true, to considerable troubles; it will take us away from home, away on untrodden ground; it is calling us into great deep waters, where we shall lose sight of land; and we would rather stay at home. If Samuel had been yourself or myself, Abinadab and Shammah and the rest would have said, "No, thank you; it is not for us; give it to Eliab;" and of course already his chance was gone. Now, my friend, you see the point. I would to God that every congregation gathered to hear preachers in London to-day could just see it! Do not pull the wool, nor let the world and the devil pull the wool over your eyes. On the one hand, do not be in the inflammation of devouring ambition; and on the other, do not be a noodle, a mere nose of wax; but, for your own sake, understand that the kingdom of heaven has come nigh unto you when the Gospel is preached. Wake up! This is worth listening to; it is worth coming into a Gospel meeting. There is a chance here that is nowhere else except in meetings like it—a chance for you, and you may have it.

I think, too, that it is depressing to read how these seven came in and went out, when I read their names, because in the Old Testament names meant something. Names nowadays mean nothing; they mean less than nothing, and vanity. The poorest sneak of a creature in your office, may be William Wallace, or Robert Bruce, or Cromwell, or Milton, or something like that. Names mean nothing. What miserable creatures one meets who have great names stuck upon them! I met, not so long ago, a poor abject creature with the glorious name of Hampden stuck upon him as a kind of sarcastic label of what he was *not!* So you have it here. One of these is Abinadab, and another Shammah; great names that have something noble in them, as many Hebrew names had. Yet, notwithstanding their names, there may be no more in the owners of them than a day's work, a day's whistling at the plough tail, an evening's pleasure, a night's sleep, and their wages. Now, is not that about the compass of what occupies your thoughts? Only get you a good "crib," a good "screw," as you call it; a comfortable salary, hours nine to five, and one on Saturdays, a prospect of advance as per scale, and that is all; you are quite contented and quite satisfied. God forbid I should be hard on anybody; but, man, I wish you would stretch yourself! Life means more than a day's work, more than a night's pleasure, more than a night's sleep; life means a chance to be saved, a chance to be redeemed, a chance to be born again, a chance to become sons and daughters of God Almighty, and to reign with Christ for ever and ever! —that is in this dull, humdrum, plodding, work-a-day life of ours, through God's grace in the Gospel. Do not let it go past; do not let these splendid days given to you here on earth go past, while you " steal inglorious to the silent grave." Wake up! and when God comes be ready for Him. "Grasp the skirts of happy chance, breast the blows of circumstance, and grapple with your evil star."

For it may be done, and gloriously done, by the furthest back and the most unlikely, if only, unlike those solid stolid sons of Jesse, we understand the situation, and yield to the call of Christ in the Gospel invitation.

Oh, they lost it, they sadly lost it; and it came so near to them, and it hung after all so far above their heads! For when we are going to be nobodies, God will treat us like that, and will not come and thrust upon you this salvation of yours, that cost Christ His precious blood and all the wonderful thirty years of His incarnate history here among men. Do you think that after Christ went through all that to found His kingdom, to found and build and set up His kingdom; do you think that after that He is going to fill it with nameless nobodies like you and me? Heaven help us! what would we be to Him? No, no, let us understand, the King wants *men*; that is why He has not some of us yet—because *anybody* won't do. He will make us men if we will only come to Him in all our loutishness and sheepishness and worldliness; for we are fairly drugged and made stupid, nine-tenths of us, by this world; it has turned our heads and made us reel. If we will only come to Him, and allow Him to do His work, He will stimulate us, rouse us, recover us from all the down-dragging tendency of this weary world, and open our eyes to see that Christ is here, and it is in our opportunity to make ourselves His, with all that that means for ever and ever.

They missed it because they deserved to miss it; because it would have been wasted on them. *Now, how did David get it?* For, don't you see, after these seven came in and went out, David's turn came? I can imagine Samuel getting a little tempery, a little peppery; he turns round to Jesse and says, "Are all your children here?" It looks as if he had come on a fool's errand. He had come to give a crown, a kingdom; and the Lord had sent him, at least he thought so, to choose a king from amongst this man's sons; they had come and gone, and still he was at a loss; and it does look as if a blush of shame would steal across Samuel's face. And what was Jesse to think, when the Lord had come by Samuel to choose a king, and there was a hitch, a mistake, or a breakdown somewhere; for all these seven had come and gone, and not one of them was chosen? Samuel, as I have described, turns round, and says, " Are they all here "? And I fancy I hear Jesse saying, " Well, when I think of it, there is the youngest, a mere stripling, out there keeping sheep."

Samuel said, " Send for him; send for him, for we will not sit down until he comes. I was sure they were not all here, though I did not know your family. I knew God did not send me on a fool's errand, I knew I came to the right house." Listen to this description: The devil has not all the fine fellows. Here David comes in, and he is described for us; just as Eliab was described so David is. And they sent and brought him. Now, he was ruddy, and withal of a beautiful countenance, and goodly to look at. The Lord has no objection to fine looks, the Lord has no objection to a fine physique, and no objection to your developing your physique, in all natural, healthful gymnastic exercises, as far as you please, and as far as you may. Oh, do not make the slightest mistake!—the Lord has no special delight in shambling people who walk on the uppers of their boots to save the soles, as some people do. The Lord has no particular delight in round shoulders and broken wind—not He. David was ruddy, comely, and goodly to look upon. As his after-history shows, a splendid fellow, a daring fellow, with a keen eye in his head, and a big brain behind his eye, and a bursting heart inside his bosom. An all-round man was David, who was shepherd, soldier and king in one lifetime, and played his part well in all three.

God never wastes Himself on nothings and nobodies. Of course, to Him be all the praise, to Him be all the glory;

it is He who makes us what we are. Oh, will you humbly return from the pride and conceit that are killing you, and come to God, for He will build you up on a new plan altogether.

In came David; and the Spirit of God said to Samuel whenever his eyes lit on him, "Arise, anoint him; for this is he." We do not profess to be thought-readers, and yet when we stand here, we preachers, or in places like this, and have no manuscript to bury our heads in—and that is a great advantage—when we can look straight into the eyes of people, we think we see men who, if they are not on Christ's side, they should be. I will give you a call to-night, in case you should start the objection that you have not yet got it. Man, you should be; you look as if you should belong to the "King's Own." There is a fine look—what you have in David—a free, open, manly, ingenuousness. No conceit, you know, no pride, no curling of the lip, with all his good looks and natural abilities; a gentleness, a nobleness, and a frankness; and on this high and holy day God anointed him, and sealed all these natural qualifications for his own, and put that extra plus to them all that comes out of His grace and His call and His anointing, sealing his youth.

> "In life's gay morn, when sprightly youth
> In vital ardour glows,
> And shines in all the fairest charms
> That Beauty can disclose;
>
> "Deep on thy soul, before its powers
> Are yet by vice enslaved,
> Be thy Redeemer's glorious name
> And character engraved."

I have kept you too long, and will let you go with one other word. I forgot that we did not begin until half-past seven, and the hour begins to wax late for some.

How did David get it?

First of all, and very briefly, let me say, he got it because he was there to get it. When his father sent for him he was keeping sheep, very likely near the house, and when they went for the stripling he was faithful to his charge. His father said he was keeping the sheep, and when the messenger went, there he was. If we had been David—you remember how we did when we were young. I remember how I did. If you had sent me to keep sheep, half-an-hour afterwards where would I have been and the sheep too? I remember once being sent to keep crows out of a field—a very important bit of work in the country—and half-an-hour afterwards there were multitudes of crows, but no boy!

Suppose somebody had come to my father and said, "I want to choose one of your family for my situation, and I had been considered likely, and that I had been sent for, expecting to find me, *faithful to little things*—namely, keeping crows away—but, lo, I was gone away hazel-nutting or bird-nesting, miles off! The point is this: Be faithful where you are; be faithful in keeping sheep; be faithful in the office; servant, be faithful down there in the kitchen; whatever your sphere, be diligent; be your best in what you are at, though it should be as humble as keeping sheep, and it does not need a great deal of intellect for that—you don't need to be a member of the Browning Society, nor to have read the hundred best books, to keep sheep. But you do need qualifications, or you will not manage. Now my brother, my sister, I do not say do not be ambitious, but I do say, in your calling be faithful and be diligent. "Seest thou a man diligent in his business," says the proverb; "he shall stand before kings—he shall not stand before mean men." And if you want the call of God in the Gospel to surely and certainly settle on your head, be on hand when the call is made, be on hand when the offer is given.

I want to say a word about non-churchgoing. Man, you are playing the devil's game, and he is winning with that trump card every time, since he got you to give up going to hear God's Gospel preachers, and since he made you think there is nothing in it. It is a lie, deep as hell; there is everything in it. Be a man, be faithful, be diligent, use all opportunities; do not miss such a splendid chance when it is going; you may rue with every vein in your heart to all eternity—the bad use to which you put the splendid opportunities that London gives *for being saved*, with all its badness and wickedness. Notwithstanding all, there is the Gospel, and God is behind it, and His offer is sincere; therefore, quit your careless ways and be on hand, be in the market when the marketing in heavenly merchandise is going on.

David got it because he was there to get it; and, last of all, *because he took it*. You can imagine David being just like the rest, and saying to Samuel, "I beg to decline. Really, Samuel, you have landed upon me too suddenly; don't you see, prophet, I have no time to think of this? I was out there keeping sheep, and I was suddenly called in; and here you are going to make me king, with all that that involves. I have no ambition that way; it is not for me; give it to Eliab"—I think they all thought Eliab was the man—" and let me go away back again."

> "The pride the devil loves best to see,
> Is the pride that apes humility."

Do not hang back and say, "It is not for me." Do not look on my face and say, "But, McNeill, man, have mercy on a fellow!" Almost unconsciously you say, "I came in to-night off the Strand, and never expected to be bombarded after this fashion. If you had only given me notice as to the lines you were going to take—really, I will need to go home and think over this." Don't! It does not need thinking over. Just as you are, and where you are, do what David did. I think there is nothing more splendid. It shows the *reach* of that young stripling's heart and mind, that when this was sprung upon him, he rose to the occasion. It was well done on both sides. Samuel did well, and David did well when he bowed his head and let the dignity and the honour with all the risk and peril, for a time, come down upon him. He stooped to conquer! So we all overcome our obstacles in connection with the acceptance of the Gospel. Do not take it home to think about it. The chances are—and here the parable of the sower comes in—that as surely as you go out into the Strand undecided, the devil will pick your pocket of my invitation and call to come to Christ. For many of us are like the wayside hearers. "The fowls of the air came," says Christ, "and picked up the seed." Before you get many blocks along the Strand, the devil with his black wing will have swept your mind bare and empty of every honest appeal that I have made to you to-night. He will, he does it; wherever the Gospel is preached, the devil is there, you may be sure. Do not take it into further consideration; but I am here to-night to make an honest offer: "Whosoever will, let him take the Son of God freely." "Him that cometh unto Me I will in no wise cast out." Do what young David did; although it spring upon you, although you did not expect it, and although it seems to interfere with your other engagements, perhaps for to-night and for to-morrow. Ah! I know what is keeping some of you from yielding to my grip—for I have a grip of you by the heart, and by the conscience to-night. "Wot ye not that such a man as I am can certainly divine?" I have got you by the truth of God, I have grappled you to me as with a hook of steel, but the devil is whispering in your ear, "That engagement to-morrow night, it will break that—what are you to do about that?" *Put thy foot on that* if thou wouldst be saved. "That man you have to meet, that guilty assignation you have to meet—what about that?" says the devil. The harlot's face comes up before your eyes. God grant that you may see the paint, and be sickened and disgusted; and, glad that you are here, clutch at my offer, and believe me, He into whose service you come to-night will stand by you to-night, will stand by you to-morrow. Break all your own engagements; allow all your own plans, your lawful plans as well as the unlawful ones—let them go to the winds. Christ has a plan for you,

Christ has a purpose for you; let it catch you, and lift you, and carry you forward to all eternity.

Ah! this great day that came to David did bring him trial, it did bring him trouble, it did bring him suffering. He was not called to the throne, nor after that to the skies,

"On flowery beds of ease;"

but he was kept, he was sustained, he came to the kingdom, and he came to the Eternal Kingdom in the fulness of time also. There were dark days when poor David was hunted amongst the hills, when he might have said that the darkest day that ever came to him was the day when Samuel came and called him from following sheep to be God's anointed king. But he held on to God, and God held on to him; and God justified all that He had said, and God fulfilled all that He had promised. Now, will you take Christ to-night, my brother, and remember that all I have said is no exaggeration; if you take Him, and He takes you, "All things are yours, for ye are Christ's, and Christ is God's." "He that overcometh shall inherit all things, and I will be his God, and he shall be My son. To him that overcometh will I grant to sit with Me on My throne, even as I overcame, and am set down with My Father on His throne."

Take Christ to-night, now, when the offer is made in the Lord's great name; and although we may never meet again, I will forecast your future before I sit down. You may never make a fortune in London nor anywhere else; you may be called upon to lose a fortune because of being faithful to Jesus Christ; you may live a long, toilsome, troubled, persecuted, seemingly undesirable life; but fifty years after this—and that is a big jump—if you are then dying, and know it, dying intelligently; if you are dying in the faith and fear of Jesus Christ, this night, this building, this unfamiliar preacher, with his unfamiliar face and his unfamiliar Scotch accent, with his rude, his seemingly rude, and rough and boisterous ways, will come back upon you, and your dying eye will brighten, and I can hear your dying tongue saying, "Aye, it is a long, long time since that night, but I accepted the preacher's call, I closed with Christ, and although I have not been what I might have been, I have fought a good fight, I have finished my course, I have kept"—what a shout!—"I have KEPT THE FAITH!" See that, oh world, oh devil, oh Babylon of London, "I have kept the faith!" It reminds me of some lines from Sir Walter Scott when he is describing the dying of Marmion: you remember how a certain name told on him,

> "The war that for a space did fail,
> Now trebly thundering swelled the gale,
>   And 'Stanley' was the cry.
> A light on Marmion's visage spread,
>   And fired his glazing eye;
> With dying hand above his head,
> He shook the fragment of his blade
>   And shouted victory!"

So with every believer. We shall live victoriously; we shall die "more than conquerors through Him that loved us." Rise to the occasion, my brother, my sister; do not be battened and flattened down to the level of the world, but bend your head and bend your heart; let the Word of God come into you, and the Spirit of God take hold of you for Christ, for ever and ever.

May we be bound up in the bundle of life with David, and with David's Greater Son. Here is our security: "Once I have sworn by My holiness that I will not lie unto David. His seed shall endure for ever; and his throne as the sun before Me" (Ps. lxxxix.). Amen and Amen.

Regent Square Pulpit.

"HOW WELL HORATIUS KEPT THE BRIDGE IN THE BRAVE DAYS OF OLD."

A Sermon

Delivered in Regent Square Church, on Sunday Morning,

Jan. 12th, 1890.

BY THE

REV. JOHN McNEILL.

Nehemiah vi.

As workers for God, and especially as those who have a special work in view, let us turn to Nehemiah, the 6th chapter, and consider how it fared with him; the difficulties he encountered; how through grace he remained steadfast, and made all difficulties only feed the flame of prayer to God, and of zeal for the welfare of Jerusalem.

Ezra's special work was to recover the ruin and the disaster that had befallen the temple, and set up again the routine and ritual of the worship of God in that dear old hallowed place. Nehemiah comes in the due course of God's providence after him; and his work is, you remember, the building up of the walls of Jerusalem. He came from Shushan, where he was cup-bearer to the Persian monarch. You remember he introduced himself to the nobles, his countrymen in Jerusalem. He took a walk by night alone round about the city. He saw how fire had laid waste the walls and destroyed the gates. After this he called the people of God together; they caught his own patriotic, God-inspired zeal, and said, "The God of heaven, He will prosper us. Therefore we His servants will arise and build." At the very beginning they had to face objectors, they had to face those who were envious; but they faced them firmly and uncomprisingly then and all through. "Ye," they said to these, "ye, have no portion, nor right, nor memorial in Jerusalem."

As we read on, we note a list, a leaf, as it has been called, taken out of the contractor's note-book, in the third chapter; where we see all the people busy on the wall, high and low, rich and poor, men and women, ladies and gentlemen; all working away busily repairing the walls, closing up the breaches, and getting ready for the finishing touches, setting up the gates, with the doors and bars.

When we come to the fourth chapter, we find the difficulties increasing. Their enemies no longer confining themselves to sneers, threats, and taunts; but gathering together and threatening to fall upon them with force of arms. This, you remember, is met by Nehemiah. He organizes his builders into soldiers. They work with sword and trowel, ready at a moment's notice to leave their actual work of building, and to rally to the trumpet note of danger.

So we read on through, until the fifth chapter, where we find Nehemiah doing a work that has more application for us to-day, although we cannot do anything more than just mention it. The rich had been oppressing the poor, although they were all Israelites, all God's people, and all suffering from the common calamity, and all brought back from exile. At this, Nehemiah's blood boiled, and his spirit burned within him; and he made what we should call to-day a ludicrously senseless proposition, namely, that the rich should disgorge, and hand back the lands they had appropriated. Strange to say, the Spirit of God was so with him that the thing was done; and the rich, in a burst of enthusiastic brotherhood, restored to their poorer brethren their oliveyards, vineyards, and houses.

Then we come to the chapter before us, in which we have some account of how Nehemiah withstood opposition of a very subtle kind. "Now it came to pass, when Sanballat, and Tobiah, and Geshem the Arabian, and the rest of our enemies, heard that I had builded the wall, and that there was no breach left therein; (though at that time I had not set up the doors upon the gates;) that Sanballat and Geshem sent unto me, saying, Come, let us meet together in some one of the villages in the plain of Ono. But they thought to do me mischief. And I sent messengers unto them, saying, I am doing a great work, so that I cannot come down: why should the work cease, whilst I leave it, and come down to you? Yet they sent unto me four times after this sort; and I answered them after the same manner."

Notice that these enemies of Nehemiah, Sanballat, Tobiah, and Gesham, the Arabian, were of a bastard race and religion. The one feature prominent in them is hatred of the peace of Jerusalem. Having tried, and failed, to cause the work to cease *by force*, they now resort to cunning.

Now, my friends, we are Israelites, and here in London; and in our own hearts we are called to a great work. We are called to set up the spiritual temple and worship of God in our own souls; and we are called to build round about that temple the wall of social, individual, family, and national righteousness and peace. There is our whole programme: that our own hearts should be the temple of God, that our own lives should be surrounded by a high wall of practical godliness and righteousness. That in politics and in business, in social life, in family life, and religious life, we should all put our hand to and build up the wall that, alas! alas! lies waste and broken down in all directions. The more we do that, the more we shall find that Nehemiah's testimony rings out even to this day with trumpet clearness; and the nearer we come to him—this grand old worker for God—the very light that shines in his eyes, I trust, will kindle in ours, and we, too, shall grasp the sword and trowel and bend our backs, get rid of our indifference, which is so ungodly, which is so unmanly, which is so unpatriotic, and put our hand to the work for God and the cities of our land. Are laziness and lust to eat up the West End? Are poverty, drunkenness, and never-ending toil to swallow up the East End? Are death and hell to prevail in God's England—God's London?

Said Nehemiah in his day "No! not if I can help it." And says every true Israelite in Regent Square this morning, "No! not if I can help it!"

Well, to come to the history, when Nehemiah was coming to an end, and thought he had got through all his difficulties, Sanballat and the others came wheedling and coaxing, and they said, "Come, Nehemiah, let us meet together in one of the villages in the plain of Ono." And they sent messengers four times to try, if they could, to prevent the thorough fulfilment and accomplishing of God's work and Nehemiah's design. Anything they would do, the enemies of Nehemiah, as our enemies also would do, to diminish our zeal for God and truth and righteousness. Thus we might paraphrase the arguments used: "Now, Nehemiah, you really are a most excellent man and, though we say it ourselves, we, too, are excellent men; and if we can only just meet together in a quiet little spot, we shall soon settle everything. You see, Nehemiah, we have misunderstood one another—a very common thing among good people. You thought we were against you, but there never was a greater mistake. We were misrepresented. Come now, and let us shake hands; and when we have looked into each other's faces, we shall discover amidst apparent diversity of purpose that our hearts, our aims, were really one, that we are seeking the same object." After such fashion, we can imagine they thought to draw Nehemiah from his purpose. "But they thought to do me mischief," says Nehemiah. And Nehemiah answers them after a Scotch fashion—if you ask us one question we ask you another—Nehemiah says, "Why should the work cease, whilst I leave it, and come down to you?" Let them put that in their pipes and smoke it; in the meantime he should go on with the work. "Why should the work cease, whilst I leave it, and come down to you?"

And you will find the more you buckle to God's work— that is to say, to strive to be first of all a sterling, righteous man in lip and life, in thought, in word, and deed— and the more you try to recover the blight and disaster in London or round about you, the more you will find opposition of different kinds, and perhaps to-day the secret, sly, and cunning opposition which is to be dreaded far more than the open, the overt.

I wonder how many invitations you will get to parties this week? because I want you to work for God in this coming ten days' mission. Very likely never so many as this week, and never so plausibly couched, asking you to come out to see some friends in the northern or western suburbs. "We have a nice little party this week. Come down, don't be righteous overmuch. Don't spoil yourself, and take all the pleasure out of life." What do you think yourself? I think that should be easily answered, shouldn't it? Let us make up our mind and heart to work, work, work. "Why should I let the work cease, and come down to you?" Let *them* answer that. Why should God's work cease while I leave it, and come down to you; so as to weaken my interest in God's work, and hinder my pace in the actual doing of God's work? Here is the test and touch stone. How do these things tell upon the work? Do they lower my temperature, and take away my energies from God's work. Then they are of the devil; and to see that, is to be kept right.

"I am doing a great work." It is easy to misunderstand a man like Nehemiah; he speaks so straight. "Why," one might say, "listen how this man rolls out his ' I's.' " That is a misunderstanding. Every soul, no matter how humble, if engaged in this work of testifying for truth and righteousness, is doing a great work. My brother, my sister, remember there is nothing small or low or mean about it. Angels and archangels might envy the doing of the work that lies around on every hand in London to-day. I am sure that if they got the chance, angels would soon change heaven for earth, and would be here, legions of them, if God only took the work out of our hands and gave it to them.

We are engaged in a great work, and nine-tenths of us don't understand it. And it is because we have low, paltry views of the high calling whereunto we are called, that we are so easily whirled around like weathercocks, and drawn aside by every temptation that comes in our way. We take up God's work, and then we run away, making a hundred excuses. Something of time, something of earth, something of self is always proved to be more urgent than that work for which Christ died and the Holy Ghost is given. But Nehemiah said, "I am engaged in a great work, and cannot come down. Why should the work cease?" "Let the dead bury their dead," but stick to your work!

"Yet they sent unto me four times after this sort, and I answered them after the same manner," Good old Nehemiah! may his number be increased!

"Then sent Sanballat his servant unto me in like manner the fifth time with an open letter in his hand; wherein was written, It is reported among the heathen, and Gashmu saith it, that thou and the Jews think to rebel: for which cause thou buildest the wall, that thou mayest be their king."

"And thou hast also appointed prophets to preach of thee at Jerusalem, saying, There is a king in Judah and now shall it be reported according to these words. Come now, therefore, and let us take counsel together." Anything, then, to get him off that wall. Anything to prevent those gates from being set up. Anything, everything, rather than the prosperity and the peace of Jerusalem. "Then I sent unto him, saying, There are no such things done as thou sayest, but thou feignest them out of thine own heart. For they all made us afraid, saying, Their hands shall be weakened from the work, that it be not done. Now therefore, O God, strengthen my hands."

How we see from this the great blessing of having pure motives and clean hands! How it gives guidance in perplexities when we are able to say like Nehemiah, when we are able to say like Paul, "One thing I do." My heart is united, my purposes are gathered together and focussed on one thing. My energies are not divided. I have one end in view, one thing to think about. Wherever I am, wherever I travel, night or day, rain or shine, I, like Nehemiah, have God's work to do; and until that is done, nothing shall seduce me to give it up.

How it enabled Nehemiah to speak out plainly, "For," said he, "there are no such things done as thou sayest, but thou feignest them out of thine own heart." Clear speaking.

> "Thrice is he armed that hath his quarrel just;
> And he but naked, though locked up in steel,
> Whose conscience with injustice is corrupted."

Oh, for this whole-heartedness in the cause of God! When our strength is like the strength of ten, because our heart is steadfast, our motives pure; then we are not driven about here and there by every wave, and by every wind, but there comes unto us a solid strength, an unshakableness, like the unshakableness of Nehemiah, and that greater than Nehemiah, the Son of God, who, when on earth, said to the Tobiahs of His day, "Go and tell that fox I works cures to-day and to-morrow, and the third day I shall be perfected." "I have a baptism to be baptized with, and how am I straitened until it be accomplished." "I seek not my own will, but the will of Him that sent Me."

Nehemiah said, "I will not cease doing the work, for I am sure it is not for my own personal ends, it is not for my own aggrandisement, my own vainglory. There are no such things as thou sayest, but thou feignest them out of thine own heart."

How it should give us courage when people talk! There is a motto engraved over the gateway of Marischal College, Aberdeen: "They say! What do they say? Let them say!" You have it here to-day. "McNeill, they say." Well, what do they say? Let them say! And they come to you Christian workers who are here bending your backs to the work, and "they say" you are doing this for your own praise. But do not listen: bend and work; don't give your ears to every idle gossiper. They say, "Oh, but Geshem says!" Well, Geshem is only a bigger liar than the rest!

They shot sore at poor Nehemiah, when they said, "Nehemiah, it is your own glory that leads you on in this work, not zeal for God." And don't think Nehemiah did not feel this; that message came with a thump to him. And what preserved him? His integrity and innocence. He could lift up his voice, and say, "It is a lie; it is *not* true. Do as you like! Say what you like! I know whom I am serving. You may try all manner of means, but you will never shake me from this, that God has sent me here, given me this work to do; and in His name I give myself to it, with singleness of heart and effort."

"For they all made us afraid, saying, Their hands shall be weakened from the work, that it be not done."

I believe the last and dreadful day will show that not a few were frightened from God's work by—"they say."

Now, if we had more Nehemiahs, these gossipers would not be so successful. If God promote you, and make you prominent in His work, remember it is He who does it; and you must stay at your post, do your day's work, and leave your reputation in the hands of the Lord. If people will say this and that and the other, let them say; you cannot leave off your work. If you draw back, they will still go on talking—people who have nothing else to do, and who are ever wanting to talk. They always have plenty to say. And if they go behind you and stab your reputation in the back, don't go back looking for them; leave your reputation to God. Soon they will meet Him face to face. Stand out to the front. Do your work, and leave your credit and reputation to your Master. It is a profitless business, beginning to defend yourself from all they say—a profitless business.

Then comes another temptation:—"Afterward I came unto the house of Shemaiah the son of Delaiah the son of Mehetabeel, who was shut up; and he said, Let us meet together in the house of God, within the temple, and let us shut the doors of the temple: for they will come to slay thee; yea, in the night will they come to slay thee. And I said, Should such a man as I flee? and who is there that, being as I am, would go into the temple to save his life? I will not go in."

That was a subtle temptation. For, I think, this man, this Shemaiah, was a man who had a particular reputation for wisdom and prudence; at any rate, Nehemiah yielded somewhat to him, for he went to his house to consult with him, and Shemaiah said to Nehemiah, "Let us meet together in the house of God, and let us shut the doors of the temple."

"Oh, Nehemiah!" he would say. "Now you are wrong, Nehemiah. You will allow me to speak plainly with you. Nobody rejoiced more than I did when you came from Persia, and I rejoice to see what is going on at Jerusalem. But the position is far different from what you think. And I have been here longer than you; and I know the currents of thought and feeling, which you don't know anything about. And, believe me, that sometimes the roundabout road is the nearest; and sometimes to go straight tramping on, you know, is the way never to reach what you want. You are carrying things, they think, with too high a hand. But if you would take time, stop, and let things blow over a little: you will get it done far more easily. Believe me, Nehemiah, I know the temper of this people (and here he spoke truly), and I tell you they are against you, and are going to seek your life. Now let us meet together in the temple, and let us shut the doors of the temple: for they will come and slay thee."

And Nehemiah said to him, "Should such a man as I flee?" He virtually stood up and said, "What, Nehemiah fleeing after all he has gone through! Get thee behind me, Satan! Thou savourest not of the things that be of God, but those that be of men." The same temptation came to the greater than Nehemiah, to the greatest Worker that ever God sent to work and to "pray for the peace of Jerusalem," even the Lord Jesus Christ. And as with the Master, so with the servant. The servant will be tempted and seduced in every way, that the work may cease, that the temperature, the heat of our zeal may go down, and the worse may appear the better reason, and carry us away from our post.

Some men go to the temple, but to them it is simply a coward's castle. This is about all that God gets from some of us. We go sneaking into our churches on the Sunday, but not to do God's work. God pity you! You never stand up for Him out there on London wall. This is what they like. Oh, to get into the church upon the Sabbath-day! Oh, to get the doors shut, and to try to forget all the misery that is outside, and the call of God to work in the world around you! You would get into the house of God, join in the service, and

"Sit and sing yourself away
To everlasting bliss."

Exactly! Well, this invitation from Shemaiah to go into the

temple was not good enough for Nehemiah—and he was about as devout a man as most of us. He was a man who feared God with all his heart, didn't he? But they were going to make the temple a coward's castle.

Listen, brother! I will bring it nearer to us. There is some young fellow here hard beset with his surroundings. You are set there on that commercial bit of the wall, to be true, to be honest, to unfurl the flag there, and to work with and for God there. And the battle is thickening, and coming to you in your business; the devil as an angel of light is trying to get you to leave your work *and go and study for the ministry!* Go into the temple to save your life. It was that kind of thing that was happening to the early Church. Men and women were going to leave the conflict and struggle, to run away into cloisters and convents, with their "dim, religious light." And so you would go and shut yourself up, and give yourself up to a life of contemplation, you say. It is a delusion; it is all moonshine; it won't do. Let us see how Nehemiah acted when asked to go into the temple. He would have been spoiled if he had yielded to that temptation. He no doubt loved the house of God, the worship of God as we do. We love all its regular services. How sweet it is to us to meet together, to hold communion, to join in our solemn feasts and hymns of love and praise! But that is on Sabbath days. And the end for which we meet is to strengthen us for the work of testifying for God and Christ. " Be faithful unto death, and I will give thee a crown of life." Oh, for Nehemiah's fidelity to-day! " Should such a man as I flee? And who is there that, being as I am, would go into the temple to save his life? I will not go in." It was the devil as an angel of light. "And, lo," said Nehemiah, " I perceived that God had not sent him; but that he pronounced this prophecy against me: for Tobiah and Sanballat had hired him." So let each one of us, in his calling wherein he is called, therein abide with God.

15 ver.—" So the wall was finished in the twenty and

fifth day of the month Elul, in fifty and two days. And it came to pass, that when all our enemies heard thereof, and all the heathen that were about us saw these things, they were much cast down in their own eyes: for they perceived that this work was wrought of our God."

That 15th verse has a ring in it like a clarion. "So the wall was finished." Their work was completed; it was done, all done, thoroughly done, men and devils notwithstanding. "So he built the wall." We don't see much just now. There is a great deal of waste and breakdown and *débris;* but let every soul be faithful in God's work, and, be sure of it, the day is coming when the truth will be brought out, for "Greater is He that is for us, than all that can be against us."

That kingdom is coming, and our business is to set it up here in London, and day and night to toil on and work on, never to give up, for "there is no discharge in this war." It may not be in my time, or my children's after me; but the work will be done. As truly as God lives, as surely as God lives, the crowning day is coming by-and-bye, and I shall be crowned, and so will you, if you do your day's work to-day. You will be there when the shout fills the universe, "*The wall is finished!* Hallelujah!" "The kingdoms of this world have become the kingdoms of our God, and of His Christ;" and ye shall reign with Him for ever and ever.

Jerusalem is yet to fill the whole earth with her godliness and righteousness. And so the wall was finished in spite of all. May we get the hope and the confidence of it to-day! when there is so much din and noise that one can hardly be sure of his little bit of building being building at all. If we could see with God's eyes, we should see far more around us of God's work and preparation for the coming kingdom than we are giving Him credit for, or ourselves either.

Now, let us take a last look at Nehemiah for the present, as we see him in the last paragraph. "Moreover in those days the nobles of Judah sent many letters unto Tobiah, and the letters of Tobiah came unto them." Now here is the point: "For there were many in Judah sworn unto him, *because he was the son-in-law* of Shechaniah the son of Arah; and his son Johanan had *taken the daughter of Meshullam* the son of Berechiah. Also they reported his good deeds before me, and uttered my words to him. And Tobiah sent letters to put me in fear." What is that? I think I see Nehemiah with his note-book in his hand after the work was all finished, and he is turning over and going through in his mind all that he had done and suffered. And he is thinking over it all, and wondering what made all the opposition to the building of these walls. "I never could rightly understand," he would say, "why that was such a tough job, and why there were continually things coming against my legs to trip me up from unexpected quarters. I felt some one was not fighting fair, that the enemy had got into our own camp and was fighting against me unfairly." And it was the *mother-in-law* that was the whole secret. They—families of God's people and their enemies—were married and inter-married with each other; and so they had their grappling-irons on the Israelitish vessel. And they pulled the vessel close by this inter-marriage relationship, and they got on board, and could not be kept off. By this marriage relation-ship Tobiah had got in with the very chief of them, and so struck hard and constantly at Nehemiah. And it was through this marriage relationship they tried to get at Nehemiah and pull him down, and thus cause God's work to cease.

Says Christ, "I am not come to send peace, but a sword; to set the father against the son, and the daughter against the mother, and the mother-in-law against the daughter-in-law: and a man's foes shall be those of his own household." Indeed, you will ofttimes be fairly per-plexed. You say, "I feel the devil at my elbow, and he is whispering in my ear with my own flesh and blood, and would overcome me unless I set watch with vigilance." This same thing is working to-day. Now, for example, I know a young fellow, he started with great vigour in the cause of God, he started with great vigour to build the wall, especially to build the total abstinence wall. But by-and-bye he married a daughter of a wine merchant, and that brought the building to a stop. Yes. He says now he thinks there are a great many excellent people among the brewers. Was not that the kind of thing they said to Nehemiah? "Moreover, they reported Tobiah's good deeds," and they said this and said that about him. "And now," I fancy Nehemiah saying, "I am so glad that I was faithful. Sometimes I thought that I was over strict, and made no allowances. But now I am able to see how they were all jumbled together. Lord, I thank Thee for keeping me so stern and uncompromising as I was. If it had not been for Thee, they would have cut the ground from under my feet, and I would have been swept away by them." So you have it. Very innocent-looking things may seduce you and take the backbone out of you. You have got married to a certain Church of England girl—a new sect to you—and you were originally a Presbyterian. You were very strict, but now you are quite the opposite; and now you make great excuses for ritualism. And why is this? It is all the influence of the mother-in-law! She is the cause of it. Your own heart's affections are as Presbyterian as ever they were. But you have got to be a coward. You dare not say "cheep"; your marriage has put you on a chain, and the mother-in-law has the pulling of the end of it!

Once upon a time you here used to be what is called "strict." Your friends called you old-fashioned and Puritanical. But lately you got married, and that has brought you into close contact with a class of people with whom you had little or no dealings before. You had nothing in common. And, to make a long story short, you were at the theatre the other evening—with your mother-in-law. She has soon called you in off the wall! Everything is altered now. And instead of your going over to carry war into the enemy's camp, they have come unto you, and have overcome you; and you have purred like a pussy-cat where before you were bold and outspoken : and the reason is the marriage, the mother-in-law; and the marrow of principle is being thereby sucked out of some of you. You need to be spoken to, and I would that my words were like fire, and would burn. Oh! that some of you would come back to your earlier faith, enthusiasm in God's work, and the blood-heat of your early zeal. For now you are as namby-pamby as the devil could wish.

"I used to think," says another, "very harshly of those who didn't hold my views. But now I have learnt to be charitable. I have discovered that many things which I thought were essential are only accidental." Softly, my friend : 'twas the mother-in-law made the discovery. You have gone off on that *charitable* dodge. Ah, God's Word has an eye in every direction.

"Also they reported his good deeds before me," and as good as said, "We know Tobiah; and, Nehemiah, you are wrong about him altogether. He is an excellent man, and he gave five shillings to this, he gave ten shillings to that; and he is a wonderful fellow altogether. He is wonderfully like yourself." Really it is such a pity that two such good men should not meet together and shake hands. But they never could, and Nehemiah kept his hands behind his back and said, "I choose my own company. I know the hands of these fellows too well."

Not long ago I was astonished at one whom I thought would be the last to play fast and loose with the Atonement and Inspiration, and with the need of conversion, and with the eternity of punishment. But now he is off the wall. And why? Because he is married into a certain circle where everything is loose and worldly; and instead of his bringing his new circle of friends up, they have brought him down. And now to see him gliding along the down-grade—with his mother-in-law—is partly ludicrous, and partly saddening, and wholly contemptible. I'm afraid there was more backbone in Nehemiah's little finger than in the whole anatomy of people I shall not name—but you can all be busy thinking. For all these reasons you should make this principle the touchstone of all friendships into which you enter, and all marriage relationships, and everything. How does it tell on the work of God? How does it tell on my walk? Does it cool or increase me in love to God, and in love for His righteous cause and His unchanging Truth? **May God bless the word!**

Regent Square Pulpit.

THE QUEEN OF THE SOUTH
VERSUS
THE MEN OF THIS GENERATION.

A Sermon

Delivered in Regent Square Church, on Sunday Morning Jan. 19th, 1890.

BY THE
REV. JOHN McNEILL.

---

1 Kings x. 4-9.

Yesterday I could not help feeling a little the reaction from incessant work in connection with our Special Meetings. I bent myself somewhat reluctantly to study a new subject. Still, as I bent over this passage, there came even from the dull printed page some glimmering of the glory, and the gladness, and the wonderment, and the mingled fainting and exhilaration of spirit that are recorded here. And my hope is that the Spirit of God may make up for my deficiency, and for yours also; that the eyes of our hearts may see the greater than Solomon, who is here with us in our own day and in our own generation, by His Word of wisdom, by His spiritual presence, with all its spiritual glory. May no ears be dull, may no eyes be dim, and may the preacher, notwithstanding all physical and mental lassitudes and drawbacks, may he also see and hear, and may he get the tongue of fire to tell out in your

No. 11.

hearing the grace and glory of the heavenly Solomon, our Lord and Saviour Jesus Christ! Oh, it is here! If the Spirit of God would only bring it out, what a sight we might get to-day for these eyes of ours, that would send us away with our very faces shining because of the abundance of the revelation of Christ's grace and glory that has been given to us!

"And when the Queen of Sheba had seen all Solomon's wisdom, and the house that he had built, and the meat of his table, and the sitting of his servants, and the attendance of his ministers, and their apparel, and his cupbearers, and his ascent by which he went up unto the house of the Lord; there was no more spirit in her. And she said to the king, It was a true report that I heard in mine own land of thy acts and of thy wisdom. Howbeit I believed not the words, until I came, and mine eyes had seen it: and, behold, the half was not told me: thy wisdom and prosperity exceedeth the fame which I heard. Happy are the men, happy are these thy servants, which stand continually before thee, and that hear thy wisdom. Blessed be the Lord thy God, which delighteth in thee, to set thee on the throne of Israel: because the Lord loved Israel for ever, therefore made He thee king, to do judgment and justice."

In those days long pilgrimages to see great persons and famous places were more remarkable, perhaps, than they are now. There were no railways, no ocean steamers, nor newspapers. Men trailed themselves for many weary miles —and travelling then was trailing in the most painful and tedious way over great leagues of country—to meet some great celebrity face to face. People travelled wearily from one country to another to see some great temple or other world's wonder. Here we have an express illustration in the Bible of that spirit which was abroad in the ancient world in ancient times. The Queen of Sheba, far, far away from the little country and kingdom of Judæa, heard of the wisdom and fame of Solomon, and with great expense and preparation, with care and toil and trouble, she started off with her retinue, and with a sample of her kingdom's wealth, and the glory of it, that she might come worthily before this greater monarch than herself, and hear his wisdom, and see his might and majesty and magnificence with her own eyes. And, let me say here, that perhaps that which most of all helped to start her out was this: she very likely heard of Solomon's fame through the widespread trading that radiated out from Judah and Jerusalem in Solomon's day.

Alas, alas! to-day we have it on indubitable, indisputable testimony that the trading of Christian Britain with certain far-off lands is not telling for Jesus Christ, but against Him. We are so trading in guns and gunpowder, and gin and rum, that far off lands are getting to hear about us, through our ships and merchants and sailors, anything but a good report. May it soon be changed, and may our commerce become one of the means by which the name and fame of Jesus Christ shall be extended to all lands, so that in the uttermost parts of the earth our trade shall be so Christian, so saturated with the Gospel and Spirit of Christ, that the far-off places of the earth shall know us as a Christian nation, the very centre and circumference of all whose grandeur and glory is Christ Jesus, whose we are, and whom we serve! May the Lord speedily take away the reproach that has fallen upon our foreign commerce, and may He make our foreign trading a foreign mission, and a means of spreading His glory! And further, the Queen of Sheba heard of the fame of Solomon "*concerning the name of the Lord.*" You see, after all, there was a spiritual element in this great fame. It was not his fame simply as a wise man and great monarch, but "concerning the name of the Lord." Wherever these traders went they evidently carried the name and the report of the great king who was in Jerusalem; but they carried this report also, that he was great, not simply in himself and from himself and because of himself, but that Jehovah, the God whom he knew, had given him this extra might and majesty, this glory and magnificence.

And that lands me at once into the heart of things, and into that line out of which I wish to make spiritual profit for Jesus Christ to-day. There is with us to-day in the land, in the city, in our assembly, One greater than Solomon, the Lord Jesus Christ; worthy to be admired, worthy to be adored, worthy of great pilgrimage and great sacrifice, if only we can get to know Him, and put our own heart-questions to Him, and taste upon our own mental palates and tongues the richness and the ripeness of His wisdom, and see with our own understanding His matchless grace and glory. He said it Himself, and He said it truly, standing in Israel, " A greater than Solomon is here ;" and He implied, " People's eyes are so filled with the things of time, people's ears are so filled with the common gossip, that although I am here, Incarnate Wisdom, the brightness of the Father's glory, and the express image of His Person, few, few, few are the people that come to see Me ; few are those who come to see My glory, to hear My wisdom, and to be blest for ever out of the abundance of My endowment of grace for all who come to get their share." May it not be so among us to-day? But if there is anything in us, if there is anything in any soul here, that draws you out of your orbit and beaten track to see with your own eyes, may that be used to move your soul into the very presence of the King to-day! And there is. Did not I see you scampering, you City man, with all your staidness and steadiness and sobriety—did not I see you with my own eyes on a recent Saturday fling all your dignity behind you, and scamper like your own office-boy, to get to some coign of vantage that you might see—umph! that thing of tinsel, of pinchbeck, and of tawdriness, the Lord Mayor's Show? Did not I see London turned out in a mass, rich London, poor London, wise London, foolish London, London lay and London clerical?—we were all there on the gape, with our very faces curled into points of interrogation, " When will he be here?—who? what? why? oh!"

Now what I want to bring out is this: *that element, my friend, is in the Gospel.* Although you are sitting there with your face as dull as the clay it is made of, that element is in the Gospel, it is in Christ. The shame is that we can go to earthly shows, and sit down at earthly banquets, and our faces sparkle, and we lick our lips over earthly wines and earthly dishes; and, alas, alas! it is so hard for us to broaden and widen and expand and strike our hands, and say, " Blessed be God! Christ is getting to be to me more than all that I have heard about Him. Glorious things are said of thee, O city of the living God, O Christ of God, and I'm beginning to find it is not rhapsody, it is not 'high falutin', not mere singing and shouting, 'It is true, and the half has not been told, or believed. The Lord Jesus Christ is a wonder; glories on Glory's head accumulate the more steadily the eyes of my heart fix upon Him and His Gospel, and all that He has done and all that He is doing, and the glorious things that He has promised, which are all yea and amen, and sure to come to pass.'" Waken up, man, waken up, let some of the brightness that fills your face at the big feast or big dinner—God save you!—let it get into your eyes and countenance, where there is a greater than Solomon and a greater than Sheba—where Christ is preached, where His Word that reveals His grace and glory to the eyes and ears of our hearts is sounding freely forth.

When the Queen of Sheba came to Jerusalem, " she came with a very great train, with camels that bare spices, and very much gold and precious stones; and when she came to Solomon, she communed." Don't you see, she came in a worthy way, not—not with one or two coppers jingling in her pocket that you fetch to the offertory; she came worthily, she came believingly, she did not expect that when she came she would find out that it was all a myth? She did not come to find fault, she did not come to drive away whatever she might see by an envious or jealous, or petulant or unbelieving, questioning disposition. She evidently was prepared for a feast, and she got it. And she came to give as well as to get, to show to Solomon that she believed that she had heard confidingly; and she was ready, as a kind of thankoffering, to pour out of the wealth and abundance that belonged to her. All the way from Arabia the blest she brought of Arabia's blessedness, that she might pour it before King Solomon. I think that is true yet. I think that element is in the Gospel. I think that element is illustrated on both sides of it in connection with Gospel preaching.

Come dull, come flat, come with the blinds pulled down and the shutters up, and you will go away thus. Come saying to yourself:—"Oh, well! what is it? Ah, yes! I will go;" or as you said to your wife this morning, "Of course, it is Sunday, and it is getting on for eleven o'clock. I have paid for a sitting, and I may as well take the worth of my money;" and you come, and you make no preparation. There is no glow, there is no gladness, there is no expectation there is no anticipation; you are at your worst when you come here. You go to hear any lecturer or any foreign traveller with more of a sparkle in your eye and more anticipation in your soul than you feel here. Now, I grant that we preachers may be somewhat to blame, but you help us in our blame: you come with such leaden ears, with such flat faces, with such vacuity, such littleness of expectation, and of desire, that the very look of you to a man who cannot bury his head in a manuscript is depressing and discouraging! Look up, as if you expected something, not in me, or through me, but because of Him who is here and who has attached certain promises to a gathering like this: "Where two or three are gathered together in My name, there am I in the midst; in all places where I record My name, I will come, and I will bless." Think of it! The doors being shut, Jesus appeared to them in the midst and showed them His hands and His side. "Then were the disciples glad"—the Queen of Sheba's spirit coming into them—"when they saw the Lord."

I think that element is in the Gospel, and the other side

of it is: come with the pure spirit, and you will get the pure blessing. Come expecting nothing, and you will get nothing What is nothing? You know the various humorous definitions of nothing—here is another: Nothing is what you get in Church, for you came for it. Oh, come expecting! Although the preacher may be very dull and very flat, the Lord will remember you, and the Lord will remember Himself, and before you, or I, are aware, through His grace, our hearts may be made like the chariots of Amminadab!

Sometimes the Lord comes with wonderful suddenness, just because there are people sitting here who are worth their room, and He cannot disappoint them. May I never get less than a houseful of people like that; and if that is not your temper or disposition, my friend, we will give you back your seat-money and let you go elsewhere! Let me say it with all my heart and soul: I have no interest in people who simply come to clap down in their pew, and who pull their very soul down into the bundle of flesh that is represented where they sit. Let your soul go up, cry to the Lord to anoint your eyes that you may see, to unstop, to dig out your ears that you may hear the fame and report of the heavenly Son, and to remember that He is standing beside you, and that you are overshadowed by the presence of His glory. It is what John said long ago that is true always, "In the beginning," he said, describing the heavenly Solomon and His magnificence, "In the beginning was the Word, and the Word was with God, and the Word was God; all things were made by Him, and without Him was not anything made that was made; and that Word became flesh and dwelt among us, and we beheld His glory, full of grace and truth." He is with us yet. Come worthily. I referred a little while ago to the money—come more worthily even in that respect. Let nothing be done heedlessly or carelessly; but as the Queen of Sheba prepared her heart and prepared her material retinue, so let us prepare our hearts and prepare our persons and prepare our substance, that we may seek this glorious Lord worthily.

And Solomon told her all her questions. There was not anything hid, or secret thing, which he told her not. And, my hearer, if this woman came from the uttermost ends of the earth, to speak of hard questions, so may we well come to the heavenly Solomon. Which of us has not his hard question — your torturing question, that tortures your own soul; your question that you can get no answer to anywhere else? Oh, what deep, hard questions, I had almost said, are natural to our minds, when we begin just to reflect and to think ever so little! Whom am I? Where am I going? My sin, my misery, this foul well of filth and dirt that for ever casts up its mire within me; my unclean heart, that there is no getting to the bottom of it, that I may lick it up and dry it up and staunch its foul overflow? These are hard questions.

My brother, my sister, you men here who want to wear it as a feather in your cap that you are thinking men, you young fellows, who want to wear it as your proudest boast that you think deeply, come here! You never carried your intellect to a more worthy place than to the place where Christ is preached as the revealer of secrets, as the answerer of hard questions. Come to Him! Come to Him as the Queen of Sheba came to Solomon; tell Him all that is in your hearts, and He will either solve your question, or He will give you grace to believe that the solution is with Him, sooner or later, if you will only wait. I do not say that He has answered all my questions; I do not say that He answers all the questions that we put to Him; but He does what is as good, He satisfies the pressing ones, those that give our conscience dispeace, those that cause gloom, fear, and alarm. He satisfies them right off, for in Him are hid the treasures of wisdom and of knowledge, oh, troubled soul, with thy hard questions! and as for the others, He says,"Wait." Blessed is he that waiteth on Him. You shall not be put to shame, if you will just wait and believingly trust in Him for all the rest that I do not seem to answer right off. Inquirer, whether you be a Royal inquirer, like the Queen, or a plain, blunt man, with your hard questions, wait, read, study, meditate My living oracles, and above all, believe, *believe*, BELIEVE; and, says Christ, thine eyes shall see; for the morning is coming when all shadows shall fly, and thou shalt stand in the perfect noonday of perfect light and perfect knowledge of thy God, and of His holy will for thee and all mankind.

Yes, there are hard questions. Come to Christ with them! The gad and fad of to-day is too much to run to the philosopher and to run to the man of science. Well, what does he say? You run to these false kings and you ask them, the men of science of to-day, "Who am I?" and they cannot tell you. They are not sure whether you are a monkey developing up or down. Oh, God help us! but the wise men have made asses of themselves in the latter part of this nineteenth century. I despise no man's researches and no man's science, but as the truth of the heavenly Solomon is in me, and is loved by me, I trust I have increasingly *a most healthy and perfect contempt for their contempt* of the Christ of God. Let us all be dowered with the hate of their hate, the scorn of their scorn. Aye, come to Him who is a greater than Solomon, and He will answer the hard questions. Put them to Him, say to Him —and it is one of the hardest questions—" What must I do that I may inherit eternal life ; what must I do to be saved ; how shall I go on growing into a perfect man, a perfect, flawless, spotless character?" And He will tell you ; and, more than that, He will secure the accomplishment of the thing if you come to Him.

Further, "And when the Queen of Sheba had seen of Solomon's wisdom, and the house that he had built, and the meat of his table, and the sitting of his servants, and the attendance of his ministers and their apparel, and his cupbearers, and the ascent by which he went to the house of the Lord, there was no more spirit in her." Now again, let me repeat that *this is in the Gospel*. I know almost as if I heard you saying it—you are sitting back there and saying, "Preacher, I wish it *were* there—well, really I wish it were ; for, do you know, that is just what I have missed in the Gospel?" And when Stanley comes to tell you about Africa, you will sit with your very mouth open for three blessed hours—you will stand on your tiptoes. I have done the same myself. I have! And what he has to tell is, after all, nothing compared with the wisdom of Christ that crieth aloud in the Gospel. A far traveller! Eternal wisdom is the far traveller. Think where Christ came from! Think what

Christ has seen! Think of what Christ has to tell of the eternity that was, and the eternity that is to be! For a far traveller, commend me to the Christ of God, Jesus of Nazareth, and this record of His journeys that shows Him travelling "in the greatness of His strength, speaking in righteousness, mighty to save." I am ashamed—with burning shame I say it—I am ashamed to think how my tongue has faltered and my heart has failed me in preaching the report of the heavenly Solomon. And you are partly to blame—the dull, stupid look on your face dulls me. God save us both!

"When she had seen,"—what? "When she had seen all Solomon's wisdom, *and the house that he had built.*" We have dealt a little with the wisdom before. "The house that he had built." Have you seen the heavenly Solomon's house? That is to say, have you seen His Person? He is fairer than the sons of men. You never saw His like. Think of His Godhead, and think of His manhood, and think of the perfect way in which these two are joined together. There He is walking by the Lake of Galilee, a Man among men; and yet the eternal glory of the Godhead is in that man from Nazareth. This is the house that the Father built for Him: this human frame, and this human flesh, and this human nature of ours; think of that! Who—what architect piled a house like the house that God's Son dwelt in and will dwell in for ever and ever? The Eternal in the human; think of it! So like ourselves after a human plan, and after a human model, bone of our bone; else we never could understand Him. His glory would just be a blinding blur and blaze that would reveal nothing to us. But God built Christ's Person a second Adam; "bone of our bone, flesh of our flesh," and yet so high and towering and over-topping, so broad and wide, like us, and yet so unlike us.

The Queen of Sheba was amazed at the house Solomon had built to live in. My dear friend, think you, walk round about the Son of God, walk about Zion and go round, consider her palaces, tell her bulwarks. Go round, man, round; you have not seen a millionth part of the magnificence of the house that God's eternal Son lives in. And if in addition to His own Person you like to regard His Church as His house, what a wonder that is! For He dwells in His Church—that is His great work, and He dwells in the midst of it, as you enter in and dwell in the house that your own hands have built. Think of His Church, think of that house, think of its erection, think of its foundations, think how it is rising and growing and spreading and filling the whole earth! Look at it, I mean to say, through Divine eyes! Look at it with the whole mind! Push up your spec's, and look at it. Get a naked view of Christ in His Church. Why, man, the eyes of angels burn like stars when they see the house that He has built that He may dwell in it for ever. And your dull eyes and mine — oh, what blindness hath happened to His people!—our eyes are holden that we do not see and do not know. We can see and grow bright, and shout "hurrah" over some trumpery thing of time, the glory of which is perishing while we look at it, and we cannot see the eternal majesty and glory of the Christ of God and the house He Himself hath built. Oh for Paul, to describe to us how Christ hath ascended far above all things, that He might fill all things, and be Head over all things to the Church, which is His Body, the fulness of Him who filleth all in all!

"And the sitting of his servants and the attendance of his ministers, and their apparel." When she saw that, then as the eight verse says, she broke out, "Happy are thy men, happy are these thy servants that stand continually before thee and hear thy wisdom." Oh believer, I want to re-echo the Queen of Sheba's word, spoken in that far-distant day! Dost thou know the Son of God? Hast thou come into the household of faith? Art thou His, and in such close relationship with Him, that thou art yielding thyself, body, soul, and spirit, a living sacrifice and help, for His service and glory? Then hear this word: "Happy art thou. Rejoice, oh man; rejoice, oh believer; lift up the hands that hang down, and the feeble knees! Wherefore art thou moping and sighing and groaning, and for ever hanging thy head like a bulrush? What! in the presence of such a King, wilt thou dare to mope and sigh? What! wilt thou sit down at such banquet as this, and begin with a soiled, tear-stained face? What! is it possible that in the presence, the real spiritual presence, of such a Saviour, we shall be dull and loutish and clownish and lumpish and sodden? You dare not do it in the presence of Queen Victoria. If you went to stand as her close attendant and servant in Windsor, or elsewhere, thou wouldst be clothed in splendid apparel; thy very outward demeanour would be compelled to show semblance at any rate of respect and obedience, and of ready attention. And, alas, alas! how is it with us, who profess to be the friends and the servants and the co-heirs of, and the co-workers with, the heavenly Solomon? Out upon thee; yea, out upon thyself, oh preacher! for who so much as thee forgets his office and its glory. Well might the Queen of Sheba break out, and I do well to re-echo her benediction this morning. Happy are Christ's men, happy are these Christ's servants, who stand continually before Him, and hear His wisdom. Take it in, for it is true. "Why art thou cast down, oh my soul, and why art thou disquieted within me?" If thou art the close servant of this King of kings and Lord of lords, be more like your work; look as if a great honour and glory had suddenly and unexpectedly come to one who was a bond-slave till this Christ, by His truth and wisdom and grace, redeemed and made thee anew, and gave thee a place in His house for ever and ever.

"The meat of His table." Have you thought of that, you diners-out, eh? You people who will talk and talk and talk to me and others about those who invited you to dine—ah, didn't we notice your tone!—you wanted us to understand under what mahogany you had stretched your legs compared with poor outcasts like us. You dined with the Blanks of Blankshire, and what a dinner that was! all along this side of the wall were powdered servants, all the other side of the wall another array of powdered servants! And what a splendid table! and the dishes on the table! and the meat in the dishes! You could not have translated the *ménu* card, if you had got a king's ransom. And you tell about it to your children, and it has filled your whole soul, and your memory, and your imagination. Well, well, if that is in the things of life, and it is genuine, and it is legitimate, there is a good thing in it—that, man, that is in religion. The meat of His table; think of it, and let your mouth water! Look at the dishes on that table! Look at the abundance provided to that people, not of the corporal and carnal kind, but the abundant feast for your reason, for your conscience, for your heart! Look at the piles that are there, the things you need, absolutely need, to fill your soul! Look at the Wine and Bread of Heaven; look at the Grace, look at the Pardon! In this mountain doth the Lord make for all people a feast of fat things; of wines upon the lees! Look at the delicacies as well as the essentials! Look—look—all things in Christ that the heart can possibly conceive : " Eye hath not seen, nor ear heard, neither hath entered into the heart of man the things which God hath prepared for them that love Him. But He hath revealed them to us by His Holy Spirit." Oh, I thank God for this! I never saw an audience so brighten up : you hardly look the same men and women as when you came in; and those who are not looking up are bending their head in their hands. That is a sign of grace. Oh that it might come over both preachers and hearers! Oh, we have well nigh put out the glory of the Gospel with our unbelief and our dulness and our slowness of heart; and I say that in this congregation which has been ministered to in spiritual wisdom and knowledge in the past, as few congregations have been! More shame to us to be so far back in brightness and grace, and work and glory—glory shining out from our faces and our works for Christ.

" The meat of his table, and the sitting of his servants, and the attendance of his ministers, *and their apparel*." The world can show great things in dress, and so can the Church ; so can Christ. Oh, poor man, poor woman, poor preacher, let us only get a look at ourselves as we are reflected in some of those flashing mirrors in the banqueting-hall of Christ's love and grace, and we will see something in the way of magnificent apparel! Clothed upon with what? With Christ Himself. With wonderful grace and power He puts Himself, as a flowing garment, right over every soul that comes into allegiance with Him. We are "clothed upon" with Christ, covered over with His righteousness, illuminated by His Holy Spirit, gloried in His own glory, made in His own image, in knowledge, in righteousness, in truth, in holiness. Well may I break out and say, " How matchless is thine apparel? Who are these in white robes, and whence came they? Whence this fine linen, the righteousness of the saints; whence this gorgeous apparel?" Ah, we have got it all, simply because we heard of the fame of the heavenly Solomon, and of the great banquet that he had spread. And we came, and when we got the length of the vestibule, He stripped us of our own foul garment and put upon us a robe worthy His presence and worthy His feast. I trust there is none of us here, when the King comes in to see the guests, none of us without the wedding-garment, the royal robe, the King's own gift—for He not only feeds us, but He clothes us before we sit down.

There is one thing more to notice that took the heart out of the Queen of Sheba. "The ascent by which Solomon went up into the house of the Lord." She was almost overcome; heart and flesh began just a little to reel and stagger at the sight of this material splendour. What is the ascent to the house of the Lord? Ah, I think I have it! When I think of the ascent by which He has gone up to the temple of the Lord; that is to say, when I think of Christ's resurrection, the splendid staircase by which, oh Lord, Thou has ascended on high; when I see Christ's resurrection; when I gaze up that shining stairway, then glories upon glories burst in upon mind and heart and imagination. "Thou hast ascended up on high, Thou has led captivity captive!" Surely, when that magnificent stairway was opened, when Christ ascended to the highest glory, then the angels and archangels burst forth, "Lift up your heads, oh ye gates, and be ye lifted up, ye everlasting doors, and let the King of glory come in."

Again I charge you, again I charge myself, look—Behold the glories of the Lamb! Look at your ascended Lord, see His resurrection glory; see His resurrection magnificence, and never let your eyes shut to it again, never. "When she saw the ascent by which he went up to the house of the Lord, there was no breath left in her." And when she recovered her breath it was to say, "Happy, happy! Blessed, blessed!" Now, what are we going to say of all this? Oh, it is a pity to criticize, but when one thinks of how people creep and crawl into God's house and sit with their hands in their pockets, and then creep and crawl out again, and begin to grumble; and instead of saying " Blessed, blessed! Happy, happy! Oh my Saviour! Oh His wisdom! Oh the depths of the riches of the wisdom and knowledge of God, how unsearchable are His judgments and His ways past finding out; may His name endure for ever, and last as long as the sun;"—no, instead of that, you drag yourself out, and what can you grumble at, and what can you find fault with, and how dark and dreary can you look! May it not be so! The Queen of Sheba came from the uttermost ends of the earth to hear the wisdom of Solomon. I am not speaking too strongly. I am speaking in my Master's name when I say, "Behold, a greater than Solomon is here," and we sadly show that we are not deserving His glory—we are not overwhelmed by His greatness and His condescending grace. But we will be. Through grace, we shall so open our hearts this very day, that the Queen of the South shall not be able to rise in the judgment and condemn us. We will go away saying, "Happy, happy, happy! Blessed, blessed, blessed! Mine eyes have seen the King in His beauty; I have got a glimpse of the land which is very far off; and now that I see Christ, mine eyes shall never close; for

> "Ah! the Master is so fair,
> He smiles so sweet on banished men,
> That they who meet it unaware
> Can never rest on earth again.
> And they who see Thee risen afar,
> At God's right hand to welcome them,
> Forgetful stand of home and land,
> Desiring fair Jerusalem.'"

It is no rhapsody, it is no mere ecstasy, or rhodomontade. As surely as the Queen of Sheba travelled those weary hundreds of miles under burning skies and across burning sands, and at last reached Solomon, and found in his presence that rest and that refreshment and that abundance for eye and ear and heart that made her sick and amazed, so surely, surely I have heard of Thy fame, oh heavenly wisdom, oh incarnate Christ, and the fame has caught my ear and told upon my heart, and I am travelling on to see Thee, and I shall! The hour is coming when we shall get in through the gates into the city, and our eyes shall see His glory and not another's. Yes, we shall see Him, we too shall fall down utterly overwhelmed and amazed as we say, "It was grand down upon the earth, what we heard from prophets and apostles: but, oh King of kings, the half was not told us of all Thy wisdom and of all Thy glory!" That hour is coming. Think of it often, revel in it often, ante-date that day, my brother, my sister, ofttimes in spiritual imagination! Spread thy wings and enter in through the gates into the city; stand upon the sea of glass; thou shalt yet stand there. Stand in faith, stand in spirit, stand in hope and expectation even now upon the sea of glass; listen to those voices that rise like the thunder of many waters, as the multitude whom no man can number rolls out the Magnificat of heaven, "Blessing and honour and glory and power be unto Him that sitteth upon the throne, and unto the Lamb for ever and ever."

> "Oh land beyond the sea,
> When will our rest be won?
> Slow-footed years more swiftly run
> Into the goal of that unsetting sun;
> Home-sick we are for thee,
> Calm land beyond the sea."

And remember, too, you who seem to care for none of these things, to whom Gospel grace has ceased to be a wonder—it is too familiar. Ye have not believed our report; and to you the arm of the Lord has not been revealed. Remember that others will come. This glorious Lord will draw multitudes to His feet. Not in vain has He lived and died, and ascended, and sent forth as on the very wings of the wind His name and fame. They will come. "Kings shall fall down before Him; all nations shall serve Him."

> "All kingdoms and all princes of the earth
> Flock to that sight; the glory of all lands
> Flows into her; unbounded is her joy
> And endless her increase.
> From every clime they come,
> To see thy beauty, and to share thy joy, O Zion!
> An assembly such as earth saw never;
> Such as heaven stoops down to see!"

Regent Square Pulpit.

REMARKS PRELIMINARY TO AN ORDINATION OF ELDERS AND DEACONS

In Regent Square Church, on Sunday Morning, Jan. 26th, 1890.

BY THE

REV. JOHN McNEILL.

Exodus xviii. 18-23.

Of course here, my friends, we are Presbyterians. This is Regent Square Presbyterian Church; and we consider that a name of joy, and a title of very high and honourable mention indeed. But it would be utterly unworthy of an occasion like this, and of a gathering like this, where we have come to worship God and to hear His Word, that I should make my sermon a Plea for and a Defence of Presbytery. We have not met for that. That may be important, and, on fitting occasion, of great use; and I trust we are ready, if there is to be controversy, to stand up for ourselves, and to show cause why we are Presbyterians rather than members of other denominations. But we shall rather take up this subject this morning because we all believe in some kind of government, we all believe in some kind of order and decency and rule in connection with the practical out-working of congregational life in the house and in the kingdom of our Lord and Saviour Jesus Christ. And we turn to this particular passage because there are here some practical ideas of universal application. You see them here, also, away from the controversy that might be too much suggested by special names and functions, such as Presbyter, Elder, Deacon, Bishop, and so on, did we find our text in some of those classical portions we have already read together in the Acts and 1st Epistle to Timothy.

The first thing I wish to notice—and I must be brief to-day, so that we may go through our Ordination Service quietly and in order—the first thing is that the organization that came out of this talk between Jethro and Moses *was marked by great common sense.* Common sense! If we are to have different organizations, different systems of working out Christ's will among His people, and carrying out His cause through all the ends of the earth, let us see to it that the tone of old Jethro is carried with us through all our plans, through all our ways, and through all our works. That is very noticeable here. It is noticeable again in the New Testament when the special order of deacons was created. The immediate feeling on the part here of one man, and in the New Testament on the part of a number of men, was "Now we are departing from sense, from common business reason and understanding. Jethro says, "This thing that thou doest is not good; thou wilt surely wear thyself away;" and the Apostles in the Book of Acts, at a critical juncture like this, say, "It is not meet that we should leave the Word of

God, to go and serve tables." Let there be a division of labour; let us find out whether among the company of ourselves, there is not all that is needed for every crisis, and for the Christian work of to-day, all to our hand." Why should one man be allowed to be eyes for everybody and ears for everybody and hands and feet for everybody! Let us have more eyes than one man's, more hands than just one pair; although we will all admit that Moses' hands were big and capacious. Let us have more hearts bent and strained over this business of looking after God's Israel than simply one when more are needed, and when we have every expectation that God will be with us in this sub-division of labour. It will be proved to be according to His will just because it is so according to common sense and right reason.

So we do not enter into any great and high arguments to-day in order to prove that Presbyterianism is the way of working out Christianity, and the only way. We will not be tempted into trying to prove that there is a text which says straight from heaven, "Thus saith the Lord, thou shalt be a Presbyterian." We will not contend that; but coming to the Old Testament story, we will see the reasonableness and common sense of having some order and some form of government. "Let all things be done decently and in order," says the Apostle Paul; and Jethro, centuries—millenniums before him, is wonderfully much on the same line. "Moses," he says, "there is a want of decency, there is a suppression of everybody's talent and everybody's endowment that yours and yours alone may be drawn upon. There is a want of decency and a want of order. this thing that thou dost is not good. Thou shalt surely wear away, both thou and this people that is with thee, for this thing is too heavy for thee; thou art not able to perform it thyself alone." And here Presbyterianism joins with other 'isms and says, " We will have no 'one man ministry' in a peculiar and special sense, on the simple ground that it is not common sense. No man is able to bear the burden of God's house and of God's work in a congregation, or in a denomination, alone. When we gather round Moses and his difficulties and dismiss all technicalities and discussions, we find we are all Jethroites—if I may name a new denomination; we are all Jethroites for the time being. We strike our hands and say, "This is reason, this is sense."

Let us trouble ourselves less—especially some of our brethren of the one Household of Faith—about *jus divinum*, &c., &c., and see to it more that Moses, the minister, is not allowed to kill himself with too much work, or somebody who differs from him with too much tyranny! All our "'isms" have a tendency to produce Popes; but the cure is grace and sense in the management.

How helpful it is occasionally, either in Old Testament or New Testament times, to have a man coming from the outside, a man to whom this whole on-going is new, and a man who will look on it with critical, but not unkindly eyes; a man related to us, like Jethro, Moses' father-in-law. The other morning I spoke of the mother-in-law, and made her a sample of what was unfortunate in relationship. Here we have the marriage relationship coming out in all that is helpful; and I was not forgetting that in connection with Nehemiah, though I did not speak of it. Here, let it be frankly admitted, is the other side, showing itself in the best and most helpful way. What a help, I say, to have outside eyes looking on us, and offering us their criticisms. You do not find Moses turning round and saying, " Now my respectable and venerable friend, mind your own business, and I shall mind mine. You may have your way of doing things down in Midian, but we do things here in our own way. This affair is my own creation; I began it, and I will see it through. When I begin to feel I am needing your help, I will call you in; meanwhile you need say nothing until you are asked."

Well, there is sometimes a "standoffishness" of tone like that. It is not reasonable nor sensible. Moses showed his greatness and his all-roundness by virtually saying, " Well, now, a man coming from the outside may see things far better than myself, for I am immersed in this business of looking after Israel; I am sunk into it to the very eyes; I am so near to it that I am perhaps not able to see matters in their true perspective. According to the old proverb, the man on the dyke always plays well; and it may be this man who is looking at us as he sits on the dyke sees weaknesses in us that we do not see, and we will listen to what he has to say." And the upshot was he did listen, and the Lord put His stamp and seal on the arrangement. It is one of the grand illustrations that we are not to look in the Bible for a special " Thus saith the Lord " for every thing. The Lord leaves certain things to us, or, shall I say, to sanctified ingenuity and sanctified common sense? The Lord leaves us free in that sense, and when we bring forward our purposes and plans, He makes them His by blessing them, by making them part of His eternal purpose. And so we find that afterwards these men were chosen without any express "Thus saith the Lord;" but the selection, springing from the crisis of the hour, and the working of a man's mind on that crisis—the men and the plan are accepted. God put His imprimatur, His stamp, His seal, His approval on this arrangement. These representative men were honoured afterwards, along with Moses, to draw near to God. "They saw God, and did eat and drink in His holy presence, on the mount."

Then, another thing that comes out of it is, a plan like this shows us *the diversity of gift and grace, and endowment which we may always expect to have in the Church of Christ;* and a reasonable and common sense arrangement like this brings out that diversity, and uses that endowment. "Moses, thou art not able to bear this burden alone; provide out of all the people able men, who shall bear the burden with thee." Now the Lord has always that in His Church. Let us not be afraid of it. We hear voices to-day filled with timidity, both for political and ecclesiastical organizations. "Do not trust the people, or if you do trust them, do it last, and do it grudgingly, and do it with the utmost reservation. The people, the people is a tiger; watch the lash of its tail and the gleam of its eye, and if you are to come near it at all, draw its teeth and muzzle it as much as possible." Presbyterianism has nothing to do with this, whatever her faults may be. We trust the people; the power is in the people. You, the congregation—and I want you to remember this—puts me here, the congregation puts the office-bearer there; and we are not here to take things out of your hands, and to come and shut ourselves up in secret conclaves, and then to come out and simply ask you to register our decrees, and march to our quick-step or slow-step—the latter, perhaps, more than the former. You put us here, and the power is in the people. I do not wish to go into controversy; indeed, I am not competent. I can accommodate a little the language of our national bard, and say—

> " For I've nae skill o' *kirks*, my lads,
> That kenna [know not] tae be free ; "

free from dictation of king or priest. But I will say that we are, as an institution, neither oligarchic, nor monarchic, nor aristocratic, but essentially democratic. We choose out from among ourselves men full of the Holy Ghost and of faith to look after our own affairs, both temporal and spiritual.

That, I say, comes out here, apart from controversy, and that is why I chose a passage in Exodus; and that comes out in our Ordination of new Office-Bearers to-day. Let us believe, dear friends, that especially in a community like the Church, called together out of the world's darkness and unbelief and sin—called together by this splendid power, the Gospel of Christ, the Word of the Eternal God, and the Spirit of God working behind the Word; let us be sure of it that in a society quickened and called together by such a power as that, there will always be gift, there will always be grace, there will always be endowment. And that system is condemned by common sense which suppresses that gift and suppresses that grace and endowment; which does not presume upon its presence, so to say, and proceed to call it out and work it up; which becomes oligarchic or monarchic, and looks to the few and the few only, or to one man only, as the fount of its wisdom and power. Let us see to it that from the broad base of the people there is rising, and there is expected to rise, the very sap and fruitfulness that comes out of the Eternal Foundation on which the people are built. Moses, good man as he was, was choking up the fountain, was keeping it from flowing out; and old Jethro coming from outside saw it at a glance. He was not one of your newspaper critics who — confound their impudence!—when they begin to write on Church matters, how flippant they become! how sneering! With what thin-lipped sarcasm they talk about "parsons" and "the ecclesiastical mind," and so on! Jethro was a kindly critic, a warm-hearted man, who looked with keen eyes and a loving heart behind the eyes. Again, I say, what a helpful chapter, simply because it takes us away from all controversy, and helps all denominations by its broad humanities, and broad divinities as well.

But to proceed. Jethro says further: "Hearken now unto my voice. I will give thee counsel, and may God be with thee. Be thou for the people to Godward, that thou mayest bring the causes unto God; and thou shall teach them ordinances and laws, and shall shew them the way wherein they must walk; and the work that they must do." From this, and from what he said elsewhere about *small matters*, Jethro, this man from outside whom we like to speak for us to-day, so as to avoid controversy, sees and admits, as we all must do—and the New Testament only brings it out more fully in its elders and deacons, the distinction in practical working between the spiritual and the temporal—the things Godward and the things manward. You notice that the men to work in both directions must alike be spiritual men. But, practically speaking, there are the spiritual things, and there are, on a lower plane, the secular things. God will always secure among His people that there shall be somebody outstanding for the great work Godward, somebody to teach, somebody to preach, to give heart and strength, time and energy of body and soul and spirit to the deeper knowledge of God and of the Word of God and of the will of God; that from that close, that consecrated, that entirely given up communion, he may come out to preach to the people who have not such opportunity, and in the actual outworking of human life and society cannot have the opportunity of studying God's Word, to know its deep Divine things in all their bearings on life and godliness, as he can.

How it all comes out, away back here. So we have the ministry, the preaching; and it is wrong to style ours, as they do who belong to those who are called "Brethren," it is wrong to call this "a one-man ministry." Our whole Ordination to-day disproves it. The one man there is, but not in the sense of being alone and of doing it all himself. Beneath him there is this broad common platform of reason and of common sense, and of business sanity. One man to do what the body of people—life being as it is—either in the Church, in the wilderness, or in New Testament times, will not do. "Be thou for the people to Godward. Teach ordinances and laws; show them the way in which they must walk and the work that they must do." How sensible! And when people rise up to say smart things about ministers; that we have run into this office in order to get an easy way of living and a comfortable salary, let us see to it that, possessed of Moses' spirit, and in our own measure doing Moses' work, we allow all such criticisms to fly past us like the idle wind. Believe me, the man is still needed in the community, and is well worth his money, is he not—even to come to that small matter—who is set apart to be for men Godward, who gives himself to prayer and to the study of God's Word. What amount of this trash—called gold—could possibly represent the value of such a man and of such a ministry in the tides of time? It cannot be valued; gold and fine gold can never be named as the price thereof. Well said Jethro and well did Moses. Perhaps Moses was not so much out among the people as before; and small-minded, pedantic, microscopic critics in Israel might say, "We do not see Moses running in and out and about the tents as he used to. I remember, dear me! he was out every morning, and we all got a hail and a word from him, and whatever was the trouble or dispute we all got to Moses himself, but now he is taking it easier; we notice he is not so much out." As some of you would say, "Oh, those black-coated gentlemen, they have nothing to do but shut themselves up in the study." We have not got to work with the hammer, or to put our hat and coat on and go to the city at ten and leave at half-past three in the evening, as some one put it in my hearing. We have nothing to do. Let us give that nonsense up. It is turned to ridicule when we look at it in the light of this Old Testament story. It was a wise plan; it conserved Moses, and it told upon the deeper spirituality of the people, who certainly greatly needed that one man should give himself up to spiritual things.

We owe, under God, among other things, the 90th Psalm —that prayer of Moses the man of God—to Jethro, humanly speaking. Jethro secured for him the time and the calm in which that Psalm was born. His work became less extensive, true; but more intensive. So with us still. As Carlyle would put it, "Of all public functionaries boarded and lodged on the industry of modern Europe, we 'speaking men,'" as he calls us, "are surely worthy of our board."

"Moreover, thou shalt provide out of all the people able men." Now, here we come to the gist of our business to-day. Ah, you had it millenniums before our presbyters and deacons are spoken of in the New Testament. "Able men, such as fear God; men of truth, hating covetousness; they shall bring to thee great matters, but every small matter they shall judge; so shall it be easier for thyself, and they shall bear the burden with thee. If thou shalt do this thing—and God command thee so—then thou shalt be able to endure, and all this people shall also go to their place in peace."

Notice the *men you want*. I do not wish to be severe at all—I never want to be so for severity's sake—but, as God is with me, I always want to speak the straight, plain, blunt truth. There is far too much of a feeling abroad in the Church to-day that prevents able men from taking office in the Church and prevents able men from taking office out there in social and civil life. That spirit belongs to the devil; that spirit is utterly unworthy of Christianity; that spirit is utterly ruinous to both Church and State, if it should spread. Let us have in Parliament, in our County Councils in London, and in all our provincial towns, able men to guide the affairs of Israel; the pick and flower of the native brain, and heart, and morality, and integrity of every kind, consecrated to the service of God and fatherland. Able men! May God sweep away from our public life over the whole nation all unworthy men. Our whole nation, like Israel of old, is a God-fearing nation, and should be ruled over in every part by men who answer to Jethro's description.

May the Lord sweep away from our magisterial benches not a few who sit there; may these be occupied by none but God-fearing men, none but men who hate covetousness. The rottenest man in the town, perhaps, morally, the deadest spiritually, is the man who sits on the bench! Any policeman out in the suburbs is able to tell shocking stories about how such a magistrate, baillie, or M.P. councillor, comes tumbling home at midnight, drunk as usual. Let us see to it that in Church and State, for the government of a *Christian nation* that claims to have Israel's place and Israel's part among the nations of the earth—a righteous nation that fears the truth and holds it forth—we remember old Jethro's word; and in all our elections of ministers, elders, deacons, guardians, councillors, justices, members of Parliament, we look for God-fearing, truth-loving, greed-hating men. But what of ability? No fear for that. This Scripture implies that all such are able men; and they are. We talk of climbing into office. Let them climb; but let us see that the ladder is that described in the 15th or 24th Psalm.

> " Who is the man that shall ascend
>   Into the hill of God ?
> Or who within His holy place
>   Shall have a firm abode ?
> Whose hands are clean, whose heart is pure,
>   And unto vanity
> Who hath not lifted up his soul,
>   Nor sworn deceitfully."

What moral thews and sinews he would need who seeks to climb into office in Israel, whether in Church or State!

Able men! Oh Jethro, I thank thee for that word. It has ever characterized—and I say it in no boastful spirit—our Presbyterian system; it has ever characterized—and I say it with devout thankfulness to God—the eldership and deaconship of this congregation; and may it ever characterize—again let me repeat—all our congregations in days to come. Be sure of it; let us take it for granted, as I have said, that in the Christian Church, the Word of God, and the Spirit of God, will provide for you able men; such as fear God, men of truth, and hating covetousness. Go forth, and pull them out. *Call them;* fetch them to the front, and by solemnly setting them apart, make them to feel their position, and to worthily exercise their functions.

Young brethren, just newly come to the knowledge of Christ, keep this in your mind, and when the next opportunity comes, take a place and part and office in the Church of Christ. I do not speak of any who declined to take such office in our last election, but I speak straight out, and I walk with a free step. What I mean to say is, please be delivered from the littleness that I have found among young men, even among Presbyterian young men, that makes you consider office in church beneath you. Do not suppose it is a thing with a big name and a big talk, but does not need brains, and does not need ability, and does not need such an endowment as yours. Your endowment is more worthily bestowed elsewhere. Now, get rid of that: that bit of dry rot of Presbyterianism. Our way of working things has come to its honourable place and its honourable name and fame in all lands, simply because men, both young and old, when they are called by the people have accepted the call thankfully, and have put themselves into the office under God and at the people's request, and found in the office something to exercise the best, the very best of both head and heart.

I ring the changes on old Jethro's word—"able men." Anything won't do for an elder; anything with a good coat on its back, with a fine and well-fed appearance—anything won't do for an office-bearer, either elder or deacon; no more than anything that may have stepped out of a clerical tailor's window, as regards dress, will do for a minister. God wants ability; "*able* men, such as fear God, men of truth, and men who hate covetousness." If my time were not gone, I should have rung the changes on that last word. Ah, I think Jethro had surely something of a divine inspiration in him when he went over those qualifications, and especially when he said, "*hating covetousness.*" Why is it you have right through the Bible, right down through the Old Testament, and all through the New, the servants of God when bidding good-bye to their work, and making ready to go; men like Samuel, men like Paul—you always have them saying, " I have coveted no man's gold, or silver, or apparel." You have them virtually washing their hands and standing before the people, and saying, "You called me to a spiritual office, and as the truth of God was in me, I was spiritual."

There might have been a duty of temporality in it, a handling of secular things; "I had to pass monies through my hands, and I saw openings where I could have made a gain of godliness; but my hands are clean; I have hated covetousness—the dry rot of everything green and bright and beautiful in Church or State." Men " who hate covetousness." Ah! perhaps—and with this I close—perhaps what is hindering the Church of Christ in all her branches, both in Dissent and in the Establishment, from getting the best men for her pulpits, the best men for all her offices, is just nothing so much as covetousness. Did I not read it as an open allegation the other day, from one who thinks himself a competent critic, that " the sons of our wealthier members in Dissent are not coming into the Church—into its ministry, for example—because the world offers a more tempting reward." And its ministry, by implication, is run upon by poor fellows who wish to get into the priest's office for a crust of bread! Let us see to it, especially I speak to those who are young and those who have the day before them, with all its honours and all its possibilities, let us see to it lest a spirit of covetousness, my brother, may be spoiling you; and you are counting your life unworthy of an office that would be an honour to you all your days, and a means of grace to yourself, and you don't know what good to the Church of Christ and to the world in which she is trying to testify, and to live for her Redeemer, and her Lord. We thank God that all through the ages His Church has had such men, and our prayer ought continually to be, and the prayer of all those who love Jerusalem, and love her prosperity, that the men indicated by Jethro, and such men as are described in the passages from the New Testament which I have read, may continually be found, and be found willing to consecrate themselves to Christ's special service in His Church, in our day even as in the best days of old.

Regent Square Pulpit.

JACOB'S CRISIS.

A Sermon

TO MIDDLE-AGED, PROSPEROUS MEN.

Delivered in Regent Square Church

BY THE

REV. JOHN McNEILL.

Genesis xxxii. 24-32.

"And Jacob was left alone." I am not going to enter into the controversy as to whether this somewhat late-dated event in Jacob's history is really the date of his conversion. I do not see that there is any great profit in it. For myself, I rather think that at Bethel he got a sight of things that never left him—that at Bethel he saw the Unseen and the Eternal with his own eyes; and although afterwards he did not greatly grow in grace and greatly grow in the knowledge of God, still his eyes never again altogether closed. But what I am sure that we are all agreed about is this, that if ever God's purposes for Jacob, and if ever God's purposes through Jacob's line were to be realized and carried forward with success, then this Jacob must be made a worthier channel through which these purposes were to work and flow.

I think, to bring this lesson home to myself and home to people, that this is somewhat the angle of incidence. Look at that lonely man there. Just try to think of him. Now he is not altogether a bad man. Sometimes we fall foul of him grievously, and we have no milder word for him than "swindler," "hypocrite," "artful dodger," and so on. Well, so he was. There was a great deal of clay in him. He was to a great extent of the earth, earthy. And yet he was not all clay. There were gleams of gold among the dirt and the rubbish. Why, see how he loved; and I have always a great hope of a man who can love. So has God. See the great, big, bursting heart that he had behind all his suppleness and craft and cunning! There burned in him that one pure, bright thing—he loved his Rachel with an intense love. See what it led him to! See what he underwent in order to secure his heart's desire! See him, tough and wiry and weather-beaten, as with splendid indignation he lifts his face into Laban's and virtually says: "For all these years the drought consumed me by day, and the frost consumed me by night. Whatever was torn I dealt with you as though I had not been your servant—as though I was accountable for it. Whatever went astray I made myself responsible for; and you know how you used me: rather you know how you abused me." All through there was in him a mixture; but that mixed condition was not to be allowed to last: it must not be allowed any further to continue. He is very much like ourselves, is he not? Sometimes we advertise sermons to young men: sometimes we advertise sermons to children. I do not think that I ever saw a sermon advertised to old men. But I am sure I never saw a sermon advertised to middle-aged men—for those who have been some twenty or thirty years in the din and hurly-burly of life. For those who, like Jacob, have been, in the main, getting on. By fair means or foul you have got on. You have not denied the faith. You have not become an infidel. You have not wholly yielded yourself to the world; neither have you wholly yielded yourself up, body and soul and spirit, on the altar of entire consecration, any more than Jacob. Ah! it has a thrilling, personal interest, I say, especially to middle-aged, to elderly, or to ageing, prosperous men.

Let us take a look at the lonely Jacob. See him there! All his company have gone. He has to meet his brother on the morrow; it has plunged him into a state of profound concern. He has sent forward a present to appease his brother's wrath. He expects that Esau is coming upon him; charging down upon him like the wolf on the fold; but he hopes that by the time he has broken through these presentations his wrath will be appeased. He hopes that he will have smothered Esau's wrath by flinging upon him such an abundance of the things that will please him, for he knows Esau as well as if he lived with him. He had walked round about Esau, and took his measurement long ago; and he has a shrewd idea that these presents will tell upon Esau if anything will. Here we have him sitting quietly alone. They have all gone across the brook, and he is just going after them when he sits down quietly and thinks, as I wish you, my middle-aged friend, and myself, and as I wish us all to sit down quietly and think. Let memory bring out of past years all that past years contain. And is not this the state of the case with a good many of us? Let us talk to our soul; let us commune in the loneliness and the solitude of a time like this, with all London there, so to speak, across the brook on the other side of the Sunday, and ourselves upon this lonely, solitary side.

Let us commune with our own own hearts and see how we stand in the sight of God. And is not this the case—that you and I are bound to say, " Well, now, undoubtedly I have got on, and I have kept up a fair character and credit and reputation among men. I am known as being sagacious and astute down in the city. I am not known as a thorough-paced blackguard, as some are down there. No; I have not flung away the faith; I have not made shipwreck of a good conscience. The most that men can say of me is that I am pretty near; and that you need to rise early to be up before me, and you need to trim your sails well, if you are to get to windward of me. But the trouble with me is this. I often wonder—you say, as I think Jacob would be wondering that night—I wonder now *how I look before God;* how do I stand before Him? This near approach of my brother Esau brings vividly before me the last twenty years, which certainly have been a strange twenty years. I believe I know God. I hope—I hope there is a something working in me, and that all this shepherding, and all this love, and all this lust,"—for the bottom of all polygamy is lust—" I hope that all these things have not drowned, and have not quenched the something in me that throbs and pulses and trembles away up to the God of my fathers. I do believe—and yet with it all there is such an amount of dirt about the mainspring—I am so clogged and hampered that I wonder how I look before God. I know how to pray, and I have prayed—yes; and God has heard me in spite of all my badness and my slipperiness, and I am as slippery as an eel, and I can go round about most men. There are not many men in Padan-aram who can beat Laban, but I have beaten him at his own game every time. I wonder how I look before God?" And, maybe,

Jacob was getting to be in danger, the danger of ourselves; and to think that God was something like him. You remember how God broke out, "Thou thoughtest that I was altogether such an one as thyself. Thou thoughtest that My notions of morality worked on as easy a sliding scale as your own, now stringent when it pays to be stringent; and again loose, and soft, and buttery and slack, when it pays to be slack! and to ride, so to speak, with a long, long length of cable between you and the anchor. Thou thoughtest that I was very much like you, for the fact remains, that you have got on at this kind of double game, half for Me and half for the world, and all the time for yourself, and all the time conscious that, in the main, the weapons of your warfare are not spiritual but carnal." Now, to-day, middle-aged and elderly brothers look clearly with daylight sincerity at yourselves, as I set you alone, before you dare to step across the stream into the Monday. You and I are, like Jacob, I believe, on the verge of eternal destruction; but God, in His great love and mercy, has gently brought us away to the quiet time of solitude on the Sabbath day, before we cross the stream and go back into the world, where perhaps we shall fatally give the loose to the worst side that is in us. God has met us to-day, *and now brother is the crisis of your soul.* Out of these doors, if God can help it, you are not to go, the shifty, tricky, subtle, half-and-half, almost contemptible creature you came in, and because He loves you, and because He knows you through and through, and because He has set His love upon you, and wants to redeem you, and the time is short, therefore He comes upon us to-day as He came upon Jacob, with a noiseless tread, and with a long stride, and He has us in His grip before we know it. You did not think, some of you, that you were to be gripped after this fashion this morning. You came into the church praying for comfort. You came in praying for comfort, and praying for soothing. It is not comfort you need, it is not soothing you need. It is the most awful through-putting that ever a man got in his life that you need. You need simply to be turned upside down and outside in, for at this rate of it you will never be made meet for the inheritance of the saints in light—never in all time—never.

I have no doubt that sitting there by the brook, sitting there with the brawling Jabbok wrestling its way through the gully on to the river, and the night winds moaning round about him, and the fear of his brother still nearer to him than the winds, surrounding his soul with its chill, Jacob was inclined to pray to God for comfort: "O, God! comfort me. O, God! help me. O, God! be good to me, O, my Father! kiss me, and put Thy arms round about me." And God did, but not to kiss him, at least not at first—not to kiss him, but to crush him, to take the Jacob in him, and simply pulverize it once for all.

I do not know how it stands with you, but I dare to say that for you, brother, this is a word in season. This is a word for most of us. Again I say, I speak in God's name to ageing, successful men who make, and have made for years, an open Christian profession. "Jacob was left alone, and there wrestled with him a man until break of the day." I can see him in the gloom sitting there, and he is thinking and fearing; he is just rising between hope and fear—rising to go over the brook and into the land of Canaan—"when suddenly one rises before him, and before he knows where he is, he is wrestling in the darkness as though for life."

It is Jacob in the crisis of his life—Jacob met along his own line, Jacob being compelled at last, singly and alone, to come face to face with that unseen, invisible One, who all through has been with him, sometimes checking him, sometimes forwarding him, sometimes taking the cup of his love, as when he thought that he was going to get Rachel, and dashing it down when he finds that he gets Leah, and yet never leaving him alone—never just making him able to say, "God is against me," but always rather making him inclined to say, "Bad and worthless as I am, God is still for me. Well, am I not good enough? And yet I know in my own conscience that I am indeed very far back." Jacob is at last brought to an end of that slipperiness and of that duplicity, and in these grips, in the silent watches of the night, compelled to come to the end, the very end, of that lubricity that was in him.

Now, my brethren, that has to come, and the sooner the better for some of us here. God is not such an one as ourselves. God does not look with approval on the tricks of trade by which we have won. God hates our sin with infinite loathing, and unless we gain the victory we are undone. Jacob's God is this kind of being: without holiness thou shalt never see Him. Hear it, O city man; none of this stuff; half dirt, half clean. Without holiness no seed of us shall ever see His face. He that doeth righteousness is righteous. No amount of justification without the deeds of the law, no amount of singing "Rock of ages cleft for me," will do if in it, and through it the strand and fibre of eternal righteousness is not being worked in. Righteousness in thought and word and deed, though the heavens fall. Righteousness!

Jacob was a man who, if you had left him, would have lived to the age of Methuselah without being a bit farther forward. Do you not know somebody vastly like him? He might have lived to the age of Methuselah, and he would just have been on the same beat—sometimes wonderfully spiritual, as we all can be on a Communion Sunday when there is a fine atmosphere round about our souls; and then away back again, back, back into the puddle before Monday night, and never getting much out of it. Now that was not to do for Jacob, and it is not to do for us. The more I study this subject in the light of all that Jacob was, and in the light of that wonderful twenty years, the more I see that in deed and in truth it is, more than words can tell, the awful crisis of his history. He is not to come out of this the same man he went in.

"And there wrestled with him a man, until the breaking of the day." There is a scene—Jacob wrestling. Oh, if there is one thing that Jacob is good at it is wrestling. We have got romantic notions about shepherds—the shepherds piping while their sheep are peacefully feeding. We remember romantic pastoral pictures that we have seen about shepherds dancing and piping on oaten straws. It is all wrong, or to a great extent wrong. You are never to think of this Jacob as a weakling—not even as a weakling physically. He was not a weakling physically, any more than was his brother Esau. He was a strong man, but his strength lay not in bigness of bulk. His strength lay in wiriness and suppleness. He is the man to make a wrestler, a man with lung and breath, sound in wind, a man with a long arm that had a deadly clutch in it—a man whose limbs always seem to land him on his feet no matter how he twists, or how he may be twisted, and that is the thing that Jacob is good at, both mentally and physically. I hear the two of them as through the night

Jacob pants, and with side, and hip, and heel he puts in every trick he knows, and tries to grass his adversary. It was a real contact and conflict. It was no dream and no vision of the night; and, as any fellow here knows, who ever tried it, there is nothing that so engages every lith and limb in you as wrestling. To wrestle, you have to have eyes, so to speak all over your body. You need to know how your antagonist is gripping you in weak places behind, you need to know where you can grip him where you do not see him. You have to put your eyes into your hands. Wrestling is mental as well as physical. No stupid, muddle-headed dolt ever made a wrestler yet—not he. And Jacob is good at it, and Jacob is being taken upon his own ground and beaten there: wiry, sagacious, crafty, cunning, now pretending to yield, and again springing like a cat; and yet all in vain; tugging, and straining, and making nothing of it, and growing desperate. "Who can this be? Not Esau. At first I thought that it was Esau. It is not Esau. I never met a man who could stand as this man is standing."

And Jacob does not give in. He grows more restless, and cunning, and impetuous, until at last *The Man* sees that—as I was almost going to put it—by fair play he is not to win. The man sees that he will not prevail against him. So he puts in and puts on what is more than mortal, and what is more than human. This unknown, this invisible Man puts on or falls back upon Divine resources. He touches him in the sinew, the hollow of his thigh; "and the hollow of Jacob's thigh was out of joint, as he wrestled with him." When that takes place wrestling is done. When the limb begins to shrink wrestling is over. You can do no more then. That strong iron sinew collapses, shrivels, and the contest is over, one would say. No, no. It grows more wonderful than ever now. Out of defeat there comes a greater and a nobler victory. The man said, "Let me go for the day breaketh." And Jacob said. "I will not let thee go except thou bless me. And he said unto him, What is thy name? and he answered, Jacob. Then said the man, Thy name shall be called no more Jacob, but Israel, for as a prince hast thou power with God and with men, and hast prevailed."

There, they are clinging now. No more wrestling. Nothing to do but just to hold on and pant. As we find it in Hosea: "He wept and made supplication." This man, strong in body, and in sinew, and in brain, and nerve — this strong man has come to an end of his tricks and of his cunning. It has been the very explanation of his life ever since he was born. Have we come to that? That crisis wears with you and me to the same point to which it wore with Jacob. Some of us for long years have just been like Jacob, as I have described—neither lost nor won, neither altogether good nor altogether bad, and yet undoubtedly on the whole the smile of God seems to have been over us, and the blessing of God has attended us and all that we have done. But He comes to us to-day, and He comes into grips with us, and He tells us calmly, and plainly, and firmly, that we cannot go one step farther into the promised land as we are—no farther road or progress in this direction. God breaks out upon us, not in judgment, but in mercy, but His mercy to-day has a grip in it that we might feel in every fibre of our soul within us. "Child of Mine," He says kindly yet firmly, as He grips us by the strong muscle and nerve which has been our stay, "Child of Mine, this has to come to an end here and now. No more trusting to yourself, no more doing of things by your own skill and your own energy; no more meeting worldly craft with craft, 'cuteness with 'cuteness, and dodge with dodge; but from to-day and forward, Jacob, I am coming to untwist you, and it is a hard business—to take the knots out of you and to make you as plain, and open, and guileless, and sincere as you ought to be." Just think of it. He took Jacob the veteran, Jacob with all his cleverness, Jacob with all his craft, to make Jacob as plain and open as the book-leaf. That is what God's grace had to do with him. That is what God's grace has to do with some of us, and for twenty years, it may be, it has striven in vain. It has to be done. When, when, in God's name, is the untwisting to come, my brother? He is asking us to-day as He asked Jacob, "What is thy name?" For when God asks, "What is thy name?" He means, "What is it that lies behind the name, that is really thee?" And Jacob had grace and honesty at last to own up and say, "Oh, unknown wrestler! my name is Trick and Quirk and Cunning. My name is Jacob. My name is Craft, my name is Cunning." He owned up at last: "I am of the earth, earthy. My name is Jacob—Supplanter."

My brother, what is your name? After bearing a Christian profession; after, it may be, being an office-bearer in God's house for twenty or forty years, the great God with whom we have to do comes in mercy to-day simply because perhaps we are soon to get to heaven, and we need a lot to make us ready; we need a lot yet to make us ready. God has to come to you this morning with my lips, and says: "What is thy name?" If you tell the truth you will say: "My name is Jacob." You will say, "My name is Money, my name is Cent Per Cent, my name is Profit—my very name is that, O God. My name is

Moderation in Religion. O God, dost Thou ask my name? My name is Lust. Right down at bottom that wriggling thing is me. My name is Lust, Uncleanness, Vileness. I have kept it in; I have veneered it over; but I admit to-day that that is me. This is the one thing in me. It is my name." "What is thy name? What is at bottom in us, that is us? What is it?" How few of us can say honestly, "My name, O God, is Religion; my name is Settled Principle; my name is Candour, Openness, Honesty, Sincerity. My name is Singleness of Heart, Childlike Simplicity." What is our name? I cannot give all the names. It is not the actual Johns and Roberts that were named over us here in baptism.

Jacob's name was a name of significance; and God gives us all a significant name, and He is asking us to-day, "What is your name? What is it?" Oh, let us be honest and tell Him. I know mine. You could stand up in this church, and in one sentence could tell this meeting what is your prevailing characteristic. Young girl, young woman, you can stand up before God and say, "My name is Frivolity. That is my prevailing characteristic. I come to church on Sunday, but the thing that engrosses and consumes me is a ball and a dance and the theatre. That is my name. That sets my whole soul abounding and a-pulsing." With some of us, our whole creed is just a determination not to yield ourselves utterly unto God, but to keep on the safe side. What is your name? Ananias is the name for some, and Sapphira is the true name for others. It was not a nice name. It may be that Jacob's swarthy cheek got a little swarthier even in the darkness, as he said, "Supplanter is my name. I am a wrestler, I depend on cunning, I call on God even occasionally, to help my cunning. I use religion for a cloak for my cunning." My name, in Thy sight, and with shame I confess it, my name is Double-tongue, or Facing-both-ways.

And the Man said, "Thy name shall be no more Jacob, but Israel (prince of God), for as a prince hast thou power with God and with men, and thou hast prevailed." The blessing came when the wrestling was over, and when the clinging came; and that is what God means, but He means all that—to come down upon us, and to stand over us, and to set Himself against us, and to seem to be the worst enemy we have—an enemy who springs upon us in the darkness, and makes our face to grow white with fear. If He puts out all His strength He could hurl us shrieking into the outer darkness from where we sit. But it is not meant for that. It is meant at last to bring us to understand Him, and to cling to Him, and to give up all duplicity, and all deceit, and all dissimulation, and all double-mindedness, both before God and men, all playing fast and loose with our own conscience, and with what we know to be right—to bring all that to an end, and with the arms of our faith round about Him, just to cling, and cling, and cling. Then we win. Then we have won against ourselves. Then also have we won with God. Jacob ceased to strive, and was broken with tears. Think of Jacob crying. Think of some before me to-day crying before God. My brother, when did you ever shed the tear before God? When did you ever shed the tear before God alone, simply because you are the wretched bundle of contradictions that you are?

When have we done it? When have we given to God these gracious drops and these gracious evidences that the fountains of the great deep at last are being broken up within us, that the old self is dying, and the new man is rising in his God-given power and beauty? Jacob weeping; Jacob clinging; Jacob pleading—he who before had been used to get at things in a far different fashion. Aye, that has to come too, and with some of us the very time of life to which we have come makes it an awful problem, whether it is ever to arrive. Aye, it has got to be soon, or it will never be with some of us. You will not for ever go on in this condition. You are not so balanced as you congratulate yourself that you are. You are far more biassed in one way than the world and the devil and your own deceitful heart are allowing you to think. When is the end to come? The true secret of spiritual success lies in that name that was given him in place of the old one: Israel in place of Jacob. The true secret of all want of success in the building up of character, and in the building up of a truly prosperous life, lies in the name "Jacob," and in the foul, ugly composite behind the name. And, contrariwise, the secret of all freshness, beauty, virility, and power in Christian character and life lies in this new name, Israel—strong with God and strong with men.

And this honour have all God's Israel. This is the stamp upon us. This is the *sine quâ non*. If we have not got this, then no wonder that we are the useless creatures we are. If we have not got this, no wonder that the world looks upon us and scarcely knows what to call us—whether hypocrite or true man. Jacob is not perfect yet. On this side of eternity we shall never be perfect. There is a limp in him where there never was a limp before. The sons of men never saw Jacob limp. Jacob with a limp—that is a new thing in the world. That strong, supple, lithe man, Jacob, limping! Oh, my brother, may it be seen to-day and from to day and forward. I would like to meet you down the town with your head a little lower than usual. It would be a good sign—Jacob, with a bowed head, and with a softened look in his eye. That would look heavenly, believe me. It has not been there. That holy light has not been the light of your countenance in past years. It has been a mingled light, a strange, shifting light, about which one never can tell whether it is going to brighten or going to fade away into the dulness of utter worldliness, and selfishness, and unspirituality. May God grant that from to-day and forward the victory may come. May we go out of these doors with the false strength utterly beaten, with our eyes open, and with the chastened look upon our faces of men and women who have gone through something, and who have been severely handled. Less than that would not have been kind to us. " Search me, O God, and know my heart; try me and know my thoughts, and see if there be any wicked way in me, and lead me in the way everlasting." That is Peniel set to music: " Lead me in the way everlasting."

We are sitting here and we are troubling ourselves about meeting somebody to-morrow, and about how we shall be able to meet to-morrow, and how we shall be able to cut and contrive against the morrow. Before to-morrow has come to-day has come, and God with it, and we have to meet Him. Let us meet God, and let us get our hearts and our lives straightened and put right. Then we shall be able to meet all the morrows that are coming. God is with us, and this great honour may come to us to-day. We might go out of that door princes with God, having power with Him and with our fellow-men. Oh, that we might break out to-day into the true dignity, and power, and privilege of spiritual manhood. You remember Wesley's hymn. It sums all up—sums up all the application of it. He says :

> " Come, O Thou Traveller unknown,
>   Whom still I hold, but cannot see :
> My company before is gone,
>   And I am left alone with Thee :
> With Thee all night I mean to stay
> And wrestle till the break of day.
>
> " I need not tell Thee who I am ;
>   My misery and sin declare ;
> Thyself hast called me by my name—
>   Look on Thy hands, and read it there.
> But who, I ask Thee—who art Thou ?
> Tell me Thy name, and tell me now.
>
> " In vain Thou strugglest to get free—
>   I never will unloose my hold !
> Art Thou the Man that died for me ?
>   The secret of Thy love unfold :
> Wrestling, I will not let Thee go
> Till I Thy name, Thy nature know !
>
> " My prayer hath power with God : the grace
>   Unspeakable I now receive,
> Through faith I see Thee face to face ;
>   I see Thee face to face, and live !
> In vain I have not wept and strove :
> Thy nature and Thy name is Love.
>
> " Lame as I am, I take the prey ;
>   Hell, earth, and sin, with ease o'ercome ;
> I leap for joy, pursue my way,
>   And, as a bounding hart, fly home,
> Through all eternity to prove
> Thy nature and Thy name is Love."

May God add His blessing to His Word ! " When I am weak, then am I strong."

Regent Square Pulpit.

FEAR NOT.

A Sermon

Delivered in Regent Square Church, on Sunday Morning, February 9th, 1890.

BY THE

REV. JOHN McNEILL.

"Then spake the Lord to Paul in the night by a vision, Be not afraid, but speak, and hold not thy peace : for I am with thee, and no man shall set on thee to hurt thee : for I have much people in this city."—
Acts xviii. 9, 10.

This was said to Paul in Corinth, and I take it up to-day to encourage all who are living and working for the Lord Jesus Christ here in London. I mention our own city specially, but what applies here will apply anywhere and everywhere. If it is difficult, humanly speaking, to push the Gospel in London, so was it in Corinth, and *vice versâ;* if it was difficult to have any real visible success in Corinth, so is it here. When we think of the two cities (and the more we compare them, the more we see they are, from a Christian worker's point of view, very much alike) is there a multitude here?—there was the same there, though not just such a multitude. Are there all sorts of people here, drawn from all parts of the earth?—so was it there. From its very position as a seaport, Corinth seemed to invite the trade and the traders alike of the eastern and western world. Was there luxury in Corinth — that enervating luxury which always accompanies too much wealth and

No. 14.

selfishness? So is there here. Was Corinth in a sense refined? Had it music and art and philosophy?—so also has London. Were there extremes of wealth and poverty? —so we, also, have them here. Was there a kind of semi-interest in religion there?—there also is here. Was there at the same time a hard, polished bone of cold indifference? —so also is there here. Was there also a persecuting spirit against the real progress of the cause and kingdom of the despised Nazarene?—so also is there here; so also is there everywhere. In fact, as a modern authority has said, "Corinth was the Vanity Fair of the Roman Empire; Corinth was the Rome and Paris in one of the century immediately after Christ." So you see we have an interest, a very close interest, in this matter. You think of Paul trying to preach the Gospel in that city, and it becomes easy to get lessons of help and stimulus for those who are trying to make their life, indoors and out of doors, in the midst of this Vanity Fair, a living epistle, a perpetual testimony, against its worldliness, its pomp, its lying vanity, its gilded sin, its grossness; and in favour of the salvation of our Lord and Saviour Jesus Christ.

Now this "open vision" speaks to us about three things, and we shall notice them briefly in the order in which they come here. First of all, a word or two comes to us from the vision about the worker, Paul; then we have something to say briefly about the worker's Master; and lastly, a word about the worker's work, from the Master's plan and point of view. According to the logic of Grace, we should begin with the Master, from whom come both the worker and the work; but we shall simply follow the order of the narrative.

Now, first of all, the worker. The worker was Paul, and Paul at a time of sore discouragement and depression. The best of men are but men at the best. We have plenty of examples all through Scripture, and plenty of examples in the continued narrative of the ongoing of Christ's cause after the record of Scripture has closed, of the fact that the strongest of men are men who know what shaking and sinking and fearing are, now and then, at any rate. The strongest of men, apart from a firm faith in the Lord God, a firm faith in Jesus Christ, a clear vision of Himself, are as weak as the weakest. They lie down even like Elijah of old, and are tempted to say, " I am spending myself in vain ; it is enough : I am not better than my fathers ; I wish I were dead."

So it is suggested to us that Paul here, as a worker for the Lord, is oppressed, discouraged, feeling overwhelmed and defeated. Now if any working Christian here, especially any Christian minister, if any real live worker for God, who is pushing the Gospel, putting his hands to the Gospel plough, feels weak and discouraged; if the opposition should appear stubborn and nearly triumphant ; and if we and our work should appear feckless, it might rally us a little to discover that no affliction has overtaken us but such as is common to men. This has been felt ever since men set themselves to be the servants of God, preachers of righteousness by lip and by life, ordained or unordained, in the face of the world's prevailing and manifold iniquity.

" Then spake the Lord, Be not afraid." Paul was spoken to in the vision as being one who was afraid. The vision brings this also to us : that our great Lord and Master knows us and sees us, just then and there, in the midst of all our weakness and discouragement, when we are lying, so to speak, upon our bed, and it is midnight as regards the time of day, and as to the prospect of our work. Then the Lord comes, and leans Himself down, and makes His first concern the individual worker. The Lord, my friend, the Lord knows you, the Lord sees you, especially *if you are weak and fainting;* if you are inclined to say as Paul might be saying, " I have spent my strength for nought and in vain ; I did not get on in Athens, it was an abortive attempt so far as I could see. Then I came here, and Jew and Gentile are against me again ; I think I will push on to the next town." So you are apt to take counsel with your fears, with the "fightings without and the fears within"—as Paul himself said when he wrote afterwards to the Corinthians and referred to this very time. "I was going to take up my bag," I can imagine him saying—but he had not got a bag—"I was going to pack up in a handkerchief, and go on to the next town, had it not been that the Lord Himself came to me with a special revelation and made me somewhat ashamed *of myself*, and more than ever strengthened and encouraged *in Him*."

We need that view of the Lord. He is not simply concerned with the whole mass and the whole movement of the spiritual campaign, like some great general or commander-in-chief who cannot be concerned with the individual soldier. The Lord is unlike that. He is concerned in the whole; the scope of the whole is before His mind from all eternity, and He will partly rebuke us and say, "Don't you take this campaign out of My hands into your thin, cold fingers: this is Mine not yours, the plan is Mine, and the power is Mine, and the glory is Mine."

But at the same time He comes and says, "I see every man who is tugging and pulling and fighting, and feeling himself discouraged." And this word which came to Paul have all God's saints; especially those of us who in great cities are seeking to stand up for Him, and are feeling a tremendous temptation either to give it up or to turn down our light so that the battle may slack a little round about us and within us.

I do not know if you have noticed it, but my former life has made me familiar with this. Have you noticed how the engine-driver in charge of a train, when he stops at a station, pays hardly any attention to the traffic at the station, no attention to who is getting into the train, or who is coming out—whether Lord So-and-so is embarking or disembarking; he leaves that to others? But whenever the train stops, he is out with the lubricator—that is the *grand* name for it!—with the little oil-flask, lifting the little brass cover and pouring in a few drops in one place, and then in another place, to cool and prevent friction, and to make everything sweet and easy in its working. Then on he goes, and if you went with him, you would see that at the next station he does exactly the same thing. Whether the platform traffic is heavy or light is simply nothing to him, his whole concern is his engine, to keep it sweet, to have all the bearings working smoothly, to prevent over-heating, for friction means breakdown, and breakdown may mean disaster.

So with Christ, my brother. Shall I call you the engine pulling and tugging away at some Church in a backward district or in an awfully godless town? My sister, are you an engine in your own way, pulling and tugging away at some Bible-class or some Sabbath-school, or tract-distribution in some wretched slum? You have hooked on to it, and do not mean to give it up; but you feel as if the wheels were barely turning, and that you are making nothing of it. Think of this: *the Lord looks after the engine*—especially after the engine. What would you think of the engine-driver who came out at every station and sauntered away down the platform, and busied himself with everybody coming in and going out, and who gossiped with people? "Who is that, and who is the other?" and so on. You know what the end would be; that train would probably not get to its destination. There must be full and close attention, and continual oiling of everything. Don't imagine, then, that our Lord Jesus Christ will neglect us. Now, think of it to-day; here He comes with oil, this comfort, and He is pouring it on to your heated, overheated spirit;—" Comfort ye, comfort ye My people, saith your God; speak ye comforably"—which means literally, speak to the heart of Jerusalem. So with us. Are we afraid, are we slowing down? Let Christ come, let Him speak to you, let Him feel you pulse, let Him take you by the hand, let Him look straight into all the turmoil, confusion, and panic that have already begun in your soul, for you will be of no use to Him if you go out in that condition; you will very likely take counsel with your fears and begin to devise plans.

Oh! may we be saved from that when we are in a depressed condition! You will find, then, that all your devisings look in the direction of the rear; there is a retreat in them, although we may blow the trumpet as if making a charge. We can't put off our Master. He sees that the heart is going back from the front, stepping back to get it easier and slacker, and, it may be, covering our retreat under prodigiously heavy artillery. We may never speak so loud as then, almost in a tone of bounce and swagger; but the Lord sees that we are going back. Take care; let Him come to you to-day when you are lying in darkness and confusion, and when London seems to have bowled you over. May the Lord come to every discouraged Paul, to every discouraged worker, to every light that is beginning to burn low and dim; let this word, "Be not afraid, I am with thee," trim the wick, put in more oil, and bring up the light to a clear and steady blaze!

The Lord spake to Paul in the night by a vision, "Be not afraid, but speak, and hold not thy peace." Notice, further, that the Lord's comfort just comes straight to the sore place. He never wastes His remedies; He never makes mistakes, as the best doctors occasionally do; He never applies the plaister to the *whole* skin, but just puts it broad and warm on the place that needs to be strengthened and toned up. Now, Paul's greatest failing and fear, no doubt— the narrative suggests it—was this, "It's no use my preaching here, there are these cultured Greeks here. To the Greeks this Gospel of mine is simply foolishness. Then those fanatical countrymen of mine, the Jews, I simply madden them whenever I preach about Christ who was crucified as the long-promised and glorious Messiah. This maddens them, and brings my bodily life into danger, so I had better stop speaking: I am speaking to the wind. To the Greeks, on the one hand, it is like the idle wind; and to the Jews, on the other, it is like the red rag to the bull. Ought not reason and sense to tell me that I had better stop; that as I left Athens, so I must leave Corinth." And the Lord speaks straight to the point: His Word goes straight to the weakness, just as medicine goes straight to the disease; His arm undergirds you just where you need undergirding. Some one has spoken about certain people who spend their lives—and it is true—coming to the help of the strong. They are always with the multitude, and always on well-filled platforms, and always where the shouting is going on, where, in fact, they are not needed. Our Lord spends the greater part of His time in coming to the help of the helpless, in being a Friend to the friendless, in being a Companion to the solitary.

This is His gracious work ever since He began to work among the sons of men. He goes straight to what is wrong, and He says to Paul, " Be not afraid "—pointing to the fact that he was afraid—" but speak, and hold not thy peace—" pointing to the fact that fear was beginning to muzzle his mouth, that fear was beginning to dry up the spoken testimony, the preaching of the Gospel of the Lord Jesus Christ. The word here used is worth noticing, for there is a lesson in it. The Lord might have used some more dignified and technical expression for describing the preaching of the Gospel, but He did not. The word used— " speak," that is the Greek word—means sometimes in the old writers, " babble away." Wasn't that spoken to the point? The noun connected with the verb is the word for gossiping, or even talking nonsense. " Up you get, Paul, and babble away. In Athens, you remember, they called you ' spermologos,' which means a chattering sparrow, a seed-picker, a man talking a kind of rant, with the suggestion that it is not his own; it was picked up somewhere else, and we can't understand it. Babble away, Paul. Speak, *speak*, SPEAK to the Jews; it may be a stumbling-block to them, and to the Greek foolishness, but I will be with you, and to those who are saved the babbling will be the power of God and the wisdom of God." Now, is not that to a great extent what the age is saying to Paul to-day? " This is only babble." Well, let it be babble. *God bless the babblers!* What has been said of prayer is perfectly true of preaching. Preaching, like prayer, is

"The simplest form of speech that infant lips can try;"

It is also:

"The sublimest strains that reach the Majesty on high."

Talk, talk, talk away! of course always remembering what you are talking about. "I have put My words into thy mouth," said the Lord to Jeremiah when he was discouraged. And so He says to-day, "I have put My words into thy mouth; therefore let thy tongue wag *My words*. Go on, speak it out; don't devise anything new; don't try to make it finer. You remember that, writing afterwards to these Corinthians, Paul told them he had determined to keep this simple speech. Said he virtually "I rather refined the babble at Athens, I rather tried to speak to the Athenians in terms, you know, of Athenian eloquence: I never spoke such fine language in my life as I did at Athens. I began loftily, and showed those Athenians that I was a man of some culture as well as themselves. But when I came to speak of the resurrection they mocked me; and they left me and I left them. So when I came to Corinth I determined to know nothing among you save Jesus Christ and Him crucified. Not with enticing words of man's wisdom, lest the Gospel of Christ should be of none effect." We must, of course, as one as said, distinguish between the foolishness of preaching and foolish preaching. But we must take care that we let the Lord speak to us when we are depressed and discouraged, and when people turn from us, and when we have fallen on times when the old Gospel "won't do," when the spirit of the age demands something more scientific and philosophical. Speak! be not afraid! but speak; talk, talk, talk, go back to your work and speak; go back to your Bible-class and speak the word that God has put into your mouth, whether they will hear or whether they will forbear. Leave that! go back to your warehouses and companions; be not afraid; open your mouth, speak for thy

God. Are there not some here who have been lowering their testimony, who have been trying to file their tongues, and to take the rough edges off the Gospel, and to smoothe and trim it a bit? Yes; "Samson is a very strong, fine fellow, but he is a little rude and uncouth; and so we'll send Samson to the barber; it will greatly improve him to get his hair cut and to shave him." Not a bit! Samson thus is weak, and like any other man. And the grand old rugged Gospel, trimmed and lopped and polished, is weak; and, like all the philosophies that have gone before it, it will have its day and cease to be. Begin to philosophize it, and you spoil it. Keep it as Christ gave it: stand and speak. Again, I repeat, the Lord took the simplest word in the Greek language to represent the articulate speech of a human being. "Speak, and hold not thy peace." Don't be silent, cast out the dumb devil—don't you feel the devil's fingers, my brother preacher, as they come up round your throat to make an end of speaking in God's name? Oh, to-day there are a lot of us getting constricted; the devil has us by the windpipe! Unhand me, Satan!

Then the Lord gave him a word, this tired worker, this engine that was going to break down; He gave him a word about personal safety; he allayed his fears, don't you see, in every way? He said to him, "No man shall set on thee to hurt thee." Now, I don't say we are in bodily danger, but at any rate we get this that Paul got, and it will do us no harm; I trust it will do us good. He will carry us through; it is the old, old bargain he laid down, "Give yourself to Me, body, soul, and spirit, and I will go bail for you; I will give you a shelter; I will give you clothes; I will give you meat. You will not wax fat and kick on what I will give you perhaps. I will not bring abundance on you, but I will keep you, and I will cover you, and I will protect you, and you will be immortal till your work is done. Therefore, go on. Leave all the chances and the chapter of accidents to Me." Let us go on with the work for which we are here. "Be thou faithful unto death." Grasp again the sword that has fallen from your nerveless hand; go on and go forward; "I am with thee, and no man shall set on thee to hurt thee."

Eighteen months afterwards the Lord fulfils that promise, if you read the chapter. Eighteen months afterwards the Jews came with a rally. Paul's life was in danger, and they brought him before Gallio, you remember. And when Paul was about to open his mouth, the Lord so splendidly remembered his promise that He put His hand over Paul's mouth. Was it to our loss that there was a speech of Paul's that we have missed? When Paul was about to open his mouth to speak for his life, Gallio contemptuously said, "I will have nothing to do with your Jewish quibbles; out you go!" The imperiousness of old Rome, and her lofty contempt, saved the Apostle Paul. He didn't even need to say a word.

"I am with thee, and no man shall hurt thee." In the same chapter the word spoken is the word accomplished and fulfilled. I wish we could learn that to-day for our own persecutions and our own trials. They will do us no harm; let them come. Don't make any preparations; don't consult; don't be afraid. Let us give ourselves to Christ, Sabbath-days and and week-days, and He stands beside us and says, "Nothing shall hurt you, nothing shall harm you." This is said to the whole Church, as well as to the individual, "No weapon that is formed against thee shall prosper." The gun was never made that will carry the bullet to kill a Christian. The plan was never framed in hell that will hurt a hair of your head, my brother, my sister. "I am with thee, and no man shall hurt thee."

You get this away back in the Psalm-book. I have no doubt when the vision was past Paul did not go back to his sleep. He gathered himself out of his bed, I fancy, and got his Psalm-book, and started the 27th Psalm. I don't know what he was as a singer: he was grand as a preacher; but that Psalm would almost make anybody a singer.

> "The Lord's my light and saving health,
>   Who shall make me dismayed?
> My life's strength is the Lord, of whom,
>   Then, shall I be afraid?
> When as mine enemies and foes,
>   Most wicked persons all,
> To eat my flesh against me rose,
>   They stumbled and did fall.
> Against me though a host encamp,
>   My heart yet fearless is;
> Though war against me rise, I will
>   Be confident in this."

No fear, no fear; preserved miraculously, in God's hand, till our warfare is accomplished. He said, "I am *with thee.*" I wish we would look to the Master this morning: He is the vision of the vision, the very soul of the comfort that was laid to Paul's soul that night. "I am with thee, I am with thee." "Paul, you are looking at yourself; Paul, you are looking at these Corinthians, these gay, dissolute, loose livers; these wretched slaves, sunk in misery and brutality; these over-fed and evil-fed Corinthian ladies and gentlemen; these pleasure-lovers, these blaspheming Jews. Paul, Paul, look at Me! Paul, I am nearer to you than your fears. Look at Me; I am with thee." A kind of "Second Coming," that always comes in the darkness of the night when the Christian is discouraged, an advent continually coming before the last one and the great one, "Lo, I am with thee alway, even to the end of the world." Now, the great point about what was said to Paul was just this. There was nothing new in it. "I will be with thee; fear not." That is not new, is it? It was said centuries before, and Paul knew it. You will find these words in the Bible over and over again long before this God repeats Himself. God tells me what before He has said in a general way, but makes it close and quick and real and new and true to me, to *me*, to ME! Now, you need that. Half of us need that. There is a vast mass of Bible words known *in the mass*, but we need them in our own heart, and for our own lives. "I am with thee." The man I am looking at down there;—I would like to single you out as though Christ looked at you through my eyes, and speak this word into your very heart. Discouraged men and woman, lad or lass, " I am with thee!" How it changes things when some of these grand "fear nots" and " I ams" come home—home! When Doctor Fisher, the Bishop of Rochester, of an earlier date, was being led out from the Tower there to martyrdom, he suddenly caught a sight of the scaffold on which he was to be executed, and the sight of it a little unnerved and depressed him. He took his New Testament out of his pocket—his Greek Testament—and sent up a prayer: " O God, send me some particular word that will help me in this awful hour ; " and he opened the book. Now, he had seen this word often before, but it then became a personal vision, a personal revelation to him—these words, " This is life eternal to know Thee, the only true God, and Jesus Christ whom Thou hast sent." He had seen that five hundred times before ; but he closed his Testament now, saying, " Blessed be God, this will suffice for all eternity." It is a different thing you see when the " fear nots " and " I ams " *come home to you* when you are cowering on your bed, and dying a thousand deaths in fearing one. " Fear not, I am with thee." That is the Master ; that changes all : God is with me. The best of all is, " God is with us."

As a commander once said to his soldiers when they came to him and represented how great was the army that was coming against them and how few they were in number, he pulled himself up and said, " How many do you count me for ? " Another general was said to be worth a whole battalion. And who shall enumerate what God is worth? " I am with thee ; the arm that built the mountains, the arm that broke Rahab in pieces, and the dragon ; I—I am with thee. Hast thou not known, hast thou not heard, that the everlasting God, the Lord, the Creator of the ends of the earth is with thee ? " Oh, fainting Paul! He fainteth not, neither is weary, there is no searching of His understanding. " I am with thee." I wish we could lay hold of Him in this word. It will make London, with all its seven abominations, as safe as the New Jerusalem. " Fear not, for I am with thee." There is the ring of an anthem in it, if our ears could hear it.

And, last of all, see the Master's verdict on the work: I have much people in this city." I almost knew what was coming. You will always find through the Bible that while the Lord is ever saving and ever comforting Elijah, and David, and Peter, and Paul, and you, and me; while He is ever comforting His children when they are nervous and frightened, there is—may I say it with reverence—there is a dry smile on His face, as much as to say, " I know what you feel and I am come to help you; but are you not foolish, Paul? Paul, you are forgetting 'I have much people in this city.' If the work had been yours, Paul; if the plan had been yours; if the energy had been yours, that were another thing. But, Paul, this Gospel is Mine, and its inception and all its development are Mine from eternity and to eternity. I am its Alpha and Omega, its Beginning and its End. I weighed this Corinthian pigsty in the scales of My eternal purposes, and from all eternity I marked out My own in Corinth, and I will get them. Go out and look for them; call them in, for they are there. They will come; the mouth of the Lord hath spoken it, and the blood of the Lamb hath purchased it." " I have much people in this city." Now, what a word that is to discouraged workers—" Much people in this city." I believe that literally, at that time, there were more Christians there than Paul thought of, and I believe to-day, my brother and sister, thou faithful testifier and worker for God, I believe your influence and mine is far wider and far more effective than in our discouraged moments we are giving either God or ourselves credit for. No word can return to Him void; and He comes and says, " Paul you are working well, and the results are at least equal to the output: you are not doing a weak thing, Paul; this is a big thing, this is a grand concern. I have got one of the best grips here and now, that I have ever got on the paganism of this century." So He had. " I have much people in this city." Whatever department of social life you look at, if you look carefully through the Epistles to the Corinthians, you will find that there was a sample of Christ's saving grace there. If Paul might be discouraged, for example, as he looked at the business circles in Corinth—and there was a deal of business and a deal of gambling speculation in Corinthian business, the same as in our own; a world of fever and excitement in Corinth just like our own. And it seems as if the pure and holy and unselfish Gospel of Jesus Christ could never tell on city men and city magnates. What could the Gospel do in

Corinth? It went right clean smash into the midst of Corinthian worldliness and commercial activity, and laid hold of Erastus, the City Chamberlain, and held him out as a sample. It saved him—a man right in the thick of it. And if Paul should say, on the other hand, "But those Corinthian households, I cannot get into the families, Lord, and that is one of my discouragements"—you remember how the Lord rebuked him. "Ye know the household of Stephanas, the firstfruits unto God in Achaia." Yes, he got the families there, and we will get them, and the old Gospel will get *nations*—" The nations of them that are saved will yet walk in the light of it." It is the biggest, grandest thing that was ever heard of, the plan of salvation through the preached Redeemer. And if he would say again, " Lord, there are people here sunken in drunkenness and in lasciviousness, men steeped—and women, too—in all abominations," what could Christ's Gospel do for them? Listen, listen, how the Gospel told. Here were the kind of people all round about Paul (1 Cor. vi. 9). "Fornicators, idolaters, effeminate, abusers of themselves with mankind, thieves, covetous, drunkards, revilers, extortioners. *And such were some of you;* but ye are washed, but ye are sanctified, but ye are justified in the name of the Lord Jesus, and by the Spirit of our God." It was no vain word, " I have much people in this city." The Gospel told; and I rejoice to believe in it to day. Oh, brother, if you work in the West End among gilded sin, go back and "speak, speak, speak." "Christ has much people in the city." We know His heart well enough to know that if He comes near to London at all, He comes to do a big thing; there is a great powerful devil here, and Christ will yet fill a big corner of heaven with saints, holy men and women out of London, out of the West End and out of the East End, and from the north, and south, and centre; He will have them from everywhere, everywhere. " I have much people in this city." And then I think how it must have encouraged Paul, alone there and apt to be discouraged, this look of things from the Master's point of view. This is the doctrine of election in its practical shape. I do not want to preach election controversially, but I may preach encouragingly to Christian workers. It referred not only to the present results of Paul's work, but I believe to what was to be. " I have people here as yet dead in sin, living in profligacy, but you have simply to go and preach." Is not that a great encouragement? I stand here to-day and do not know you, but I know my Master's plan and purpose, and know that He could not look at a gathering like this; I cannot without wishing to God that you in the gallery and you down here—I cannot look at you without wishing that you were washed, that you were sanctified, that you were justified; and shall the man, shall the servant be greater than the master? I know that when Christ looks at an audience like this, He whispers in my ear, " I will get Mine own, oh preacher, out of this company. Call them out; they are sitting there, hard, cold, and far gone; but speak, speak My words—call them." And I call you to believe on the Lord Jesus Christ. In His great name I command you this Sabbath morning. Trust Him, give Him your heart, give Him your sins, give Him your all, just as you are and where you are; for from all eternity He purposed this Sabbath morning, by my word, to call His own unto Him out of this company; and if any man says, " But am I His own ? " the proof is, accept the call, believe in Christ, give Him your life, yield to His voice by my lips in the Gospel to-day.

I like this election plan; it does not say that all will be saved—that is universalism, it is simply wind; all evidently are not being saved, but this is the old way of putting it. Well, it is not so windy and does not make so large a show as other ways of putting it; but it infallibly says that somebody will come, and that is what I want. I want no big talk and no gas about all coming back to the Father's bosom and so on; I like the old election predestination Gospel because it secures that *somebody will come, i.e.,* the Gospel will not be preached in vain. " I have much people—not all—but I have much people in the city; some of them already quickened, others of them marked out to be quickened. Go on and preach the Gospel, and My own shall come to Me."

I remember what happened to me when I was a lad and my bones were very young and green. On one cold, dark, winter's night when the snow lay heavy on the ground, it had been coming down for nearly a week, and there had been frost, but a thaw had come. You know what that means on a country road. I was sent on a message of life and death for the doctor. We had no doctor in our village, and the nearest place was a good many miles away. I started off at too dashing a pace; my muscles soon demonstrated this to me. There was no purchase or grip for your foot, as soon as you put it down it slipped away, and, if I may use an old familiar Irishism, for every step forward you took two backward. More than once I felt that awful temptation to fall asleep, but I staggered on, and struggled on, slipping, sliding, and tumbling—but on, on, with every bone in my body and every muscle proclaiming itself, and a weariness that no tongue can describe. And I shall never forget when I came trembling, floundering, and plunging, and at last my foot struck the plain stones at the far end of the town I was making for. The pavement there, of course, was swept, and I suddenly plunged through the toll-bar, and my feet struck good hard ground; it shot the sense of firmness and grip through my whole frame. I remember it yet:—the grip of the hard solid road beneath my feet. No more pushing, forcing, and struggling. So with Paul. He was floundering in Corinth. He seemed to be slipping, sinking back; and the more he tried to push himself forward, the more tired and weary he became. Then, suddenly, Christ put beneath him the Bed-rock of the Eternal Purpose. His heel grated on it; and the strength of it shot through him, body and soul and spirit. Let others preach the Gospel as they please; I will not be controversial, if I can help it, but this is my plan: I stand on the Rock of the Eternal Purpose. As a fisher of men I stand on this Rock in the great Stream; and, standing there, I cast my "invitations" all around, sure of it that by an eternal decree, out of those dark waters *something will rise* to my rod most certainly. "I have much people in this city," and all that we have to do is to go out and call them in.

Don't go out to preach election. But, grounded on that, preach the Gospel to every creature. And the Lord will look after the rest. His own will come to Him. And, as one has said, if you should happen to save anybody who wasn't "chosen in Christ before the world began," Christ will forgive you! Now, let us away to a work in which failure is impossible, and discouragement should be unknown. The Lord bless His Word. Amen.

HENDERSON & SPALDING, Printers, 1, 3 and 5, Marylebone Lane, London, W.

Regent Square Pulpit.

THE THREE CROSSES.

A Sermon

DELIVERED IN REGENT SQUARE CHURCH,

BY THE

REV. JOHN McNEILL.

Luke xxiii. 23-39.

We are hampered by an embarrassment of riches when we come to the 23rd of Luke; we scarcely know where to begin, or where to end. And even when we descend on this particular passage, there is so much, not only in connection with the three crosses, and with each one, but there is so much in those who are gathered round the crosses, that it is difficult to keep the eye from wandering, and to settle it steadily for a little on one particular place and aspect of teaching. Two words, however, two words of mighty meaning, will focus for us the lights (and shades) of this solemn scene. Guilt and Grace, Sin and Salvation, and each at its height—these are the terms, the thoughts, that shape themselves most vividly before our minds. These are the bright and the black bands, may we say, in this "spectrum analysis." "By one man sin entered into the world, and death by sin." It is a scene of death three times repeated; and therefore the power and dominion, the doom and gloom of sin receive a threefold emphasis. Christ, the Grace of God, as we may well call Him, on the Central Cross, *dying unto sin*, as the Scripture says; or *for* sin, in the true, real, substitutionary sense. On one side of Him a man *dying in sin*—cold, hard, twice dead, with all such sensibilities as repentance and faith utterly plucked out by the roots. On the other hand, again, a man—a sinner, but *dying in faith*, in hope, in expectation!

Now let us look for a little at these three crosses, and try to get something out of each. Let us take, first of all, he who is mentioned first: "One of the malefactors which were hanged railed on Christ, saying, If Thou be Christ, save Thyself and us." Here, in this awful scene let us expect to see everything in connection with sin and death, with grace and salvation, made most wonderfully vivid, quick, and powerful. And surely we see in this man the power of sin in its most awful aspect. What is sin? I think the Catechism, on which a number of us were fed, gives the best answer. That old teaching of ours always lands sin up close against the very throne of God and the very person of God Himself. It makes sin to be " Any want of conformity unto, transgression of, the Law of God." "Against Thee, Thee only, have I sinned." What is a sinner? A sinner, if I might use an illustration which has some freshness to-day, is a poor, puny wretch of a creature, steeped in ignorance and error; debauched, infatuated, and intoxicated; an incarnation of all ideas dark and devilish—a little insignificant wretch of a creature whom God could crush into nothing in a moment, whom God could have obliterated the first moment that his infatuation possessed him, but whom, strange to say, in His inscrutable grace and mercy, He permits to live! This wretched little creature goes and tries to explode his own little parcel of dynamite against the very throne of God! As you have it in Exodus xvii. 16 (margin)—A hand lifted against the thrones of Jehovah! That is what sin is; let that be an illustration of the sinner. I suppose, whatever be our politics (and you know mine), we have a horror here of the people who use dynamite. My friend, did you ever think how like them you are? We all admit that there is no more dastardly wretch on earth than the dynamitard; none more infatuated, none so utterly out of reason, none so possessed of all notions diabolical, as the man who would blow up London Bridge and destroy the Houses of Parliament, and cause bloodshed and wreck and ruin and general Hell. For what?—he could not tell for what. But have you ever thought how like him you are; to come away from politics and away from all in that direction that might irritate or distract? What is my sin, and your sin? Just exactly like this man's. Let it be foreshortened, and made vivid to us. Sin and sinners! We are just wretches with parcels of dynamite, slipping forward in the dark—nay, "in Thy sight," laying it against God's very throne, and trying to explode it, no matter what the wreck and howling desolation may be!

No saved sinner has any hesitation in repeating, "Christ Jesus came into the world to save sinners, OF WHOM I AM CHIEF."

As I have often said, so it is here. Sin and sinners never look well in the Bible; and in this scene, the cross of Christ makes sin look at its ugliest and its blackest; it here assumes its most hellish and diabolic form. A man is there dying, dying justly, dying because of his crimes; there is no relenting in him, no melting in him, no yielding in him—in the very article of death, using his last breath, to spit in the face of his Redeemer. Now, that is sin. We have invented fine names for it, to-day. We talk about "infirmity," and we say, "There is something wrong;" and we say, "Alas! poor humanity is very weak, and poor humanity ofttimes makes mistakes." But sin is more than weakness, and more than making mistakes. Sin, when it is finished, is a principle, marked by a baleful stubbornness and determination; sin knows that it is sin, and knows what it is doing. I say, how that comes out—far more than any tongue of angel could tell. And oh, the utter inexcusableness of this thing, this power, principle, or whatever you like to call it, that has got into the hearts and thoughts of men and women! One of the malefactors who were hanged "railed on *Him.*" Go away back to the Book of Genesis, and hold the two places in your hand; take the devil's word in the Book of Genesis about God, and take this word of the servant of the devil who hangs dying in sin; and how Genesis and this chapter come together! What did the devil do when he came to our first parents? He railed against God; he sneered at Him; he insinuated those subtle lies against His love, and against His truth, and against His power. "Never mind," he virtually said in his railings, "never mind what He has promised, and give as little heed to what He has threatened. God! Treat Him as I do—treat Him as nothing. Has He said, 'Thou shalt surely die?' Put your foot on what He has said: Thou shalt *not* surely die." He railed against Him.

Go right down through the Bible until you come to this awful, stupendous scene on the cross, and round about the cross. Here you have the re-echo of the railing of the Book of Genesis. He railed and said, "If Thou be the Christ, save Thyself and us." The same old thing. "He has said something, and it isn't true," so said the devil; so says every sinner; so have we all said. I examined myself, and I examined that man all through yesterday, to find out wherein by nature he and I were unlike; and I stand with shame to-day to confess for myself, as I trust for all souls here, that I could not find the difference. None! or whatever difference is, is in this man's favour! There is your likeness and mine, *railing against Him.* And not railing *in absolute ignorance*, but shutting one's eyes to all that might bring light, and just simply railing. "*If Thou be the Christ*"—he knew something about it; he was not in ignorance—"If Thou be the Messiah, save Thyself and us."

Especially let me speak to any this morning who are hard of heart and stout of countenance against God, and against the truth of God, but who perhaps are deluding themselves with this: that they are superior to this malignant, infatuated kind of sin that is represented in the impenitent robber. My friend, do not delude yourself so; the likelihood is, that except for a miracle of grace—and that is a miracle from which you are turning away—save for a miracle of grace, you will die the death of this man. Do not look forward and say, "Ah, surely, the time is coming, when I shall change, and especially when I come to the end." When you come to the end, the leading passion will be strong, not weak, in death; you will probably die as you have lived. To-day you are cool, hard, and polished as the mahogany you sit at all the week; and at death, too, you will be cool, hard, and polished. You will die, very likely, as you live: giving no sign; or if you give any, it will, as in the case of this man, show the irremediable hardness of your heart against the love and the fear of God. When on your death-bed you are asked, "Shall I send for the missionary? Shall I send for the minister? Shall I send for some good man to pray with you?" you will rail, and say, "No!" Men die as they live; but for a miracle of grace somewhere between the cradle and the death-bed. That is the old way of preaching as to the nature and course of sin; it is my way of preaching. Standing with this scene to work on, what else could I do? How would you preach if you were here? Tell me. I ask especially any intelligent young man here who is beginning to waver about the doctrines of grace, because, although they may be very healing, they are first of all so desperately humbling. Now, my dear fellow, how would you expound that man? Be consistent with your book, with all that goes before, and all that comes after. That is the thing; not merely to spin theories. You would be logical and theological—and I trust you would do it better than I—but from this scene this application must come. Dying, stout and hard and firm, and without a quiver, in the face of the atoning Redeemer! You can die, when your death-bed comes, thus, in the face of the Redeemer! If you can live through this service in face of that atoning Saviour, and refuse to yield to Him and be saved by Him, you can so live when you go out from here, and on to the end. Sin! that awful, stubborn principle within you, enabled you hitherto to refuse to know this Christ except as a dim, vague name; and it will also, unless battled with, enable you to resist Him to-day. Ah, I could not expound this man to this congregation—some of us penitent and some of us impenitent thieves—if I said a syllable less than I am saying. I say, logically and theologically, that is where the sin that begins in Genesis lands itself in this last awful scene; where sin is either finished on Christ's Cross, or for ever confirmed upon the damned sinner's own head—one or the other.

But here is another side. See the 40th verse. "The other man answering rebuked him, saying, Dost not thou fear God, seeing thou art in the same condemnation? And we indeed justly; for we receive the due reward of our deeds." *How the one man answers the other.* There is a word comes out of that which we need to-day, and it is just this: There is a great deal of controversy about Christ and about Christianity to-day. Now, God has so ordered it and so provided it, that, if we would let it alone, a good deal of it would answer itself. It is very refreshing and edifying to see one objector answering another and shutting his mouth. I think, if we preachers would look at that, we would get the help of it and learn the lesson, and instead of answering so learnedly and laboriously and painstakingly, what are, after all, but the wild and infatuated words of poor, ignorant sinners, just let them answer themselves. Let one dying thief answer another. We have other work to do, viz., to point both to Christ. "The *other* answering rebuked him, saying, Dost thou not fear God, seeing thou art in the same condemnation?" And then he adds the qualification, "We indeed justly; for we receive the due reward of our deeds; but this Man hath done nothing amiss." Now see how far forward this man is! I will take him just on that last word—"we receive the due reward of our deeds." That is what the man says when he is come to the end, when sin has finished its course, when it has brought forth death, and all its present misery, and all its future gloom and doom! He says "justly"—justly! "I wrought for this, I fought for this, I lived for this; and why should I begin now to be amazed or alarmed? I have got what I have worked for—'We indeed justly, for we receive the due reward of our deeds.'"

My friend, if since you were born you have lived a life that was a hell on earth for misery, and you should die thus racked in every limb upon a cross actually, physically, decent, respectable though you may be, if the truth of God in that solemn hour worked into your heart, your dying utterance would be "Justly, *justly!* It is the due reward of the life that I lived, and of the thoughts that possessed me, and of the motives that moved me before God and towards God, all the days of my life." Now, that is the old preaching too, and no wonder it is not very popular. It never is popular as long as the human heart is blown up with sin. "The due reward of our deeds." The man is saying it on the cross. He is not railing; he is not bringing in, as he might have done, that awful dark question, "Well, well, after all, I have been a bad fellow, and I might have been better; but I know other bad fellows." He might have nodded his head in the direction of old greybeards and pharisees, scribes and elders and said, "Do you see that rotten old hypocrite there, he is going about respected, and I am strung up here dying like a dog!" No, he did not. "We indeed justly." In this awful scene every man is speaking by himself and for himself. And that impenitent thief is speaking for himself, and he is railing; while this one, speaking for himself, takes the other view—"We receive the due reward of our deeds."

It is worth while tarrying on that, for it prepares us for what is coming afterwards. I wish that over all this audience there would come that wave over the heart of conviction of sin and guilt and ill-desert. Come, my decent friends; come, my own heart; let us stand in the light of this awful scene to day, and say "Justly, *justly!* My sin deserved all manner of misery for the life that now is, and eternal misery and death for the life that is to come." Let us be convicted of sin and of ill-desert. That is the old preaching, that is the old theology; and as we would preach the truth of God, we must never, never leave it out. It is this kind of preaching that brings down our pride and our carnal self-security, and makes us to understand the awful mystery of Christ upon the cross, and makes us ready to receive the pardon and the peace, and the wealth of heaven's blessings that come to poor self-convicted and law-condemned sinners through the Lord Jesus Christ, the sinner's Substitute and Saviour. I trust we have come to that. Are you in misery; are you in perplexity; are you in distress of body or soul? Have you ever taken the trouble to trace it to its true root? Do not, oh wretched heart, be behind the dying thief! Wonderful light was breaking on his dying head; for oh, the death-bed is a revealing time, is it not? We talk of the darkness and of the gloom of the death-bed. I rather think that if we could see as God sees, death-beds are not so dark. I rather think that in the dying hour tremendous floods of light break in. Even when we think them unconscious, God alone knows how, in the dying hour, floods of light are illuminating the past life; floods of light are streaming into the spirit, and the awful realities of life;—sin, death, hell, guilt, salvation, judgment, Christ, are seen just flashing with light, light, light, meaning, meaning, power, power. I do not believe it is so dark, in the sense of being confused, as we sometimes think, and as the poor body's condition would lead us to think.

What a wonderful, clear, calm, logical utterance, coming from a man racked in every limb, and suffering unspeakable pain! No doctor of divinity, after years of study of the subject, coming before a class of students in all his robes of dignity and calmness, and paper and manuscript, could utter a more clear word as to the doctrine of sin on its practical side, than the ignorant, dying thief. "We indeed justly, for we receive the due reward of our deeds : but this Man hath done nothing amiss."

All hope comes out of this exception. This one clear exception to the common, the general, the universal run. "This Man has done nothing over the line," no transgression, nothing amiss. Would God that to-day all of us might accept it! I do not ask you to come into a state of excitement, but I do ask that the Spirit of God may come and convince this audience of sin, of righteousness, and of judgment to come. I grant that His name is the "Comforter," but His very first work is a very comfortless work. He is called the Comforter, but His first work is to trouble us. "When He, the Comforter, is come, the Spirit of Truth, He convinces of sin." That is the proof that He is here with us, that He is what the Lord said He is, that He is carrying out the Divine programme along the divinely indicated line. May He come to-day, and in the presence of Christ on the cross silently, secretly, but powerfully, convince us, each man, each woman apart, of sin, of righteousness, and judgment to come ! "The due reward of the deeds done in the body."

And he said unto Jesus, "Lord, remember me when Thou comest into Thy kingdom. And Jesus said unto him, "Verily I say to thee, To-day shalt thou be with Me in Paradise." Brief words these, so also is the Lord's answer to this dying thief, this one whom the old authors call "*Bonus Latro,*" "the good robber," "blessed bandit." Let us listen.

Now, as we have seen some of the essential attributes and outcomes of sin, let us hear some of the essential attributes and outcomes of faith, or rather, of that grace which makes faith possible. We are all agreed with grand John Calvin about this instance of the dying thief. "Never," he says, "never since the world began was there a more remarkable instance of faith, and, therefore, never since the world began was there such a remarkable instance of the grace of the Holy Spirit than that which is herein magnificently displayed." That blessed Spirit works in the dead sinner's heart true ideas about sin and about the Saviour, and leads us to that faith that saves the soul and delivers us from sin's guilt and power here and hereafter. "Lord!" Well then, an essential element or characteristic of saving faith, that great antidote of sin is this—that it looks to Christ *on the Cross*, and calls Him Lord!

Brethren, to-day we are preaching Christ, and Him crucified. In many a pulpit to-day Christ is preached, but not *Him crucified;* the Christ of history, the ideal Christ of an ideal humanity that is to be, of which He is the Pattern, and so on; or even the Christ who is coming again. "Christ crucified," says Paul. "I determined to know nothing but Christ, and *Him crucified.*" I find myself in a sinful city and in a sinful world; and if I am to begin where God would have me, my plan and purpose must be this: Rear in the midst of London's sin, wherever I get a congregation, Christ and Him crucified: the Cross! yea, rather the Three Crosses, and try to show you yourselves as impaled on one or other of them. That is the preacher's programme, and God will withhold His blessing from any man who tries another. No enticing words of man's wisdom. Perish philosophy! perish rhetoric! The Three Crosses! Which are you on? for impaled on one or the other all of you are: either crucified with Christ, or crucified (dying) without Him! Now faith essentially is this: faith sees in the Central Cross, with all its weakness, with all its shame, with all its lowliness, faith sees a King, faith sees One to whom it says intelligently, "Lord, *Lord*, Lord!"

We call ourselves believers here this morning. Where did our faith begin? Has it got this element about it? As we stand round about the cross—the three crosses—this morning, and look at the central one, is your heart saying with more intelligence than the dying thief,

" Lord, there Thou art, a Man among men; there Thou art condemned by man, condemned as an impostor, condemned as a transgressor, condemned because Thou didst claim to be the Son of God. *And Thou art the Son of God;* Thou art not an impostor. Thou art more than simply Jesus of Nazareth, the reputed son of Joseph and Mary." What do we say about Him? It is good just to see the Central Cross, to carry it round about this audience, and ask every man and woman here, " *Who is He?*" Is there one soul here as I preach Christ crucified, although in weakness, and in fear, and in trembling—is there one soul here not upon its knees—one? I would not be in your place for a thousand worlds. Down! Christ on the cross, *who is He?* Come now, my brother—I would almost single you out if I knew your name—what do you say? You see what the dying thief said in that awful hour, and the Holy Ghost thought fit to record it. That is what I say. What do you say? "Lord!" I know that surely you are wanting to say it, though you don't speak it out. His dying ears were quick to catch the word, and on the throne of His Glory, to-day, His ear is open. He listens still for that whisper, " Lord!" Thou art Lord and Christ to me. " Lord, I believe!" Then the darkness is passing, and the ignorance is going away, and heaven is beginning, and the kingdom and your place in it are coming. " Lord "—is that it now? Then flesh and blood never revealed it unto thee: thou art the subject of Divine illumination. What a wonder! What a mystery! What a miracle! Oh, what a delight in the actual experience. " Lord, Lord!" he said. Oh, how difficult it was to say it then, and yet in all the dimness and darkness and confusion, his eyes opened to see that He is a King. Not just now, but " when Thou comest in Thy kingdom." " It is coming. I don't know how; I don't see how; many things are dark and confused, and I cannot apprehend." But his heart leaped, and grasped and fastened on that: " Lord, remember me when Thou comest in Thy kingdom."

I go no further than that with his prayer, but I emphasize that, and bring it out. What dost thou call Him? What is the testimony of thy heart, especially concerning this Jesus on the cross in the hour of His greatest weakness and shame and humiliation? Again I say, come and stand near the cross; is there any one here who can dare to wag his head? They did it then. Sin is such an awful thing! Oh God, forgive us! Sin enables us to look blank into the stricken face of the Christ of God and wag our heads. That is sin. Grace enables us to come into the same presence, and to say, like Thomas, " My Lord and my God." Groaning, bleeding, dying, but *for me*. King here! Triumphant here! A something here that is kingly, regal, splendid, and that shall tell to all eternity.

And what did Jesus say? " Jesus saith unto him, Verily I say unto thee, To-day shalt thou be with Me in Paradise." As Bossuet, the great French orator, says, " ' To-day! ' What promptitude! ' With me,' what company! ' In Paradise,' what repose!" " To-day with Me in Paradise." See how the old way of preaching gets its illustration here! You have often heard us saying it was to-day, not to-morrow. You have often heard us talking about the reality of conversion. Is it any wonder? There it is: what other kind of conversion would you have than instantaneous conversion? If life be what it is, if sin be what it is, if the future be the awful irrevocable affair that God represents it to be, and if there is but a very step between me and eternity, I may make that step at any moment; I may never get home to day. My brethren and sisters in London, according to the flesh, are to-day making the passage from time to eternity, and my day is coming. Why should I find fault with instantaneous conversion? Why should I sneer at it as being unphilosophical? Why talk about the " evolution " of the good that is in me? My dear brother, unless that evolution makes more progress in the next million years than it has made in your lifetime, so far as I know you, it will do little for you.

When I speak to you, I speak to myself. If it is to be evolution, it should be showing something by this time to give you some courage to face the future with your good that has been evolved out of the seeds which you say are undoubtedly in your heart. Don't you think it is time that at least a blade of that mighty harvest that is to be was beginning to push out from the soil? and if there is none appearing above the ground, is it not time to turn over the soil to find out if the thing is dead? The seed is turned rotten under the clod, with a rottenness that yields no life. Why should we object to this to-day—this instantaneous conversion, the passage from death to life *to-day*, the passage from sin to grace to-day, the passage from condemnation to acceptation and pardon to-day? Instantaneous! We are glad of it here. How logical it is here; how natural it is here; how it fits into the narrative here! What a wonderful consistency it has here! And from this one learn all. Believe me, that in the end of the day God will show that his much-derided way of salvation had an eternal wisdom planning all its processes, that nothing was done "*per saltum*," but everything done consistently; concentrically, not eccentrically; harmoniously, step by step and in due order, although to our minds there may seem to be abruptness and break, almost inconceivable paradox and inconsistency. To the dying thief, a man who had lived a lifetime in sin and crime, He said, "To-day shalt thou be with Me in Paradise." I look for the eternal day to show that God was wise and just and logical, and all that belongs to the term reasonable, when He did that. I look to see that in my case as well as in His. It is not capriciousness; it will be seen that the salvation is bottomed and grounded upon the Eternal Rock of Justice and Judgment, as well as marked by unspeakable and unexplainable love and mercy. To-day! Is not that a grand Gospel to preach to a company of perishing men and women gathered here in London? I may never see you here again; you may never see me. Bless God we do not need to care!

To-day we can have Christ; to-day we can be forgiven—*to-day!* You came trailing away from the south side; you have not been here for months, you will not be here for months again—perhaps never! What a grand thing to be able to stand up to-day and say, "Thou mayest be with Christ on the throne to-day; to-day certainly thou canst trust HIM; to-day thou canst have the infinite benefit of His righteousness and His atoning death and His intercession, to-day—now at thirty-one minutes past twelve o'clock to-day—*to-day*—TO-DAY!

When you tumbled out of your boat last summer, down at the coast, you wanted instantaneous salvation, didn't you, from drowning? You didn't want people to come and discuss the situation, and propose plans, and begin to lecture you about your stupidity for getting in, and to give you discourses on swimming, and tell you that if you would do so-and-so all would be right! You were yelling, as far as your water-logged mouth would let you, for help, and it came; and it could not have come too quickly, could it? So we preach to perishing sinners to-day. As Bossuet says, "What promptitude!" The arm of the Lord is among us to-day; do not put it away, oh man! oh woman! Will you have this salvation that comes when Christ turns His head and looks at you from the cross of His shame, from the throne of His glory, and as He says, "I have seen you, I have heard you, I know you; to-day shalt thou be with Me in Paradise." "He that believeth *hath* everlasting life, and shall not come into condemnation." Will you have it to-day?

A poor man was journeying in a steamer down one of our lovely friths, and suddenly an awful cry got up; for he took a race along the deck, got on to the rail, and plunged into the sea! The steamer was immediately stopped and backed, a rope was thrown to him, and the utter horror that went through those passengers no tongue can tell, as the man used his last strength to throw the rope away, and, with a howl, disappeared beneath the waves! Of course, the man was a maniac, and his keeper had been slack and allowed him to get out of his hands. Such a maniac is the man in this congregation to-day who in the presence of the Cross of Christ, and of this Gospel that is preached, refuses instantaneously to close therewith! May there be no such madmen among us!

"*With Me in Paradise!*" I cannot dwell on "with Me." I don't know what it means; the Bible does not tell us; Paul could only say, "I have a desire to depart, to be with Thee—with Christ, for it is far better." But, at any rate, it is heaven. That is the next thing after the sermon, if sudden death should come. Now, is not that something? Isn't that certitude? Isn't that something to grip and to hang on to? After the sermon, if you should die before you get home, that is the next thing. First of all, believing on Him, and then to be with Him. With Him, *with Him*, WITH HIM!

"The Lamb is all the glory in Emmanuel's land." To be "absent from the body," is to be present with the Lord." No purgatory! No intervening time, or space, or place, but with Him! With *Me*—with Me "on My throne, as I also am with My Father on His throne." That is what grace has done; that is the mighty work it has done; it has cut between me and my sins, and joined me with the Lord Jesus Christ my Saviour.

But it is worth while just looking at the word that Christ used to the poor man. "In Paradise." Where is Paradise? I don't know. What is Paradise? I don't know. It is only referred to by St. Paul in 2nd Corinthians, when he speaks of one who was "caught up to Paradise and heard words that it would be impossible for man to utter;" and again in Revelation, where it is said, "To Him that overcometh will I grant to eat of the Tree of Life that is in the midst of the Paradise of God." It was taken very likely by the Old Testament Church, just as we take it, from that wonderful scene the sinless Eden, with all its gardens and waters, and its innocence and beauty. And I think, apart from all controversy, what Christ meant was this: That was a poor ignorant man as regards much systematized, definite Bible knowledge that he might have had. Very ignorant; but he was Jew, an Israelite, who had been brought up, I think, to better things; and what the Lord meant when He used the word was to bring him away back, even in his dying hour, to childhood's days. He used a word that very likely Hebrew mothers used. You know when you talk to your child you do not talk logically and theologically and in the set, formal terms even of the Bible about the things of religion You talk to your boy and girl about "the Happy Land," don't you? And "the Good Man," don't you? And in these simple ways you bring these things near to them. Now, what "Happy Land" is to our children, Paradise was to a Hebrew child—a place of all beauty and all verdure and all delight. It was "the Happy Land, far, far away;" and Christ worked upon that in the man's dying hour. He virtually said, "Don't be troubled about when I am coming; don't be troubled about My kingdom. I see that you are confused about that, and you don't know; you have been living in sin and misery and ignorance." He virtually said to him, "The Happy Land that your mother told you about, it is true; it is not a myth, it is not a dream; we are going to it together. We are within sight! Land ahead! We are almost there 'in the Paradise'"—the Happy Land that you heard about in earlier, brighter, and sunnier days."

Do I speak to somebody here to-day who has drifted away from home-influences and home-trainings; who has drank of sin; who has poisoned his mind with scepticism? My brother, let a simple illustration, a simple word, be used of God to bring to an end the dark power of unbelief and of the devil in your hardened, sceptical soul. It is no myth, it is no phantom—"the Happy Land far, far away," that you and your mother sang about twenty, thirty, forty, fifty years ago. *It is true!* Christ says it is true! "If it were not so, He would have told you." In an awful crisis like this, would He have deceived us? Would He have put sand beneath our sinking feet when rock, and nothing less than rock, was needed? Surely not! Will you trust Him then? Look to Jesus, dying sinner. He is all you need. There may be much to learn; yea, there is much to learn of this "mystery made manifest"—Christ dying that He may establish a kingdom, and make me a living member of it for ever. But, oh! be quick; begin to call Him Lord!

> "Upon a life you did not live,
> Upon a death you did not die,
> Another's life, Another's death,
> You stake your whole Eternity."

Yes, poor thief, He loved thee, He gave Himself for thee; and, blessed be His name, also for me, thy fellow-sinner. The Lord save us at the Cross to-day. Amen.

Regent Square Pulpit.

THE LORD OUR SHEPHERD.*

A Sermon

DELIVERED IN REGENT SQUARE CHURCH ON A COMMUNION SABBATH, BY THE

REV. JOHN McNEILL.

PSALM xxiii.

ON Wednesday evening, dear friends, we sought to prepare ourselves for the Communion by sitting down at the Master's feet—at the feet of our risen Lord, and listening to His own word, as He said to us, His disciples of to-day, the word that He spoke to His disciples on that morning, beside the Lake of Galilee, "Come and dine." I feel that in taking up this sweet spiritual, pastoral Psalm this morning, we are keeping ourselves in line with whatever the Holy Spirit brought to us then, and whatever He may have brought to us since, of what is helpful for a Communion Sabbath in the meditations of our hearts within us. I shall try to be brief, and get to the Table as quickly as possible, for that is the centre of attraction to-day. We long to be there, to

---

* Mr. McNeill has to visit Liverpool and Manchester this week. He cannot, therefore, prepare for publication the Sermon delivered last Sunday morning. But several enquiries were made at the time for the discourse now issued. It was found to be helpful when preached;—may the Lord bless the reading of it now.

cease from man, and to have once more in our hands those precious memorials of the death of the Great Shepherd of the sheep. What shall we say more about this Psalm than has been said already? The finest-minded saints who have ever lived since it was written have exhausted themselves in describing its beauties. All are agreed that this beauty is of a quiet, tender, spiritual type. May we enter into its beauty to-day!

"Oh, may my heart in tune be found,
Like David's harp of solemn sound."

Sometimes the preacher's voice has to be rough, strong, keen, and somewhat cutting. He has to cry aloud and spare not: to lift up his voice like a trumpet, and to show God's people their transgressions and sins, and warn them, that they be not partakers of coming judgments. But on an occasion like this, and with a Psalm like this, we could wish that we had the tongues of men and of angels. May our whole soul, may our very voice, to-day, like the dyer's hand, be subdued to what it works in! May the Spirit Himself breathe the sweet gracious melody of this sweet gracious Psalm into your heart and mind.

The prevailing note that throbs through it all is the Lord's presence with us. There are just two words on which the changes are rung, "I" and "Thou"—"He" and "Me." Martin Luther said that the most of experimental religion lay in the pronouns—the possessive pronouns and the personal ones. Certainly that remark is illustrated by this Psalm, which he again called "a little Bible." I and Thou, He and Me. "The Lord is *my* Shepherd. *He* leadeth *me*. *I* will fear no evil, for *Thou* art with *me*." And just because it is of that quiet kind, just because it is a stream which, like the waters of Siloah, go softly, the Psalm, I might say, is a test and a touchstone of spirituality—of true spiritual experience. I do not think that Mr. Talkative would like this Psalm. It is too quiet. And I do not think that your argumentative, very logical Christian gets a great deal of marrow and fatness out of this Psalm. I am reminded of what McCheyne said about the Song of Solomon, and I would apply it to this Psalm. He said that the Song of Solomon is such a touchstone because the man who is rather logical in his turn of mind, whose religion is in his head rather than his heart, would not get much good out of it; so I would say that he would not get much good out of this Psalm.

There is logic in it, there is argument in it ; but it is not great and solid and massive. There are little links, little argumentative links, which, like hooks of steel, bind *the theme* into a unity. There is that; but not broadly and strongly and massively, like the piers and spans, shall I say, of the rising Forth Bridge. Then, again, for those who are very fond of the imaginative—the soaring and the fanciful, there is not much here. There is imagination in it, but it is very quiet, very simple. It is a very quiet singing-bird, and there are those who are not spiritual at all, who will find far grander flights of imagination in this same Psalm book. There is nothing in literature, for example, for a description of a thunderstorm better than David's great Psalm on that subject, when he describes the rending heavens, and the forests being laid bare, and the Lord's voice upon the waters, and the God of Glory thundering. Here *all* is very quiet ; very subdued. It is the song, very likely, of an aged man, who had been a shepherd, and a courtier, and a king. He had come through great trials, and in his old age is musing over all these things, and singing to himself this sweet and heavenly melody. It begins, "The Lord is my Shepherd;" and it ends, "I shall dwell in His fold for ever." Ah! to-day, at the Lord's Table, especially do we enjoy it all the more for its sweet, profound simplicity. It is a Psalm of which, as you read, you say to yourself, "I might have written that myself:" that is the touch of genius in it. "I might have said that myself. Why could not I have said it: 'The Lord is my Shepherd, I shall not want: He makes me to lie down in green pastures, He leads me beside the still waters'?" I am sure we all agree with what Henry Ward Beecher has said most beautifully about this exquisite little Psalm. I cannot give the exact words; but here is the substance. "Blessed be the day," he says, "when this Psalm was born. It is the opening of a man's heart, only, as it were, for a moment, and yet between the opening and the shutting there has gushed out a spiritual melody that has throbbed in the very air ever since." I could spend our whole time in simply quoting versions and appreciative criticisms of this Psalm.

I think it was Beecher who said that this Psalm is among psalms what the nightingale is among birds. It is a small bird, he says, and of homely plumage; but with what throbbing melody he pours out his notes! and he goes on to describe what it has done ever since it was penned: how it has soothed the sorrowful, cheered the lonely, dried the eyes of the mourners, comforted those who were dying, and consoled those who were left behind. And then he says, that its work is not done. It was at first full of quiet, but intense spiritual power, like the heaving of a silent sea, and it is as full of it as ever it was. It will go on singing to your children and my children, and will not fold its wings and cease until the last pilgrim has reached the Father's house, to dwell there for evermore.

Then, he says, it will fold its wings and fly away back to the God who gave it, to mingle its song with the mighty anthems which for ever shall circle round the throne. Oh that we might begin where it begins, and end where it ends! It is a short Psalm. If I may say so, it is a little step-ladder, but a little step-ladder will suffice to lift a man from the pavement up to the shining street-lamp. So may it be with this little Psalm; although it has only six verses, it is always long enough to stretch from the gloom and the darkness of this present evil world to the breakings of the brightness which shall shine more and more till the perfect day. As I have said, the note that throbs all through this nightingale Psalm is that exquisitely melodious spiritual note—"God is with me, and I am with Him;" so simple, so profound—so simple, that the smallest child here can, in a measure, understand it—so profound, that to all eternity we shall never have done wondering at it, and admiring its beauty.

"God is with me, and I am with Him."

> "Rise, my soul, adore and wonder,
> Why, O Lord, such love to me !
> Grace has put me in the number
> Of the Saviour's family.
> Hallelujah ! Thanks, eternal thanks, to Thee."

"The Lord is my Shepherd, I shall not want." Let us begin with this confidence, dear friends, especially as we are gathered round the Communion Table this morning. It is a plain proposition, as logical as logical can be, and therefore most helpful and encouraging to us in spiritual things; for, oh, we are apt to think that the ordinary rules of logic that apply to ordinary themes, and the treatment of them, do not quite apply in spiritual things and in spiritual experiences. They do.

"The Lord is my Shepherd, I shall not want." There is to be no argument then. Says the writer of this Psalm, "I am not going to examine foundations. I am not going into doctrine. I am not going into history. I am simply to muse, and treat of my own experience, and as I muse, the fire burns, and out comes this ruddy glow of simple assurance, 'The Lord is my Shepherd, I shall not want.'" Say it in your heart. Begin with it. Look round about upon all that would cause trouble and distress, and look up then to the Great Shepherd; "The Lord is my Shepherd, I shall not want." How these two things go together, and, alas! alas! how often we separate them. I was at a marriage here during the week. Down there the two knelt, and they made their covenant, and I sealed it with a lifelong seal, with the words, "Whom God hath joined together let no man put asunder." So have we come to Christ, if we have come at all.

We have made our covenant with Him. Both sides of it are expressed in this very opening line: "The Lord is my Shepherd, I shall not want." And yet how often what God hath joined, our unbelief violently divorces. With the one breath we say, "The Lord is my shepherd," with the other breath, there are a thousand disquietudes, and fears, and alarms, and perplexities, and murmurings. It is not easy to say the simplest of God's words. On the surface they seem to be only like other words. But how round and full, how vast and wide they are when we enter into them. "The Lord is my Shepherd, I shall not want." That is a fact. If the first be a fact, so is the second. Then bid "good-bye" to fear and care, O soul of mine, if thou canst say, like the Psalmist, "The Lord is my Shepherd." Be gone, dull care, I prithee, begone from me, for "The Lord is my Shepherd, I shall not want." These two things go together. I shall want for nothing—for the body, for time, for eternity, for the life that now is or for that which is to come. We shall want for nothing as regards ourselves, as regards our business, or as regards our children. All is included within the sweep and grasp of the heavenly covenant. What a good shepherd is to his sheep, that surely, and more, the heavenly Shepherd will be to us. "The King of Love my Shepherd is." It was well for David to sing a Psalm through this metaphor, for he knew what shepherding was; he knew the faithfulness which it needed; he knew the perils which it brought a man into. He knew the temptation to become a hireling, and save his own skin and secure his own comfort, by leaving the sheep to the present danger. But just because he knew so well what a tax shepherding puts on body and heart and brain, therefore he is entitled to say, "The Lord is my Shepherd; and if I risked my life, as I did—for I have wrestled with the lion and the bear to save the helpless lamb of my flock—how much more will He, the Lord Jehovah, extend to me His power and faithfulness! 'The Lord is my Shepherd, I shall not want.' No, I shall not!" Here is your bank. It will never fail. There is a vast deal more of ready money in there than the poor saints have ever yet taken out of it. There is a deal more of present help in perplexity than troubled and perplexed saints have ever taken out of it. There is everything that we need in that God who has revealed Himself to us indubitably, in these last days, in the person of His Son, who has expressly said to us, "I am the Good Shepherd; I give My life for the sheep." He has done the deed, and this morning we are celebrating the memorial thereof. Come near Him, man. Come near Him, woman. Gather round about this great Good Shepherd. Lay hold, at any rate, of the skirts of His garments; and, as you cling to them, get some sense and feeling of the mighty shoulders from which those garments depend.

I once said in this same church to a servant girl who had got into a good family, "Are you happy where you are?" She had got what for a servant was a good situation, and I shall not forget the quietly confident way in which with beaming face she said, "Oh yes, sir, I have £22 a year, *and all found.*" "The Lord is my Shepherd," and all is found. "I shall not want." "All found." That was evidently more to her than the small sum total of the actual pounds. She dwelt upon that, and said with emphasis, "and all found."

"He maketh me to lie down in green pastures. He leadeth me beside the still waters." How simply, how artlessly this Psalm is composed. That is what makes it so difficult to expound—it is artlessly artful. David, in his riper years, is just beating out his own experience. He sees himself once more a shepherd lad back on the hillsides of Judæa, and he hears in his ears the bleating of his flock. There are few who keep close to him, but see yonder wild one, and this other, dashing off here, and breaking off there. All his shepherd experience comes upon him as he details in the second and third verses, "He maketh me to lie down in green pastures. He leadeth me beside the still waters. He restoreth my soul. He leadeth me in the paths of righteousness for His name's sake." How David here puts all things into the category of the sovereignty of grace.

I am sure there is none of us who will feel that his part in grace is being overlooked, because David lifts God up so high and so splendidly. *He* makes all right. *He* maketh me to lie down. The very syntax helps us. "*He* causeth me to lie down in green pastures. *He* leadeth me beside the still waters. *He* restoreth my soul. *He* leadeth me in the paths of righteousness for His name's sake," for He is the Shepherd, and the shepherd keeps the sheep, not the sheep the shepherd, as has often been remarked.

May we enter just now into this gracious simplicity of the relationship that exists between us and the Lord Jesus, the great Shepherd and Bishop of our souls.

"Green pastures, still waters," or, as the margin has it, "waters of quietness." The vision before David's mind, no doubt, is a vision of a sunny day in some quiet place in Israel—one of the days that instinctively made him sing —one of the days when he was preparing himself to be the sweet psalmist and harper of Israel; just such a day as you saw this past summer, when, perhaps, this very scene was before your eyes. Out came the sheep, and out came the shepherd, and in a short time they were scattering themselves through the meadow, or all along the gentle slopes of the hill, and, as you looked, this scene rose up before your eyes.

"He maketh me to lie down." He is seeking to do that to-day; for very often, like sheep, we are very restless, and we need to be made to lie down. We need to be urged to come off the wing; we need to have our souls steadied and settled and brought to rest. To change the figure. He needs to say to us, as He said to the wind and the agitated sea, "Peace! Be still!" You need to say it to your children. The bed is very soft and downy and white. The resting-time has come, and the child is lying on the bed, and ought to be enjoying it, but the little thing is so restless that there is something more needed. The mother, the father, or the nurse needs to say, " My child, lie still." So does God. May it be a word of power to our hot and restless hearts to-day. " Lie still. What is it that aileth thee?"

" He restoreth my soul." That is hard work. I think that we are rather apt to have romantic notions about shepherds. I do not know anything about it practically, but I did once make the acquaintance of a shepherd, and I went with him two or three times, and I got to see that it was not so romantic as poets would make out. It is a toilsome, unromantic business. I had no idea that sheep caused so much trouble until I went with him. I remember him smilingly saying to me, " Oh, you people think that ours is a very romantic life, and that the whole current of our life tends somewhat to the making of poetry. Now," he said, " do you not see that it is a very prosy business?" And so it was. I had no idea that there was such disease among sheep. I had no idea that the shepherd needed to be so much (if you will allow the term) a veterinary surgeon. I had no idea whatever of the hard, rough—shall I say dirty—work that a shepherd has to go through. It all comes out, I think, in one line of this Psalm, " He restoreth my soul: He leadeth me in the paths of righteousness." There is a good deal of doctoring needed. It is not at all romantic and superfine.

A shepherd needs to be a man with a pair of open eyes and ears, and ready hands and strong limbs. He needs to be in it, and all in it, and always in it. So does our blessed Master. He needs to be about and around us continually, for we are always going wrong. The sheep is said to be, for its size, the animal with the least brain in the animal creation. And will you allow — not me, but God, just because of that, to speak to us in this type and figure. Like a sheep, my brother, you have a genius for going wrong — a genius for going astray. I have seen how easily they will go through a gap in the hedge, and then, when they seem to be looking for it, in order to come back, they cannot find it. How easily we break out. How easily we get tangled and torn. With what infinite difficulty, as regards ourselves, we get back, and are restored. How thankful it ought to make us that the Lord Jesus Christ stands among us not only as a great Shepherd, but as a great Physician : "Jehovah Rophi "— "I am the Lord that healeth thee." He says, "There is no trouble known to sin-sick men and women that I do not know, and that I cannot cure." None ! "He restoreth my soul." How often the roaring lion has sprung upon us, and how often he might rejoice and say, "Now I have prevailed. Now I have rent them limb from limb." But, lo ! we do not die. "He restoreth my soul." Not dead yet, oh devil, but alive and here, notwithstanding all that has happened ; here, in this quiet sheepfold, resting myself among the green pastures and beside the still waters of His Word and Sacrament.

"That's a dead 'un," said one of the Hospital Staff, as he pointed to one of the bodies in the trenches before Sebastopol. "Oh no," said "the body"; "I'm worth a great many dead men yet." And the "dead 'un" is now known to fame as Lord Wolseley !

"He leadeth me in the paths of righteousness." A man in Glasgow translated the Psalms into broad Scotch, because he thought that broad Scotch had wonderful affinities in its idiom to simple, old-world Hebrew ; and I think he was right. He said here, "He leadeth me in richt roddins." There are little bits of country road that seem to lead nowhere, but the farmer needs them all and uses them all. You tourists, if you struck them, would find that they led you nowhere, but the farmer uses them, and the shepherd uses them, and the dairymaid knows all about them for her charge. So with the Lord Jesus Christ. He leads us by little bits. He does not lay out a whole champaign of country, and cast us on the great highway. No; but He leads us along this sheep-track to-day, and another sheep-track to-morrow. And these tracks never lose themselves in the moor, for He will always be with us, and it will always be found that there was a track and a path, and that it was the right path. Literally translated, it is, "He leadeth me in the straight paths." They have an expected end and termination because He is Leader and He is Guide.

"Yea, though I walk through the valley of the shadow of death, I will fear no evil; for Thou art with me; Thy rod and Thy staff they comfort me." This is a lamp that has often been lit on death-beds, and yet, primarily, it is not meant as a lamp for a dying chamber. It is rather meant as a light for a dark valley—for those troubles and sudden distresses, or prolonged distresses, that come to God's pilgrim folk as they go up through the wilderness of this world. David had before him instances in his own experience when he had to lead his flock through some gorge or some deep defile—through some valley filled with gloom and shadow; and there, lurking in that corner, and here, lurking in the other corner, is the wild beast of prey, ready to spring, watching for its chance, but kept back by the watchful eyes and the sturdy arm of the shepherd with his rod and with his staff.

"The valley of the shadow of death." Sometimes we say, "Oh, it is only children who are afraid of shadows." And the point is brought out for our encouragement, that death has been vanquished by Jesus Christ, and that all that is left is only a shadow. It is said that only children are afraid of shadows. I do not know. I am not a child, but I frankly admit that I do not like darkness. With all my years, and with all my height and weight, I am naturally nervous. How does that nervousness come? Nervousness springs originally, I suppose, from sin, and it needs grace to cure it; and even the valley of the shadow is a gruesome place. I do not know that you would care to go from the top to the bottom of your house at night, especially if there is nobody in it but yourself, without at least a candle or a taper. Try it; and, unless you are very brave, I rather think you will admit that your heart beats. And if there is a sudden, unusual sound, you feel your hair almost beginning to rise. Darkness needs light, and the valley of the shadow needs nothing less than the Divine light. "Though I walk through the valley of the shadow." What a blessing that the Lord Jesus Christ understands nervousness—for a great many folks do not. Even your best friends, my good woman, my dear man, laugh at you for your nervousness, because you are so timid, and because you are so shrinking, and because you are so easily put about; and they say, "What is wrong with you? There is nothing. You are alarmed and frightened even at your own shadow." And the commentators, brave fellows, tell us so smartly, that the shadow of a sword doesn't cut; and the shadow of a dog won't bite. Well, no; but the shadow of a dog means a dog *somewhere round here*, doesn't it? Ah, anyway, what a Saviour Christ is for nervous people! Even among the shadows, He gives us His own substantial presence. He wants to ally every fear by taking away the very source of fear. He wants Himself to be with us in the darkness and the gloom. "Though I walk through the valley of the shadow of death, I will fear no evil; for Thou art with me; Thy rod and Thy staff they comfort me."

Are you in darkness to-day? Hear this voice. Take this rod and Him that appointed it. Come near to Christ and listen to Him: "When thou passeth through the waters I will be with thee, and through the rivers they shall not overflow thee. When thou walkest through the fire thou shalt not be burned, neither shall the flame kindle upon thee, for I am with thee; I have redeemed thee; thou art Mine." What does that mean? It means what it says. Take it in, in all its strong, majestic simplicity. Some of us are a long while in the valley of the shadow, and we need to work away at that verse, or at something like it.

Did you ever hear such an exquisite song in the night as the 4th verse? Did you ever hear a song in the night? Here is one. Oh, what an exquisite melody it appears, as you think of David in some time of darkness and distress and danger! And how darkness and distress and danger were multiplied to him, let his life show. Just think of him, in the midst of it all, saying, "I will fear no evil, for Thou art with me."

I remember having this borne in upon myself (if you will pardon a personal reminiscence) in a way that I have never forgotten. One night, when I was a lad, lying in my bed at home, long ago, I awoke, and it was dark, and I heard a voice in the night—not a song, but I heard the voice of my mother as she lay upon her bed of pain. She was twenty-five years in the valley of the shadow of death. Her "light affliction" endured for a quarter of a century, but it was "but for a moment," seeing that it led to the "eternal weight of glory." I shall never forget how the sound of her voice floated into my dark room and my disquieted heart—"Yea, though I walk through the valley"—think of it rising in the air at two o'clock on a dark winter morning with the wind howling round your house—"Yea, though I walk through the valley of the shadow of death I will fear no evil, for Thou art with me." I am saying it in a rough, unmelodious man's voice. I heard it hymned in the exquisite tone that only a man's mother's voice can ever have to his own ear. Sing it! Sing it in the darkness. Sing it now all the more if the valley seems long. You are passing through it, remember. "Though I walk *through* the valley." It is a tunnel, but only a tunnel, and, like all tunnels, it has light at both ends, and certainly it has light at that end to which you are travelling. Most of the railway stations, I notice, are entered through tunnels. I do not know why, but it so happens that coming into most of our London termini you shoot through a long, dreary, ghostly, rattling tunnel, and then there is the terminus, and your father there, or your wife there on the platform, and then the embrace and the kiss and the hearty welcome. We are going through the tunnel, and at the end of it is the terminus, and, please God, we shall soon be there. It is dark and noisome and spectral, and a little awesome and fearsome just now. Sing. Sing this Psalm of heart-confidence, and the shadows will become somewhat luminous with the light that is about to reveal itself—the light of heaven, our eternal home.

I heard again a song in the night. I do not know whether I can faithfully set it forth to you. I remember going down one night, about twelve o'clock, to the seaside, and I stood in the shadow of a gloomy wood. In the front of me for miles stretched the frith of the sea. Away across yonder were the Argyleshire hills, and up above them, again, the gloomy heavens, with here and there a star peeping out. It was like the valley of the shadow of death. The sea was lapping at my feet, and a gentle breeze was blowing over it, when suddenly I heard a sound. I listened and strained my ear, and that sound turned out to be the sound, first of all, of oars in the rowlocks—a dull, thumping sound as some fishermen urged their boat along its way. And still I listened, and what I heard was the sound of music; and as the boat came nearer, there was borne to me across the waves the sound of singing.

Those fishermen were Christians, and even while tugging at the weary oar in the dark and lonely night they were cheering themselves with the songs of Zion. I have changed the figure a little from David's valley of the shadow. I have brought it from the country down to the sea, but the teaching is the same. That song told upon me in a wonderful way. I cannot describe how that simple music came into me—those voices and that sound of the rowing. How the singing changed it all. Apart from the singing, that dull thumping on the rowlocks would only have told me of hard-toiling men tugging at the weary oar; but when the sound of the music came, that dull thump became a musical beat, and the whole of the drudgery of their work disappeared It became the musical beat of that song with which they helped themselves along in their toilsome task. We are down here in the valley. We are out here upon the dark seas of time and sin; but as I stood upon the shore and listened, so God stands upon the eternal shore and listens. Sing this Psalm of quiet confidence. Sing this song in the darkness and in the night. It will tell on God, surely, as no other singing does. There is something peculiarly plaintive in singing that comes across the waters. The water takes a something out of it, and puts an exquisite something into it, which I cannot describe, but which we have all felt. So let us sing amid these seas of time and sin. The very winds will carry our songs. Let us send across to the great God who stands upon the shore our quiet psalm of hearty cheer. Let it rise in the darkness, and it will tell upon God's ear and tell upon His heart as even the mighty hallelujahs round the throne do not tell. Pull out this *vox hamana* stop of the great organ, and let God hear it as we sing to Him this quiet psalm in the night of trouble and storm and adversity, " I will fear no evil, for Thou art with me : Thy rod and Thy staff they comfort me." We shall never be without cause for praise ; not even in the shadowless land.

> " Our days of praise will ne'er be past,
> While life and thought and being last,
> And immortality endures."

In this quiet, trustful confidence, may we have the Lord continuing with us at His Table !

[The rest of the Psalm was taken " after Supper."]

Regent Square Pulpit.

THE WORTH AND WORTHLESSNESS OF MUSIC.

A Sermon

Delivered in Regent Square Church on Sunday, March 2nd, by the

REV. JOHN McNEILL.

"And it came to pass, when the evil spirit from God was upon Saul, that David took an harp, and played with his hand : so Saul was refreshed, and was well, and the evil spirit departed from him."—1 Sam. xvi. 23.

In this chapter we have Saul and David brought together; and round the combination of these two names, as you well know, a wonderful history gathers. Saul and David! How bright is the halo that surrounds one of those heads, and how dark is the cloud that settles on the brow of the other! how increasingly bright the one; how increasingly dark the other! And let me say that these two men represent two great but opposing principles. David represents the man of grace. A man he is with many faults, with many things which make him like other men at their worst, but a man who is, notwithstanding, worthy of the title, "a man according to God's own heart." A man *subdued by grace*, although with all his own individual points and characteristics; a man who could be Saul, a man who could be and might be Saul at his worst, but who, with all this, *knows* that he is bad, sincerely repents of his evil, and asks for grace that he may be better. And Saul is a man after, not *God's own* heart, but a man after *his own* heart. Saul, notwithstanding many points wherein he seems to be a David, is of a totally different spirit from David. How bright he was at the beginning! how frank, how modest, how generous, how ingenuous! David himself could scarcely have played the part better than Saul played it at the time when he was chosen to be king by Samuel, and suddenly exalted to that high dignity. And yet Saul, after all, was so centred in himself, so proud, so rebellious, so possessed of an evil spirit, that his day went down into deep and deepening darkness. When we think of him at the end, or try to forecast how it fared with him beyond the end, we feel that the best we can say, apart from the well-known lament, is to shake our heads and say nothing.

Now these two are brought together in this chapter. We have seen David already, on a former occasion. Let us look at Saul as he comes before us here. "The Spirit of the Lord departed from Saul, and an evil spirit from the Lord troubled him." See the way in which these Hebrews explain things. That is hardly the way in which philosophy, either of history or of mind—these are hardly the terms in which it speaks to-day; but I am prepared to stand to them. This is biblical psychology; this is the Scriptural keynote to all individual history, and all collective history. "The Lord"—that is the grand feature of this Book; in its personal histories, or in its national histories. "The Lord"— either the presence of Him or the want of Him—the Lord's presence, the explanation of all a man's goodness, his intellect, his power, his valour, his industry, his success, either for himself or for his time. The absence of the Lord, the opposite of the Lord, is also the explanation of all that is dark and calamitous in the same directions.

Notice further how the old Book does not hesitate to trace everything up to God. The writers of this Book, whenever they come across a dark, perplexing problem, are men of this stamp—they get themselves to rest, to mental rest and consistency, when otherwise all things would rock and reel, by pressing everything up to God and letting it lie there. I find, speaking for myself in my day, and for my heart-breaking problems, that I get the same rest by letting everything go up to Him too. To put the very devil into God's hands gives rest: I can wait now; he is on a chain. No wonder Calvinism, as it is called, will always hold its own. It is because it is the most logical system, at any rate, to say the least of it. There is a thorough-going logic about it. We may call it *iron*, or may call it gloomy; I am not troubled about that. I seem to feel in my own heart what is the reason of it. Once you put God in the heart of the difficulty, I grant it does not untie the knot, but I expect to see it untie all knots and straighten out all problems in the end. Put the Lord in, and don't get nervous about His reputation. There is a problem for every system, a great difficulty. Why is evil here? And it is remarkable how the writers of the Bible, without making God responsible, put Him in there in the meantime. We rest here. "Shall not the Judge of all the earth do right?" You see how the problem breaks out upon us. "An evil spirit from the Lord troubled Saul." What is this? What imp from hell crept up to the Bible and wrote that in it? "An evil spirit from the Lord." Well, but that rings all through the Bible! The Lord is put in, in the meantime, for us short-sighted mortals, and He seems to say, "Rest here; see as far along the difficulty as Me, and do not ask anything further. And although it seems hard for Me, and although it seems awkward for Me, I will bear the brunt; and in the end of the day I will be just and justified, and clear Myself when I am judged."

"An evil spirit from the Lord troubled him." But has not the Revised Version done something with such a reckless sentence as that? No, my friend, it has not. The Revisers were only revisers. A number of people, we know, expected them to be *re-versers*. Ah, then, how many nice, smooth sentences would have taken the place of this, and many another awfully rugged utterance like it!

But I do not dwell upon that, I rather come upon another point. Here is a man in an iron cage, as Bunyan would say. Look at him—dark, gloomy, miserable, melancholy man. What is wrong with him? There are several elements in his trouble. The Spirit of the Lord left Saul, and an evil spirit from the Lord troubled him. Look at that man; for the longer I live, the more I get to see that there are many such still in Israel. My friends, I would like to be a better counsellor to you than Saul's servants were to Saul. I would like to go along their line, but to go a great deal farther, while I am at it. Will you listen? Heads up, hearts up, those who are troubled, those who are moody, those who are melancholy, those who are in distress in mind or heart, if not in body. Listen! Let us deal firmly with your disease, my atrabilious friend. First of all, as I see in Saul, so I see in you—*a good man gone wrong*. You are not bad, utterly bad, as yet. No, there are grand elements in you, and there are great possibilities yet, God be praised! there are great possibilities in connection with you.

> "The blackest night that veils the sky
> Of beauty hath a share;
> The darkest heart hath signs to tell
> That God still lingers there."

He only goes at the last, and then it is with weeping as He goes. You are moody and melancholy, because you look back on a happier beginning. That is one thing. Years ago, "in life's morning march, when your bosom was young," you started out like Saul. Life was to you a kingdom, and you were climbing up to its very throne. You began well; bright and fair and happy was everything on your horizon.

Yet to-day you sit in moodiness, bitterness, and hardness of spirit. You cannot help thinking of those earlier years, when the soft south wind blew, and you spread the sail to the breeze, "and let loose from Crete."

> "A wet sheet and a flowing sea,
> And a wind that followed fast,
> That filled the white and rustling sail,
> And bent the gallant mast."

The south wind blew, and all things in nature and Providence seemed to concur and smile upon you. The memory of it to-day increases the present blackness and the future foreboding. Is that not so? Why should we speak of these Old Testament characters as if they were dead mummies in a museum! My friend, is not that the reason of the darkness gathered here on your very face? Although you are come to the house of God, although you still keep to the worship of God, although you are not an infidel or a scoffer, your religion, whatever it is, is not a religion which brings peace and power with it. Are you, like Saul, getting darker, heavier, and blacker as the days and years go on, with, in some respects, a true knowledge of God, yet no light, no power, no peace? That was Saul.

But now we will come at once, for we must hasten, to the real explanation of his misery. It was this—*secret sin;* but I will give that sin a name: secret sin, taking the shape of *self-will,* which was not repented of and done away with.

Self-will was the secret explanation of all Saul's inward and outward misery, of all the still heavier distress which overtook him later on. Poor man! "whom unmerciful disaster followed fast, and followed faster:" and yet he began so well. Secret sin! I said at the beginning that I wanted to do my best for you; and the Lord wants to do His best for us all. My friends, what is the use of going about sighing and moping? What is the use of our going about cross with ourselves and each other as two sticks, when we know what is the matter? You know you are cherishing some secret sin. The Spirit of God has laid Saul bare to the very backbone, and we know what was his disease.

When will we understand that the Lord is always trying to lay us bare to ourselves? There is a stone in the machine: may it soon be detected and put away, then all the wheels shall move swiftly and without friction, as they used to do. There is war in your own heart, my friend. I grant there are troubles without—external sources of trouble and annoyance—but how many of us here to-day can say that we are free from the battle that raged in Saul's breast —that worst of all fights: the fight between a man and his conscience; between a man and his God? Said one not long ago, "You think I am a Christian; you think I am a Christian worker. Sir, I am the vilest hypocrite that ever was. You are utterly mistaken about me. When I put my hat on in the morning to go down town I feel like a brute." I probed him and probed him, and I found that he knew what was wrong. What was wrong was sin; not sin in the abstract—the Bible knows nothing about sin in the abstract, neither do I—but sin in the concrete. Sin in a particular form—a particular lust cherished and loved, although it is causing all this intense bitterness, and makes him say he is a hypocrite and a brute. Well, out of that I trust his salvation will yet come, for he knows his sin, and ceases to attempt any excuse for it.

Saul's lust was a lust for power, a lust for his own way. But he cloaked it, he covered it, he disguised it, he twisted it into religious phrases, he kept justifying himself to himself and to Samuel. But he is laid bare, and all subterfuges are torn to pieces. All refuges of lies in which he would hide himself are laid low, that God may show to him and show to us, that if we cover our sin we cannot prosper; but "if we confess our sins, He is faithful and just to forgive us our sins, and to cleanse us from all unrighteousness."

"The wicked is like the troubled sea when it cannot rest: whose waters heave up mire and dirt!" Now we know it. This man in the iron cage is not Saul of centuries ago; he becomes you, John Brown, in Regent Square, this morning. It is you, hemmed in, shut up, wrecked and wretched, with a war in your own breast. Alas! alas! peace so near, and we won't have it. Sin in the definite, particular, active, concrete form is practised and cherished and loved.

May the Lord deliver us from our besetting sin! May He come in the power of His Word and Spirit to-day, all the more because I feel so feeble and helpless in the face of the gigantic work which needs to be done. May Almighty God come, and may He—for it is His great prerogative—may He strike off all the spiritual chains which bite into our soul, as no iron-chain can! May He unloose the prisoners; may He take us out of our bondage! Poor soul! a sight to make angels and men shed bitter tears—a man of great capacity, great powers, and great discernment, and the devil has wound round about him the chain of evil habit, and he is pulling it tighter and tighter. First of all one act of sin; which seems so simple, so natural; and, on the spur of the moment, the right thing to do! But out of that egg there is hatched a whole habit and disposition. Oh, young man, young woman, let me speak to you on behalf of some of your elders sitting about you; let me interpret the bitterness of many a heart in London—some known to you, and some not known! Oh, let me, as God's minister of grace, warn you this morning of your responsibility!

Resist the beginning; resist the start; break with lust of flesh and mind when it seems to be filmy as a spider's web, for that spider's web may become a chain-cable, and bring down your honour in the dust.

Never forget that splendid spiritual drama, that spiritual tragedy that Christ has unfolded for us in the Gospels. "When the unclean, the evil spirit goeth out of a man"—as he went out of Saul and Judas for a while, as he went out of Achan, as he went out of Ananias and Sapphira, and as he went out of Demas for a time. When the evil spirit goeth out of one's manhood and womanhood, because I come into contact with Christ and His Gospel, I am empty of the devil, I am empty of lust. My bosom is unburdened, my skies are bright, heaven is opening up, and there is Paradise all around me. "When the unclean spirit goeth out of a man, he walketh through dry places seeking rest, and finding none, that unclean spirit saith, I will return unto my house (the impudence of him!)— I will return unto my house from which I came out; and when he cometh, he finds it empty, swept, and garnished." And then comes the crisis for your soul. Oh, Saul! Oh, Achan! Oh, Judas! Oh, Demas! Then, when he comes back to get in, then is the crisis of the soul. God help us to fight on the threshold of our house, which is God's house! And the evil spirit who says, "My house, let me in," is a liar; he must be rooted out, and routed on the spot. He will murder us if we don't overcome him. He cometh, as he came to Saul, and says, "*My* house," for he finds it empty, swept, and garnished. "My house, I used to live here. What a fine place it is; and how much better it is since I left. This place has been swept; it was a filthy, dirty, tumble-down place when I was here. It is greatly improved, I can live here better than ever." "Then he taketh seven spirits worse than himself, and they enter in and dwell there." And the last state of poor Saul, Achan, Judas, Ananias, Sapphira, and Demas—and God forbid it may be you and me!—the last state is worse than the first. It would have been better not to have known the way of life, than, having known it, to turn from it into the way of perdition. There is an awful blackness as well as a glorious brightness in the Gospel story—the brightest light throws the blackest shadow.

Then just a word about another thing: a word about the too cheap and slim and utterly inadequate remedy that was tried for Saul. I cannot go into all the narrative, but you will remember it brings out this point. The help and the helplessness, the worth and the worthlessness of music—the use and the uselessness of recreation, of change, of pleasure, of relaxation. How far these go; and how far they don't go! His servants came around Saul and virtually said, "What you need, dear master, is change; what you need is relaxation; what you need is music. We see the cloud upon your brow." And they were distressed for the poor man, the poor king. "Uneasy lies the head that wears a crown." Uneasy lies any head that belongs to a heart that is not right with God: that is hell begun in either king or cobbler. No treasures, says the poet of my country—

> "Nae treasures, nae pleasures can mak us happy lang,
> The heart's aye, the pairt aye, that maks us richt or wrang."

And if God is not in the heart, then the evil spirit is in it. Music! Well, we will say nothing against music, shall we? Music hath charms of every kind; who has not felt its power? The man who is not influenced and softened by music, we are almost inclined to say with Shakespeare, "Let no such man be trusted." We feel naturally suspicious of him. And yet how little it does! When we see what music sets itself to cure—London's music, London's sacred music, or its secular music—when we see what it is called in to cure, it is no wonder if I should get a little outspoken about it. Music for a madman!—whenever did it cure madness? Music for a man who needs Almighty God!—what a pitiful remedy! And is not that what the very Church of God is saying to-day? The masses —the squirming, wretched, howling masses—fiddle to them, oh, fiddle to them; get up music for them, get up popular entertainments for them. Cast out the devil with the fiddle!

Well, if he can be cast out with the fiddle, I am taking a wrong plan. It is a ludicrous mistake for me to have gone eight years through a college, when I ought to have been learning the banjo; was it not? If that is going to do it, we are on the wrong system. Now, I do not say a word against music. Let us have music, more music and better music; let it be done by the best talent we can get, the very best. The devil should not have all the good music, the Lord should have it, and I believe it is coming to that. But see here—this is the point—*see what our music is called in to do*. You talk about curing earthquakes with pills, it is very much the same as curing poor Saul's trouble by getting a man who was skilful with his hands upon the harp.

And a word, let me put in here, to people who are susceptible of music. My dear friends, this which was meant to do good to Saul, I rather think that in the end it only deepened his trouble; for medicine, when brought in in a case like this, if it does not permanently benefit, it will permanently injure. Now, I speak to people here who speak thus:—Said a young man to me, "When I go into a church where there is an organ, even before the sermon begins, and there is 'the long-drawn aisle and fretted vault;' when the music from the organ begins to peal and to steal, I almost begin to think I am a new creature." Well, if the organ is going to do it, it was an awful mistake for Christ to have climbed upon the cross. That was the blunder of all time—the Crucifixion was not needed if music and organs and choirs can cast out the evil spirit from a man. That is the trouble. Yes, I grant that you feel it, and *I* feel it—those inexpressible shivers that go all through us when there is splendid music, either of instrument, or the splendid musical crash of well-trained and well-balanced choirs. But tell me, you people, you emotional people, and I am one of you, what good does it do in the end? How does it leave you afterwards? There are plenty of people in London who, to-day and to-morrow and the next day, will go about simply to get the best music, and they, if they will tell the truth, can speak with bitterness as to how little it does for them. It leaves the heart as wicked as ever. David's harp! Ah, I would like to have heard him on his harp; I would like to have heard the sweet songs of Israel as David accompanied his harp with his voice.

> "Ten thousand times the man were blest,
> That might that musing hear!"

No doubt it was sacred music that he discoursed. Sacred music! But even that is not enough; it can stir for a little that muddy, drumly pool of our emotions; but when the exciting cause is withdrawn, the heart gets flatter and more stagnant than ever. Oh, man and woman, here in Regent Square this morning, turn from all physicians who would heal your wounds *slightly*, saying, "Peace! Peace! when there is no peace." Your wound is no slight wound; your wound is desperate, your wound is deadly. Nothing will cure thy heart but the almighty grace from the Lord Jesus Christ, through the Word and the Truth of His Gospel.

No; one of the sad things of this story is to find how near Saul came to a cure, and how far he remained from it. One could almost cry out, "Oh, Saul, you are on the right track, and yet you are altogether wrong! Oh, Saul, take not only the harp and the music, but if you would take the harper to your heart, that would cure you!"

What was all Saul's trouble? It was David. David was the stone, the stumbling-stone, over which he tripped and fell. The story gets breathless in its sad interest: David brought so near; and if Saul had only lent his heart as well as his ears, and taken David in and loved him, David would have been his salvation.

My parable is easily applied. Look here, friend, you do make a certain use of Christ; like Saul, you make a certain use of David and a certain use of religion, and you admit its power so far as you use it. Now, in the name of salvation, come farther; let me plead with you on this my first anniversary morning, come on a little bit farther! You like music, you like sacred music; I have seen it on your faces—how the eye gets filled over the singing, and for the time being, a brief but holy light settles upon your troubled face, and I believe that a corresponding peace comes into your war-broken soul. But if that is all, if it is only these sounds and strains and these sweet words, that is not enough. The devil in you can stand that, and still be what he is. If, however, you would take in not only the praise, but Him who is praised, if you would take in Christ, you would be saved. You are very near it to-day. Again and again and again we have sung His praise, and the singing went into your ear and flooded your soul; you felt, "Ah, yes, it is good for me to be here; I am glad I came to Regent Square this morning; I am glad I did not go for a walk; I am glad I did not go to some secular lecture or some Sunday concert; I am glad I came here into this sacred atmosphere." But oh, my friends, there is the awful danger! How many stop at that? How many are deluding themselves? Because the worship of God, beautifully and æsthetically and refinedly conducted, tells upon them emotionally, they think that is all, that is everything. "Ah," they say to themselves, "I who can be conscious, I who can be susceptible of these gushes and rushes of emotion and feeling, surely I am not the devil's prey, surely I am a child of God, surely it is all right with me!" My friends, say not so. There was Saul, and Saul felt all that; but as we know, poor man, he was allowing his wound to be *slightly* healed, to be slightly skimmed over, and soon it broke out with worse virulence than ever. The evil spirit departed from him when David took the harp and played with his hands; Saul was refreshed, but, as we know, *only for a season.*

Now I close with that. You are as near to the perfect cure as Saul was. *See that you get it.* And the perfect cure is to take the Lord Jesus Christ, who is the centre of the Church's service, and the centre of the preacher's preaching. Let him be as eloquent as he may, what is the use of eloquence, if you have not taken into your heart Him of whom the eloquent tongue preaches? Yet, let the preacher lack eloquence as much as he may, his preaching will tell upon you, as though he had the tongues of men and of angels, if he speaks of Jesus, and if your heart believes in Jesus while he speaks. Let the singing be what it may, what good will it do you permanently, unless you take in Christ, the burden of all our song, the theme of all our praise. And He is with you, He is beside you, He stands in front of you, He is related to you, as David was to Saul on this memorable occasion. Open the arms of your heart and take in Christ. Then you have got all heaven begun. But for your own sake —and I stand in doubt of not a few of you—as God would make me faithful, I tremble and I am anxious for you. You come so far, and then, God pity you! you stop short. Come on, come away forward; take Christ; come the whole way; do not stop at half measures, do not be contented with merely having your nervous system, and your physical frame, and your lower feelings soothed or gently excited, and moved either by singing or speaking, but come and get your very heart filled with all peace, all-abiding peace, by taking to your bosom Him who is at once David's Son and David's Lord. Get past the singing, go past all our service, go past the preacher. I am but a harp, and a very poor harp, with little more than one string; but if the Spirit of God struck me, what wonderful tones He might bring out. Go past the harp, go past the sound that comes from the harp, and see to it that you discern Him; See that you discern the heavenly David who holds this rude instrument in His hand. Yea, I say unto you, "See that you discern Him and love Him; take Him in to you; then shall the devil of discord leave thy breast, and thy soul shall begin to fill with heaven's own melody.

David was more than a mere strolling minstrel, whose art might beguile Saul's heart into a brief forgetfulness of its misery. Religion is more, much more, than simply what you are making it: a soothing, pleasant way of spending an idle hour of a particular day. Religion is submission of the heart to Christ. Use it *for all it is worth;* not merely for part, and that such a small part.

He who stood before Saul as a poor player is thus described: "Behold, I have seen a son of Jesse the Bethlehemite, that is cunning in playing (but far more than that). He is a mighty valiant man, and a man of war, and prudent in matters, and a comely person, and the Lord is with him." Such also is the Saviour I offer you to-day!

Regent Square Pulpit.

CONCERNING AUDIENCES, PREACHERS, SERMONS, AND CONVERSIONS.

A Sermon

DELIVERED IN REGENT SQUARE CHURCH ON SUNDAY, MARCH 9TH, BY THE

REV. JOHN McNEILL.

"Now therefore are we all here present before God, to hear all things that are commanded thee of God."—ACTS x. 33.

THIS chapter, as you are aware, notes for us the beginning, the entering-in of the Gospel among the Gentiles. That is its great interest. That is why, no doubt, so much detail is given of this gathering and of this sermon. The Lord is here doing a new thing. For generations, for centuries, He had committed the revelation of Himself and the working-out of His gracious purpose among men, to one narrow channel. To Israel's people mainly He had confined Himself; but now that Christ has come, that narrow channel was to be broken down, and the stream that was flowing in it was to overflow all its banks. Here, in this chapter, is the beginning of the breaking down of all Jewish dykes, and the outbursting and overflowing of that brimming river of grace and salvation, the waves of which are gently lapping at our feet to-day. So we have a special interest in taking up this text, because the Spirit of God seems to point to this audience through it, and to be saying to us, "Now, watch this people; see how they gathered together, and learn from them something about audiences and preachers and sermons, as long as audiences shall gather, and preachers shall confront them, to open their mouths, like Peter, to testify of God and His Son Jesus Christ." May we be helped to-day with this familiar Scripture to see where we are, and to know that this is no vain gathering. It is not a gathering of chance, neither is it a gathering entirely explained by long familiar custom and routine. The arm of the Lord has been shepherding you to meet me, and the same arm of the Lord has brought me forth, as out of His own very presence, to speak to you; and the Spirit of God, who fell upon the hearer's heart then, is the same Spirit who seeks to-day to fall, with all His gracious power, upon thy heart and life, even while thou art waiting here.

"Now therefore are we all here present before God, to hear all things that are commanded thee of God." There is something unusual in the text, in this, namely, that before the preacher began his sermon this "innovation" takes place—the audience spoke up to the preacher, the pew spoke up to the pulpit, and said, "Now therefore are we all here present." It was a splendid audience, though not so very large; but splendid when you look at it from the point of view of the narrative. How earnestly they came together! What a solidarity there was in this company! How these people were all bound together as one! Eyes front, heart front, mind front, conscience front. No wandering thought or eye, but all was focussed and settled; calm and purposeful both in body and soul; so that ere the preacher began, one man could speak for the whole company, and say in truth and soberness, "Now therefore, are we all here present before God." I should like to have seen that company. Well, I trust I see it as often as I am here, and that all of us preachers have the same conditions given us, in the midst of many difficulties with which we have to contend, without and within. May this audience bring its contribution to the preacher and the sermon, while it expects the preacher certainly to bring his! The contribution he has a right to expect is, that the people should come to hear—that the people should come united, full of expectation, led into the temple like Simeon of old, who was led into the temple by the Spirit of God, at the very moment when the parents of Jesus came to present Him before God, according to the custom of the law. No chance, no hap-hazard in this gathering. We have not come here to spend an idle hour. It is wrong to say, as, perhaps, some may say carelessly, when they go out of this place and are asked, " Where have you been this morning?"—it is wrong to answer the question by saying, " Oh, I dropped in to Regent Square." You did not drop in, my friend, nor drop out. You came in purposely. The Lord's providences for the whole of the week, like so many collie dogs, have been barking you in here, hedging up your way, and securing that to-day, at a certain time, you should be here. Fall in with God's arrangement. Let all depressing feeling which comes from custom and routine be taken away. I know you are apt to say, " Yes, there is something very vivid and fresh in this idea, as it relates to the first gathering; but you know, preacher, that was many centuries ago, and to come to church is now so regular and steady a thing, that it is hardly just to apply this text to this gathering to-day." My friend, all things here are spiritual, and belong to faith; they do not belong to sense and sight and mere human arrangement. Do not regard your presence here, on this lower plane of your own habit and intention; but see how the Word of God sets this hour in a strong, clear, and eternal light. God brought the people there, and had a great purpose in view concerning them. As it was then, so it is for ever—God has a purpose in bringing us to His house this day and hour.

I like to dwell on the word *all*. The people were invited. Cornelius invited his kinsmen and his near friends, and the invited people came. This morning the very hour invites us, "the bell invites me" to this place. I trust we have *all* come—that we are *all* here present. The husband is here, the wife is here, the children are here—no, they are not. It is of no use pretending they are, for they are not. That is one of the drawbacks in the gathering. We have not the young people as we should have them. We are not *all* here, and I feel when we haven't the children we lack a splendid part of the audience. I know there are explanations. I do not go into them, but let us try our utmost to fulfil this condition : "We are *all* here present before God." I know there are many excuses. I know you can tell me about young children, and sickness, and waiting on the sick; about fogs, and bitter east winds, and long distances, and wet days, and I don't know what besides. But making full allowance for all these things, there is still great need for the preacher, now and again, even with a full congregation, to take up this text, and insist upon this word being repeated every Sabbath as far as may be, "We are all here present before God." For there is often, with all our talk about this place and day, when you come to the practical point, there is often a heavy discount to be taken off. There is a great discrepancy between our creed about the Sabbath day and our actual conduct. In many families, at ten o'clock on the Sabbath morning, attendance at church is still an open question. Often in a working man's house, and in others that are not working men's, after waking, after dressing, after breakfasting, it is an open question, "Will you go out to-day?" It is no open question on the Monday morning, "John, will you go to work to-day?" They never dream of asking such a thing. "Oh," said a farmer in Scotland, when a minister rebuked him for not attending church, and said, "You know, John, you are never absent from the market." "Oh," was the reply, "we maun gang to the market." (We must go the market.) Unconsciously it came out. But to come to the house of God was not to be put on the same level, for urgency. Oh, there is a difference between our creed and our actual conduct and custom. But when we look at this audience we see the great benefit of continually setting ourselves the task of coming with a purpose to God's house. It will need plan and purpose to accomplish this. Some of you are here to-day only because you have trampled upon a hundred obstacles in order to get here. If you had given way you would not have been here. And some are not here who might have been included in this "*all* here present," because they have given way to things which will not be allowed for a moment to stand in the way of the world's engagements to-morrow. I know there are difficulties and obstacles and young children, and so on; but in the case of many there are no difficulties that could not be overcome. You have not all young children and babies at the breast. In many households "the key could keep the castle," and nothing would either burn or boil over if all came out, and not a hoof was left behind.

And then, when we do that, when we all come, don't you think the Lord notices that, and marks how we have pressed forward to meet Him. I think there is no sweeter sight to His holy eyes in London and in England to-day than to see the people wending their way to the house of God—to see them in cities and towns and villages and in quiet hamlets all going up to worship the Lord. All things the same as on another day, and yet all things different.

> "How sweet the morning of the Sabbath day!
> Hushed the ploughboy's whistle, and the merry milkmaid's song,
> The scythe lies glittering in the dewy wreath of tedded grass,
> Which yestermorn bloomed, waving in the breeze,
> The blackbird's note comes mellower from the dale,
> And sweeter from the sky the gladsome lark pours forth his song."

All the same, and yet all different, on the Sabbath day
And says another:—

> "O sweeter than the marriage feast,
> 'Tis sweeter far to me,
> To walk together to the kirk with a goodly company !
> To walk together to the kirk, and all together pray,
> While each to his great Father bends,
> Old men, and babes, and loving friends,
> And youths, and maidens gay !"

Long may such gatherings be the crown and flower of our land! "Forsake not the assembling of yourselves together, as the manner of some is, and so much the more, as ye see the day approaching." Oh, there is a great deal in determining to be there, and to be always there, and making it the key-note of all Sabbath morning arrangements.

You womenfolk, my heart is with *you*. You have great burdens in connection with domestic arrangements, and I would sometimes that you could get a longer sleep and take it easier; but not on the Sabbath morning, if you please. Be up a little earlier, and see to it that that day you take everything into prayerful hands, and shape and guide everything to help me and my Master behind me. You have a great deal in your hands—a great deal of responsibility And when you come in this expectant way, how it helps the reception of the sermon! How we have all suffered from coming to the house of God in a disorderly, hurried way, both as regards body and soul! We come tumbling in late, because we only made up our minds half an hour ago that we would come at all, and the service is half over before you know where you are, or what you are, or how you are, or what is being said. Then you look up to the preacher and expect him to work miracles on your higgledy-piggledy soul. Your very clothes are not on as well as you would like, and you are distressing yourself as to whether your personal attire is becoming. And yet you look to me, and expect me to soothe and smoothe you, and make you feel that this is the house of God and the gate of heaven. It is not so in our text. What a sight is here—every eye eager; everything prompting with the suggestion, a great business is on hand, and God and man are straitened till it be accomplished. "Now, therefore, are we all here present before God," they said. Ah! there is another point. They realized God's presence. May He grant that we may realize it to-day and always!

Try to realize God's presence; get past outward and temporal things, and call upon your soul to pass into the secret place of the tabernacle of the Most High. Compel your soul to grasp the thought—God is here! God is here! I am in His presence. This is the house of God; the Lord is with us in this place. "Surely God is in this place;" and instead of saying, "I knew it not," our heart is saying eagerly, "We know it, and wait to see a still clearer revelation of His presence. He made me, and redeemed me, and sustains me, and before Him ere another Sabbath I may stand in judgment. This is holy ground. The burning bush is here, with the voice of God speaking out of it, and saying "Draw not nigh rashly, heedlessly; put off thy shoes from off thy feet, for the place whereon thou standest is holy ground."

Do you know that where you are sitting God, by His Word, has converted men ere now? Canst thou come and sit in these pews, where God has done His mightiest work, carelessly, heedlessly, and merely as a matter of custom and routine? Yes, here and there, and all over —could we see this holy place with God's eyes—we should see that this man, and that man, was born there, and there, for God is present in this place. How canst thou sit carelessly, when right from where thou art souls have gone to their eternal home? Thou art occupying the room and space of men and women who to-day are before the eternal throne. The church is a grand place; it is the house of God. This word is true: "We are all present before *God*"—and therefore let there be nothing mean or low; nothing unworthy of such a Presence and such a place.

And how the thought of God's presence will help still further to focus our attention; to take our eyes off each other, and off the preacher! How it will help to prepare us to receive God's Word! How it will reduce to the irreducible minimum the over-critical spirit! Said a preacher to myself, "I notice when I give out my text, my people settle down and settle back; but, I am afraid, not so much to hear what I have to say as to watch how I get through." I wonder if that is how the congregation does at Regent Square—if they settle back to see how I get on, and to observe with what dexterity, or want of it, I shall handle the theme? I do not wish that we should turn the pulpit into a coward's castle, in which, speak as I may, I am safe from remark as to my message—either its matter or delivery. Yet there is a bound to be set to our critical tendencies—a very definite bound; and many of us every day overstep it, sadly overstep it, and we get no good, but much harm, thereby. Now, the thought of God's presence puts us in our right place as regards our neighbour and our minister, and the minister in his right place as regards the audience. May the Holy Ghost come upon us, and the power of the Highest overshadow us! Oh, what a place this would be now, if He came into our hearts! He *is* here; *and we are here, in the sight of God.*

And then Cornelius said further, " Now therefore are we all here present before God, *to hear all things* that are commanded thee of God." They came to listen, to hear God's Word. You know that to-day there is a tendency to revise the Directory for Public Worship; to say, " Oh, the hearing"—meaning the hearing of God's Word at the preacher's mouth—" has been too much magnified. We shall change all that." We have made a mistake. " What I come to God's house for," says one, " is to worship; what I come for is to join in prayer and in praise. The preacher gets far too much place and far too much space. There is so much room given to him in the programme that it is no wonder if he exalts himself and wearies or bewitches us with the display of his eloquence or learning, or both." There may be something in that, but it is seriously exaggerated. What was central here, and what must always be central in a gathering of saints or sinners, in evangelistic missions, or regular services like our own; what must always be central is the preaching of God's Word, and the attending thereto by the hearer. That is worship at its highest. All the powers of the soul get their highest use and their fullest freedom when God's Word is faithfully and lovingly proclaimed. We are here to hear. Faith cometh by hearing. The large, central, integral, essential part of our work is to preach and to hear what is commanded from God.

And Cornelius said they had met to hear " all things *that are commanded thee of God.*" I have been speaking strongly and straightly to you, but now your turn comes. This is the portion for the preacher, when the pew says to the preacher, " Now, give us to-day what God has told you. There are many things that might interestingly occupy an hour; give us, however, the thing that brought us here, that for which the house is built, and for which the ministry is appointed—the Word of God, the Gospel of the grace of God that bringeth salvation unto men. We need that to-day." And I should like always to be kept right by being pushed hard here. *We* must study. We look ahead to the Sabbath day. It is our special work: we are not engaged in secular work. There were great preachers in olden days who worked at, say, tent-making through the week, and did not utter slim discourses either when the Sabbath day came round. We haven't got to the bottom of them yet. But, so it is; we preachers are given up to this business. Now, out of this room and time for study there may come a serious detriment to the Gospel. We get so immersed in favourite lines of reading and study, and this may so unconsciously tincture and colour our utterances on the Sabbath day, that we may need, severely need, that the audience should approach us here, and say, " Now, preacher, God's Word and truth ; all things from Him to-day, and nothing else—*nothing else.* Never mind about reconciling science and revelation to-day ; we can live without that ; we can get that in our own magazines and periodicals for sixpence a month. We can read that at home, on the sofa, in the afternoon, when dinner is over, unless we fall asleep. We are really so little concerned about it that we give it the sleepy hour. But give us to-day what really concerns us—the Word of God as the Word of God, and what is meant to save our souls, to purify our hearts, and to guide the practical daily life we are living—' All things commanded thee of God.'" Oh, see what it suggests ! It suggests that the preacher comes from God's hand. I say it suggests that the preacher comes from the secret place. "Now, then, we are ambassadors for Christ, as though God did beseech you by us, we pray you, in Christ's stead, be ye reconciled to God." Before we came to meet you this morning, we were in before the Lord the King, and had our message from Him. Aye, we do need to be reminded, sharply in these days, that we exist to feed the hungry with bread.

Peter needed that. It needed a great work of God's Spirit and providence on Peter's mind and heart and imagination to enable him to preach that day. Peter was a narrow, bigoted Jew, if left to himself, and he would never, of himself, have preached to Cornelius and his company the sermon they needed. And so the Lord had to widen the preacher's views, and by a vision from heaven He had to prepare Peter to preach to the Gentiles salvation through faith in Jesus Christ. At the best we are but men, and of narrowness and prejudice we have our share. Therefore there is tremendous need that the preacher should be in God's hand, and come from God's presence with his soul and voice attuned to a large, full, free, and glorious utterance of the Gospel of the grace of God. Leave us to ourselves, and even the largest heart and most liberal culture may be found preaching away at something that is as narrow as a razor's edge, and quite " FROM the purpose " of preaching. There may be some little glimmering light in it, but it is only a little; there may be light from every quarter, to use the phrase of the day; from every quarter—save the Sun! The Lord blow out all OUR penny candles His light has come.

We need to come forth from God, He having poured into us something of the breadth and fulness of God's mind and heart, and of God's love for those to whom we are to speak. "All things commanded of God." What a word for the preacher! How it humbles us, and makes us tremble! How it would make Peter stand at "Attention!" as he looked into hungry eyes and hungry hearts, and said to himself, "What am I to say?" I stand before you to-day, and the very look is enough to shake either man or angel to the very foundation. What have you come for? Why are you there? Why are you there, and why am I here? Almighty God, give us the explanation! You are here because God has a purpose to save and bless you, and that purpose is to be accomplished by my mouth to-day.

Now, what was the sermon? "Then Peter opened his mouth." Do not run over that phrase and say, "Of course Peter opened his mouth." Not "of course" at all. A number of us cannot open our mouths when we preach—it is the most pitiable mumbling ever was heard. It is said of our Lord, He went up into a mountain, and, when His disciples were gathered around Him, "*He opened His mouth and taught them.*" Do not run over it. It is not an "of course." Sabbath-school teacher, Bible-class teacher, when you meet with your company to-day, preacher—for I speak to brethren here who before this sun sets will be doing the very thing I am trying to do now—to all of you I say "Open your mouth, and teach the people." Let it be seen in the very manner of our speech that our mouth is open.

for our heart is enlarged; that it comes, not feebly and faint and constricted, but glad and full and free, for the Lord is with us. Do not say, "I have no eloquence." I could say it, and with truth. Do not say, "I have a stammering tongue." Who made man's mouth? "Have not I the Lord? Open thy mouth; behold I put My words into thy mouth." What does Isaiah say? "Lift up," he says— and how much it is needed in this namby-pamby, over-refined, hypercritical age — "Lift up thy voice with strength, lift it up; be not afraid; say unto the cities of Judah, Behold your God." It is as if Isaiah had seen the nineteenth century, and had seen that we have fallen upon such over-refined times, that to speak with open mouth and full heart is to be vulgar, and lacks refinement; and that to chirrup, chirrup, chirrup, so as not to be heard beyond the choir seats, or to be as white in the face as the paper you are reading from, is to be surrounded by tokens of thoughtfulness; aye, that is the word, *thoughtfulness*, and culture. "Peter opened his mouth." He lifted up his head, *and let go!* We put down ours, *and hold on!*

I won't go into his sermon, but will only read from the forty-third verse: "To him gave all the prophets witness, that through His name whosoever believeth in Him shall receive remission of sins. While Peter yet spake these words, the Holy Ghost fell on all them which heard the word." There is the sermon, and the effect of the sermon. We have spoken of the audience; then the preacher; now the sermon, and the result of the sermon. What was the sermon? It was the Gospel, the old Gospel. It was new and fresh then; it had only been "finished" a few weeks before! That is one thing that one does sometimes envy the first preachers for. They had seen Him; they were with Him on the holy mount, and had seen His glory; they heard His words, they were at the Cross, and saw Him crucified, dead, and buried. He appeared unto them after His Passion; as Peter says here, "not to all people," but to us, His witnesses, who did eat and drink with Him after

He rose from the dead. He preached Christ, you see. It is not theology, not a creed. I am fond of theology, and have a very definite creed, as many of you, and those in my communicants' class well know. I have a definite theology and creed; I took it in with my mother's milk, so to speak, and I believe it as strongly as ever, though perhaps with more charity towards people whose creed has not at all the points the firm, sharp outline of my own. But what Peter preached was not so much a creed or formulated truth as Jesus, sent for a particular purpose from God and by God; how that, carrying out that purpose, He had died on the cross and risen again, and that through Him is preached forgiveness of sins. It was no Jewish ritual. The Jewish ritual is for ever swallowed up and done away with. You have simply to bow your heart, and give your heart to this Jesus whom I, Peter, saw on the cross, and after He came out of the tomb. I am witness for Him. I am His witness, and this is the burden of my message to you to-day, "that through Him you may receive forgiveness of sins."

That is where the Gospel began then, and where it begins to-day—forgiveness of sins to the man who is described in the same passage as being a devout man, and one that feared God, and made prayers, and gave alms. Yet he needed to have forgiveness of sins, if he would become a true evangelical believer. Here was one who prayed and gave alms, yet Peter dared to begin with Him at this low level of remission—forgiveness of sins. "Oh," people would have said to-day, "with an audience like that, what you want to do is not to take them to the cross; do not begin with them at forgiveness of sins, you will only make them stumble. Show them Christ, of course; but Christ as the great ideal and embodiment of all that is pure and noble and beneficent; and ask them to be loyal to Him, and as like Him as possible. Show him Jesus Christ, and a devout, God-fearing man like Cornelius will be enamoured with Christ and make Him his Leader and Pattern. Preach

Christ to him, but not Christ crucified." "No," says Peter; "we preach the Christ who died for sin to everybody, to everything human." Do not dare to begin. unless you begin down there, and at men's sins—preach forgiveness through a crucified, divinely-appointed Redeemer. If not, the people will be still in the gall of bitterness and in the bond of iniquity.

By Him I preach the forgiveness of sins, men and brethren. Now, are you forgiven? After coming forty years to Regent Square, are you forgiven? Christ is our atoning Redeemer *first*, or He is nothing—*nothing*.

Woe be unto us if we do not preach Christ and Him crucified; not because you are good, but because you are bad, and nothing less could satisfy either your conscience or the justice of God. A French officer, whose ship had been taken by Nelson, was brought on board Nelson's vessel, and he walked up to the great admiral and gave him his hand. "No," said Nelson; "your sword first, if you please." That is the Gospel. Oh, there are great companies of people to-day who are going to take the preacher's hand and Christ's hand! "Jesus is such a noble character," say they; "we are enamoured with Him; we will walk with Him." Nay, nay! not so fast. Your sword first, please. Give up your rebellious will first; admit your guilt, then Christ will take your hand with a grip that He will never relinquish. That is the Gospel. You are either forgiven through faith in His blood, or you are remaining in your sins. Where are you? "To Him gave all the prophets and apostles witness;" and I stand in the Apostolic succession, in a straight line from the cross and the resurrection, down and down and down, through the great multitude of witnesses.

I speak to-day as with a thousand tongues, when I speak with heart and voice, and say that the Gospel is this—That Jesus died for our sins, that He lives again, and is with us, and begins by blotting out all our sins for His own great name sake. And when I utter that Paul is with me, and Peter, and John, and Isaiah, and David, and Moses—all are standing with me in this pulpit. "To Him gave all the prophets and apostles witness." There is no doubt about it. Forgiveness of sins is preached through Him who died and rose again. Now, are you giving up the sword? Are you giving up yourself to Him as a poor lost sinner? I believe I am speaking this to not a few Corneliuses. You are devout men and women, and fear God to such an extent as makes you depart from flagrant iniquity. You conform your ways wonderfully in some things, outwardly, to the ten commandments. You pray and give, and your prayers and alms are come up for a memorial before God. He would not have you standing in the outer court. He has sent me to-day to ask you to come in, but you can only do so as a poor sinner. Oh, be washed from sin; be saved by the pardoning grace of Jesus Christ to-day!

While Peter yet spake these words—there is a new name brought in here. I have talked of Cornelius and of the audience. I have talked of Peter and of Jesus. I have talked of God the Father, but here is another name. While Peter yet spake these words about Jesus, "The Holy Ghost fell on all them that heard the word," on Cornelius and his kinsmen and his near friends round about him. There was no visible flame, as at Pentecost; but they felt the fire in their hearts. Cornelius possibly had only heard of Jesus as a name of reproach and rebuke and blasphemy. Now, Jesus leapt up into his heart as his Friend and Saviour, and Redeemer and God. That is the miracle of the Gospel. That is the miracle of to-day. That was the miracle wrought for me on a day never to be forgotten.

I heard these words, or truths conveyed in words like them, and the Holy Ghost fell along with the word; and that Jesus, who before was only a name in history to me, became *my Redeemer, who died for me,* who lives for me, who is with me here, and intercedes for me yonder. That is what the Holy Ghost does. If you know Jesus Christ, flesh and blood hath not revealed it unto you, but the Holy Ghost. Peter was there, as the preacher is here; and the sermon, with its appeal and arguments and illustrations; but the Holy Ghost gives the increase and blesses the word. The Holy Ghost brings forth fruit unto everlasting life; and without Him fruit cannot be.

I am not going to leave you in a puzzle. I used to get puzzled between Jesus and the Holy Spirit. I was told (and it is true), "You are saved by Jesus. He died; He has done the work; His blood and righteousness are your salvation; and you have nothing to do but to believe in Him." But I was also told I could not trust Him without the help of the Holy Spirit; and what between looking to Jesus and the Spirit one gets into a little dilemma. My friend, you have nothing to do with the Holy Spirit—*not now*. You have not to do directly with Him. The Holy Spirit does His work by getting you *to look to Jesus;* but when, by this sermon, He lifts up Jesus before you, and seeks to fasten the eyes of your understanding upon Him, this word comes in as the explanation of the great result that follows. As an explanation to serve for all time, and to give us the assurance that it was not the eloquent preacher, nor wonderful arguments, nor special appeals, but the supernatural work of the Holy Ghost on an otherwise dead and dark heart, that revealed to us Jesus as our Saviour, who loved us and gave Himself for us. So do not be in a dilemma.

I preach to you Jesus; but I tell you to encourage you that there are more at work upon you than myself. The Holy Spirit is preaching to you Jesus. Would you obey the Holy Spirit and satisfy all that He requires? Then simply say in your heart, "Yes, I take this Jesus to be my Saviour, I give up myself into His hands." Then all Godhead is satisfied. Oh, how familiar! Will you believe Him to-day? Come to Him. Here is no room for the display of eloquence. Will you believe in Christ to-day? Hear the word of this salvation: believe in Him to-day; trust in Him to-day; then thy sins are blotted out. It will have to be done some day, if ever it is to be done. While these words are being spoken may the Holy Ghost fall upon your hearts, and all who receive the word will be saved! God could save the whole congregation at once. May God come and save this twelve hundred in Regent Square! It would only be a lift for the little finger of such a mighty Saviour. We can hardly take it in. We think God comes to pick out one here, and another over there. We think that God's election is a narrow thing. We have forgotten the sweep and scope and embrace of the Gospel. We have forgotten that there is One amongst us to-day whose arms are long enough and whose heart is big enough to draw all within these four walls into His embrace and keep us there for ever and for ever. O Blessed Spirit, we have lifted up Christ! Now, let sinners find a refuge in His cleansing blood. Amen.

Regent Square Pulpit.

"SANS EYES, SANS TASTE, SANS EVERYTHING"
—BUT GOD AND HOPE.

A Sermon

DELIVERED IN REGENT SQUARE CHURCH ON SUNDAY,
MARCH 16TH, BY THE

REV. JOHN McNEILL.

"And even to your old age I am He; and even to hoar hairs will I carry you: I have made, and I will bear; even I will carry, and will deliver you."—ISA. xlvi. 4.

You will sympathize with me, my friends, in the difficulty I feel in preaching from a text like this; not because it is a complicated utterance, but because it is so open and self-evident; not because it is thin, with too little in it; but because it is so wide, and deep, and full. That is my difficulty. *There is so much of God in it* that I am steadied somewhat between desire to preach it and despair of being able, in any sufficient degree, to bring out its fulness. That wonderful "I" occurs in the short compass of our text some half-dozen times; so you will sympathize with me. What man or angel is fit worthily to preach a Scripture that rings throughout with the voice of God, a passage that is so peculiarly shining with His immediate presence. "Even to your old age I am He; and even to hoar hairs will I carry you: I have made, and I will bear; even I will carry,

No. 19.

and will deliver you." May the Lord, the Spirit, ring out this text from the page, and may His voice sound into your very hearts!

If only the ears of our hearts somehow or other catch the echo of these blessed tones, catch something of this splendid emphasis regarding the presence of God, and the power of God, and the perpetual salvation of God, then the eldest shall have their strength renewed, and the youngest shall have theirs multiplied like the strength of ten. Why I have directed your thoughts to this text to-day is not far to seek. If you stood here where I stand, you would see how our company is adorned with not a few white and whitening heads. The Lord, since last we met here, has taken to Himself a sister, or mother, rather, from that "Bright Band." For the comfort of those "who are alive and remain"—well, for the comfort, and instruction, and stimulus of all, I turn to this portion of Scripture.

I do not mean to speak here of our friend's years and labours, except to say, in one word, that they were long, abundant, and self-denying. My hope is rather that through our sister's departure, the Lord has created among such an atmosphere as shall give special brightness and blessedness to the gracious words we are considering this morning.

We are speaking, then, to those who have come to what is called poetically "the vale of years"—to our aged friends. Sometimes the pulpit speaks specially to the young, to children; sometimes specially to young men and women; sometimes, again, it speaks specially to those in middle life. To-day the pulpit addresses those who are advanced in life; who have gone onward, far along the pilgrim journey. The end to them is drawing near; somewhat sensibly, and almost visibly, the road is getting shorter, and the terminus, the bound of life, is coming more clearly into view.

Notice, first of all, then, that the comfort, the solid, substantial comfort, in God's estimation, for the aged pilgrim, is this—*the thought of His own presence.* "I am He." God Himself is seen here to be thinking for you, and feeling for you, if I may put it so. Eternal God although He be, without beginning of days, or end of years, yet He knows how you feel and what you feel; He understands how the burden of years tells upon you physically, mentally, emotionally, imaginatively, and every way. He knows how sorely the burden and battle of life press upon you. He understands all this as I, for example, do not and cannot understand it. If I had not God's Word in my mouth to-day, I might not know what to preach; you have so far outstripped me in years and experience. It would be an impertinence in every sense for me to dare to speak if I had not God's Word; but I have God's Word, and God's Word at its best, for an aged pilgrim.

He sees what you need, and therefore this message. You well know these things, of course; but I wish to establish you in the present truth. Therefore, I call your attention to this splendid emphasis; this bringing out of the personal "*I*"—"*I am*," "*I* have borne," "*I* will carry," and "*I* will deliver," as long as danger and need require deliverance and relief. Think, then, upon this thought. Your eyes are waxing dim, and the burden of years is getting heavy upon you; allow me to come and remind you to-day of that God in whom you have put your trust. He is entirely unaffected by the flight of time. "Thou art the same: and thy years shall not fail." Your sight grows dim; His keen as ever. You arm is shortened; His almighty as ever. "Even to your old age He is the same (for so it has been rendered); and to hoar hairs will He carry you." The Lord, in His infinite, eternal, and unchangeable presence; that is the great strong Rock that lifts itself upon the view of those who are stooping and fainting in the long and weary ways of life. Your physical life is ebbing away, and its very sources are being dried up. My friends, use your remaining strength to-day to do this; use your strength not to travel, or run, or climb. I shall not ask for any eagle-wing exercise of faith; I do not ask you to mount up as with wings, or run without being wearied, or to walk without fainting. All I ask of you is simply—lie down. To an "old body" that should be easy, should it not? You say you are old and tottering. Lie down, then—now, here—under the shelter of this great Rock. "To your old age I am He!" Yes, lie close in against the root of this sheltering Rock; and see how all fears and troubles, like careering clouds, pass high over head. And as you look up sing thus :—

"Who but the Lord is God? but He
Who is a Rock and Stay?
'Tis God that girdeth me with strength,
And perfect makes my way."
—Ps. xviii. 31.

Then see how He emphasizes this. If we look back to the previous verse, we read, "Hearken unto me, O house of Jacob, and all the remnant of the house of Israel, which are borne by me from the belly, which are carried from the womb." This verse takes you back to the beginning of your earthly existence. Remember how you came here. It is a fact that you were once an infant. Since then you have passed through many experiences, so varied, and, perhaps, wonderful, that you might stand to-day, after seventy or eighty years, and say, "Am I the same being?" I find myself in such strange circumstances to-day. Why, I began life hundreds, or even thousands of miles away from here, with all things different, and under different skies. In how many different lands have I pitched my tent? What sights I have seen, and with how many people I have met and parted! What ups and downs I have had! What disasters I have come through, when hundreds, it may be, were swept away in epidemic visitations! And yet here am I. But I could almost wonder "am I really myself. Has my identity really been preserved? I have had so many troubles and trials; so many and great have been my changes and experiences." Well, friends, but suppose we leave all that has come between, and go back to the solid, unalterable, substantial fact of your first coming into this world. You hung upon a mother's breast, and were dandled, a helpless infant, upon her knees. God takes that unalterable fact, and says, "I was there;" and, lo! seventy years afterwards, "I am here, as close to you as ever. I formed you in the womb, and hung you upon the breast; it was My hands that handled you first. 'Twas I who fastened your mouth upon those breasts; 'twas I who dandled you; 'twas I who heard your infant cries, and preserved you when your life was like a gossamer-thread, and when any rude puff of wind might have broken it. When you were launched upon the stream of being, the last bubble, so to speak, that had appeared upon its waves, it was I who kept the bubble from bursting, and your life from vanishing almost before it became visible. When you were at the lowest and feeblest, I, the Almighty, the Eternal God was with you: *then* I was by you." "Shall I leave you now," is the argument, "when you are coming round to second childhood, which is even more pathetic, in some senses, than infancy? What did I bring you up for? Why did I see you through all the perils that throng thick and fast round infancy? Was it to forsake the work of My own hands? Was it to stultify Myself by abandoning you when old age and hoary hairs have come?" I press that argument upon us all.

These "scientific" days of ours are going to corrupt us everywhere. We will soon be praising and magnifying the great god, Evolution, for everything. We will make father and mother out of it; and giving no thanks to them, or nurse, or doctor, transfer them all to "Evolution." I am face to face with a company of people, and I am one of them myself, who are all monuments of God's handiwork. The explanation of your presence in that seat to-day is this: God was with you from *the very beginning*. "Thine eyes," says David, that old Bible philosopher—"Thine eyes did see my substance, yet being unperfect; and in Thy book all my members were written, which in continuance were fashioned, when as yet there was none of them." I speak to you, young men and women, and to you, middle-aged men and women, who have waxed strong and grown great. Come down off your high horse as quickly as you can. You were not born on horse-back, remember. Let me remind you, yea, let God remind you, how you began life. You are very clever and intellectual now; but let me remind you of the days when to pull at your mother's breasts was the utmost you could do! You can utter great speeches to-day, and talk very philosophically; but allow me to remind you, Mr. Robert Elsmere, of the days when the most you could do was to lie and cry, *and you did it*. May the Lord take us down in His own unspeakably gentle yet thorough fashion!

Let us think of those two under-nurses, under God—our dear nursing mother and father. Let us think of the cradle in which we lay; and in the light of this text let us see the Overshadowing God. I say again, this is of worth for all of us; but especially for all aged and ageing friends. It is good for you, is it not, my friends, to have your life stream traced back to this Well-head? For the Well-head is God : the presence of God, the intention of God, from eternity and to eternity. The gates of life through which you issued as an helpless infant, this is the Divine philosophy of our being and becoming—these gates never open but at His command. And He said thou shalt be; therefore thou art. He formed thee in the womb, and brought thee forth by His own hand. He touched thee and handled thee before any mortal in this world. How precious, how comforting, how sustaining to an aged saint! And how full of Gospel to an aged sinner! Remember *the former mercies*, and return.

Then go on: "To hoar hairs will I carry you: I have made and I will bear; even I will carry, and will deliver you." I don't know if you have noticed the connection between this and the beginning of this chapter. When we were boys and girls, this was a strange chapter to us. "Bel boweth down, Nebo stoopeth." Bel and Nebo were great gods of the oppressors of ancient Israel. The prophet here is getting very sarcastic. He speaks of the time when their captors shall be overthrown, and their very gods shall be taken captive. These idol gods shall be pitched into some old lumber waggon; and, he says, the beasts will be weary pulling the dead burden of these man-made gods, and will be glad to get rid of them. The gods could not save themselves, but should be carried into captivity. And here comes the argument, "I have made you, and will bear you." These other gods, these gods of the heathen, they needs must be carried by their worshippers;—they are senseless, dumb, useless things: needing to be carried, and, when danger comes to their devotees, unable to save themselves. But "I," says God—"I carry My worshippers; they do not carry Me. I look after them; they do not look after Me." He is demolishing idols with every stroke of this tremendous, magnificent "I"—"I have made, I will bear, yea, I will carry, and will deliver you."

The same demolition of idols is needed with us. Are we not all tempted, in our hot and fiery youth and mid-manhood, with its pride, to make gods out of our strength? Yea, to think that God is somewhat indebted to us. As the idolaters did with their divinities—you can see them still in old sculptures—carrying their gods upon their shoulders, so we carried on our shoulders heaven and earth. We were so strong and mighty, we were of so much importance, that if we had not taken care, and taken trouble, where would earth, and God, and heaven have gone? The Lord is reminding us in our old age, when we take it in better than in lusty youth and manhood, the Lord is saying to us, "Now, this was always the case, only you will believe it to-day. I never required your fears, and anxious cares. I have got a good opportunity now, when your mighty shoulders are getting sharp, and thin, and poor, to tell you that your dependence all along was on My shoulders, and on My strength, and on My wisdom, and on My presence. I made, and I will bear; even I will carry, and will deliver you." Lie back in His bosom, oh little helpless child of seventy years!

"Cast me not off," said David, "in the time of old age," when I am feeble and failing; when the young are outstripping me, and getting to the front; and I am being sent as so much impedimenta to the rear. "O God, cast me not off!" To which cry God says, "I will not; I am here—here in the growing, gathering darkness: let My presence be your light at eventide." How it rings out in the darkness of your gathering years, my aged friends! God is with you. He was always with you. Lean back on His strength. You were foolish, even at your lustiest, if ever you did less. But when the limbs are strong, and all our powers in full force, we are prone to make our strength our god. Now, in old age, when your powers are but a remnant, find your strength in the strength of God. " He giveth power to the faint; and to them that have no might He increaseth strength. Even the youths shall faint and be weary, and young men shall utterly fall; but they that wait upon the Lord shall renew their strength."

> " And in old age, when others fade,
> They fruit still forth shall bring;
> They shall be fat, and full of sap,
> And aye be flourishing."

I remember, one night, when I was a lad, I took a long walk from the place where I was working, late on a Saturday night, to my father's house; and all the way along that walk the night increased about me, the darkness got thicker and thicker. I knew that just before I should reach home I should pass through what to me was the gloomiest and thickest wood that ever was. It was gloomy even at midday. And I remember I was feeling my way through that dense wood, when suddenly my heart leapt to my mouth, and the same instant almost all my fears vanished. For a great, strong voice rang through every timber of the wood—"Are you coming, Johnny?" 'Twas my father coming to meet me! Oh, the night became almost light about me. I could almost fancy I saw the outline of a great, strong man flashed upon the darkness—so vivid was the impression, not only on the ear, but also on the imagination. Then the whole darkness was vocal with the crash of his voice. Some of you are in darkness. It is wearing late, my brother. It is getting dark, and late, and lonely, and not many people are tramping your road now. Time was when the road was filled with your friends. Lover and friend have been put far from you, and best and dearest acquaintances have gone out into the darkness. You are like one who sits up far into the night, and sees the lights in the neighbours' houses one by one put out, while the darkness and silence are deepening round about him. But suddenly, suddenly, in this darkness and loneliness, God's voice rings out, "I am here; fear not; never nearer than now, in your hoar hairs and old age." May the dimness and darkness be light about you; and may the air be full and palpitating with the ringing voice of God's good cheer!

Now, I want to say a word or two of a practical kind, by way of application in closing. This is your text, my aged friend, isn't it? If not, whose is it? I looked at myself in the glass before I came out this morning, and it is plainly not for me. And as I look at you and see you from here, it is as evidently for you, and you, and you. Listen to me if it is so. I do not wish to be impertinent; I remember your years and honours, and how, beside you, I am but of yesterday. But I am God's ambassador here; therefore suffer me to speak in His behalf. Why are you so peevish, let me ask, as you sometimes are, if this text is your text; and it is? Why so discontented as you sometimes are? Some of you (I am glad I don't know you) are ageing, but you are not ageing well. You are not going to make a bonny old man or a bonny old woman. You might be growing old in a more beautiful way. If this text is true, and if it is for you, you ought to be the sweetest, nicest, homeliest, heavenliest body that one could meet in a day's journey. What lights ought to settle round about your head! When I, in the fume and fever and fret of mid-manhood, pushing my head against walls, and knocking doors out of windows, when I come in contact with you, the very shake of your hand should take some of this superfluous electricity out of me. The shake of your hand and the look in your eyes ought to soothe and pacify me. By this time you are so calm, and stable, and matured—at least, you should be. But are you so? Are you what this text should make you? without fear, or care, or peevishness, or querulousness; without a great many of the things that disfigure some old people. Dr. Oliver Wendell Holmes has said that men, like peaches, begin to grow sweet just a little while before they begin to decay. It is a pity if it is true; but I am afraid there is too much truth in it. I wish you would sweeten, then.

Nothing is more pitiful than to go to some aged character, as one would approach a tree in autumn, and pull off a fruit that you expect to be large and luscious as a ripe apple, and behold it is a crab-apple, sour and harsh as can be. The fruit is there, but it has not ripened, nor mellowed. I speak this to your shame and blame. If this text be true, again I repeat, What are we fretting for? What are these anxieties, and fears, and alarms for? Will not God Himself be enough for you as He has been in all days gone by? He has pledged and promised it. See what He has done already. I charge my aged friends to be strong in the Lord, and in the power of His might, and to show forth to us, who are younger, God's faithfulness, and to speak with a clearer testimony for Him. If *you* begin to complain, then heaven help *us!* The whole household of faith will become a howling menagerie of discontent. Cease, for example, that harking back upon the past, as if both God and man did something then—when you were young; but now, neither God, nor man, nor minister can put light into your countenance. The former times were *not* better than these.

My one sorrow for you is that you are so far through, for all the best is yet to come! If aged people begin to fail in their trust in God, where will the rest of us be? So I ask and insist, upon the ground of this text, and all it says and implies, let its light break upon you, let your very face be filled with the light of the city you are so near. How many of us are like old Caleb, in the Book of Joshua, at eighty-five years of age. Listen to him, see what grace can do to resist all the wear and tear of time and sin! Caleb says, "Forty years old was I when Moses the servant of the Lord sent me from Kadesh Barnea to spy out the land. . . . . And now, lo, I am this day four score and five years old. As yet I am as strong this day as I was in the day that Moses sent me: as my strength was then, even so is my strength now—for war, both to go out and to come in." And while I am speaking of him I remember old Barzillai, on whom years had told more heavily. You remember how he speaks to David, when, it is said, " Barzillai was a very aged man, even fourscore years old. . . . . And the king said unto Barzillai, Come now over with me, and I will feed thee with me in Jerusalem. Barzillai said unto the king, How long have I to live that I should go up with the king unto Jerusalem? I am this day fourscore years old; can I discern between good and evil? can thy servant taste what I eat or what I drink? Can I hear any more the voice of singing men and women? Wherefore, then, should thy servant be yet a burden to my lord the king? Thy servant will go a little way over Jordan with the king; why should the king recompense me with such a reward? Let thy servant, I pray thee, turn back again that I may die in my own city, and be buried by the grave of my father and mother. But behold thy servant Chimham; let him go over with my lord the king; and do to him what shall seem good unto thee." You see in the one the vigour of old age; and in the other the contentment, the calm, quiet, blessed, unspeakable contentment, of the man who has grown old and grey, and has gone through many trials, but in and through them all God has been his strength, and now he waits till God shall call him home. His soul is like a weaned child.

> "The scathed and leafless trunk may seem
>   Old age's mournful sign;
> Yet on its bark may sunshine gleam,
>   And moonbeams softly shine.
>
> "So on the cheek of age should rest,
>   The light of days gone by,
> Calm as the glories of the west
>   When night is drawing nigh."

My friends, may God give you an abundant entrance into His own presence! And to this end He has sent me to-day to prepare you for the things that must shortly come to pass. Oh, I charge you, make God your strength more than ever! Feed upon His Word more than ever; live by faith, live by prayer more than ever; and concern yourself with His cause and with His kingdom in the only ways that now are left to you. The more the outward activities are limited, let your life be more intense, and full, and abundant in your own soul; in faith and in prayer, for yourself and others.

"It is a favourite speculation of mine," says Dr. Chalmers, "that, if spared to sixty, we then enter on the seventh decade of human life, and that this, if possible, should be turned into the Sabbath of our earthly pilgrimage. It should be spent Sabbatically—as if on the shores of an eternal world, or in the outer courts, as it were, of the temple that is above, the tabernacle that is in heaven."

Soon thy feet shall stand within the city of the Blessed One, thy tears all past, thy joy for ever sure. Therefore, in these last miles of the journey let your whole soul be filled with brightest hope and loftiest expectation. You have lived long and seen much, and all of it should tend to this. You have not seen the righteous forsaken, nor his seed begging bread; but you have seen it, again and again, well with the righteous. You have seen the wicked in great power, and spreading himself like a green bay-tree; but while you looked the crash came. Of a sudden God's axe was laid to the root of the wicked, and he passed away, and his memory began to rot in your own life-time. You have seen the hand of the Lord in all your wilderness journey now for perhaps seventy years; and now, at last, shall you turn from God in peevishness and querulousness? It cannot be. Your light from this day forward shall shine more brightly and more instructively than ever. You will bring forth fruit in old age, the special fruit of old age—calmness, patience, brightness, cheerfulness, unfailing and unfaltering trust in your Redeemer, God, and in every word of promise He has spoken.

And no matter, if that be so, what special trials old age may yet bring—and it may bring many trials. You may be neglected by your own flesh and blood. A poor old woman came to my door the other day—poor old body, drifted about, like a cork on a stream, from one married daughter to another. And one can easily see the meaning of such treatment. It is how most cheaply to get rid of the mother in whose womb they lay, and at whose breast they drew their nourishment. Well, that may come. It has come to the godly. That sort of trial, and other trials, may come while we are here. We may expect tribulation to the very end; but the deeper the darkness, the brighter the light of God's presence.

Remember all that He has done. Remember all the love of His heart, and never allow yourselves to think that this can be the end. These fading eyes, and closing ears, and palsied hands, and opening graves, and increasing poverty, and friendlessness—can this be the end of all the wonderful providences that God has showed to you? Is that to be the end? It cannot be. Did God lavish upon you such wisdom, and power, and love, and is this to be the end—to grow weaker, and dimmer, and duller, and at length to mingle with the clods—defeated and disappointed? That cannot be. The worm, surely, shall not outlive the man— the man of our text.

Thy days are only in the beginning. Thy Maker and Redeemer has been working for eternity, through all these years of thine earthly sojourn.

> "Earth changes; but thy soul and God stand sure;
> What entered into thee,
> That was, is, and shall be:
> Time's wheel runs back or stops: potter and clay endure."

Regent Square Pulpit.

BREAD TO THE FULL.

A Sermon

Delivered in Regent Square Church on Sunday, February 23rd, by the

REV. JOHN McNEILL.

Mark vi., from the 35th verse.

Feeding five thousand. As this narrative is set down here, and still more when read in the light of those other portions of Scripture where the same event is recorded, we are made to feel that the Lord purposely, on this occasion, put his disciples into a difficulty. He Himself was in no difficulty; although from their tone, when they came to Him, they almost implied that not only were *they* in a difficulty, but that He also had been placed in a crisis for which He had no ready relief.

Now, it is very helpful to plunge into the middle of things at once, to notice (and you will read the narratives for yourselves, I trust, when you go home) how Christ allowed this crisis deliberately to come upon Himself and upon His followers. He had been teaching the people many things; a great multitude had gathered round Him, and they were out in a lonely desert place. There were no supplies near, and the disciples almost seemed to have thought that the

Master had been so enthusiastic in His teaching, so swallowed up with His spiritual work, as to have forgotten the course of time. He seemed not to have noticed the westering wheel of the sun, and to be oblivious to the panic, or, at any rate, the grave difficulty which would shortly present itself to Him, and them, and to all that great multitude, when night should have fallen, with no accommodation near at hand either for rest or refreshment. But, I say, it is when you read the other narratives that you see how, earlier in the day, Christ foresaw the difficulty. Not that He was in any strait. " He Himself knew what He would do;" but He asked the disciples, " Whence shall we buy bread that these may eat?" to prove and to try them; to see if they understood where their resources lay; and to teach them, and to teach His Church in time to come, that although the work before us may seem to be overwhelming, although the demands may seem to be immense, and the supply utterly deficient, we are thereby urged to fling ourselves back the more certainly and quickly upon the infinite supply that is always ours, because Christ is with us. No crisis to Him; no difficulty to Him. "And when the day was now far spent, His disciples came unto Him, and said, This is a desert place, and now the time is far passed." Exactly! The Lord is so spiritual that He does not keep a watch and ask what o'clock it is. It is a desert place, and the disciples seem to say, " Send them away, that they may forage for themselves; relieve us of the responsibility. We did not ask them to come here; and although it may look a little harsh to send them helter-skelter, as fast as they can go, to the little villages, with their white walls glimmering away in the distance, yet it is the only thing left, and there is still time if they make speed. We grant, as regards the children, there is a difficulty, but, none the less, send them away quickly, that they make the best of it, and that we may be relieved; for every moment increases our uneasiness. Send them away, that they may go into the country round about, and into the villages, and buy themselves bread, for they have nothing to eat."

Now, is it not a great pity, my friends, when you look at "Church History" up till to-day, that that tone has far too much been the prevailing tone of our counsel and labour? "Send them away." I thank God that to-day the Church of Christ is waking up to speak another word. I thank God that in our own day and generation, although for hundreds of years the tone of the Church to this multitudinous world, as a world, as a whole, as a perishing, famine-stricken whole, has been "keep away, keep back; we have nothing for you, and barely enough for ourselves"—I bless God that in this century, and I had almost said every year, every month we live, the Church of Christ is seeing her mistake and is retrieving her error. Instead now of keeping the famishing faces of the world away at a distance, she is waving them back, and crying aloud! "Come back, India! Ho, there, China! we have made a mistake. Ye need not depart, oh, Africa! there is bread enough and to spare, we have happened upon great supplies. Verily the Church of God needs it. For far too long we have repeated the foolish words of the disciples, "Send them away, we have nothing. We can scarce manage for ourselves with these five loaves and two fishes, we can barely manage just to keep the life in."

And it is always true that so long as the Church of God treats the multitude with indifference, *she has justly barely enough for herself,* she is always in a kind of half-famishing state, with her five loaves and two fishes—not much, truly, for twelve Galilean fishermen! At the moment she begins to divide, to scatter, and to spread, that moment she gets fatter herself, as well as being able to supply the need of others. "There is that scattereth and yet increaseth."

"Send them away." Another narrative gives us our Lord's reply, "They need not depart." A direct contradiction—"Send them away." "*They need not depart.*" "We have nothing; they have nothing;" and again, "*Give ye them to eat.*" Now, which is right? Whether did Christ, or His disciples, gauge the situation most accurately. Was it not Christ?

Although it is easy for us to see with Him to-day, it was rather difficult then. Yet, as regards our own day, the problems are just where the disciples were. If the Church would rise to her strength, she would to-morrow send messengers with the Bread of Life in a hundred-fold degree as compared with anything she has yet done. A kind of work that cannot run into foolish enthusiasm this sending the Bread of Life to the perishing thousands, the multitudinous millions of our flesh and blood, and scattering the Bread over the surface of the whole earth!

"He answered and said unto them, "Give ye them to eat." And they said unto Him, "Shall we go and buy two hundred pennyworth of bread and give them to eat?"

Ah! friends, when we are left to ourselves, how far we wander! When we gather together in conferences, as we sometimes do, I often think of this story. When the wise man, the grey-headed man, the old, experienced minister gets up to speak, there is a little of the tone of Philip in him. It seems to be wise according to the rule of the multiplication table, or the estimate of a pastry-cook contracting for a big picnic! What they say, looked at from that point of view, is quite right: according to human ways of handling figures, our figures seem to be justifiable. But when we look at things through Christ's eyes, in the light of God's Word, and in the light of the precious promises, how foolish, and feckless, and inept is this—" Shall we go and buy two hundred pennyworth of bread and give them to eat?"

When will we learn the lesson? Each individual, even the whole Church of God, has wisdom which is only foolishness; and if we would be wise, as Paul says, we must first become fools. If we would be wise with heavenly wisdom, let us ask of God who giveth to all men liberally, and upbraideth not, and it shall be given. "He said unto them, How many loaves have ye? Go and see. And when they knew, they say, Five, and two fishes."

He flings us back again upon ourselves. He will bless us, He will use us; but He will make us bring out what we have. Now, what have we? I speak to some Christian worker here to-day who was just about to give up, and I might myself say, "What am I? Ted, what are you, what are any of us, what are all of us, in the midst of London's millions—millions perishing for lack of knowledge, for lack of the Bread of Life?" Ah! we are so feeble, so helpless. Yet what have we got? Oh, my brother, my sister, in the Sunday-school, with the Bible-class, you women in your own families, the Lord would fling us all back upon what we have got. Have we got anything at all?

Then let us take it, although to us foolishly inadequate; let us bring it to Him. "Only five loaves and two fishes!" Ludicrous, in the face of five thousand men, besides women and children. But fetch it, find it out, and bring it to Him. I like that to-day! Preacher, what have you got? Here are a thousand or twelve hundred people to be fed. In the session-house, in the vestry, before we came out, a brother prayed that the people might be fed, *fed ;* and I sadly said, "What have I got? what have I here to feed the people with? I am empty;" or, "What is the use of trying, with the little, the very little I have got?"

But the Lord says, "Bring it unto Me: fetch Me whatever you have; fetch the ready mind; bring the loving heart. And I believe the disciples—it was shown afterwards — were delivered from their panic and distress, humanly speaking, by the ready mind and the loving heart. Do you wish to have a part in feeding London's famine? *Then bring that wish.* Have you a desire to save sinners? *Then fetch that desire.* Do not hold back, moaning and complaining, and joining in the general loleful lamentation. But whatever you have, bring it to-day.

We all have something, *if we know Him at all.* Don't say, "I have nothing." Were you ever converted, do you think? Then bring that, and He will bless that, and make it *bread* to others. Have you had experience of the power of prayer to deliver you from darkness, and give you victory over sin. Then bring that, and He will bless it to others. I pin you and myself down to these personal possessions *that we are bound to have* if we are His. They must be in the cupboard somewhere. Fetch them out. "Go and see." For the half of us are thinking that what we need is college learning, and some conspicuous intellectual endowment Do you know His Word *at all?* You must know it, again I repeat, if you are His. I don't ask for a Bibleful of knowledge; but bring what you know indubitably and experimentally. Bring that; He will bless it to others. It will be bread.

Cast about, friends; "go and see." You are not *so empty* as you think.

I feel burdened as the disciples felt—only it becomes maddening and heart-breaking. Lord, see what we have brought upon ourselves. Thousands of men, women, and children; and only five loaves and two fishes, as if the very devil were beginning to fill the air with mocking laughter. The Lord wants us to do something. Look, here is this mighty London swinging down to hell—men, women, and children; and *where, where, where* are the Christians? The Christians! they are the most feeble, useless creatures imaginable; whole cart-loads of them doing nothing, and worse than nothing. Christians by churchfuls, by hundreds upon hundreds, doing nothing; nothing but asking questions, "How?" "What?" "Why?" "Where?" "Whether?" and so on. Let us stop asking questions and begin buckling to. There is no panic with Him, all the panic is in our own hearts. An awful round of panic is here—the main thing we seem to keep our hearts for is panic; we have no room for aught else but fear and trepidation

Now, we have Christ with us; let us give Him all we have Bring your nothings. Do you say you are nothing? Yet nothing with Christ, as the unit in front of it, makes ten; and if you are double nothing, twice nothing, yet with. Christ in front you make a hundred. That is how He works. The emptier you are the better, if you will just come to Him.

"How many loaves have ye? Go and see." And the great surprise is that they were not insufficient and utterly useless, as they thought they were. Oh, we have something—we have the wish, we have the will, we have the desire, we have the Word, we have "oor ain ken," (our own knowledge); and out of that shall come bread, yea, abundance of bread!

"And He commanded them to make all sit down by companies on the green grass. And they sat down in ranks, by hundreds, and by fifties." I should have liked to have looked at Christ then. He takes this business in hand with the air of one who means to do it. I have no doubt that the disciples' eyes fairly burned in their heads when He gave them this notice, " Make all sit down in companies on the green grass."

He handled the crowd in a way that would suggest to them that there was an abundance somewhere, and that they were to sit down in expectation of being fed. It was not to be a dumb show. " Cut them up; make them get-at-able; make them workable."

I like to hear of that aged minister who is now gone to his rest, the venerable Dr. Andrew Somerville, how he prayed on his knees for the whole world *with the atlas spread out before him*. Upon that he divided mankind; he took mankind in companies—the nationalities, and companies in which God in His providence has divided us—and he then prayed for them one by one—for the Indian company, the African division, the islands of the sea, the colonies, and so on. Why, my friends, it is going to turn out that this great national family arrangement is in the interest of the Gospel, not against the Gospel; and that God for Gospel purposes has set the world in companies, in communities, in cities, and in nations. And as for getting at them—" The seas now join the lands they did divide." Everything is ready and plain for us. Oh, that the Church of Jesus Christ could see!—and bless God, she is seeing it, and. looking more at the world, not as a great heaving, unwieldy mass upon which she can make no impact, no impression. A world the very sight of which makes her head bow down, and her heart ache and faint with a feeling of hopelessness. No; the world is beginning already to fall in order, and we are beginning to see the world as planned out for the furtherance of the Gospel. It is just capitally laid out for starting on with your bread-basket and doing your best.

"He commanded them to make all sit down in companies upon the green grass. And they sat down in ranks, by hundreds, and by fifties." The very organization suggested to the disciples and to the people that they were being competently, skilfully handled. "This thing is to be done," thought they. "We may sit down in expectation, for we are going to be fed." "And when He had taken the five loaves and the two fishes, He looked up to heaven, and blessed, and brake the loaves, and gave them to His disciples to set before them, and the two fishes divided He among them all." Notice His action. We are going to do it now. It is a great work to which we are called to feed the world's famine. Now, see how He does it. When He had taken the five loaves and two fishes, He looked up to heaven. My brother, my sister, in working for God, first look to heaven. It is a grand plan. Over and over again our Lord Jesus Christ looked up to heaven, and said, "Father." He looked up into heaven's peace, and heaven's power when he was standing here a man of our own height. His feet down here on our own earth. Let us imitate Him: although standing on the earth, let us have our conversation in heaven. Before you go out, if you would feed the world, if you would be a blessing in the midst of spiritual dearth and famine, lift up your head to heaven. Be up there and back again before you go out of this place, then your very face will shine, your very garments will smell of myrrh and aloes and cassia, out of the ivory palaces where you have been with your God and Saviour. Then those among whom you labour will take notice that you have been with Jesus: there will be stamped upon you the dignity and power of the service of the Most High God. "This is the way the Master trod." "Should not the servant tread it still?" But if you run away without prayer, you run away without your Master, without power; and the bread will break the eater's teeth, for it will be as hard and stale and sapless as the stones of the street. "He looked up to heaven, and then He blessed the bread." What does that mean? I do not know, except by the results. But I do know that between one act and the other that bread was different. His blessing makes all the difference. Go into His presence to-day, poor man, poor woman, helpless toiler, for if you get utterly frightened and pressed down under the magnificence of the command, and the littleness of your supply, and if He just blesses you, to the eye you may look the same; but you are different; you are what you were *plus Christ*, plus the blessing of God. Who shall fathom what the blessing of God means? The blessing of God, oh, it maketh rich! What wonderful things have been done in London, and are being done to day, by men and women without wealth, without rank, or anything which the world calls power or endowment; but simply and solely because God Almighty has *blessed*, BLESSED, BLESSED them. And they do what great intellects in the world, and even doctors of divinity and popular preachers in the Church may not accomplish —they save souls, they quicken the dead, *for God has blessed them.* May their numbers be multiplied. It almost makes one mad to think how little we are, and how great we might be on the showing of this Book. "*He* blessed them." If He blesses us, then our words, that otherwise would be so feeble, so feckless, so helpless, will be all-powerful. Here is the history of the conversion of a young fellow. He had been trying to feed himself, like some of you, in his awful hunger, and in the madness which gnawing hunger brings, he was trying to feed upon the husks that swine do eat. But one never-to-be-forgotten day just for a few moments he met a former companion whom Christ had saved. That companion, who was vastly below him in intellect, in power, and in many other ways, just spoke a word, but it was a Christ-blessed word, and that word of testimony led him to Christ. Oh, congregation, I charge you before the risen Christ to-day—" What are ye here for?" For God's sake, and for your own sake, for the sake of that damned city around about us, living as a hell above ground, before it gets to the hell underground, I ask, "What are ye here for?" Come forward with what you have to the Master: then, with His blessing on your effort, before bed-time London will be the better somewhat for it.

That is the great word—He blessed the bread. I cannot, I say, explain it. But there is what He did, and He would do nothing foolishly. The thousands of people there were hungry, and He would not waste time and put them off. No! But He took time to bless that bread. He "brake the loaves, and gave them to the disciples, and the two fishes. And they did all eat, and were filled." Again, I say, I cannot describe it. The closer you come to these miracles, and hold your very finger on the critical place, you say, "Steady, steady!" I want to keep this from deceiving my eye. I want to see precisely where the miracle came in. You put your thumb down here, and the other here, and say, "Now, I want to see just exactly *where* these loaves were multiplied." Ah, but you can't! They were multiplied; the result, the effect, is patent; the "how" is as mysterious as ever.

Now, that was a merry time, wasn't it? You never saw a picnic like it. I wish I had been there. And in spirit let us all be there, where fear and gloom disappeared, and one said to his neighbour, "Hold your peace, Simon; it's all right. These people are going to provide for us. There is a look there in the face of Him who is in the centre—a look of confidence, a look of calmness, and a look of power. I do not see any great supply of bread about, but it's all right." And so it was. "He brake the bread, and gave to the disciples, and the disciples to the multitude. And they did all eat, and were filled."

Now do we see it? *Him* first, last, in the midst, and to the end. "He led them out as far as Bethany, and lifted His hands upon them, and blessed them," and these dozen weak, ignorant men they have shaken the world ever since. Twelve fishermen from Galilee, blessed of the Lord, have become the most powerful men on the face of the earth; and to-day the power of their word is increasing while we speak, and every day we live.

Now, let us up and distribute; do not keep it to yourselves. Oh, friends, what a horrible story this would have been, if it had read as follows: "And when He had blessed the bread and broken it, they sat down to eat it among themselves." That is the kind of disgraceful guzzle some of us are turning the Gospel feast into; keeping it to ourselves.

Here am I; and I have preached within these walls inside of two months some thirty Gospel discourses. The

Lord knows why we keep it up. Are you not sick, tired of me, and I of you? It may be so. I will come to this: that you shall get so fastidious and so critical that I won't be able to please you; nor will any man, no, nor angel either, be able to please people who do nothing but come to get and get more, and there is an end of it. The blessing will turn to a curse; the manna will breed worms, and stink; the flesh will come out at your nostrils, as God said to His overfed and fattened people who ate themselves stupid in the wilderness long, long ago. That is what is troubling many of our congregations to-day. There is a wail of discontent. We hear that such and such a congregation is not very happy; the minister is not getting on with the people, nor the people with the minister, and there is trouble rising among the office-bearers, and so on. Now, I believe nine-tenths of the reason is this: there is too much food, the blood has got hot and wanton from over-feeding. Scatter what you have got; go out and give, and then you will come back, and on almost any given Sunday the poorest preacher that ever stood here you will think is just the best preacher you have ever heard, because you are hungry and thirsty, not only for yourselves, but for what you have to give away to others. I know it in my little experience that the best people to preach to are not the people who know a great deal. These are often the worst. The best are earnest ministers and Christian workers, those who have to distribute to others.

My pampered hearer, sermons are for eating, and not for criticizing. God's Word is for taking in. The preacher is here to-day to give you Christ, and I might have done or undone a lot of things, but as God is true, and I would be true, surely I have lifted Him up, I have given you Him,

His Word, His power, and His magnificence. Take Him, eat Him, man, eat Him, *eat*—believe, that is to say, take Him. Christ is with us, and the moment your soul goes out to Him in confidence, it is like the hungry man eating, or the thirsty man drinking the bubbling water. Then eat! Oh, eat! When will the congregation learn that? I am standing as it were close over you; and I am here with my hands filled with the Bread of Life; my mouth filled with "Believe on the Lord Jesus Christ, and thou shalt be saved." Your famine will leave you, and your soul will take on flesh the moment you begin to eat. Now, will you do it? How strangely it would have read if there had been a statement to this effect: That when Simon Peter went with his hand full to some crusty old Jew, he, instead of eating, began to ask questions, and to say, "Can you explain this to me? Look here, Peter, just sit down a minute, I have some views about this." I think Peter would have sat upon him in a minute, and told him, "You and your views perish together; I am too busy. I have really other work to do than to stand here with bread talking to a man who should be eating. Sit back, let me get past; there is a hungry man next to you with his mouth watering. Let me get ahead." Oh, I wish the same power would come to all preachers of the Gospel in this critical 19th century! Perish criticism; I had almost said, perish you. No, God forbid: that would be an awful thing. I will stop up your critical mouths with bread, and give your critical teeth something to do that is more worthy of their function. Eat! eat! eat! "They did all eat." The Lord give me a congregation like that! The men and women might have asked many questions, I grant; and might have thought that the servitors possibly should have been more mannerly. So you want me to serve you out of a silver cake-basket, I suppose, and to be as mild and whispering as a waiter! But, dear me, you cannot eat silver cake-baskets. Eat the bread, and be strong enough and hungry enough to keep from these grumblings and these discussions. And as to my manner and "style," I will not do you a bit of harm if you take what I am bringing—the Bread of Life from Christ's own hands.

"They did all eat," and the last word is, "they were filled." Now, my friends, when you go home to-day, when you go back to mix with your people, it will be a very poor certificate of me, a very poor certificate of my Master, if you go home with that lean, hungry look that you had when you came here. Go away; I had almost said, assume the virtue, if you possess it not; at any rate, try to get up a fed look. It will encourage some of them at home to come back. But if you go home fretful and critical, of course it is all up with Regent Square. They will say, "It is no use my going to that church, for the people I know who do go there do not seem to get anything. They never come back, but grumble and find fault, saying, it is not a bread-shop, I won't go." "They did all eat, and were filled." You go up to this man here, this orra man in the crowd, any man upon whom your eye lingers, and you say, "Well, friend, satisfied?" "Satisfied!" he says, "I never tasted bread like it." Now, tell me, and I will let you go in another minute, "Are you satisfied?" I do not mean with me, nor with the sermon, but with *Him*. The Bread is His, the Water of Life is His—yea, He Himself, the living, loving Saviour, is the Food of the soul; and if you have come to the reality of things, you have come to Him. Now, do not insult Him; do what you like with me. I know I might serve you much better, and your criticisms might be perfectly just towards me; but looked at in the highest, best, and truest light, I cannot diminish Him; and the one chance of this hour is to get your hungry heart close to His fulness. If you have listened, oh, tell me, is not Christ sweet to your taste? You do not mean to say that you are dissatisfied with Him? "They did all eat, and were filled." What a great and full salvation Christ is able to supply! " He that eateth Me, the same shall live by Me." " I am the Living Bread, which came down out of heaven. If any man eat—(ah, there it is again!)—*if any man eat* of this Bread, he shall live for ever." Lord, bless this word, and make it go over us all. Amen

Regent Square Pulpit.

THE TRANSFIGURATION.

A Sermon

Delivered in Regent Square Church, on Sunday, March 30, 1890, by the

REV. JOHN M' NEILL.

Luke ix. 27-35.

If time had permitted, we might have read the account three times over, for it is given us three times, not always in the same way, but each telling of it supplements and increases the force and brightness and beauty of the other. In taking up this subject, I feel, and I am sure you sympathize with me very much, as Peter felt: "I wist not what to say." Every commentator on the subject has expressed pretty much the same feeling. It is so bright, that we are conscious of a feeling of straining ourselves, of standing too much on tip-toe, and of allowing ourselves to be tempted to indulge too much in word-painting, so as to reproduce as vividly as possible this solemn, awful, glorious scene.

The best way would be to handle it with strict exegesis, to show the point at which Christ in His own earthly ministry has arrived when we come to the Transfiguration, for this is one of the great watersheds, so to speak, which turn the current of the narrative of His earthly history into a particular direction. That would lead us to dwell not only upon its bearing on Christ Himself, and upon the great work that brought Him here to tread the ways of time, but its bearing also on the disciples, those slow scholars, after Christ and with Christ, who here are eye-witnesses of His majesty.

However, it is our Communion Sabbath, and I would rather use the subject simply as a quiet, spiritual meditation. We shall be content with anything that may help us to sit down at the Lord's Table, and to get nearer and nearer still to the Saviour, who has glorified Himself for ever by the decease which He accomplished at Jerusalem.

"It came to pass about eight days after, He took Peter and John and James, and went up into a mountain to pray;" and, as another narrative says, "He was transfigured before them." After a week. It was a wonderful week, although Scripture says nothing about it. Its very silence is striking. What happened six or eight days before? Ah, what happened was this: our Saviour, as we have read in Matthew's Gospel, began to show His disciples that one thing they always turned their backs upon, the one thing that brought Him here. He began to show them that He must suffer many things, that He must be rejected of the chief priests and the leaders of the people, and that He must be killed, and be raised again on the third day. The disciples hung upon that mournful word "killed!" And Peter, with the best intentions in the world, said, "Lord, pity Thyself. Lord, spare Thyself. Lord, there is no one who can possibly kill Thee. We know that about Thee, at any rate. No one can possibly do Thee harm, if Thou dost only stand up and defend Thyself. Thou art the Christ: Thou art the Son of the living God: save Thyself. If there is to be danger, carry Thyself through it alive and victorious." It was a loving heart that spoke, although it was a foolish tongue. Christ was sorely pained; very much as we are when we set our hearts upon some darling object. We communicate our intentions to our best friends, and we try to show them that we are really girding ourselves for this; that it is not sudden and spasmodic, nor hastily conceived. But they will not take to it. How painful it is to us when, after we have done our best to open to them the solid contents of our mind on some darling object, they become our stumblingblocks. Instead of encouraging us and sympathizing with us, and doing their best to understand us, they only wave their hands and say, "Don't! don't! Do not talk about that at all. You will do no such thing." It is very apt to make us change our minds. It is very apt to make us think twice, with a second thought that is not better than the first; but which contradicts the first, and brings our mind under the influence of others. And then, our mind being feeble of purpose, its "current turns awry." Christ was just there. He loved nobody more than Peter, and Peter could not hold his tongue. Peter spoke to Him in just that human tone that has so much impression upon us to turn us aside from our dearest wish. And the Lord found relief in a strange way. "Get thee behind Me, Satan." He speaks as though the very whisper of the devil that had come to Him on the mountain of temptation had come again from the lips of His own beloved disciple. "Get thee behind Me, Satan. Thou art a stumblingblock unto Me, thou savourest not the things that be of God, but those that be of men." Then silence fell; Peter said no more, and the Saviour said no more, and we lose sight of them for a week. There comes a blank or a gap in history. But here the chain is taken up again. "Eight days after these sayings, He took Peter and John and James, and went up into a mountain to pray." His mind never wavered; His thought never wandered from what He said last. The decease, with its agony and shame and suffering, is vividly before His mind, if I may say so, somewhat more vividly, for He has travelled eight days nearer to that humiliating and triumphant time, the Cross, the Death, and the Rising again. And so He comes back to it in a wonderful way. The inevitable Cross appears in a new light for them, even as it was set by His Father in a helpful and glorious light for Him. "Eight days after, He called Peter and John and James, and went up into a mountain to pray." May we be up on the mountain with Him, and see what the few moments there will reveal!

Well, let us be thankful that He is the same Jesus still. Still, He has among us those whom He takes up with Him into close and peculiar fellowship. All along the history of the Church the Lord has had His Peters and Jameses and Johns—those who get very close to Him in work, in meditation, and in prayer. That is something helpful. Most of us, perhaps, feel as if—like the rest of the disciples—we are always down there in the world; down at the mountain-foot, contending with the world and the devil and the flesh. At this time they were being sorely set upon their defence by the Scribes and Pharisees, because, as you remember, they could not cast the devil out of the demoniac boy.

But these three were having a glorious time! So, I say, let us thank God that it is not all fighting and worrying. He still preserves among His people those souls to whom He reveals Himself, and let us ask to be among them. Peter and James and John were among them. I cannot say that they were so promoted because they were choice spirits. All along through this Gospel narrative you do not see much that is choice in them. Any other three, as far as we can see, would have done just as well if they had got the same training. They do not seem to have been particularly bright; and they did not seem to benefit particularly at the first by the extra training opportunities they got. So there is a chance for any of us, there is a chance for all of us, to serve ourselves heirs to this peculiar fellowship, and this intimate discipleship.

Come close to Him, He may take you, my friend—obscure *you* down there. He may take you to-day up into the mountain-top, for where He took Peter and James and John—Peter, with his blundering, and James and John, those sons of Thunder, who, time and again, so utterly misunderstood their Master and His mission—there is no reason why He should not take you. You can hardly be farther back than they were. So don't shut yourself out of it, and say, "Ah, these wonderful visions and revelations of the Lord are for choice spirits. They are for an election within the election." They may be for you. The Lord will come to those that are " humble and of a contrite heart, and who tremble at His Word." Far back and ignorant and feeble though you may feel yourself to be, come to Him, and He will come to you. Expect much from the Lord, and this very day the Lord may come to you and give you such a lift, such exaltation, and exaltation of soul as you never had before. He did it for Peter and John and James, and there are *lots* of Peters and Johns and Jameses here. May it be done again! If we could now see the household of faith, as we shall see it by-and-bye, we should see that every day we live He is picking up some of us all through London, all through the toil and moil and sweat and grind of this pilgrim life of faith. Every day He is coming and giving us our turn. "Come on! come up! Come, and I will show you something. Come, and I will give you a new view. Come, and I will climb this hill with you, and let you see things from a different angle and from a loftier elevation." I am speaking to souls here whose faces are brightening at the very remembrance of times of such refreshing from the Lord.

" He went up into a mountain to pray. And as He prayed, the fashion of His countenance was altered, and His raiment was white and glistening." Luke alone notices the praying, and we are thankful to him for it. It was not so much outward glory that shone down upon Him and covered Him externally. It was an inward glory, the glory that always was there, but was veiled by "this muddy vesture of decay." The flesh, even His holy flesh, banked up those fires that burned within Him; but on this occasion, drawn near to His Father in prayer, the fires within broke through. They flamed out. "The glory of the Lord filled the Lord's house." "*While He prayed*, the fashion of His countenance was altered, and His garments became white and shining." He is white-heat human holiness. He is also the eternal Son of the eternal Father. We are glad of that glimpse. That is our Saviour always. He was always like that to His Father's eyes. His spotless soul always had that white flame, that dazzling lustre, in it and round about it. The inner man of Jesus possessed the outer man for one bright, brief moment, in the depth of His humiliation; and it was prayer that brought it out. There is Christ on the lonely mountain, and the night has come down upon Him, and He is praying. What a prayer that would be! No word of it is given to us, but He is so laying hold of God, and God is so coming to Him, that at last the flesh could no longer conceal the spirit, and there bursts out this glory, this uncreated splendour, which He has by right of His eternal Sonship, and which He had with the Father before the world was. That is His very garment now where He sits, the Father's equal on the eternal throne. There was a means used, if I may say so. While He prayed, this spiritual glory blazed and burned till the very sin-bleared eyes of the disciples saw it on His face and on His garments. You have sometimes been greatly dissatisfied with the photograph or picture of a dear friend. You have been very intimate with that friend. You have not only known him in the street; you have not only known him as regards public appearances; but you have known him in private and quiet times. You have lifted some photographs, good enough in their way, but you have flung them down, and said, "No; that is like, but there is a something that has not caught. The real friend has not yet come out." Now, here is a view of our Saviour (oh, we need to get it!), a view that never left Peter's mind, at any rate. Long afterwards, writing in that Epistle, his mind is filled with this very scene in which he got a sight of Jesus, the true Jesus, Jesus as He is. Have we seen that sight of Him with our own eyes—Jesus as He is, as He shall be for ever and for ever? The fashion of His face altered, and yet the same face. It was not another Jesus. That would not be a blessing. Any change that comes over Christ that would make Him really different from what He was would be no help. It is a change so far, and yet the substance, the substratum is the same. It was the dear familiar face, but with light, light ineffable, bathing its every feature. It was the same height, the same form, and yet not the same, transfigured before them; the fashion altered, the substance, the identity remaining the same. "While He prayed." Oh, that it might be given to us in prayer to tread more than we do in the Master's footsteps! Have we not seen it sometimes?

Have you not been present at the death-bed of some dear friend, say, your father, and while upon his death-bed that friend prayed, just before he died, and you got a new glimpse of your father. You never in your life saw him before. You got a glimpse of your dear friend as he is now—as he shall be in the resurrection morning. Just when time was receding, when earth was fading, when the flesh was getting faint and weak, he clasped his hands, and, as he prayed, his soul hasted to reach its goal. The very fashion of his countenance was altered. Ay, there broke from within the glory of a soul that was soon to be one with Christ in His glory—the glory of the Head, the same glory covering this particular living member of Christ's glorious, mystical body. Oh, friends, we are not what we seem to be, any more than Jesus was! There He is, treading the ways of time, with His form and His visage more marred than the sons of men —quiet, silent, homeless, lonely. "When we shall see Him," says the prophet, "He is a root out of a dry ground: having neither form nor comeliness; and there is no beauty that we should desire Him." But there He is, even in His humiliation. There is what is in Him, that is native to Him. So we are not what we seem.

I would like you to dwell on this for yourself. Dwell on it. There is more in us than the eye sees. If we are Christ's—if we are born again, ah, we shall be wonderful one day. Christ in us—the hope of glory. Would that that which is ours in Him might be more often realized, and it will be realized if oftener we seek for quiet, private times when we get "far ben" into communion by our own secret prayer. I believe that the most of us do not yet know what prayer might do to change us, to bring us down into the world the same, and yet not the same. There would be a moral excellence, a refulgence; and men would take knowledge of us that we had been on some heaven-kissing hill on the Sabbath day, and that we had brought down some of heaven's beauty and brightness with us.

" And, behold, there talked with Him two men, which were Moses and Elias: who appeared in glory, and spake of His decease which He should accomplish at Jerusalem." You see how subjects pour into the mind as we read the verses. "There talked with Him two men, Moses and Elias." Hundreds of years ago these men had departed from earth, and here they reappeared. See the subject that is before us. Our dead—where are they? Here is Moses back again—the man whom God buried, as the Scripture says, " with His own hand, in a valley over against Beth-peor, and no man knoweth the place of his sepulchre until this day." And here is Elias, who went up in a chariot of fire, not having tasted death. Here, centuries after the event, is the personal, living Elijah.

They came with their identity whole, absolute, undiminished, unimpaired, known to be Moses, and known to be Elias. The disciples knew them, recognized them, and named them. There is an air of reality about the whole story which makes it difficult for any but the most determined sceptic to make out that this was a mere apparition.

"Two men talked with Him, which were Moses and Elias." I feel better than I can express it what a wonderful world Christ has opened up to us. What a wonderful difference Jesus has made by His birth and death and resurrection. Why, one almost feels inclined to stand and say, " Moses is within hail. For all we know to the contrary, Elijah may be beside us; and the great and good of all time, like a cloud of witnesses round about us. " We are come to Mount Zion, the city of the living God, to an innumerable company of angels, to the general assembly and Church of the firstborn, whose names are written in heaven, and to the spirits of just men made perfect."

> "They sing the Lamb in hymns above,
> And we in hymns below."

What a wonderful Church is this Church of the living God—the whole community of people who have been begotten again from the dead by the Lord Jesus Christ, one great company, a company upon whom death and the grave have absolutely no power—none! Already we are superior to their sway.

> "O Death, where is thy sting?
> O Grave, where is thy victory?"

Yes; here are two men like ourselves. About one of them the Scripture is careful to say that he is a man of like passions with ourselves. There is Elijah in his immortal youth, notwithstanding all his troubles. I almost wish that I had been there. Very likely I should have spoken as foolishly as Peter, but my folly would have taken another turn. I would have been tempted to ask Moses, "Now, Moses, what do you think of that day when you got so mad with the Israelites? Elijah, what do you think of that day when you ran away at the curse of a woman, and lay beneath a juniper-tree, and wished to God that you might die, for you were not better than your fathers?" To think that we are all called to honour, glory, immortality, and eternal life, and we are forgetting it in this little miserable tick of the clock called "to-day!" Because something has its little thorn in my mortal side *to-day*, I am forgetting the glory, and the honour, and the immortality, and the eternal life; forgetting that it is all coming to me, and that I, too, shall reach that state from which I shall look away back, and all these present troubles shall be swallowed up. I shall not be able to see them in the blaze and flood of light and peace and heaven that are actually mine for ever and for ever. I say that we are brought near to it here. Away up on this mountain-top our heads get into heaven; it comes very near.

May we just have a moment there. Oh, that all his company of believers in Jesus Christ would get to realize what faith has done, and the difference that Christ has made already! We are come! Faith has a tinge of glory in it. We are raised together, and sit in heavenly places with Christ Jesus. From where you sit the hand of faith can reach Moses and Elijah. You are in fellowship with Isaiah; burning Ezekiel is in the same Church with you, in a higher part of it, but in the same blessed company. And so with our Luthers and our John Knoxes and our Chalmerses and our Guthries and our sainted James Hamiltons. They are with us. They can never leave us. They can never forsake us. We are one! We are one! That the dead are not dead is signified, not only by what God said at the bush when He called Himself the God of Abraham, and showed that He is not the God of the dead, but of the living; but it is signified here, also, with great and unspeakable strength, when Moses and Elias, two men in glory, appeared and talked with Him. How it changes all! I am not sure that we should go so often to the graveyards as we do. I am not sure that it is just the best thing for us. It seems rather to be going down into the valley than climbing up to the mountain-top, where all is transfigured and flooded with heaven's own light; and that is what we need.

And what did they say? Ah, how Peter's ears open! "They spoke of His decease which He should accomplish at Jerusalem." The thing that Peter would not hear about, the thing that we ourselves are so slow to understand, that suffering is the appointed path to glory, that is what they spoke of. Moses, the representative of the law, and the fiery prophet, Elijah, who was sent of God to restore the law, you remember, when people were breaking out into all manner of idolatry, and rejection of their covenant God-the Alpha and the Omega of Israel's law as a system—there they both are, uniting and sympathizing and harmonizing with that to which Peter would not listen: to the decease (literally, the exodus) which Christ should shortly accomplish at Jerusalem. My friend, it is the theme of heaven; the great interest of heaven. To talk to the Saviour about it upon the mountain-top, Moses and Elijah lift themselves from their ivory couches where they rest in peace, in God's own rest; and they come to talk with God's dear Son about the decease which He should accomplish at Jerusalem. There, you see, in the midst of all the glory, the cross is set. These two hills look at each other—this mountain where the glorious transfiguration takes place; and that other, away down south, at Jerusalem, where the crucifixion takes place. Here the cross is seen embedded in the glory, and there again you have the same thing. The one shines to the other: and this looks back to that. This mountain and that other, Hermon and Calvary, " North and south Christ hath created them. Hermon and Calvary rejoice in His name." We have to put these two things, the sufferings and the glory, the glory and the sufferings. It took a long while before the disciples put them together. Are we in our own day putting them together?

Away down at Clydeside, where I spent a part of my early days, there is what people call " the measured mile." Vessels that are newly launched and engined are taken down there, to test their engines and to test their speed. Thus, there are two poles upon the river's bank, one here and the other behind it; and a mile farther down there are two poles, one close to the shore, and another farther back behind. The captain stands upon the bridge of the vessel as it comes drifting down the stream, and he waits for the moment to take out his stop-watch and accurately measure when the pressure begins. Thus, when these two poles are seen to be no longer two, but when, by the drifting of his vessel past the two poles, become to his eye one, then he looks at the stop-watch; then the pressure is put on, and on goes the vessel at the utmost speed; and when, at the end of the mile, the two poles again are one, the mile has been run, and all that is wanted to be made known is known. Well, now, from this point always these two things are everything with Christ: the sufferings and the glory, and the glory and the sufferings. Here is Christ at the great trial, the crisis of His life. He is entering into the last stretch of the tremendous race that He came here to run, and He begins here. On the Mount of Transfiguration there is a definite girding of Himself for all that the cross means.

From this point on, He runs to the very last yard of the appointed course, when, you remember, the sufferings and the glory are one again. In His death these two again come together. In the very article of dying the glory burst out, when this Mighty Runner cried, "It is finished!" and He bowed His head, and gave up the ghost; and the earth quaked, and the rocks rent, and the graves were opened, so splendid was the exodus that He accomplished at Jerusalem. The sufferings and the glory. The Cross is the way to the Crown, and the Crown sheds its lustre aways on the Cross. Let us not fail, or falter, or shrink, or hesitate.

"But Peter and they that were with Him were heavy with sleep: and when they were awake (or rather, suddenly starting awake), they saw His glory, and the two men that stood with Him." The climbing of the mountain was plenty for them. When they got to the hill-top they fell asleep. Coming to church is plenty for a good many people. When they have managed to drop themselves there, then sleep begins. It is then that the eye should be opened. It is then that the glory, if there is any, is to be revealed. Alas, alas! many of us make the mere coming here our terminus. They climbed the mountain and fell asleep. How many people in this benighted England are doing it every Sabbath day! They climb the mountain of ordinances, and that is the end. We are content now. We have got to the end of our journey, and mind and imagination drop off asleep, instead of stirring ourselves up with all the powers within us, to be at our highest pitch of wakefulness and activity. Oh, may we be awake and alive! I feel the drowsiness. You feel it. I have not felt as drowsy, I think, on any theme of Scripture for months on end, as I have felt on this one. The light here is too bright for mortal eye. It is hardly for preaching about. We ought to call on our souls and all that is within us to look at it, and think about and pray over it. It is filled with light; but on looking at subjects of this kind in the Bible, the nearer we come, the more our wings seem to begin to droop. How heavy we are to-day, how dull, how languid; and Christ's Transfiguration is the theme! Christ's death is soon to be represented to us in this broken bread and this poured-out wine. We are so apt, it is so easy, to blame the disciples. When the Master was in the agony in the garden, again they fell asleep. But it is not so strange. "The spirit is willing, but the flesh is weak."

I believe, friends, that it will need eternity to show what an awful risk God's Son ran when He covered His soul with mortal flesh. The wonder is that the flesh did not in some way or other dim the glory and break Him down. It does it for the best that ever lived, even with the Spirit to help them. At some point or other the flesh overcomes the spirit, and we shall never be right till we get rid of it—never! Never till we get rid of it. What a risk the Saviour ran when "for us and our salvation" He took flesh! What a soul He must have had to lift and glorify a garment and a vesture which was as much flesh and blood as our own!

"Peter and they that were with him were heavy with sleep;" and they started awake, and they saw the two men. "And as they departed, Peter said unto Jesus, Master, it is good for us to be here: and let us make three tabernacles; one for Thee, and one for Moses, and one for Elias: not knowing what he said." As Peter did not know what he said himself, you will not ask me to make sense out of it. He did not know, and I do not know. What in all the world was he talking about? What notion came into his head, I do not know. The Lord only knows **the vagaries** that come into some good people's heads. They are for ever wanting to build some sticks and wattles, and they are for ever wanting to have their glory down here. They are wanting to get into some kind of fool's paradise. What did Peter mean? In the name of sense, what did he mean? "We will build three things of wattles—a little hut made of bushes and twigs—one for Thee, and one for Moses, and one for Elias."

Well, what then? What good is it going to do? So we might say about a great many things. For example, I feel myself pretty near to some of our premillenarian notions. That seems to me to be making things of wattles—building three tabernacles. We shall not have our glory here. Suppose the Master, even in His glory, came and stood with His feet on Mount Sion. That would be an anticlimax, a pitiful anticlimax. We are looking for far more than that, something greater and grander than that. "And while He thus spake, there came a cloud"—a bright cloud, like the Shekinah glory of which you read in Exodus, and from which God spoke to His people in the Old Testament Church. That Shekinah glory overshadowed them; "And there came a voice out of the cloud, saying, This is My beloved Son: hear Him." It is God's voice attesting the divinity, and attesting the work and mission of His Son. Moses and Elias had been there confirming Him in His work and in His mission; and when Moses and Elias departed, the Lord Himself speaks, saying, "Listen to My beloved Son: hear ye Him." My friends, are we listening to God's voice as to-day He points to His dear Son, and says to us, "My beloved Son, in whom I am well pleased: hear ye Him." Oh, you who are sitting down here, and all you people in these galleries, with this subject before us to-day, I would charge it on you, and charge it on myself.

Have we been listening to Jesus Christ, and have we opened our ears to receive His instruction? "Hear ye Him." You may be ignorant of Moses; you may not know much about Elijah. Well, bless God, He has done better for us than to give us either Moses or Elijah. They were not suffered to abide. Their ministry was temporary, and passed away; but there is One in these last days who speaks with the authority of a Son; and how great shall be our condemnation if we do not hear Him? Fasten your soul upon Him. Would you know about God? would you know about sin? would you know about salvation? would you know about the life to come? Are you troubled with scepticism? are you troubled with doubt and fears of any or every kind? Come to the Last and Best; the only Refuge and the only Remedy. God's last word to us. God Himself can do no more for us than this—to send forth His Son into the world, and command men everywhere to hear Him.

Why are we so long coming to Him? There is my gospel. There is my message. There is my sermon. There is the culmination of the wonderful scene upon the holy mount. "The Lamb is all the glory"—God Himself pointing at Him, and saying, "This is My last, this is My best Beloved. Beyond Him I have nothing. Come unto Him. Hear Him." Are there any of us to-day who have come to years of understanding, and are bound to admit that we have never yet heard Jesus Christ, that we do not know Him, that we have not heard, have not obeyed, and have not understood, and that this greatest revelation of God in Christ has been made in vain, although it has received such certificate and such attestation? Here we are in the darkness and stupidity of unbelief. So far as your life is concerned, God might never have sent Christ, and the cross might never have been erected, and the resurrection of Jesus from the dead might never have been accomplished and verified. To you—to you that for which all eternity was travailing as in birth, Jesus, "the brightness of the Father's glory," and the express Image of the Person of the eternal God, is a blank: nothing! nothing! You have never seen; you have never heard; you have never believed. May it be different to-day! I thank God that it is different. It is changing. For a while there will be unbelief, and for a while there will be scepticism; but the transfiguration is coming.

Swiftly there comes for all of us the putting off of this tabernacle. One day the Lord will come with a shout, and the very air that is so stagnant to-day with unbelief, and with rejection of the Son of God, will rend with the shoutings of the saints: "Thou art the King of Glory, oh, Christ!" Heaven and earth shall be filled with a magnificent Te Deum. It is coming; it is bound to come. God Himself has put His seal on His Son as He sent Him forth; and, in the end of the day, a great multitude, whom no man can number, of all nations and kindreds, and peoples and tongues, shall set forth Christ as the Father set Him forth, and shall re-echo the Father's word, "God's beloved Son," in whom we are well pleased; and we have heard Him, believed in Him, and we know in deed and in truth that He is the Christ, the Saviour of the world.

"When the voice had passed, Jesus was found alone." I am glad of that. I sometimes think that that was a critical moment. Think how toilsome this world was to Him. Think how He was misunderstood on every hand. The disciples did not then understand what He came here for. And when that glory comes out, I could wonder that He did not go back with Moses and Elias, and leave Peter and James and John, and leave this dark, damned world to go on its own course. He sent back Moses, and He sent Elijah. Let them go, so long as He abides. I will do without you, Moses, for a little. I will do without you, Elijah. Isaiah, Ezekiel, John the Baptist, Paul, Peter, James, John —they are all gone. Luther is gone; Calvin is gone; Chalmers is gone; Whitfield is gone; Wesley is gone; and we seem to be a small company to-day. Never mind, Christ abides with us for ever. He did not go away with them. He came back with the feeble, ignorant disciples. "Lo, I am with you alway, even to the end of the world." We are not going to build tabernacles, we have not His bodily Presence with us; but to-day at His own Table we have Him specially, we have Him in a peculiar sense. This is a mount of transfiguration. Here is the cross. Here also is the glory. We are in fellowship to-day at once with the suffering and with the glorified Jesus. Hear ye Him, as He says, "As often as ye eat this bread, and drink this cup, ye do show the Lord's death till He come." Here is no bright cloud, here are no visitants from glory. The voice also is passed. May Jesus be found alone. May He show Himself to us, for His own name's sake. Amen.

Regent Square Pulpit.

NAAMAN, THE SYRIAN.

A Sermon

DELIVERED IN REGENT SQUARE CHURCH

BY THE

REV. JOHN McNEILL.

2 KINGS v. 1-14.

LEPROSY, of course, is a type of sin. How much teaching is in the type, you and I scarcely know. When I had the honour to preach in Mr. Spurgeon's Tabernacle on "The cleansing of one of the New Testament lepers," I said that I thought the sight of a leper would greatly tend to quicken, and give practical meaning and force in our minds to all Bible teaching about the exceeding sinfulness of sin. I have since seen a returned foreign missionary who almost wanted just at that point to set me aside, and to stand up for five minutes himself and describe to the audience what leprosy really is, and the awful effect which the first acquaintance with it has upon English eyes and English hearts and understandings. I will not attempt to set it forth. I cannot. I have not seen it, neither have the bulk of us seen it; but let us understand that leprosy is one of the Bible's representations of the intense malignity and defilement of the mortal malady that has attacked you and me, namely, sin. Naaman, then, was a typical man, a man afflicted and covered with this typical disease; and we have to follow the turnings and windings of the narrative, which he made somewhat unnecessarily protracted, in order to see how this typical sinner fares when he comes into contact with the Lord God Almighty, the only God of grace and salvation for a leprous sinner.

Notice how, in the very first verse, then, the Bible puts this doctrine of the *depth of our need* as represented in the disease of leprosy. Many people are stumbled at it. The vision of a leper is a sermon to every one who sees him, as to what sin is in its insidious, but mortal, and, but for one cure, incurable ravages upon the inner man, the soul within us. I am stating the doctrine roughly, harshly. I may so put it as to state it, as you think, in a somewhat unbalanced way. Do not blame the Bible. The Bible is wonderfully considerate. As it states the case of Naaman, so it is willing to state the case of every one here. It puts it, but see how softly it puts it: " Now Naaman, captain of the host of the king of Syria "—it admits that he was a captain—" was a great man "—the Bible admits that he was great—" and honourable; "—the Bible admits that—" because by him the Lord had given deliverance unto Syria "—quite a special man. The Bible admits that—" he was also a mighty man in valour; "—good general: perhaps the only general. The Bible admits that; but making all admissions, and taking in everything by the way, it does say, and it dares to say, and it insists upon saying—" *but he was a leper.*" As it is put there, so I would like to put it here. You are amiable. I grant that you are amiable. You are not a drunkard, or a harlot, or a debauchee. I am willing to admit it; but at the bottom, the last analysis of all that you are, yields this, that you are a sinner: you are a leper. That is the last analysis. Taken into God's scales, tested in His crucible, weighed in His balances, here is the end, " *but he was a leper.*" Amiable, but an amiable sinner; refined, a refined sinner; wealthy, a wealthy sinner; a peer of the realm, a sinner as regards your spiritual condition.

The Bible makes all allowances. It is not rude; it takes everything into consideration, but it will not speak false words. It will not say "Peace," when there is no peace. It will not give you a clean bill, and allow you to come into port, when you ought to be riding quarantine because there is infectious disease on board. The Bible will be honest with you: and while it makes all admissions, on certain grounds, as to what differentiates you from other people who are dishonourable and dishonest and every way broken down outwardly and visibly, it goes straight into the conscience, and says, "After all, however, you may differ: you are a sinner. You are smitten with an incurable disease, which knows no remedy save one, the knowledge of which, and the experience of which, come not from earth, but straight and miraculously from heaven.

"And the Syrians had gone out by companies, and had brought away captive out of the land of Israel a little maid; and she waited on Naaman's wife." Now, does it not look as if this was a roundabout road to the well? After all this about Naaman, and who Naaman was, and what was wrong with him, then in the second verse we are away off to the Syrians. What about them, and what about this little maid who waited on Naaman's wife? Ah, out of little seeds great oaks grow. Out of little events great events come. Great doors turn upon small hinges; and such a thing as this wonderful story of God's gracious dealing with poor Naaman turns upon that seemingly trivial incident, that a marauding, thieving band of Syrians, when they crossed the borders and went into Israel, took away captive this little maid. They "builded better than they knew." I can imagine that the band of Syrians came back, and all their booty was a little maid. Oh, how their companions laughed at them! It seemed to have been a poor excursion, a great deal of toil and trouble and effort for very little, when they came back with only this little girl. Perhaps they brought more, but I almost think that the narrative wishes to emphasize that that was about the size of the haul on that occasion. They fetched with them a little Hebrew maid. "Who hath despised the day of small things?" No wise man. Fools do it every day. Do not despise little folk. Do no despise little things. Do not despise the day of small things. What a great work this little maid did. She has found for herself a conspicuous place in the picture-gallery of God's Word. She shall be exhibited to all eternity. Were there not kings and queens and mighty men that burnt and blazed, and paraded for a little, and then went down to dusty death? Their name and their memorial have perished with them. But that little lass, a stranger in a strange land, away there in Syria, lives for ever, here in the imperishable record of the Word of God.

"She waited on Naaman's wife. And she said unto her mistress, Would God my lord were with the prophet that is in Samaria! for he would recover him of his leprosy. And one went in, and told his lord, saying, Thus and thus said the maid that is of the land of Israel." What a simple testimony she bore. Pardon me for, perhaps, beginning to spiritualize too suddenly, but it is the main part of our work here.

What interest there is in this old story! Just the interest which comes from the story in so far as it represents spiritual and eternal verities for ourselves to-night. Ought not preachers of the Gospel to be like this little lass, just knowing one thing, and knowing that one thing well enough to say it, and to say it boldly, and to say it again and again, to fill people's ears with it, and, although at first they may laugh, and at first they may scoff, and at first they may jeer, to keep saying it? "Would God my lord were with the prophet that is in Samaria! for he would recover him of his leprosy." What a splendid preacher she was! She had all the qualifications of a first-rate, successful preacher. She had a message, and she spoke that message simply and directly, and she spoke it with great assurance. The world has always had a great many more philosophers than it knew what to do with. Do not be proud, my young fellow, and pull your moustache, and put a glass in your eye, and talk about "philosophy." It is about the windiest of nonsense, and it has filled the ears of intelligent people for far too long a time. Philosophy has had its innings, and scored very little. We might give a chance to the Gospel, might we not? Now, we ought to be all like this girl. She is really a type for all preachers and Sabbath-school teachers. She spoke what she knew. There was a ring of sincerity and conviction in what she said, and it told on her mistress. At any rate, it told on somebody who heard it; and that somebody went and told Naaman, and it so told upon him that he said, "There is something in it."

Now, the same thing is working in and through the Gospel yet. On the surface it seems to be a weak, foolish, despised and despicable thing—the word of a witless lassie against all the misery and blighting power of leprosy. But God has chosen the weak things, the base things, things that are despised, to do His work, to bring to naught things that are, to save souls, to give to Him eternal fame and honour.

Do we know this Gospel? Do we know the prophet that is in Israel—no longer Elisha, but the Lord Jesus Christ, the Prophet of prophets, the King and Lord and Head of them all, the Incarnation and Embodiment of all healing power and spiritual virtue? Then, if we know Him, let us not only know Him in our hearts, but let us simply and sincerely testify for Him, and He will spread our testimony on the wings of the wind, and make it tell as He did with this little girl, "One went in and told his lord." The king of Syria writes to the king of Israel. Crowns sometimes drop upon very unworthy heads. Both of these kings cut very sorry figures, do they not? The king of Syria was going to do it all, and he said, "Go to, go, and I will send a letter to the king of Israel." "And Naaman departed, and took with him ten talents of silver, and six thousand pieces of gold, and ten changes of raiment." How this poor girl's little simple gospel is being spoiled! Did she say a single word about kings, or about talents of silver, or about changes of raiment? Then see how they have corrupted the simplicity of her simple testimony. Does not the Gospel suffer in the same way still? Is it not being muddled, and meddled with, and interfered with to its detriment, just in the same way? Many people are coming, as they think, to spread it, when they are really hindering it. They are coming to help it on a bit, when they are really taking off both its feet and its wings, and turning it into no Gospel at all. I know nothing more difficult (I speak from the depths of my heart) than it is to stand to-day four-square to all the philosophical, scientific, intellectual, critical, social, political cross currents and winds that are blowing, and notwithstanding them all to speak the simple Gospel as you get it from the Lord Jesus Christ. Try it and prove its difficulty, and you will have more sympathy with those who are trying to do it than perhaps you have. It is not just so easy to speak as this little girl spoke as some of you are thinking. You cry for the whole Gospel, and the simple Gospel. Do not simply cry to us, but cry to the Lord Jesus Christ, for it will need all the baptism and anointing and indwelling of His own Spirit to keep us at the true, simple Gospel. There are a thousand things round about us that tend to spoil us and to spoil the simplicity of our testimony; and this old trouble is just here to-day still—the king of Syria saying, "I will send a letter to the king of Israel." Well, what did they make of it? He brought the letter to the king of Israel, saying, " Now when this letter is come unto thee, behold, I have therewith sent Naaman my servant to thee, that thou mayest recover him of his leprosy. And it came to pass, when the king of Israel had read the letter, he rent his clothes, and said, Am I God, to kill and to make alive, that this man doth send unto me to recover a man of his leprosy? Wherefore consider, I pray you, and see how he seeketh a quarrel against me."

There are some things that kings and councillors and parliaments cannot do. This is one of them. They are utterly at their wits' end, and God will not give this glory but in one way, and this blessing but along a particular line. One thing does come out of it clearly, and that is the emphasizing of the point with which I began. Leprosy evidently was regarded as incurable. "Consider, I pray you, and see how he seeketh a quarrel against me. Am I God, to kill and to make alive?" Oh, that we had the same notion to-day about sin! Oh, that men and women were revived to a simple and intense conviction of this: "Sin is incurable: there is no remedy except the heavenly, the supernatural!" Where is the wise man's wisdom? Where is all the power of kings and lords and princes and councillors to save a sinner? It is reduced to utter contempt.

"And it was so, when Elisha the man of God had heard that the king of Israel had rent his clothes, that he sent to the king, saying, Wherefore has thou rent thy clothes? let him come now to me, and he shall know that there is a prophet in Israel." Does not that look a little like boasting at first? "Let him come to me." Yes, it is boasting, but it is boasting of the right kind. When a man boasts in God, "the humble hear thereof, and are glad." The meek hear of a testimony like this, and instead of being offended at it, and calling it vainglory, they glory in it; for Elisha is here lifting up, not himself, but the God who gave him all the power that he had. And here again is a great lesson for those of us who would really serve the deepest need of our generation. Let us not magnify ourselves, but let us magnify our office; let us magnify our message; let us magnify Him whom we preach to men. Let us challenge the world's need and the world's problem. Let us call upon men and women to come and look our way, and give us a trial. You ran here and ran there, and ran the otherwhere to get rid of your leprosy. Now, have you got soul peace, and power, and strength? Then, if not, will you come at length to us? "I magnify my office." In myself I am poor and weak and vile and nothing; but

I stand here to-night and dare to say that I preach a Gospel which could send every sinner within these walls outside of the walls as mightily changed as was Naaman before Elisha had done with him. That makes it worth your while to come here. Oh, that God would revive preachers in a simple faith in the message which we have to deliver. "Let him come unto me," said Elisha—and it was no boasting or vainglory. He dared not say less for God's sake and for Naaman's sake. He dared not say less than he said, neither dare we. Come to us. After all, things are at a very sad pass, I grant you. There is awful trouble in the land. There is an awful problem, and we cannot untie it; and the power of the State, and the power of the world's wisdom, and the power of the world's deepest sympathy, seems to make no more impression upon it than the king's advice and the king's sympathy made upon the sickness of his beloved general. But yet "there is balm in Gilead, and there is a physician there," and the problem is not so insoluble as we think it is, and the distress is not so dire; for there is one voice rising sharp and clear above all the Babel voices of a thousand counsellors who are darkening counsel by words without knowledge; and this is the voice: "Believe on the Lord Jesus Christ, and thou shalt be saved, and thy house." It is a message straight from Jesus Christ, who died and rose again. Oh, that it might be rung out! "Let him come now to me, and he shall know that there is a prophet in Israel."

"So Naaman came with his horses"—it is a sarcastic book, this old Bible—"so Naaman came with his horses." They were not lepers, but he fetched them. "So Naaman came with his horses and with his chariot." The Revised Version is more sarcastic. It says, "With his *chariots;* and stood at the door of the house of Elisha." Now, Elisha, you are on your trial. Now, Elisha, you never were in such a perilous place as you are now, after all that has been said about Israel and Israel's God. It is a trying time for you now. Very likely some young gentleman who has come in here this evening said, not out loud, but by his whole attitude, as he sat down in that pew, and as I came up into this pulpit — for wot ye not that such a man I can certainly divine? — "Now, preacher, you may have been criticized a little before, but it was gentleness and mercy, compared with what you will have now, since *I* have come. I am none of your ordinary church-goers. I am" — what do you suppose you are? I am very glad to see you, dear friend, but less of your airs, if you please, and less criticism! Understand the situation. I am master of the situation, and the situation is this: there is no problem up here. The whole problem is down there. Will you at length open your eyes? Will you at last be humbled in your own eyes? Will you at last cease from criticizing, cease from pulling yourself up all your inches, and strutting, and spreading, and accept the Gospel as a helpless leper, like you, should? Will you? I hope that is plain enough. If you will give me plainer English, I will hand it back to you, for, as God is my witness, I do believe that if you have not been washed by the blood of Christ, Naaman, for loathsomeness, is but a poor picture of your condition in the sight of God.

No, Elisha was not on his trial, and God was not on His trial; but Naaman was upon his, and he did not come through it very well at first. Elisha sent a messenger to him, saying, "Go and wash in Jordan seven times, and thy flesh shall come again to thee, and thou shalt be clean. But Naaman was wroth, and went away;" and you remember what he said, "Behold, I thought he will surely come to me." "*To me.*" "Granted that I am a leper, but I am not an ordinary leper. I am an extraordinary leper. I am a general. I am a prince. I am a captain. I am here with these jingling horses and chariots. May he deal thus with me?" Have you never heard or witnessed that rage? Is it not in your veins at this moment? Are you not sorry that you came in? Sit still. You may be sorry before you go out. After all, the worst kind of Gospel hearer is that one who comes and goes, and comes and goes, and you never find him either sad, or glad, or mad—never. There they are, like a ditch without fall or flood—like the Mediterranean, without ebb or flow—at the one fall-less and floodless, contemptible level. I like to see men mad. When a man like Naaman is being led along a line like this —when he is taken so far away out of his own orbit, or so far off the beaten track, so completely away from what he expects, when the Lord's message through Elisha falls upon him at an angle of incidence so unexpected—I can quite understand him. I do not suppose that the Lord was angry, and I do not suppose that Elisha was angry. They thoroughly understood it. They knew exactly what the effect would be. When men are wakened up from a deep sleep, and wakened up in a hurry because there is something urgent and imminent, they often wake up cross—they often wake up angry. I suppose that if I were to come to you to-morrow morning, with all your amiability and your sweetness and your gentleness— and I do not despise it—and seized you by the hand, and put my hand on your shoulder and shook you rudely and woke you up, when you arose you would not have all your "Polite Letter Writer" phrases just ready at the time. You would be likely to be a little indignant, and you would be likely to think that I was very inconsiderate; but if in the midst of all your ruffledness and all your anger I showed you that I had a just cause for what I had done, and that there was a fire, and that the fire was not in the next street or even in the next house, but was in your own house, I think when you got to know *that*, you would thank me, and you would say that if I had been polite, and had stood upon ceremony, I should not have been your friend. So with the Gospel preachers, so with Elisha. Poor Naaman was far gone, and what he needed was quick medicine: what he needed was something which went straight to the point. I grant there was seeming rudeness in the wording; I grant there was imperiousness, for when God speaks you must allow Him to be imperious and imperial—never forget that. The Gospel does beseech, but in it all and through it all the Gospel is a command, and you disobey it at peril of eternal damnation —let every soul of us know it before we go out. The Gospel is a command. Believe: repent. Go wash, and go as quickly as you can for your own sake. That is the Gospel— a command; and it is in your interest, oh sinner, that the Gospel is on the surface as seemingly rude and inconsiderate and urgent as it is.

Naaman was wroth, and said, " I thought : " that is what is wrong with some of us here until this hour. Why are you not as happy and rejoicing a Christian as there is in all London? I will tell you why in a word. You are just troubled with the same disease that troubled Naaman inwardly. Leprosy was his trouble outwardly, and the leprosy of pride was his trouble inwardly. He needed to be humbled before he could be healed. Now, your pride is very likely intellectual pride, intellectual vanity, intellectual conceit. I speak to men and women here who have read a little. If you had read more you would be very fine material for preaching the Gospel to, but you have read a little, just a little. You have got the names of Huxley and Spencer and Darwin on your tongues, and you could not very likely tell for the life of you what Huxley and Spencer and Darwin had particularly said; but you have got a hold of the names on your tongues, and you juggle, juggle, juggle away with these words and names, and you want to impress and overawe the poor preacher with a sense of your opinion, and "I think so and so, " and you say, "When I go to hear a sermon, I think, and I wish, and I like," and when you do not get what you like, the preacher gets your ugliest verdict. Now, my dear friend, come away from that, if you please. We are met here for far more serious work. You are a poor hopeless, helpless, condemned sinner; until you receive this Gospel in childlike simplicity you cannot be saved; you are neither fit to live nor fit to die, and you have both to do, so do come down off your horse of pride and headiness and high-mindedness and self-conceit, and sit there as quietly and humbly as though you had never read a book. Forget your wisdom and forget your knowledge, and remember that in all past ages, and even in this nineteenth century, thanks to God, wise men and learned who have forgotten more about literature and science and philosophy than you ever learnt, have with all their knowledge, contrived to be as simple, genuine, evangelical believers in the blood of the Lamb as any that ever lived. You "thought." Thank you for nothing. What did you think? Let us hear it. Well, here it is, " I thought that he would surely come out to me, and stand, and call on the name of the Lord his God, and wave his hand over the place, and recover me of the leprosy." That is "I thought that he was a trickster and a juggler, and that he would come and and say, ' Hey ! Presto ! Pass !' and the thing would be done." Yes, is not that about the length and breadth and and depth and height, my friend, of your notions of what genuine religion is? The thoughts of people in Naaman's condition—oh, they are worth little ! Naaman spoke out his thought, and there it is. That is what he thought. When salvation comes to us, it comes when we get rid of our own thought, or we hold in our own thought, whatever it may be, and we choke it down, and we allow God to speak; for God's thoughts are what we need to know; and God says in this business, " My thoughts are not your thoughts, neither are My ways your ways, for as the heaven is high above the earth, so are My thoughts higher than your thoughts, and My ways than your ways." Oh, hush, be still, and know that God is here—that God is speaking, and that you ought to bow the head and keep silence and believe !

" Are not Abana and Pharpar—?" Oh, yes! With what contempt men sometimes speak of the Gospel until they have tried it.

> "What's Yarrow but a river bare,
>   That rolls the dark hills under;
> There are a thousand streams elsewhere
>   As worthy of your wonder."

Naaman dear, if Abana and Pharpar were waters that could have cleansed you, why did you not go to them? Why did you come here at all? That was a witless speech, surely! And have not some of us spoken in the same rude and contemptuous way about what we call old, narrow-minded, bigoted, Puritanical doctrines, until we have tried them? But when the day came when our sins were fastening upon us, and the sorrows of death compassed us, and the pains of hell got hold upon us, and we found trouble and sorrow, then we changed our tune. When we were heart-whole and we were well, when no spiritual pains had fastened upon us, we could speak contemptuously of the old Gospel, and call it a " doctrine of the shambles," this salvation by blood; but when we stand naked and shivering and ready to perish, then this old Gospel of the Cross—the Gospel of salvation through the doing and dying of Another—is to us like a peal of heaven's own music. Do not talk against the Gospel, my friend. You are only showing your want of heart or the depth of your ignorance.

"And his servants came near, and spoke, and said, If the prophet had bid thee do some great thing, wouldst thou not have done it? How much rather, then, when he said, Wash, and be clean?" "Then went he down, and dipped himself seven times in the Jordan"—*verbatim et literatim* according to the saying of the man of God. He had to humble himself to obey the Gospel. And you and I must do the same. We do not give up intellectuality, we do not give up the powers of the mind. We simply crucify their pride; that is all.

"And his flesh came unto him like unto the flesh of a little child, and he was clean." This is the Gospel. Will you try it? Now, after all that we have said to-night, and after all the comings and goings between some of us here and religion, and the preachers of Christ's religion, will you do, my friend, what you never did before? Will you humble yourself simply to believe? The Gospel will never prove its power in anybody as long as he criticizes, and as long as he questions. The Gospel is for believing; the Gospel is for receiving. "Oh, taste and see that God is good: blessed is the man who trusteth in Him." At last Naaman is a sadder and a wiser man. He is kindly spoken to by his servant. Naaman had his good points about him. But after all, you see, there was the leprosy. There was no arguing against that. There was this sentence of death eating into him. So with you, man, you are dying while you are criticizing; hell opens its mouth to receive you while you are quibbling and wanting another gospel to suit you. Do not forget that. It does not become beggars to be choosers; and you are an absolute beggar at heaven's gate—an absolute dependant upon God's bounty; and when it is offered to you, it ill becomes you to adopt the sneer or the angry tone which you do adopt. Let us cease to-night from all such superfluity of haughtiness, and in simplicity, like the poor dying lepers that we are, let us receive salvation through Jesus Christ, through His atonement.

That dark, muddy Jordan was not a nice stream. It was really a very poor river from an artistic point of view; but it was in Israel, it was an Israelitish river; and away to it Naaman must go, great man and all as he was. And he went. He swallowed down his pride. He very likely said to himself, "Well, that servant of mine is true; he is right; I am a leper, and of course I am dying, and after all, I may as well try it. It would be a pity to come all this distance, with all these jingling horses and chariots, and go home, and admit that I had come on a fool's errand; and maybe there is something in it." And he went down. "He stooped to conquer, and he conquered by stooping;" he gave in to God, and he won. For a time he seemed to be no better, only much wetter. But, dipping seven times, when he came up the seventh time he had left his leprosy in the last plunge. The flesh came to him as with that leper in the New Testament to whom Christ said, "Be thou made clean, and immediately he was made whole." As the poet says:

> " And his dry palms grew moist,
>   And the blood coursed with delicious coolness through his veins;
>   And on his brow the dewy softness of an infant stole,
>   His leprosy was cleansed, and he fell down—
>   At Jesus' feet and worshipped Him."

That is the Gospel for lepers, Old Testament or New.

I am sorry, in one way, that my time is up; but I do trust that, although our time is up, we have had sufficient time to come near to the cleansing fountain, and that all of us here, ere we go hence, are, in absolute abject simplicity, plunging into it.

> "There is a fountain filled with blood."

Not long ago that hymn was severely objected to, and scornfully criticized. It was said that this was a religion of gore and of the shambles, unfit for ears intellectual and polite. Still, let me preach it. If it angers you at first, that may be just the road to your salvation.

> " There is a fountain filled with blood,
>   Drawn from Emmanuel's veins;
>   And sinners plunged beneath that flood
>   Lose all their guilty stains."

I trust I have read a book or two. I hope I know a little about philosophy. I trust I know a little about science. I went for eight winters to a college and a divinity hall, and I was lectured and taught by the most cultured and eminent men of the day. But if to-morrow I am upon my death-bed, and if you want to come and give me a parting word, come, and I will tell you before you come what you may say. Do not mention this nineteenth century; do not mention these new gospels, which are no gospels. If you have no word, and if you have no text, that old hymn that I have quoted will do, and especially the verse that I am going to quote now :

> " The dying thief rejoiced to see
> That fountain in his day ;
> And there may I, though vile as he,
> Wash all my sins away."

Ah, my lad, you may despise this old Gospel, but your mother died rejoicing in it. So did your father; and if you are ever to see them and meet with them ; if you are ever to sit down with the truly refined people, you must be washed in the blood of the Lamb. May the Lord, the Spirit, graciously plead His own cause, and ere we go hence, may all of us come to the simplicity of faith in Jesus Christ, who died for our sins, and rose again for our justification !

Regent Square Pulpit.

THE FARMER WHO FED *HIS SOUL* WITH CORN.

A Sermon

Delivered in Regent Square Church on Sunday, April 13th, 1890, by the

REV. JOHN McNEILL.

Luke xii.—Read from the 13th verse to 21st.

The Parable of the Rich Farmer.

The key to this parable, as Matthew Henry would say, hangs at the door. It is meant to rebuke covetousness; it is therefore a parable of widespread application. Who among us to-day can say, "My heart is clean from covetousness?" None of us. No specific form of sin, perhaps, is more common in the thoughts and actions of men than covetousness. "I had not known lust," says one whose outward life was blameless, except the law had said, "Thou shalt not covet." "Take heed," says Christ—the very emphasis of His tone is meant to waken us up to the lesson—"Take heed, and beware of covetousness." The rich need beware of it, the poor need beware of it; those who are too rich, those who are too poor, and the mass of the middle folk lying between. I do not need to take time to prove this. Those among us who belong to the various classes mentioned will, I am sure, frankly admit that the parable has meaning and force, and that there is need for it in the case of all us. These hearts of ours, because of sin, are hot, hungry, and restless. In their lustings and longings and breathings they go out everywhere; after every conceivable thing, except for that intense desire which would be no sin, but would satisfy every wish of the immortal soul. Oh, that we may earnestly covet the best gift! "God so loved the world that He gave His only begotten Son." May our hearts to-day be smitten with covetousness for God's great gift—Jesus Christ! Then shall we be rich toward God.

"A man's life consisteth not in the abundance of the things that he possesseth," and contrariwise, a man's death consisteth not in the dearth or absence of material possessions. I may be miserable when corn and wine abound; and I may live and enjoy good days with God's blessing on bread and water.

See, then, how our Lord, by bringing before us a well-to-do, prosperous Jewish farmer, would rebuke covetousness, would set us right, would deliver us from the down-dragging power of this world, and would so succour us that even when this world flows in upon us, we shall be helped to use it without abusing it; we shall be able, when our hands are filled, to keep their palms as open and level as though there was nothing in them.

"The ground of a certain rich man brought forth plentifully." It looks as though the Lord would emphasize, in putting the case so, that greed, selfishness, and covetousness—a heart that lusts after material abundance, and seeks to find its satisfaction therein, is here particularly, especially, horribly out of order. A farmer, a man whose wealth comes out of the soil, is peculiarly dependent upon a thousand and one things over which he has no control.

What a lesson there ought to be for those of us here whose trade depends on clouds or want of clouds; a lesson to farmers, and those whose wealth, for example, comes by the way of the sea—shippers, and seafaring folk generally If such are making money and getting substance beyond what they actually need, how peculiarly thankful to God Almighty they should be! For there are some ways of making money, such as all that modern juggling and financing in stocks and shares, that I scarcely understand— but concerning which I do not wonder that men should lose sight of God, and not see precisely where God comes into their business.

But here, in this kind of merchandise, the thought of God ought to be in the farmer's mind all the year round, and ought to animate his dreams at night; he is so fairly and squarely, so nakedly dependent upon Him. Says the Scripture—just to emphasize this—"The farmer is a man who puts his precious seed into the earth, and sleeps and rises night and day, and the seed springeth up, he knoweth not how." If he were to tear out his hair by handfuls he could not bring a drop of rain, supposing it was wanted, while he could not keep a drop away if too much were to come. If the heavens were to be like brass, and the earth beneath his feet like iron, what could he do? God has the farmer in a vice. If any man ought, at the close of a prosperous season, to be fairly bubbling over with thankfulness to God, surely it ought to be a farmer. And yet, that is the kind of man used to exemplify the sin of covetousness, and to make it gross, awful, and hideous. Christ, in this inimitable way of His, shows us a prosperous Jewish farmer rubbing his fat hands at the close of a good season, and saying, "*My* fruits, and *my* goods, and *my* barns!" Me and mine, and not a word about God, or his needy brother man.

As if the man had put the chemical properties into the soil, he takes all the credit and all the increase and all the abundance to himself. "And what for no." Hasn't he been rainmaker and cloud-compeller; charioteer of the sun, aye, and man in the moon for the last six months. Therefore when the crop, his crop, is gathered into his barn, he sets his soul to swallow it all down; and what he cannot swallow, he shall "big (build) it roon aboot," and keep it safe from heavenly God or hungry man. The fat-hearted fool!

"He thought within himself." That is the Bible. "He thought within himself"—yourself when you are alone. Prosperous man, watch yourself when you are alone, thinking; man with too much or too little, watch yourself when you are alone, because then God is there, God is looking on, and God is reading the heart, He sees not as man sees. The Lord looked in upon this prosperous Jewish farmer's heart, and here is the blank, blatant, most tremendous atheism which He saw. No God, no thankfulness! Nothing about the great Lord God Almighty. "Me! my fruits, my goods! Sit back, oh world, and make room for me and my barns!" You have him to-day. He will root us all out, and send us miles across the sea to make room for his sheep and his deer, and will huddle us into the odd corners of the globe, as good enough for us.

"What shall I do?" said this man. Ah! we never should have known this if Christ had not turned this man inside out, for we are deep and desperate puzzles to ourselves, and we can delude each the other. Remember, this was a man who on the Sabbath, after this jolly little confab with himself, supposing he had been spared, on the Sabbath day would have gone to the synagogue or temple, and would have had to sing the psalm we have just sung. Here was a man who, if you pass by what he thinks within himself, says this outside of himself: "Thou visitest the earth, and waterest it: Thou greatly enrichest it with the river of God, which is full of water: Thou preparest them corn, when Thou hast so provided for it. Thou waterest"— (here is the Great Husbandman out with the watering-can) —"Thou waterest the ridges thereof abundantly: Thou settlest the furrows thereof: Thou makest it soft with showers: Thou blessest the springing thereof. Thou crownest the year with Thy goodness; and Thy paths drop fatness. They drop upon the pastures of the wilderness: and the little hills rejoice on every side. The pastures are clothed with flocks; the valleys also are covered over with corn; *they* "—(not *I*)—" they shout for joy, they also sing." That is the tongue and the teeth of this rich Jewish farmer in his pew on Sunday! It is also the prosperous London City merchant in Regent Square Church on Sunday. It is all God to-day. This old Book of ours, and our ritual, compel our tongue and teeth to be right. But the same Lord that looked into the Jewish farmer's heart looks into your heart and my heart to-day, and He may see this ugly thing in us that He saw in him. Behind the psalm, and behind the prayer, this hideous, gaping covetousness, "My fruit, my goods."

Now, let us remember that when we are thinking within ourselves, the Lord hears the whirring wheels of our mental machinery, and bends His ear down just then. That is when I should like to get a look into your hearts, and when you would like to get a look into mine. Is it not when we are all alone by ourselves and hidden, that the time comes to know what a man is inside? Well, understand friends, that there is present with us to-day One who knows what we are inside, who knows the heart's creed and the heart's confession of faith or faithlessness; He knows the blank atheism that may be in the heart of a professing Christian; the Sahara barrenness. No green sprout of gratitude to God, any more than on the sands of the sea; not a green blade! This is a man whose Bible, whose creed, as well as his very occupation, that of a farmer, all prompted to remembrance of a present God. But the knowledge of God has left him; he is suffering, he is dying from that very common disease, fatty degeneration of the heart.

"And he thought within himself, saying, What shall I do, because I have no room where to bestow my fruits? And he said, This will I do: I will pull down my barns, and build greater; and there will I bestow all my fruits and goods." Now, think of what that man should have done at the close of the harvest home, when it was all in, and stacked, and cleared. How he ought to have sat down in the evening in his chair, and then said to himself, "What a poor fool I am! Dear me; there are those barns chock-full, and I remember one day back in the spring I really shed tears of disappointment; so utterly did the weather seem to go against me, that I lost hope and heart. And I said to myself and to my servants in the fields, We have had all this trouble and anxiety, and have put this good grain into soil, and now look at this weather; we shall be ruined! Although I am a believer in the God of Israel, I am ashamed to say it, but it wrung tears of bitter disappointment from my heart; and now, what a fool I was! See now, notwithstanding all my over-anxiety, my fear for the day I never saw—here are my barns full; I have never had such a prosperous year." And then he would call all his domestics together, and make them sing—what is it?—the 139th Psalm, or that Psalm I have already read, the 65th, and read those grand old passages filled with promises and warnings for farming folks out of the Book of Deuteronomy. Especially should he have charged himself not to forget those words: "Honour the Lord with thy substance and with the first-fruits of all thine increase: so shall thy barns be filled with plenty, and thy presses burst with new wine." For surely in his case, through God's goodness, he that went forth weeping, bearing precious seed, had come again with rejoicing, bringing his sheaves with him. That is how he ought to have done, that is how *he ought* to have "thought within himself." He should have said to his soul, "How good God has been; how He has disappointed all my fears; how He has exceeded all my hopes! God could have made the earth to have been dry, cracked, and barren; God could have ruined me, and I would have deserved it. I am such a sinner; but He has filled me and blest me, and my soul stands amazed at His goodness." That is what some of us ought to be doing. Oh, greyheaded man, it is getting late in the day with you; let me hold up this mirror before you, and if you see one lineament in that face like your own, go down before God with awful shame, before you pass to meet Him! Just let some of us remember how God has blessed us. Let me remind you of the days when you came to London with half-a-crown in your pocket, and spent it, and it did not bring another half-crown, and yet you are sitting to-day, well-to-do and with a comfortable competence. What is the explanation of it? Who did it for you?—you did not. I am not forgetting your industry; I am not forgetting how you rose up early and sat up late; I am not forgetting anything about the human qualities that you have used and developed. But do not forget God, my friends. If God were to take away *His* share out of your successes, the devil himself would not be made up with what is left. Suppose God took away His share out of all that has been at work in bringing this betterment, this unearned increment, what would be left? Suppose God took His share out of your brains, and out of your business, what would be left?—"less than nothing, and vanity." Suppose God had withheld His blessing when you were at a crisis in your business, when you had to take a leap in the dark, and when you landed, not in the ditch, but on the firm ground. He guided you over the ditch. Oh, man, put in God somewhere! God grant you may get to see and acknowledge more of Him than you have yet done! You have not been quite so hard as some, yet you are still far behind in giving back to Him who gave you every copper you have; and as to any coppers and any gold we may have which God did *not* give us, may we get rid of that, for we will rue it with every vein in our hearts that we ever took a penny that God did not give us; we will be sorry for that success, as sure as we live!

Then, see his action and purpose: "I will pull down my barns, and build greater," and so on. Now, my hearers, perish all thought to-day of being eloquent, or of being eloquent on any day; but let us stick to God's work! If I have any power among my fellow-men, I know it has only come through this—a gripping, perhaps, more than many other men of the naked truth of God's Word. Now, look here, do not let us hold up our hands in mock horror at this Jewish farmer, for we are doing the same things ourselves every day. The Lord is not guilty of coarse daubing when He paints this man. This is a character which is true to life. This awful exposition of what is in our hearts, especially in time of prosperity, is needed.

"I will pull down my barns, and build greater; and there will I bestow all my fruits and my goods." How to invest, and invest, and invest is the dry rot, and I fear will be the downright damnation of not a few professing Christians! Simply how to keep, and how to keep, so that it shall grow, and I shall die rich! Men are bending their whole energies to that for seven days of the week. It is only six days on which they can actually work, but the seventh is chock-full of thinking about it. Do not let us hold up our hands in mock horror, as though Christ could be guilty of exaggeration. No words of mine could make this poor doit of a creature look worse than he is. Just look at him. Whereas he ought to have said as he dried the tears out of his eyes, where I left him at the last soliloquy, "Now, what will I do? Let me see. I wonder if I paid my men? Good, honest fellows! How they toiled and tugged hard all through the working time!" Do you remember what James says in his Epistle? "Go to now, ye rich men, howl and weep." When did ever we preachers dare to take that as a text? "Howl and weep!" Why? "Because the hire of your labourers that reaped down your fields, which is by you kept back through fraud, crieth, and the cry of your labourers has entered into the ears of the Lord of Sabaoth." You are doing well, my friend. Have you paid everybody who helped you to your success? Go back yonder to your miserable quill-drivers, and for heaven's sake give them a few more shillings a week! You have not all the credit and all the glory. No man can say, "I did it, and I did it all." And that very thing to which James refers was a current scandal at the time this fat farmer was rubbing his hands, as if he were quits with God and with every mortal being.

Now, let us look around; let us go abroad through the city, and see the want, and the hunger, and the nakedness, and the famine, and the wretchedness. Open your gate, my brother. You live out in a villa, just a little too self-contained; open your gate, and step out and see that you don't tumble over some Lazarus into hell. Take care; Lazarus is set there to keep you out of it, in mercy. Look abroad.

> "Is there no beggar at your gate?
> Are there no poor about your lands?"

Am not I the son of a man who toiled hard for another man, who took his skill and labour, and ground him down to the last shilling? Ground him down; and because old John McNeill wanted a shilling more, he let him go, and then went sneaking after him when he found out his worth, saying, "I will give you another shilling." Oh, the curse of it—"I will give you another shilling!" That a Christian man, a leader in a Christian Church, should say to another Christian who has a wife and family, "I will give you another shilling. You are worth pounds and pounds to me; I cannot do without you, in fact; therefore I will give you another shilling!" The wonder is that, with a Bible like this to preach, we do not pull men out of their seats. There is such an awful grip in the Word I have got to-day.

"And he said, I will pull down my barns, and build greater; and there will I bestow my goods." And God's cause in the land, and God's poor, crying for money! The Sustentation Fund collector round at the back door getting snubbed and driven away, told by the servant, "You come too often; master says he has nothing more for you. It is give, give, all the time." The Lord save us from this! Do I speak to any poor person here? My friend, listen. When that cold east wind flutters your rags, when it bites you to the very marrow, thank God for your coldness, and for your emptiness, thank God for your poverty, if it has saved you from this black atheism! Thank God for your poverty and rags and all manner of emptiness, if it has cooled this lustful fever in your blood, and taken this devouring flame of covetousness out of your bones! Thank God for it!

Thy goods!—thou infinite liar! Hands off, thou thief! *God's* goods, every ear of it, God's own grain! Thou unjust steward, thou fraudulent trustee!

"And I will say to my *soul!*"—(but thou canst not; thy soul is gone, thou corn-chest)—" I will say to my soul, Soul, thou hast much goods laid up for many years; take thine ease, eat, drink, and be merry." Now, what should he have said? How pitiful to think that this soliloquy, time and again, was very near the right path, and yet went wrong. For we should talk with our heart occasionally. If you are well to-day, if you are prosperous, if you have more than you need, it is right you should talk to your soul. But talk to it after a different fashion. Just sit down with your soul, and put your soul there into a corner, and hold it tightly in the corner, and say, "Now, my soul, look here; soul, look at me, you and I are getting on very well. Soul, we are making money; soul, you know the balance at the bank; now, my soul, for God's sake, and thine own, let me talk to thee. Soul, soul, take care, thou art on the brink of a precipice over which other souls have gone, and there was no recovery. Soul, take care—for thine own eternal interests, take care—when thy hands are being filled and filled, that thou dost keep them open, flat out; for God has many a hungry sparrow flying about, looking for a pick."

Oh, soul of mine, take care of that cramp that is coming in thine hand; fight against it, keep thy palm open; though millions lay upon it, do not let thy fingers clutch upon them. Talk to your heart like that. But what are words of mine. Hear these Divine words with which he might have filled his mouth in sacred soliloquy: "When thou hast eaten and art full, then thou shalt bless the Lord thy God for the good land which He hath given thee. Beware that thou forget not the Lord thy God; lest when thou hast eaten and art full, and hast built goodly houses and dwelt therein . . . . and all that thou hast is multiplied: then thy heart is lifted up, and thou forgettest the Lord thy God. But thou shalt remember the Lord thy God, for it is He that giveth thee power to get wealth." Put your soul in a corner. Tell your soul about the infinite danger of the body running off with the soul, even as the swine ran down the steep place into the sea and were choked. Tell your heart about the danger of swinishness and lustfulness, and of becoming material in all the finer susceptibilities, until any throb of gratitude to God or of desire to help your helpless brother has become petrified or withered away.

"But God said unto him, Thou fool, this night thy soul shall be required of thee: then whose shall those things be which thou hast provided?" Now, perhaps, you are inclined to say at this point, " Well, preacher, about the last thing to make an impression on men is to talk of sudden death. Here we are in Regent Square Church all right, sound and well, sound in wind and limb, healthy, prosperous in body, and prosperous in estate; do not talk to us of death, do not talk to us of eternity; that is bad art; you cannot make any impression." No, and yet that is how the parable closes, for that is true to life, and to fact, that is true to nature; and the preacher must use this arrow from God's own quiver. My friend, the greatest of all reasons why you and I should be open-handed and open-hearted, why we should give and give—and I am not talking about indiscriminate charity; no, no, no, I do not think we have ruined many people with our indiscriminate charity, God will forgive us for the damage we have done in this direction—I say the greatest reason why we should be open-handed and open-hearted *is the thought of death.* Tell your heart, talk to your heart about death, say to yourself with all your abundance round about you, sitting at the parlour window looking out on the stack-yard and seeing all its fulness, lay down your hand on your head, and say, " Now, stack-yard, what a fool I'd be to choke myself with you! I am a dying man."

> "The numbered hour is on the wing
> That lays me with the dead."

The hour is coming, I do not know how soon, and the preachers have said it, and God's Word rings with it, while I have also found it out in the case of others round about me; my turn is coming. Oh, world, I see through thee! Oh, stackyard, I am delivered from thee! for between me and all my possessions I put the opening grave, the great white throne, and Him who sits upon it. Ah! if you do that you can take all manner of wealth and abundance, all manner of goods and gear; if only between thee and it thou dost put the opening grave and the day of reckoning. Then I will trust you with a million of money, for you will be very anxious to get rid of it before the reckoning comes. That is what the poor soul forgot — his highest interests. He was closed up with the very fatness of his cheeks. I am not coarse; I am not exaggerating; David was a very fine-souled man, and David has described this man when he says—

> "Their hearts, with worldly ease and wealth,
> As fat as grease they be."

Again he says, "They spend their days in mirth, and in a moment go down to the grave." Oh, that God would give me a tongue to reach the Mansion House corner yonder, to lift up this magnificent old Scripture. In the midst of your marts and markets and exchanges, remember death and judgment and eternity. May the subject cool the fever in our blood, and may those that have be as though they had not, and may those that weep be as though they wept not; and those that are poor, may they be as though such a thing as poverty were unknown; for the fashion of this world passeth away, and we are all on the road to a scene and a world in which a big purse and a long rent-roll, blessed be God, count for nothing!

> "Naked as to the earth we came,
> And entered life at first;
> Naked we to the earth return,
> And mix with kindred dust."

"How much did he leave?" said a man when the death of a wealthy friend was mentioned; and the answer came, with a sly touch of quiet sarcasm, "How much did he leave? why, of course, he left it all." Yes, he left it all.

"This night,"—*This* night! Oh, how it brings eternity near! That man sitting there thinking of nothing but time, time, time, as we are apt to sit here and think of nothing but our circumstances, our family, our stocks, our shares, our business. Time, time, time; and there in the background is God telling that angel, "Angel, start down to London for the soul of a certain man, to whom I shall guide thee, who is now sitting in Regent's Square Church." While you are saying to yourself, "Much goods," the pocketless shroud is waiting for you; while you are saying to yourself, "Many years," your name is being called in the other world; and presently you shall appear to answer it. Have you ever had any experience something like this? I remember one evening when I was staying in the country. It was growing late and dark, and I had not lit the lamp; the house was getting dark, and I was sitting there quietly thinking, when suddenly my whole flesh began to move, and my hair almost to stand on end. It was next to nothing, but it was just the most nervous thing that can happen to one—a sudden look of a face peering in at the window at you—just a moment, and then the face vanishes. May we all get that stagger to-day! May you just get one brief look at God's face, for God looks in at the window of your soul when you are thinking, "My fruits, my goods, my ease, my abundance! What I am going to do if I can only get the Benediction pronounced and the Sunday turned into Monday." Just then God is looking in at the window; just one brief, swift glance to tell you He is there. And remember, that He who looks in at the window is not far from the door; He can quickly be in on the floor, with His hand on your shoulder. God is as near as that. He is looking in at the window, and He will be round at the door some of these days, and we will then have to go out whether we like it or no. We shall be "required" to go. Exit, rich farmer! Enter the relatives, to fight about the will! Oh, the sarcasm of such a life! May the Lord to-day help us to look up to Him, sick or well, rich or poor, young or old, and let us see to it that we are rich towards God, rich in prayer, rich in work, rich in spiritual ambition and in spiritual covetousness!

For death shall only usher us into a more abundant possession.

May the Lord bless the preaching of His Word!

Regent Square Pulpit.

THE IMPERIAL STANDARD FOR MEASURING RECRUITS.

A Sermon

DELIVERED IN REGENT SQUARE CHURCH ON SUNDAY MORNING, APRIL 20TH, 1890, BY THE

REV. JOHN McNEILL.

LUKE ix. 57-62.

IT is evident, then, the very first reflection that comes into one's mind after reading such a passage as this—reading it in the light partly of its own setting, its own date and generation; and reading it also in the light of our own surroundings—our obvious reflection is that Christ's cause and kingdom may not be expected to go on by leaps and bounds.

Not because it is not a grand cause and kingdom, not because He is not a great King and Leader, but simply because men are men. Christ is here to set up His kingdom among men, among us men and women. And therein lies the difficulty. Christ wants to count, not heads, but hearts. It is nothing to Him, evidently it is nothing to the Lord Jesus Christ, who is here to set up His great society, His great eternal rule and sway, with all its personal and social characteristics, with all its beneficent purposes now and for evermore—it is evidently nothing to Him, I say, to have a flock of people coming to-day, if they are going to leave Him to-morrow. He is delivered—this great King and Lord and Leader of men, who comes to form His new society—He is delivered from many of those mistakes and false ambitions, which, although for the time they seem to serve the purpose of great leaders, by-and-bye become the very destruction of all progress.

See how Christ lifts Himself up to our view as delivered from all mean, low, and petty aims and methods of accomplishing His purpose. He will part company with you, with me, with anybody, in order to be on terms of absolute sincerity with us. He will say to us, " Come, and I am glad to see you ; but let us understand the terms. I would rather that you never began than that you should begin on a false notion, a false understanding, and perhaps afterwards have some kind of just occasion to say that I held out bright hopes at the beginning, which were falsified as time went on." And let us remember, that if Christ could afford to deal thus with candidates for His fellowship then, in those small and despised days, when He could count His actual, devoted followers without going very deep into arithmetic ; if He could afford to do this *then*, to put on the riddle, the sieve, so to speak, and sift so thoroughly, much more can He afford to do it to-day. So we need to turn to a passage like this every now and then, especially in times of increase, outward increase, in times of outward prosperity, in times of outward and visible success, in order that we may be delivered from any delusion; for it is utterly impossible to delude or glamour our Master. He is delivered from all wrong use of numbers and figures; from all that the eye sees, and from the shouts and hosannas that may fill the ear. From all *that* He is absolutely free. Are we?

"And it came to pass, that, as they went in the way, a certain man said unto Him, Lord, I will follow Thee whithersoever Thou goest. And Jesus said unto him, Foxes have holes, and birds of the air have nests; but the Son of Man hath not where to lay His head." Now let me test myself, first of all, by this man. The great question for you and me is this: Christ is going through the land. I have heard much about Him, glorious things are said about Him, glorious things are in His gift and offer for me, for whomsoever will. Now let us go back to the beginning. Am I really with Him, am I really in the inner circle of Christ's own true, faithful, devoted followers? For with Him *it is all inner circle.* Can I encourage myself, then, this morning; can I, dare I encourage my heart with the honest assurance, "Through grace I do believe I have heard Christ's call, and from the heart I have obeyed. I am His irrevocably, by my own sincere, honest, day-light decision in His own presence." What kind of man is this? You may be like him.

The Lord did not fasten him by *a* "Follow Me," as He did with others. But neither is he turned away by the Lord saying, "No, My friend; I am going through the land, and whomsoever I wish to have for My purposes, I call individually. I give to each express, clear monition and indication on the tympanum of his own ear that My voice has spoken, and I have called him by his name." Now I believe in eternity that will be found to be true. When all tests have been applied, and all winds of judgment have blown their utmost, and the last speck of chaff has gone drifting away on the last gust that will ever blow out of the judgment quarter, I believe it will be found that all of us who are left, all who are saved, did receive a personal call, to which in the depths of our soul we responded. But even supposing we should be in doubt about that; supposing that down here to-day that should trouble us, the Lord virtually says to us by this first man, "Don't stumble yourself. Are you directed to Me? In any of the ordinary ways by which men are moved and brought into contact with Me, have you been drawn towards Me?" This first man had no special call, like Peter, for example, so far as we know. But he had heard of Jesus, and he was a man to whom Christ seems to have been most attractive. His person drew him; the look in His face, the tone of His conversation, and, above all, the things He said and did. He was what we would call a man of sanguine temperament, warm-blooded, quick, open, free; a man who does not need much telling; a man who does not wait; a man who sees the drift of your argument before you have got through it. He knows the appeal before it is uttered, and there he is saying, "All right; I understand. You want me? Here I am." And one would think it seems hard to take such a quick-pulsed man, all boiling over for Christ, to give him a sousing in this cold bath two or three times, and then to set him down all dripping and say, "Now, what do you think of it?" It seems to be hard; but as there can be no hardness and no harshness with Christ, this must be the way of perfect wisdom. I must take Christ for Himself alone.

Suppose I am sanguine—suppose somebody here is of a sanguine temperament; you are easily wrought upon by a preacher of the Gospel. Now here is where the danger comes out. You may think that because you are easily made to shed tears when I picture the sufferings of my

Master, or some other more skilful preacher does so, that therefore you are Christ's. And when other sides of the Gospel are represented, your heart beats quick and warm, and your whole soul thrills and fills and swells. Ah! it is the thrilling, filling, swelling kind of people who are tested here. And you know we need testing. I speak unto you as unto honest men. My brethren and my sisters, those of us who are quick and warm and sympathetic—now crying in sympathy, our eyes filled and our whole being quivering, and in another moment shouting with triumph—don't we come to be as near to hypocrites as anything that deserves that name, if there is such a thing going? If it be hypocrisy to be hot and full-blooded this minute and then to be as cold as the world before an hour is over—if that is hypocrisy, then have we not been desperately near it? And is it not kind of Christ to take us when we are quick and warm and give us a sousing in this cold bath : " Foxes have holes, and birds of the air have nests; but the Son of Man hath not where to lay His head."

"Yes, come to Me," we may with reverence imagine our Lord saying, "but I may as well settle and sober you at the beginning; in fact, better now than later on. I may just as well tell you eager, quick, sympathetic people that I may turn out to be a slow Christ to you." "To people like you," Christ says, " I sometimes seem to be very aggravating. When you want to carry things *per saltum*, and you are going to crush into a day a thousand years, I sit down, and keep sitting—I seem to fold My hands. And that will try you ; and you will be apt to think that you have found Me out, and that we had better part company. You began with Me thinking it was all going on from strength to strength, and from one exploit and victory to another·

whereas you find there are long campaigns, and long, dull, fagging days, as well as weary nights, that never seem to come to an end. Now, will you understand that Mine is a cause that is going to be for ever on a flood of popularity. To-day I am popular; to-morrow another wind will blow. 'Foxes have holes, and birds of the air have nests; but the Son of Man hath not where to lay His head.' I will be despised, will you bear the despite with Me? I will be lonely, will you have companionship with a lonely man?"

It is like our old story from the Old Testament of Naomi and Ruth. How marvellously like Christ is that old widow Naomi! "A root out of a dry ground," and not much prospect along the road that the lonely, bereaved widow is taking. Now, can you, like Ruth, take Christ at the lowest level; and can you see His true spiritual glory, and all the promise and prophecy about Him for Himself and for us that are bound up in Him? Can we put our arms round Him when He comes before us, the despised and rejected of men, and say to Him, "Entreat me not to leave Thee, nor to return from following after Thee, my Master. I am uncertain, I know it—now hot, now cold, now strong, now weak, now all for going forward, and again all for flinging up everything, because I have got a little checked and disillusionized. But, Master, take me into Thine own hands, and be firm with me. Shake that nonsense out of me; take away what is merely natural and of the flesh; for that which is born of the flesh is flesh, and will pass away, and come to nothing. By Thy grace I am becoming deeper, O Christ, than I thought I was. Entreat me not to leave Thee, nor to return from following after Thee: where Thou goest, I will go; and where Thou lodgest, let it be on the cold hillside of loneliness and unpopularity, I will lodge; Thy people shall be my people, and Thy God my God. I will try to give another answer than the expected one to the question, Doth Job serve God for naught?"

When you go to see a doctor, you are not altogether relieved if your doctor is too suave and smiling; if he pooh-poohs everything, and seems almost as if he does not take the trouble to find out what is the matter, you suspect there is something; that is why you have come. Now, this great Physician knows us and deals with us; even when He seems to grip us hard and to make us wince, that is the time when He is doing most, and doing His best for us. Then let us understand.

The kingdom of Christ is not of this world. Now, let me be plain with you. Am I not speaking to some here to-day who profess to be His? It is the best factor in your life, so to speak, your Christian profession. *But is there anything in common between you and Christ?* Christ was so dead to the ambitions of the world that He could fare as He did; and take it calmly. Are you like that? Am I like that? If I am not, am I His? What is the use of my hugging a delusion to my heart and living a minute longer in a fool's paradise? Am I in any honest sense becoming dead to the world?

Are we people who have so seen and heard and observed Christ, and have been so taught by Him that the world is altogether changed? The world's glory is gone. We have seen through it, and we are content now to go along any path so long as His feet are travelling just immediately in front of us. "Whom have I in heaven or on the earth but *Thee*, O Jesus, the once crucified, the for ever-glorious Saviour. For Thee I will part with everything."

> "For ah, the Master is so fair,
> His smile so sweet on banished men,
> That they who meet it unaware
> Can never rest on earth again.
>
> "And they who see Him risen afar
> At God's right hand to welcome them,
> Forgetful stand of home and land,
> Desiring fair Jerusalem."

Has Christ detached you from the world? from this mere bread-and-butter existence, with its bread-and-butter ambitions—has He? Has He made me a pilgrim and a stranger on the earth?

"And He said unto another, Follow me. But he said, Lord, suffer me first to go and bury my father. And Jesus said unto him, Let the dead bury their dead: but go thou and preach the kingdom of God." Now, let us test ourselves by this man. He is a man in a dilemma, and I speak now to men and women in Regent Square who may be in the same dilemma. Let us see. Here is a man who has no doubt as to his call; it is ringing in his ear. You are in no doubt as to your call; it is ringing in your ear still. You have been attending this very Church for some time, and the conviction is coming to you every day: "The Lord Jesus Christ looks on me and claims me; He calls me; and I have no rational doubt about it. He means me." "But," you say, "preacher, what am I to do? For it so happens that when the call comes, it always seems to come just at the wrong time of day. If it would come an hour sooner, when that engagement was not on, or an hour later, when that other engagement was off." The Lord said to this man, "Follow Me. But he said, Lord, suffer me first to go and bury my father." He did not say no; it is an honest human difficulty. As if he would say, "Now, don't be extreme; don't be inconsiderate, remember

I am only flesh and blood. Lord, remember how when Thou didst come to me, I was tangled and twisted into all this coil of a world, and how am I to get out?" The first man was what the Scotch would say "ower quick," the second "ower slow."

The first is a man who sees too little; who under-estimates; who, in fact, does not count the cost. His eyes are too narrow in range, and he wants to leap before he looks. While the other man, he may be a very good leaper, for he is in good form, comes running forward, and is just going to jump, but he looks too much. He looks too much at the high hedge and at the ditch on the other side. Then he goes back and begins again. He is again going to clear it, when his courage fails, and he says to himself, " What if I should land in that ditch?" Discretion with him becomes the better part of valour. He is a man who would be a good runner, but that a loose garment about his legs is for ever flapping about him and tripping him up. Now, my hearer, it is wise and loving in Christ to give some of us this treatment. To give us, that is to say, no quarter and no consideration; to seem to be one who does not know human feelings and failings, that He may get us over the bar across the line, into decided, open fellowship with Himself once for all. If I could see with Christ's eyes, I believe I should see a number of people here not over the bar, but stuck on the bar; and of all places for a boat, inward or outward bound, to be stranded, this seems the worst.

I have got some of you, by God's grace, very near; you have come from indifference, chill, utter disregard, to the real claims of the Christ of God. You have been brought down south, into warm latitudes, and you are coming still nearer, when lo! just at the door, somebody comes running up to you to say, "Your father is dead, and the funeral must be attended to." Now, Christ does feel for you; His eyes are filled with tears. He knows what a tug that is on your heart-strings. You know it, you feel it. You say, "Surely this is a legitimate occasion for pausing a moment, doing this first and the other next." In my own measure I have had that experience. Last summer all this came vividly upon me. My father died hundreds of miles away, in Scotland. Is there anything that would have been better for me, apparently, anything more urgent upon me, than to have gone and laid his honoured dust beside my mother in the churchyard on the hill-side? But just at that very time I was placarded all over a Midland town to preach the Gospel. The minister had just written—I am telling you about it frankly, as though it were of some other man—he had written telling me that people were coming in from far and near to hear. Then in came a letter by the next post, saying that my father had died; and because of the date when, in God's providence, he had been taken away, there was no other day on which to bury him than that on which I was down to preach in that Midland town. Well, don't you think I felt the tug: "Shall I wire and say the meeting must be abandoned—my father dead?" I thought that would be a sufficient excuse. People might be disappointed, but what, after all, could they say? But I dared not send it, for this same Jesus stood by me, and seemed to say, "Now, look, I have you. You go and preach the Gospel to those people. Whether would you rather bury the dead or raise the dead?" And I went to preach.

The folks away in yon Scottish village do not understand it yet. They are inclined to say it was heartless; and even this explanation does not suffice some. The little company of villagers going along the Manse brae on that day were all asking naturally, "Where's John?" What do you think of it, friends? It just comes to this: when Christ's call is working in you, let that break all engagements.

This call seems to have come, you say, at an awkward hour; and it seems so natural to say this *first*, "Let me bury my father first." But Christ dares to interfere with the tenderest ties and the most urgent calls that come from the natural side, and to say, "Me first. That will not suffer, that can be done without. Come to Me, I want you; yield to Me immediately."

Now, friends, that same call is in our ears to-day. We are apt to say, "Lord, suffer me first to do this thing or the other." Jesus said, and it does look harsh, "Let the dead bury their dead: but go thou and preach the kingdom of God." By the time that man went to the funeral and came back, he would likely be a different man. Christ knows best; and very likely Christ saw that if he went there, he would not come back. Very often when death comes in to a family in this fashion, a great many things happen that do not help a man into the kingdom. He says he will go and bury his father, and then he will be back after the burial. They go back to the house, and there are the lawyers, and the will is read, and the things of time come very near, and this candidate for the kingdom says to himself, "It is a good thing I did not attach myself to that Jesus, for, you see, all the current of my life is altered." And he lets the matter go, and it vanishes away like a dream when one awaketh. The Lord pity some of you here to-day! You were as near to Christ not long ago as that man, and now you are away from Him. Something of the world came to you and presented a more **urgent** claim. You yielded, and said, "I am not going to take the one and drop the other. Oh, preacher, you are inconsiderate. I am going to have the two: I shall bury my father, and come back." And you buried your father, and you are not back. Do you think Christ is going to stand for ever waiting till you come back from that funeral? Not likely. If births, deaths, and marriages are to come in between, when will we ever be free? We go to attend to this other thing, and we delude ourselves to believe that it is only a short delay. We say, "I cannot decide for Christ to-day. I cannot rise up to tell you, preacher, of another thing that is coming first; but if I told you, you would quite understand that I cannot decide to-day. But I'll be back next Sunday, and I shall then make a splendid surrender." Exactly. The devil knows all about it. His side is full of men like that. The way to hell is paved with good intentions, filled with people dressed in mourning, burying their friends, too busy digging graves to serve the Lord. I must get a little sarcastic, for it is there. Say whether would you rather work with a sexton's shovel, or blow the resurrection trumpet? God help you! and are you going to take the spade? This man was meant to be a trumpet blower, to be a raiser of the dead, a preacher of the kingdom, and he was in danger of falling down to the sexton's task. And so are you, so am I. The Lord deliver us from our danger! Take the trumpet, and go and blow it, and it will be found that when you take this engagement *first*, all others settle into their places round about it.

I have but little time left in which to test ourselves by the third man. "Another also said, Lord, I will follow Thee; but let me first go bid them farewell, which are at home at my house. And Jesus said unto him, No man, having put his hand to the plough, and looking back, is fit for the kingdom of God." "Lord, here am I." He is there, he is all there; there is no doubt about that, and a capital fellow, a man who has, no doubt, a fine opinion of himself; he almost seems inclined to say, "Lord, when you got me, you got somebody; I am not one of those half-and-half creatures. I am here, all here; only let me run down and bid them farewell at home." You are a social man; popular at home; the delight of the house—the light and spirit of all things at home. He liked home, and *the Lord knows all about that feeling.* He is homely; He is as human as we are. He liked home, and is able to understand how it tells upon us. He understands its sweet atmosphere, its music, its spell, its peace. He knew Himself what it was to open the door and to step out of His mother's home, never to go back. To open the door; to pause upon the threshold; to salute His mother; gently yet firmly to disengage Himself, and then to pass out to coldness, suspicion, and loneliness. None but Himself could have done it. He knows how "home" would have shut him in from His work, and therefore urges for decision now. Aye, He knows it all; He has been through it all. Man, He has tasted every cup that seems bitter to you and me. He has left the fragrance of His lips on the cup; and that gives it sweetness still to you and me, and enables us to drink it.

"Do not, then, think He is hard; do not think He does not understand; do not go back to the genial circle at home with this great claim undecided; but, before you go home, while I am speaking, trust Christ; give yourself to Him altogether, henceforth, for ever more. Go back home, taking Him with you. Run the flag up to the mast-head, and nail it there, never to come down again. What a great relief will come to our lives if all of us gathered here to-day, in the light of Christ's presence, in the light of Christ's Word, and yielding to the Spirit that worketh on us and in us, decided for Him. Those of us who have done it before, let us do it again. Grip Him, as I said on Wednesday, grip Him somewhat higher up; and those of us who have never decided, let us decide at last. Decide, *decide*; Christ first; everything after that. "No man having put his hand to the plough, and looking back, is fit for the kingdom of God." Do not overtax yourself, my friend; you mean well, but if you go back home, there are influences even there, and you know them, which will hinder you. You mean to be brave, and you mean to bid them farewell, and you mean a great many things. Do not overtax your strength; there are things at home—alas, alas! that it should be so—there are things in all our homes that are telling against decision for Christ. There are subtle temptations at home, different from the temptations along those public streets of ours, or the temptations of business. There are subtle temptations at home, that whenever you step in under the door-way, begin to beat against you and to undermine your foundations. Before you go home be decided for Christ. "No man putting his hand to the plough, and looking back, is fit for the kingdom of Christ." "If a man forsake not father, mother, wife, life, all that he hath, he cannot be My disciple."

You cannot plough, and put your hands in your pockets. You cannot take ploughing easy; and yet you are taking religion easy, my friend. You are giving it one hand only, and you have lots of energy to spare for other things. You are " broad," you are " liberal," a great deal too liberal; the plough is dropping out of your too liberal hands. Take care!

Now come "*in between,*" all of us, and let us grip these stilts. Let both hands be so full and firm that we shall, as it were, grow into the plough, and the plough grow into us, till we cannot let go—as you do when you catch those electric handles; you catch them, yes, but you notice that they catch you, and there you are! Thank God for that electric throb that tingles through the stilts of the plough! Many a time, we are such ingrates, we would go back, we would drop it. It is cold work ploughing, in cold, sharp days—perishing work. Have you ever tried it? It needs skill; and it needs that you shall be all there. I have tried it; I was never anything great at it. I broke the plough; it was far too much for me. It is not nearly so easy as you think.

But oh, do not go back! Many a sermon of mine does not seem to have done any good; but I stand here to-day, and I am not going back. Many a poor discourse I have uttered, but if God spares me to the afternoon I will be at it again. So let it be with you. Many a poor day you have had in your Bible-class and in your Sunday school. Are you going to stop? Stop? Never! We are going at it better than ever. We thank Thee, O Christ, for that solemn warning. Thou hast told us to our faces that it is possible we may be condemning ourselves; that we are too soft and flabby, and unfit for the kingdom of God. "Stick in, man; stick till't."

How like, or how unlike, we are to Him who could say, "It is My meat and drink to do the will of Him that sent Me, and to finish His work." Plough out your furrow, for Christ is at the far end to receive you, and to say, "Well done, well ploughed!" Amen.

Regent Square Pulpit.

AWAKE! ARISE!

Evangelistic Address

Delivered in Regent Square Church on Tuesday, January 21st, 1890, by the

REV. JOHN McNEILL.

"Awake thou that sleepest, and arise from the dead, and Christ shall give thee light."—Eph. v. 14.

"Awake thou that sleepest." We have this in substance and in different forms elsewhere, but in actual form here. Luther said, you remember, that certain texts were little Bibles. For instance, "God so loved the world that He gave His only begotten Son, that whosoever believeth on Him should not perish, but have everlasting life." Well, that *is* a little Bible. And another one is like unto it: "Behold I stand at the door and knock; if any man hear My voice, let him open the door, and I will come in, and sup with him, and he with Me." And I think this is one, too, at any rate, this is a text which is a little sermon: "Awake thou that sleepest, and arise from the dead, and Christ shall give thee light." That is an evangelistic text; it is

---

As Mr. McNeill must attend the meetings of Synod in Liverpool, last Sabbath morning's discourse must be delayed. Would friends kindly read and circulate this Gospel message.

No. 25.

an evangelistic address; it is put in the very form that conveys it to the people to whom you are talking. So that if any of you are budding preachers—and whatever good or ill I have done, either in Scotland or England, I have always been charged with this, that I started people off to preach—if any of you are starting off to preach, take my text with you, and although what I say may have more of darkness than light in it, you will at any rate have a good text, and if the people remember the text, they have got a bit of God's Word. Now here is a text that is a sermon. You may forget what I say, but I want you to remember the text. I would put the trumpet to my lips and sound this text over and over again, "Awake thou that sleepest, and arise from the dead, and Christ shall give thee light."

There is the sinner described; there is the sinner addressed; there is the sinner pointed to the Saviour. What more would you have? "Awake thou that sleepest." See how the sinner is described here, and the backslider, for the backslider has just gone back again into sin, and has lost communion with his Saviour, and needs to be called back by the Word by which he was brought at first out of darkness into light. He needs to be recovered. See how our life away from Christ, the life of unbelief, the life of worldliness, the life of sin that you are living, is described here as a life of sleep. Elsewhere the figure is changed, and it is described as death. The Bible often changes its figures. "Awake thou that sleepest." The man who is not converted, the soul here that is not walking in the light of Christ's grace, is asleep; you are like one who at twelve o'clock in the day is still soundly snoring on his bed. It is not a complimentary description, is it? The Bible never was complimentary to a sinner; the Bible always speaks the plain, bare truth: that is why folks don't like the Bible, and don't like the preacher. If, my dear friends, you have big notions about yourself, and you think, Oh, well, you may be a sinner, but you are a superior sort of a sinner, then you need not come to hear me, and you need not attend any preacher of the Bible, for you will never get those big notions flattered, you will get them contradicted. "Awake thou that sleepest." And I can imagine a man saying, "Oh, this is overdone, you know; we must draw the line at this." You say, "I have been here every night, McNeill, and one night you called me a leper, another night blind, and another night paralytic; and now you have it that I am snoring;—these are surely rather hard speeches." But it is the Bible; I stand on the Bible every time, and the Bible said it all to me first. I kicked against it just like my neighbours, but found it true, and I am not going to let you off. Not only does the Bible back me up, but my own experience does, and plenty of people also, who first of all were ruffled by God's Word and irritated; but by-and-bye they found out that the Bible was a faithful friend. Because the Bible loved them, it dared their rebuke and told them the truth. "Yes, yes," you say, "but I draw the line at that; I do not think I am asleep." You say to me, "If you only knew the people who know me, they would tell you that I am rather wide-awake; I am not one of your sleepy chicks, I am a wide-awake person." Well, I have not denied it; I believe, in the affairs of this world, you are very wide-awake. A man would have to rise early to be up before you, and would have to sit up late to outwatch you. If there was anything to be got by it, you are on the night-shift to make overtime. I believe you are all agog; you would turn night into day, and make Sunday into Saturday, if it got you something as regards this present world. Yet making that admission, that you are not stupid and you are not asleep, that you are keen in business and intellectual activity, a great reader, a great thinker, earnest in attendance at evening classes, and in legitimately employing your time, still, man, if you are not converted, if you do not know Jesus Christ, where in the world have you been living for the last thirty years? You are a poor Rip Van Winkle; I tell you to your face. You remember the story of the man who went to sleep, and when he awakened up the generations had meanwhile passed away. He came to the village and noticed how everything round him was mildewed and rusty, and nobody knew him. The only place where he felt familiar was in the graveyard, where the names of the headstones were the names of the people he had known before he fell on his sleep. Now every unconverted man will, after his awakening up, admit that he was sound asleep, and that the realities of life had never dawned upon him. Thus the texts holds true: "Awake thou that sleepest."

If you have not wakened up to a knowledge of sin, a painful knowledge of sin, as a plague and a disease that has fastened on your vitals which you cannot shake off; if you have not wakened up to a knowledge of God, and of the judgment, of heaven and of hell, where are you but sleeping — soundly sleeping? The awful realities of existence are all round about you, but are unheard and unappreciated. Suffer my blunt speech. If you want to rouse a man, you have got to rouse him; you will never rouse a heavy sleeper, like some of you, by standing up and washing your hands in invisible soap and water, and whispering polite nothings. You will never arouse me, and I am not an extraordinary sleeper; though I can do a good sleep—you will never arouse me by coming to my bedside to-morrow morning, and by whispering scarcely above your breath, by putting on your sweetest manner and saying, "Sir, Sir, I would not disturb you for the world, but it is nearly twelve o'clock." I will stand that, or rather I will lie that; I will keep sound and stiff. If you want to be my friend, you had better come, especially if there is anything worth wakening me for, and grip me, shake me, and tell me there is a letter come giving me a fortune, or tell me that the house is on fire, and I will show you a jump. Make it worth my while to waken, and I will wake. Well, it is the same thing with the preacher. I am not here to say hard things about your natural condition simply for the sake of saying them, or simply to show that I have the best of the argument according to the Bible, or that I have the whip by the handle, and will make you feel the supple end of it. It is not for that; it is not to turn the contention against you, and to pain you, and to flatten you, that I may crow over you. I am speaking in the rousing way I am doing because I am right. But more than that: because it is high time you were out of sleep; and if you are only wakened up, you will admit all I am saying. I will go bail for it, that you come to me to-morrow night, if you take Christ to-night, and you would say, "Preacher, you were right; my past unconverted life was just as good as a sleep, a dream—unreal; and I only woke up to the realities of existence, to the realities of time and eternity some time between eight and nine o'clock in Regent Square Church, on Tuesday, 21st January, in the year of grace 1890." A man never forgets the time of his awakening The day I awoke from indifference and formality, the sounds of eternity came rushing like a cold sharp east wind into my ears. I remember the day I woke; and the next day when I got the light. I remember those two days. Now, " Awake thou that sleepest." Wake up; believe these things ; sit back and listen. Say to yourselves, " Well, well, it is true at any rate." Say to yourselves, " I would need to contradict the Bible, and a multitude of honest people, to make myself right and them wrong." You can't do it. Say to yourself, " Suppose it is true, what then ? Well, then, the next thing is wake up, get up, listen, be interested, be concerned. You can be interested, you can be concerned.

Let me come to you and be the means of wakening you to concern about conversion, about your own personal interest in Christ, to personal concern about the things which await you in eternity, which is always coming nearer. Believe in eternity, believe in God, believe in Christ; take the Bible view of things in regard to yourself and in regard to sin, and the Saviour, and eternity, and the blessings which come through faith in Him. " Awake thou that sleepest " to reality, to consciousness, to some dim understanding, at least, of existence, as represented by the eternal Word of the eternal God. " Awake thou that sleepest," and thank God that the message is so plain—a trumpet call, something rolling, resounding, and no mistake about it. It is no world for sleeping in, this. Ah ! my careless friend, or my busy friend, busy or careless with the things of time, but asleep as to the things of eternity, this is no world for sleeping in. There may be circumstances where sleep is appropriate, but that sleep of your soul is awfully inappropriate just now. When you know Christ, and have come to Christ, lie down in Him and take a grand sleep; and as to all your affairs and all your interest, let them go to sleep. When you have come to Christ, rest in Him all your length, all your weight, all your destiny. Rest in Him as a tired labouring man rests at the close of a long journey, or after an exhausting day's work. Sweet is the sleep of the resting soul.

But oh, outside of Christ, how dare you sleep?—outside of Christ, how dare you rest? It is no world for sleeping in, poor sinner. Do you know where I once caught a man sleeping? I once caught a man lying asleep—a drunken sleep—between the four-foot, as it is called, of the railway, and the midnight express coming thundering down the bank. Such is thy state, oh, unconverted soul. Thou art asleep between the rails, and God's judgment express is coming down, and is almost on top of you. I say again, it is no world for a sinner to go to sleep in. And as that express sounds forth its signals and sends news in advance of it, so God, who is coming to judge the world in mercy, is sending a sound before Him. Awake and listen, and you will hear the far-off sound of that judgment which is coming. Get upon your feet, and get into the six-foot. Even that will save you. Get out from between the rails altogether; get out, shift your body, get yourself clear. I wakened that man, didn't I? How could I pass him? And didn't I wake him rather roughly? Wouldn't I have been a fool if I had sat down and said polite things to him? Was I not his best friend when I gripped him and held him, and, half asleep and half awake, got him into safety. And am I not your friend to stand in the face of you to-night and tell you the truth? Oh man, awake; listen :—

> "This is no time to trifle;
> Life is brief and sin is here;
> Our age is like the falling of a leaf,
> The dropping of a tear.
> This is no place to dream away the hours;
> All should be earnest in a world like ours."

"Awake thou that sleepeth, and arise from the dead." First of all, awake thou that sleepest. But then in this wonderful little text of mine *there is another trumpet blast—* two trumpet calls in one text: not many texts like that! "Awake thou that sleepest, and "—and what? "and arise from the dead." What does that mean? Oh, I think there is a beautiful sequence in these two trumpet calls, in these two evangelical cries out from the preacher's heart, and out from God's heart, and out from the Holy Ghost's heart. First of all "awake;" that's the first thing. Then the second thing is, of course, "get up, arise from the dead," for every man who awakens is not a man who is up, is he? Oh, no, no, no! We are illustrating this every morning. Some of us make a big difference between awakening and getting up. It is not so hard to awaken some of you, but oh, it is a job to get you over on to your feet! You will awaken, and you will get on your elbow, and you will crack away with anybody for an hour like a pop-gun; you will talk and talk, and drink a cup of coffee in your bed—oh, how you like it!—yes, anything to postpone the actual having to get up, and put on your clothes, and go back again to the old treadmill of the world's work. And if it were not for the spur that you *have* to go, some of you don't know when you would go. Oh, some of us don't know how lazy we can be, for we have never been tried. If you had been the eldest son of a duke, you might have been just as much a lie-a-bed and a trifler as those swells whom you always denounce, that don't need to get up in the morning. We, maybe, you are more like them than you think. You don't need to get up every *Sunday morning*. Are you over-smart then? No, verily.

We will not go much farther on that line, but allow me to insist on this: it is one thing to be wakened up, and another thing to get up. How many things come in between these! And, spiritually, how true that is! I believe it has been illustrated every night at these meetings, and will be illustrated at every evangelical meeting in London. If we are preaching the Word of God, we will have people interested, and they will sit back and say, "That is true, that is straight, this is plain; now that's the kind of preaching that doesn't fly over a fellow's head." You admit that this is true, you are awakened; but alas, alas! that's all. You don't rise, you don't get up, you don't come to Christ. You sit there and talk back; you are only awake. You know there is one thing which keeps people from getting up; sometimes it keeps me. I awaken sometimes, I don't know whether it is the same with you? I take these homely illustrations that cause a smile because they are true. And I hope there is a smile on your heart of intelligent appreciation. Now, I have wakened and not got up; this was the fatal thing: *I fell over again, and dreamed that I was up*. Haven't you done that? I dreamed that I was up and dressed, and then afterwards woke with a start and an awful disappointment, to find that it was all to do yet. I'm afraid there are a lot of people that way in religion. They only think.

Now, my friends—I speak with all tender and affectionate solicitude—I stand in doubt of you; if I could but get nearer to you, to look into the very eyes of your soul, and to shake you, and say, " Now, John, you're not up yet, you are still lying on the bed of self-pleasing and worldliness and indulgence; your tongue is awake, but you are talking in your sleep, you are not up yet, you are not in the daylight of eternity yet—no, not yet—but you may be this minute while I speak. Come, wake, man; *arise, take the step forward* and outward away from sleep, away from your past, away from every consideration that would keep you down, and step out and get clear of the bed, and be able to say, " I am up, bless God, I'm up, I know that I'm up, and I know that I have left my bed by the very shivers that are going through me in the cold. Ah, yes! you will hear a great many people talking about the joy of conversion. Well, that's true; but there is often before the joy, a wee while, as they say in Scotland, a little time of a kind of mortal shivering, when a man wakens up to the realities before him. Ah! it is cold, it is an unfamiliar state, and you are awfully prone to go back, saying, " I'll take another forty winks." Now, don't; oh, don't! it's an awful thing. You'll go back, and you will oversleep yourself almost as sure as sure can be. You will; you know it in the affairs of this world. You have got to distrust yourself there. You know that if you turn over after waking and take another forty winks in the morning you are too late, and you go shivering and shambling and ashamed to the gate of your workshop—*late*, and the foreman meets you and says, " Look here, if you can't come in the morning when the men's work begins, you can stay away all day; we don't need you." I have known men to whom that has happened, and it cured them of their heavy-headedness and their trifling. And, oh, my friend, I know that while I am speaking concerning the bed on which you are lying, the devil is making it appear to you never so easy, soft, and delicious as now, that I want you to arise.

The life of unbelief and worldliness, and of taking the day as it comes—the devil is whispering how sweet it is, how pleasant! But to come to Christ is to come under obligations; he is telling you that to come to Christ is to come to a new Master who is hard, and whom there is no pleasing; and as to wages, nobody ever saw them. The devil says, "You know I pay you cash down." He is a liar; he does not. But he will dare to say it all the same. "I make my service one of ready money; I give you pleasure and all that you want right off." "No, you don't; you tickle and trick and cheat us to our very faces." No, no, no! come away to Christ; don't yield to the whispering seductions of the devil and the flesh. "Awake, arise from the dead, and Christ shall give thee light." Spring to your feet like a man; it is high time—it is almost past time. "What meanest thou, oh sleeper? Arise and call upon thy God." And then, to help you to arise, do you notice what the text says? "Arise *from the dead.*" Oh, what does that mean, and what is that intended for? Well, that is the counter-blast to those seductions that are trying to grip you in their soft embraces while I am trying to arouse you. There is the truth, too, to describe what is round about you and the state you are in. Who would sleep in a graveyard? Who would live among bones and decay? And that is where you are living, unconverted sinner. "Arise from the dead." That is to help you to make a jump; for you will be like them if you stay with them much longer, utterly dead, no more impressed at all with the rousing call of the Gospel; and the very Spirit of God Himself may say at last, "Sleep on, sleep on. Ephraim is joined to his idols, let him alone." "You have made your bed, now lie upon it." That hour, that awful moment may come; for God's sake and thine own, be wise this minute; there is a time when God's Spirit ceases to strive with men who say, "A little more sleep, and a little more slumber, and a little more folding of the hands." If you love it, sleep on.

> "There is a time, I know not when,
> A point, I know not where,
> That marks the destiny of men
> For glory or despair."

"Awake thou that sleepest, and arise from the dead." Don't live among the dying and the dead and the rotting. Live! Oh, come, arise!

What next? See the beautiful sequence of the text: first of all to awaken you, then to get you up, and then "Christ shall give thee light." It is just as though I came in in the morning when all is dark; I waken you and shake you, for two things compel me: I have a great offer to make to you, and I have an awful danger to warn you from. That is why I am so urgent, and that is why I am shaking you by the shoulder. A great offer for you, "Christ shall give thee light;" and the great danger to warn you from, the awful death, the awful danger of passing away in your sleep, as we read of people doing every day in the newspapers, passing away in their sleep. God save us! There may be numbers of people who *spiritually* pass away in their sleep, and have never awoke. They never gave to minister or missionary one single solitary sign that ever they awoke to the realities of sin and salvation—never one. They passed away in their sleep; they died as they lived! Now, "Christ shall give thee light." It is like this. When a man wakens under the preaching of the Gospel to the eternal verities of God's Word and truth, and springs up into activity, he usually finds that he wakens up to darkness and perplexity, and often in more or less of alarm, with fright upon his spirit. "Oh, oh! What is it? Where am I now?" Why, the other night in Oakley Square I woke after midnight, and I heard pouring through the Square the rush of feet and the sound of voices. I sprang out of bed and went to the window, and there, just outside of the window, I saw the whole sky blazing with the reflected flame of a great fire, and people rushing from all parts—for there are Londoners who never seem to go to bed. Let a fire blaze up at any time, and you will have a crowd of dressed men and women pouring to that sight. Well, ofttimes when a sinner first awakes, he awakes with the red, lurid glare coming in at his window; he awakens up—to put it in Old Testament fashion—with Sinai gleaming in upon his soul. That sight, "that blackness and darkness, and voice of the trumpet, and sound of words," that lightning and thunder, and there is no peace and no rest. A man is not comfortable when he wakens; he wakens with his face to Sinai, and there sweep through his soul these considerations: "God is holy, God is my Lawgiver; I have broken His laws. I was made by Him, and am accountable to Him, and my life has been a transgression, a trampling under foot of His commands, and of His grace and mercy." And nothing about him seems to give peace. It is like the glare of the midnight fire. If I waken up and discover that there is a fire, and that the fire is not in the next street, that it is not in the next house, but that it has fastened upon *my own* house, it keeps me from going back to bed and to sleep. I begin to make shift, to get out of the house; I am glad to hear then about escapes, fire-engines, and ladders, and all that kind of thing. So when a sinner wakens up to know God, and the holiness of God, and the law, with its curse, to the thought of meeting with God, his peace vanishes as a dream when one waketh. He is awakened, and he is up, and now what is he to do? Now, my friend, if you are awakened, I don't say that you are to put yourself in a state of terror. Every one is not alarmed by a fire. Some, when a fire is in their house, are wonderfully cool, others are wonderfully excited; but all are making their way out. Now, whether cool or not, you are wanting peace, you are wanting rest, you are wanting salvation. You have wakened up to know that there is nothing around you but condemnation and destruction. Steady your nerve a minute, it is a critical state; you may take a wrong step now; and as you have obeyed the rest of the text, will you obey this: "Christ shall give thee light"? Stand just where you are now, don't take a step, wait a minute, wait for the firemen. The escape is already reared against the window, and the brave fellows are coming up; don't rush in a panic, don't go helter-skelter here and there, for there is blinding smoke, and there is confusion, with the possibility of your taking a wrong turning and doing something in a panic that you may never undo. Wait. Whenever a soul is awakened and aroused, then the Bible, that has been talking in thunder tones to you all along, suddenly changes, and brings in a new word, a new name that I never mentioned before, " Christ shall give thee light."

First of all, you are sleeping in the midst of your danger and distress; then, when you are awakened to it all, " Christ shall give thee light." Do you ask, " Where is He?" He is beside you, He has come in; *He* is the brave fireman; He has come into your burning building, and has wanted to fill His arms with you. Will you let Him? It is like this. I think I have told you this illustration before; I will tell it again, for it is true. In Edinburgh, one night—and if any of you know Edinburgh, you know the Register House, and you know the very high block of buildings behind the Register House—I think, in West Register Street yonder, just straight from the Post Office, there stands a very high, towering building. Some friends of mine lived in one of the "flats," as they are called. A fire broke out in the night—a raging, destroying, desolating fire. The people heard the noise, they heard the crackling, they heard the shouts, and they awakened the sleepers. They arose, though, alas, alas! they afterwards went wrong. They arose, they gathered themselves together, they came downstairs till they came to the passage, the entry, the "close," as they call it there, that leads out into the street. They were almost safe, but in that entry leading to the street they were met by a blinding rush of smoke, and, in the terror and alarm of the moment, instead of going straight out through the smoke, they turned into a door that was standing deceitfully open, a door into a chamber, and before they could recover from their mistake they were suffocated; they perished in the smoke.

What would have saved my friends? This, if in that moment of panic and terror and confusion, by fire on the one hand and smoke on the other, and danger all round about, if there could have pierced through the blinding smoke one, only one, clear ray of God's daylight from outside, it would have met their eyes, it would have guided them out into the street, and to safety and peace. For want of light, they perished in the smoke and darkness. *So need perish none who come to Christ.* What my friends did *not* get, and for lack of which they were lost, is what you do get when you come to Christ. He is thy Light. Oh, awaken! Oh trembling, oh anxious soul, look to Jesus! and the more you turn away your eyes from Sinai to another hill, the moment you turn your eyes to Calvary, you will get peace. Look to Him, the Light on the cross. He is the Light that calms my fears, that delivers me from all my guilt and condemnation. Look to Jesus.

> " I once was a stranger to grace and to God,
> I knew not the danger, and felt not the load;
> Though friends spoke in rapture of Christ on the tree,
> Jehovah Tsidkenu was nothing to me."

Then you remember how he was aroused :—

> "When free grace awoke me by light from on high,
> Then legal fears shook me, I trembled to die;
> No refuge, no safety, no help could I see:
> Jehovah Tsidkenu my Saviour must be."

Then he looked to the Saviour, you remember :—

> "My terrors all vanished before the sweet name,
> My guilty fears banished, with boldness I came
> To drink of the fountain, life-giving and free;
> Jehovah Tsidkenu was all things to me."

So He is. Christ shall give thee *light, light, light!* Light to see by, light to walk by, light for all your path along the road; and light, you know, means everything here. Darkness means all that is fearful and gloomy and paralyzing; light means everything that is helpful and hopeful, and liberating and enriching. Come to Christ, and He shall give thee light; oh, come, trust Him! that is to say, let in the light of peace and pardon that streams from the crucified and gloried Saviour. Let Him shine on you, and let Him shine *in* you. Faith in Him is the opening of the eyes to let in the saving light—the calming, the cheering, the guiding light. "I heard," says Dr. Horatius Bonar, the sweet singer of Israel lately fallen asleep—

> "I heard the voice of Jesus say,
> 'I am this dark world's light,
> Look unto me, thy morn shall rise
> And all thy day be bright.'
> I looked to Jesus, and I found
> In Him my star, my sun,
> And in that light of life I'll walk
> Till travelling days are done." Amen.

Regent Square Pulpit.

THE SALVATION OF ZACCHÆUS.

A Sermon

Delivered in the Great Central Hall,
Holborn, London,
on Sabbath Afternoon, May 4th, 1890, by the

REV. JOHN McNEILL.

"For the Son of Man is come to seek and to save that which was lost."—Luke xix. 10.

This story of the salvation of Zacchæus on the roadside, by Jesus of Nazareth, the Son of God in human flesh, in all His love and grace, is an illustration of the statement made in the tenth verse, "The Son of Man is come to seek and to save that which was lost." Of the real and awful meaning of the word "lost," every man and woman born is the vivid, particular illustration. The lost coin, the lost sheep, the lost son or daughter, are illustrations on a lower level. But the awful reality and fact of "lostness" lies here: I have lost God, and God has lost me. And the Gospel of the Gospel lies in that sentence, "The Son of Man is come to seek and to save that which was lost."

Now, says the narrative, here you see the Lord Jesus Christ at His work. How does He do it? Here is how He does it. Here is an illustration of the Son of Man at

No. 26.

His work. There is something refreshing and exhilarating in seeing a competent man—not a bungler, the sight of him puts a pain in your very face, but a competent man doing the thing that he has come to do; seeing him taking off his coat and girding himself for the work with the air of a man who says, "I have come to do this, and I will do it. I will not leave it till it is finished." Here is the Son of God at His best, the Son of God at His work of ferreting out, seeking, and saving a lost sinner. It needs skill to find out a thing that is lost. Some of us have not got it. You know that in your own house yonder, at home, if anything is lost, your wife tells you about it; but when the hunt begins, she very likely says to you, "Oh, you had better sit down. You will never find it out." You have not got the turn for finding out lost things. You could not see it—not you. Others of us, again, have a kind of happy knack of ferreting out lost things. Now, on every ground, will you watch this intensely interesting matter, with a throb, if you please, of personal concern, and see how the Son of Man, the Son of God, comes to find out and bring back home again a lost sinner? If you know yourself that you are not saved yet, bring your whole soul up to your eyes and ears, for unless the Son of God does upon you a work such as He did upon Zacchæus, your life is not worth living. This is salvation, as I have said, salvation at work.

Now, how does He do it? See how He does it. First of all He comes to the lost sinner's town. Sin and sinners, you know, to God are realities. Theologians and writers in magazines sometimes write about a thing called "s-i-n" as if it were an abstraction, and discuss it in polysyllabic, philosophical terms. When we come to the Bible we do not find any of these polysyllabic discussions. We find sin is a reality. Sin has its power in the hearts of men and women. Sin is a something concrete, definite, substantial, incarnate. "Sinner" is not a mere combination of letters in the alphabet. If you will tell me your name and address, I will tell you the name and address of one specimen of what a sinner is. That is what I want to bring out. Now the Son of Man is here on a practical business—to seek and to save lost sinners—and here is how He does it. Says the narrative, "He entered and passed through Jericho"—that is to say, He came to the lost sinner's town. That was something. He came there, just as He has entered and come into London to-day. He was the first in London this morning when the sun broke. He will be the last to leave it to-night; and His greatest interest in London to-day is to get a hold on lost sinners. He entered this Hall at the beginning of the service, and He will be the last to leave it. His whole interest in this Hall is, "Is Zacchæus here?" I would not stand up to preach on this subject if I did not believe from the depths of my soul that that same Jesus is here, and that somewhere between the beginning and the end of this discourse He shall find how to lay hold of some lost sinner or backslider. He comes to Zacchæus's town, but more than that, He comes to the particular street in the town where Zacchæus is. More than that, He comes to the particular tree, on the roadside, in the branches of which that particular sinner is sitting; and He calls him by his name, and says to him, "Zacchæus, make haste, and come down; for to-day I must abide at thy house. And he made haste, and came down, and received Him joyfully;" and that salvation story ends. Well, no, it does not end, for they are together yet. Of course, there is no end to it. Jesus and Zacchæus met together then at the foot of that tree, and they are together this afternoon. They shall never, never be separated. Whithersoever through the vast eternity Christ conducts to-day His magnificent procession, Zacchæus is there, be sure.

Now, notice one or two points. To come just at once to what I want to say, *this was a man who needed saving*. If any of you do not need saving, you may rise and go, for, of course, this is not for you. If you have already been found by the Saviour, you are the one who will be glued to the seat; because there is nothing you like to hear better than the old story over again. But if any of you think that you are *above the need of being saved*, then I would only tell you to go out, on the plea that you may send in some other listener. But don't go. Give me your whole attention. Zacchæus was a man who needed saving, and so are you. The one trouble of your life, if you are not saved, is just that you do not know Jesus Christ, and have not given your heart to Him; and you will never have anything worth living for, either in present possession or in expectation, if you do not get to know Him. I would not have your life for a thousand worlds. If you do not know the Lord Jesus Christ, what is your life worth?

Zacchæus needed saving. He was a publican; and he was a chief among the publicans; and he was rich. Now, " publican " does not mean drink-seller in this connection; although if there are any drink-sellers here, they might listen, because I believe that those in that trade need saving every way. Zacchæus was a tax-gatherer. Israel, you remember, had lost her independence, and was under the conquering heel of Rome; and she had to pay tax. The taxes were farmed out, and a particular class of men lifted the taxes for the hated Roman power. Now, you can see that when a Jew gave himself to the business of lifting the tax, he must have been a case-hardened Jew, a man who had lost all patriotic and religious feeling before he could come to this low level, that he would soil his soul and his fingers making money by lifting the hated tax. The very sight of a tax-collector reminded an Israelite that his proud nation had the chain of conquest about its neck. Suppose that London were under the conquering heel of France, and we had to pay a tax to that country, what would you think of the Englishman who made his money by lifting the tax for the hated usurping Frenchman? How you would spurn him and scorn him! He would not be a man popular in any circle. Now, that kind of a broken down man was Zacchæus. He was not popular either at church or at market. The world was against him, and he was against the world. He brazened it out with society. "You give your scoff to me—I will scoff you back again. I have taken this in hand, and I can make money at it,"—as they all could. They not only lifted what was legal for Rome, but they could grind: they could put on the screw: they could feather their own nest. Aye, they were a hated class of men, these turncoat renegade Jews.

Now, that is the kind of man we have in Zacchæus.

Oh, I wonder whether there is anybody here who is considered particularly unsalvable, particularly "out of it." Maybe I should not say it, but sometimes it does look as if we wasted our breath on these decent people whom you cannot call riotous sinners, and equally, you cannot call them saints. God pity them, there they are—a kind of nondescript, well-dressed creatures. They wash like a wave into church, and they wash out again. They wash into Holborn Hall, and they wash out again. Are there any big thumping sinners in? Then to you is the word of this salvation sent! Holborn Hall was built for the sinner in it this afternoon—the man concerning whom the very devil would say that his was a very off chance of ever being saved. These are they upon whom Christ's grace and mercy continually are lighting.

Now, here is how it began. See how the Lord works along human lines, and plays upon all our stops. For He knows us; He made us. "Jesus entered and passed through Jericho. And a certain man named Zacchæus," an "outsider" to religion and to good repute, as I have described, comes out of his toll-booth, his custom-house box, where he sat levying the tax, for there is a great surging crowd of people passing along, like the procession that is even now on its way to Hyde Park. Zacchæus came out, for there was a great crowd of people, and Jesus was passing through. The town was filled with the noise about Him, and Zacchæus wanted "to see Jesus who He was." He was a new Teacher, a new Prophet. Great things were said about Him—what He could do in the way of miracles, and what He claimed to be. And another thing: Zacchæus had very likely heard that this same new Prophet, Jesus, had said some very straight things to the natural enemies of Zacchæus, the religious leaders, the Scribes and Pharisees. Zacchæus had heard that He had even dared to call them hypocrites; and, between you and me, that was Zacchæus's own opinion about these gentry. There was no love lost between Zacchæus and the Pharisees; and what he had heard about Him would rather draw Zacchæus to Jesus—that He was a man into whose eyes the Scribes and

Pharisees could not throw one particle of dust. He estimated their religious ongoings at their true worth, and said, "Woe unto you, Scribes and Pharisees, hypocrites!" Well, do you not see, Zacchæus would be rather drawn to an outspoken Prophet like that? When Jesus is entering and passing through, Zacchæus is wakened up with a kind of natural curiosity: "He wanted to see Jesus"—*to see "the Man."* God often works upon curiosity. It is a little thing in the start, but it is a great thing in the end. Living faith in a living Saviour often comes at the end of curiosity—quite often. Fools have come to a meeting to scoff, and have before now remained to pray: have they not? You came in to see, and to hear, and to get a look at things for yourselves, and the Lord is at the back of that. He is using that to bring you into the Hall, not to me, but to Himself, even as through curiosity he gets a hold for ever of Zacchæus. Zacchæus wanted " to see Jesus who He was."

Thank God for curiosity! That is what led you astray. Do you remember how the devil took advantage of curiosity to lead you away from God? Listen: "When the woman" —away back in Genesis—" When the woman saw that the tree was "—what?—" When she saw that it was good for food, and pleasant to the eyes, and a tree to be desired to make one wise," she forgot all other trees of the garden, and went and stood there.—"Ah! I would like to taste that tree—that fruit." Curiosity was the beginning, and curiosity deepened into a determination so strong that the woman dashed her fist through God's commandment. "She took of the fruit," and I am here preaching salvation because we are the sons and daughters of a too curious woman. Now, the Lord likes to break the devil's back with his own stick, and He takes this curiosity which has led, and which still leads, so many to the devil, in order to lead Zacchæus from sin and the devil, back to salvation in Jesus Christ.

Lad, look here. Here is the history of many a lad. He comes from the country into London. In the country he was mainly and fairly decent; but he has heard about that Regent Street and Piccadilly hell at midnight, and the poor lad, through curiosity, says, "I will go only to see—only just to look at it;" and the poor lad goes to look at it, and, as Jeremiah would say, "The eye affects the heart." The eye kindles the heart, and he goes, and he goes again, and at last he makes common cause with the sinners. He never meant it. It began in curiosity. Now, I say that the Lord uses that to bring us back. You hear about a preacher, for example, as Zacchæus heard about Jesus, and you hear this and that and the other thing, and through very curiosity you come. Bless God for that! Curiosity limes the twig, and the bird lights upon it, and Christ comes and catches it.

But now notice the difficulties in the way of seeing Jesus. There was Jesus passing through, and there was poor Zacchæus out on the roadside, and there was just a chance to see Him, but he is going to lose it. There is a great crowd of people, and Zacchæus is an undersized man. Oh, I can imagine the devil laughing at Zacchæus, saying, "Ha, ha, ha! you little wretch! I have you now. You would go to see Jesus, would you? Come in behind here. Zacchæus, you are mine, mine for ever." But he was not; the devil lost him, as I trust he will lose you, for "Greater is He that is for us than all that can be against us;" and that is a good deal in the case of some. How did he act? What did he do? He could not see Him for the crowd, because he was of little stature. If he had been a great, big, six-foot, porridge-fed Scotchman he could have dashed into that crowd, and scattered it right and left, and made a lane for himself right into the heart of the crowd, where Jesus was. But being a little man, and an undersized man, what was he to do? If he had gone pushing and boring, there were men there who hated him, and they would have been glad to hustle him back. They would have been glad almost to take him neck and crop and pitch him back into the side walk again, and say, " Zacchæus, you have nothing to do with this. Stick to your accursed tax-lifting. That is good enough for you." Is not that what the devil hisses in the ears of some of you? " *You* go to hear McNeill? *You* go to Holborn Hall? *You* go to hear these Gospellers?" says your master the devil. " Come in behind here. You forget," says Satan, " that you are not free. You forget that you are on a chain. I will lengthen the chain to allow you to go to the theatre. I will lengthen the chain to allow you to go to the circus. I will lengthen the chain to allow you to prowl through music-halls and shady places as much as you like." But when you would take a turn into Holborn Hall on Sunday afternoon, he hauls you in, hand over hand. "Come in behind." Ah! he knows. He knows that it is dangerous to let a man come near a Gospel preacher, even under the influence of curiosity. He has lost not a few, to his great disgust, in that same way. May he lose a good many more!

What did Zacchæus do then? "He ran." I always like that fourth verse. Zacchæus could not see Jesus, although He was there; for Jesus was in the heart of the crowd, and Zacchæus was undersized. What then? He put his hands in his pockets, and said, " All right, I am too low; it is not for me;" and he went away back again, and sat down in his toll-booth, and that was the end of it? No, my friends, that is not what he did, and that was not the end of it; but I am afraid that will be the end of some of you. You are going sheer, plumb to hell *for want of pluck.* When Zacchæus saw that there were difficulties, little man and all as he was, he was splendid "grit"—the little fragment!—when he saw that there were difficulties, instead of giving in and becoming as soft as putty in the hands of circumstances, and instead of saying, "Ah, circumstances are against me; it won't do;" he girded at the difficulties. "He ran before;" he said to himself, "I will not be done; I came out to see Him in mere curiosity, and these difficulties only make me more determined. I am not the man to give in for a trifle." Pluck up heart of grace, man! Do you want to be saved? Then put your foot on the neck of your softness and laziness and milksoppiness. That is how to be saved. Do you think that we are going to be saved in the way we speak of in the hymn.

> "Shall I be carried to the skies
> On flowery beds of ease?"

No, my good friend, you will not. There is no use in putting the question. It answers itself. You will get to heaven, I trust, but you will know about it on the road. Do you understand? In a word, you will have to put your feet below you and run for it. If you think that it is worth while, show it by your pace. What effort are you making to be saved? What effort are you making to break from the devil's chain? Well, I can imagine a man who says, "It is of no use for me to make an effort; I am too weak, and the chain too strong." Give a good tug, my brother. Put out your best. Rise, weak and all as you are, only rise, and God Almighty will rise with you and in you and for you. Although Alps were piled on Appenines, God the Lord will lay them in dust. Thy feet shall stand in heaven, if thou shalt but begin. That is how we are saved. We begin. God is the bottom of it and the top of it; but He works along these natural, human lines of self-determination. Now, man or woman, do not any longer be a football of the world and the devil and the flesh, and the sport of circumstances.

> "Break your birth's invidious bar,
> And grasp the skirts of happy chance,
> And breast the blows of circumstance,
> And grapple with your evil star."

It can be done. That is the difference which Christ has made by His coming, for every otherwise hopeless and helpless sinner. Pluck up heart of grace! You can be saved, and the devil can be cheated of you as he was of Zacchæus.

"And he ran before, and climbed into a sycamore to see Him; for He was to pass that way." I think I hear the scamper of his feet on the road. And people would jeer; for there is nothing so easy, my friend, as to waste your little wit on "anxious souls." The Lord pity you for it! There is nothing so easy. I can imagine that the Scribes and Pharisees, who were content to be merely in the crowd, were scoffing and saying, "Do you see him? See, he is going up like a squirrel"—if they knew what squirrels were. They laughed, I have no doubt of it. And they scoffed, I have no doubt. But, blessed be God, Zacchæus ran on. Put your feet below you, and run for it, man.

"Let them laugh that win." "They laugh best who laugh last." And who do you think is going to laugh last? "He that sitteth in the heavens shall laugh. The Lord shall have them in derision." Run for it. They may laugh you into hell, but they will never laugh you out again. Do you think I care what you say? Do you think I care what you think? Laugh, scoff, sneer as you please. I know my own mind; I know my Master; I know what I would be at; I know what I need. You can do as you like. Here I am; I can do no other. So help me, God!

Since I have become a minister of the Lord Jesus Christ, they have laughed and scoffed and sneered at me, and I am fourteen stone and a half this blessed day with people laughing at me. It has not done me much harm, then? Not a bit of it. And I apply it to you, my timid friend. Put your feet below you, and be determined to know Christ, and let them laugh that win. God speed your feet on the road to Christ!

I have spoken about Zacchæus. I have hardly left time to speak about a greater matter.

Zacchæus "ran before, and climbed up into a tree." Now, if you read the narrative when you go home, you will see at a glance that the Bible is inspired. You will see at a glance the Divine skilfulness of its simplicity. "When Jesus came to the place"—what?—"He looked up, and saw him, and said unto him, Zacchæus, make haste, and come down." Do your part, and Christ will do His. Do not lie back in the devil's lap, and expect that any good will ever come to you there; but spring up and out, and away and forward, and Christ will meet you.

He is always going about looking for you. Have no doubt about that. He "*came to the place, and looked up, and saw him.*"

What does that mean? It just means the same thing to-day. My hearer, you are getting what Zacchæus got in that tree by the roadside. You are getting a personal call to a personal Saviour. He said to him, "Zacchæus, be quick, and come down. I am wanting to stay with you." That is the Gospel.

Now, I do not read that Zacchæus looked all round about

the tree and said, " Well, I wonder whether He means me."
There were not a score of Zacchæuses up that tree. There
was just one little man with that name, and the little man
answered to the name, and, quicker than I am taking time
to tell it, he came down to meet the Saviour—and that is
salvation. Answer, answer to your name! What is your
name? Your name is "lost sinner." But that is the
thing. You do not admit your name. You bridle up and
say, "Now, now, preacher, that is what I will not stand.
That is not my name." All right. If it is not your name,
you never were called. *There is nothing between you and
Christ yet*, if you have not answered to this name. I know
that I am smashing into a lot of cheap, pinchbeck, Brummagem gospels of the day, but God help me to do it! There
is no point of contact between you and Christ if you are
not a lost, guilty, hopeless, helpless sinner.

"The Son of Man is come to seek and save the lost." If
you are not lost, you are not in Christ's programme. It is
time we understood that. You belong to a class He never
contemplated when He came here, if you are not lost.
Now, what are we to do? My friend, be honest and
answer to your name. If I had called your dog by its name
half as often as I have called you by that which is your
true name in God's sight, the brute would have been up
here wagging its tail beside me. And we poor preachers
have to stand and call to you loud and long, as you are
sitting in the branches of Gospel ordinances. "Come
down! Come down! Come down! And be quick! Be
quick! Be quick!" And—God pity you—you sit, and
sit, and sit in the branches, and gape and stare all round
about you, and drop off dead; but you do not come to
Christ. It was all very well for Zacchæus to climb up the
tree. It *was* a grand place for seeing. But it was better
for him to climb down out of the tree, and come to the
living Saviour at the foot of it. It is good to come to
Holborn Hall. I trust that you came here to see Jesus,

for He is to pass this way. But come to Christ in the Hall. That is the best. He is standing looking at you, and giving you this personal message, "Make haste, and come down!"

Oh sinner, are you willing to come down? It is not safe to be higher up than Christ. Come down! Come down! You are sitting up in those galleries in a state of spectatorhood. Come down, if you please, good friend—a long way down—off your high horse. Come away down; the Lord cannot save you and the horse. He is not interested in the horse. He will save you. Dismount! Come down! Come down out of pride! Come down out of headiness! Come down out of high-mindedness! Come down out of sympathetic interest!—Come down out of even that! I can imagine Zacchæus sitting up there as the representative of people who are deeply interested, in a way, in religion, and saying to himself, "Now, I have got a comfortable seat, and I will see Jesus, and I will see His disciples. I will see the whole show, and a wonderful show it is." Alas! that is all that some of you have got to do with true religion. You are sitting as spectators—that is all. You are deeply interested spectators, I grant you. Come down out of mere spectatorhood, no matter how interested. You are interested in me. You are interested in Holborn Hall. Thank you for nothing. What is your interest in the Blessed Lamb of God, who came here and died for the salvation of your soul? That is the measure of your interest in religion. Do you know Him? If you do not know Him, you are in Egyptian darkness about the whole business.

Have you come to Christ? Do not stand up and say you do not know. You do. No man can touch Christ with the tip of his little finger and not be thrilled to the very core of the heart within him. Now, where are you? Sitting in churches and chapels and halls looking on; or down at the foot in close grips with the Christ of God Himself? Go home with Him, first to your home, and then to His home in heaven. Where are you? We are getting the same chance this afternoon that Zacchæus got.

"Zacchæus made haste, and came down, and received Him joyfully;" and they went away home together. And this is my last picture. I see them at home, and Jesus sitting down at table with Zacchæus. He is a homely Saviour. Oh man, you need Him under the roof at home. And He will come. He is not there, because you have never asked Him. He went home with Zacchæus, and the table was spread, and Jesus sat down at it. He did not look across the table like thunder, and say, "Now, you little wretch, I have got you now," and shake him over the pit, and cast his sins in his teeth. No; He sat down with him, and He asked him for his wife, if he had one, and got introduced to her, and was amazingly pleasant and easy to deal with. And He asked for the children, and very likely He took the youngest child, and set him on His knee, and put one hand under his chin. I have done it; would the Master be less human than I, the servant, would be? To win the father and mother, I have worked with the children, and kissed them, and been kind to them.

And He took the youngest child, and put him on His knee; and with His hand below his chin, He turned up the bairn's face, and kissed him, and said, "My little man, did you ever see Me before?" And the child looked up at Him, as though He were strangely familiar; for "in heaven their angels do always behold the face of His Father." And when Zacchæus saw that, "then burst his wicked heart." Christ killed him with kindness. He broke his heart with love. He stood, and he bubbled over, and said, "Behold, Lord, the half of my goods I give to the poor; and if I have taken anything from any man by false accusation, I will make it a good 'spec' for any man that ever I defrauded. I will restore him fourfold." And this, not to win Christ's grace, but because he had got it; not good works to merit salvation, but good works because Christ had got into

His heart. He had seen Him, and his very heart-strings were breaking for Him. And that is what Christ does. Get the love of Jesus into your heart, and the lust for woman, and man, the lust for gold, and the lust for drink—you will get rid of them.

Money! It was for money that Zacchæus was damning his soul; but Jesus has so taken his heart that he virtually says, "Lord, as to money, I will fling it away by the shovelful, now that I know Thee. I will give, and give, and restore." That is a splendid evidence of being converted. You say that you are converted. Show me your hands. Show me your purse. Humph! Do not pretend that you know Jesus, if you have got a purse as tight as a miser's fist. You do not know Him. You say that you are converted. Have you done with drinking? Are you doing without it? Are you delivered from that which, before, was dragging you down to the pit? That is the proof, the test. Folks go about scorning conversion. There was nobody in Jericho who scorned and scoffed at the conversion of Zacchæus. It had all the signs of a genuine turning of the man inside out and outside in. He was truly and really and radically changed, and it was the love of Christ that did it.

Now, my time is gone, and yours also. I leave you with this great Saviour. He wants to go home with you. He wants you to love Him, and to join yourself to Him.

Zacchæus came, out of curiosity, to see this man Jesus who He was; and he saw Him; he got such a close look at Him that his heart within him rose up and said, "This is the Lord." That is faith, saving faith. It works by love, and purifies the heart, and overcomes the world. Lord draw us; and we shall run after Thee. Amen and Amen.

HENDERSON & SPALDING, Printers, 1, 3 and 5, Marylebone Lane, London, W.

www.ingramcontent.com/pod-product-compliance
Lightning Source LLC
Chambersburg PA
CBHW022108290426
44112CB00008B/589